Nightwatch

A BOOK IN THE SERIES

Latin America Otherwise: Languages, Empires, Nations

Series editors:

Walter D. Mignolo, Duke University

Irene Silverblatt, Duke University

Sonia Saldívar-Hull, University of California at Los Angeles

NIGHTWATCH

The Politics of Protest in the Andes

Orin Starn

Duke University Press   Durham and London

1999

© 1999 Duke University Press

All rights reserved Printed in the United States of America

on acid-free paper ∞

Designed by C.H. Westmoreland

Typeset in Adobe Garamond with Twentieth Century display

by Tseng Information Systems, Inc.

Library of Congress Cataloging-in-Publication Data

appear on the last printed page of this book.

Frontispiece photograph: Oscar Berrú on the nightwatch,

Tunnel Six, 1986

About the Series

Latin America Otherwise: Languages, Empires, Nations is a critical series. It aims to explore the emergence and consequences of concepts used to define "Latin America" while at the same time exploring the broad interplay of political, economic, and cultural practices that have shaped Latin American worlds. Latin America, at the crossroads of competing imperial designs and local responses, has been construed as a geocultural and geopolitical entity since the nineteenth century. This series provides a starting point to redefine Latin America as a configuration of political, linguistic, cultural, and economic intersections that demand a continuous reappraisal of the role of the Americas in history and of the ongoing process of globalization and the relocation of people and cultures that have characterized Latin America's experience. *Latin America Otherwise: Languages, Empires, Nations* is a forum that confronts established geocultural constructions, that rethinks area studies and disciplinary boundaries, that assesses convictions of the academy and of public policy, and that, correspondingly, demands that the practices through which we produce knowledge and understanding about and from Latin America be subject to rigorous and critical scrutiny.

Grounded in extensive ethnographic and archival research, *Nightwatch* investigates the making of an Andean social movement—the *rondas campesinas* or peasant patrols, formed by villagers in Peru's northern sierra as a defense against theft and state corruption. But it is also much more. *Nightwatch* reflects the innovations in method and theory that characterize the best of contemporary thinking. Focusing on a localized struggle for social change (the Zapatistas would be another example), Starn confronts assumptions linked to the orthodoxies of the Right and Left. At the same time, *Nightwatch* challenges assumptions that have long shaped Andean anthropology and history. Starn addresses these issues by exploring imaginative analytical strategies. Moreover, and perhaps most remarkably, Starn does not shy away from confronting difficult and often painful questions regarding the politics and morality of anthropology and anthropologists — himself included.

Nightwatch forces us to simultaneously rethink the Andes and how bodies of knowledge are produced. Its unswerving critical stance furthers the intent of Latin American Otherwise and makes *Nightwatch* a significant contribution to the series.

To Robin

CONTENTS

Acknowledgments xi

Introduction 1

1 Origin Stories 36

2 Nightwatch 70

3 Nightcourt 105

4 Women and the Rondas 155

5 The Rondas in the Age of the NGO 192

6 Leaders and Followers 224

Epilogue 261

Notes 277

Bibliography 303

Index 325

ACKNOWLEDGMENTS

Which French literary critic announced the "death of the author"? I do not remember. I do know that for me it would have been impossible to write this book on my own. The advice and warmth of dozens of people encouraged me at every step in the journey. They much more than I are the reason I found my way to the end.

I am grateful in the first place to the villagers of Tunnel Six. After a rocky start, they received me with kindness and generosity. I remember especially those that became my compadres: Margarito Guaygua and Dalinda Aguilar, Graciela Calle and Teobaldo Jiménez, Clemente Jiménez and Teresa Córdova, Luis Jiménez and Amalia Piñín, Catalino Llacsahuache and Lidia Alvarado. To their children, and my godchildren, Duberly, Ildebrando, Martín, Oscar, and Dimás, I wish every happiness. The same goes for my stalwart compadres Indolfa Morocho and Ilarión Llacsahuache in the nearby town of Paimas, who asked me to be the godfather of their daughter Mercedes. I am indebted as well to village leaders in Tunnel Six, among them Martín Llacsahuache, Natividad Domador, Manuel Guerrero, and José Paz. Above all, I want to thank the president of the ronda committee and his family: my compadres Víctor Córdova and Francisca Paz and their children Profelinda, Jesús María, Jorge, Cristina, Luz, and my beloved godson Edwin. They live in the city of Piura now, but I cannot forget everything they did for me back in Tunnel Six in 1986, when they took me into their family.

I made new friendships in the mountains of Cajamarca at the beginning of the 1990s. For their help there, I am heavily indebted to Régulo Oblitas, Eladio Idrogo, Daniel Idrogo, Oscar Sánchez, Juana Vásquez, Pascual Ruiz, Diego Sánchez, and Omelia López, among others. Those were also the years in Peru that I met cherished friends Alejandro Coronado, Enrique Bossio, Lucien Chauvin, Cromwell Castillo, Carmen Paz and my compadres Nancy

Angeles and Líder Maguiña, whose daughter Francesca is also my godchild.

Many people shaped my thinking in *Nightwatch*. As a graduate student at Stanford University a decade ago, I was fortunate to have the guidance of George Collier, Renato Rosaldo, and Sylvia Yanagisako. I am thankful for friendship and conversation, among others, with Bruno Revesz, Walter Mignolo, Paul Gelles, Katherine Ewing, Carlos Iván Degregori, Miguel Díaz-Barriga, Gustavo Gorriti, Catherine Lutz, Irene Silverblatt, Walter Mignolo, Telmo Rojas, Steve J. Stern, Ponciano del Pino, Nora Bonifaz, and José Coronel. Ralph Litzinger, Christopher Welna, Caroline Yezer, Ya-Chung Chuang, Marro Inoue, Marisol de la Cadena, Sangeeta Luthra, Ayşe Gül Karayazgan, Nilgün Uygun, Víctor Vich, Arif Dirlik, Lewis Taylor, Bruce Kay, Deborah Billings, and Sonia Alvarez astutely read parts of the manuscript. Lewis Taylor was additionally generous in providing copies of old documents on peasant organizing in northern Peru. Jacqueline Brown and Lisa Rofel invited me to talk about the book in a seminar at the University of California, Santa Cruz; they and their students gave me valuable feedback. Richard G. Fox has been a generous friend and mentor to me over these last years, and I want here to express my special thanks to him. The chairs of the Department of Cultural Anthropology at Duke University, Naomi Quinn and William O'Barr, supported my writing, and William O'Barr also gave me insightful comments on the manuscript. I am also grateful to Deborah Jakubs and Natalie Hartman of the Duke University Council on Latin American Studies. The research for the book would not have been possible without grants from the Inter-American Foundation, Wenner-Gren Foundation for Anthropological Research, and American Council of Learned Societies. Besides being one of the smartest people I know, Ken Wissoker at Duke University Press has been a good friend and a pleasure to work with on *Nightwatch*.

Five people offered counsel and encouragement far beyond the call of duty. I am profoundly grateful to Anne Allison, Arturo Escobar, Charles Hale, Donald Moore, and Charles Piot for doing the wonderful scholarship that makes me think that anthropology may actually have a future and for the many and vital ways they helped me through writing *Nightwatch*. I am only too aware of the book's imperfections; without the guidance and advice of these friends, there would have been far more.

Finally, I want to thank my parents, Frances Starn and Randolph Starn. They spent innumerable hours editing the manuscript's murky prose, and they always offered a reliable sounding board for new ideas. More than this, they were a constant source of solace and strength through difficult times. To them, my daughter, Frances, and Robin, I will always owe far more than I can say.

INTRODUCTION

It was always hot in Tunnel Six, and this day in 1986 was no exception. I followed José Paz down the ridge of this village of 100 families in the Andean foothills of northern Peru.[1] José was my age, twenty-six, a short, strong man who had just returned from a year of military service in the city of Sullana, three hours by truck toward the coast across the dust-choked track that passed for a highway. That day in October we were on our way to harvest corn in his small field just a half-mile down from the string of adobe farmhouses on the ridge. It was customary in this part of the Andes to allow the ears to dry on the stalk, the desiccated plants swaying and crackling in the sticky breeze. After José showed me how to whittle a wood knife to pull the parched husk from each cob, we went through the field—yanking off the ears, stripping the husks, and flinging the cobs into a pile.

José surveyed the harvest at day's end. The ears of corn were beautiful, the red and purple kernels like rows of tiny gems. It would be enough to keep José, his widowed mother, his wife, and his baby daughter in tamales for a month or two. Having risen before dawn to pasture his two cows in the chaparral above Tunnel Six, José was tired from ten hours in the cornfield under the fierce sun, and nicks and blisters from the plants ran up his arms. Yet his day was not done. That night, José would take his weekly turn on patrol for the *ronda campesina,* the system of nightwatch against rustlers and thieves established in Tunnel Six three years before. As we climbed back up the ridge in the twilight, José explained that patrolling was burdensome, but also a point of satisfaction and pride for him and other villagers. "It's so much better without having to worry about assaults, losing a cow, break-ins, and the other dangers of the days before the rondas."

I had arrived in Tunnel Six a month before to study the *ron-*

das campesinas for my doctoral dissertation in anthropology. *Ronda campesina* means "peasant round," and the organization had started as a nightwatch to protect the village from the theft of crops and animals. It was an initiative born of desperation. In 1983, the flooding connected to the El Niño weather pattern had destroyed roads, crops, and houses and had set off a spiral of crime and lawlessness in the desperate, hungry countryside. Only a few men patrolled at the start, José among them. Yet the nightwatch proved successful at deterring crime, especially after the villagers captured, whipped, and dunked in an irrigation canal the district's most notorious rustler, warning him never to return to Tunnel Six. Other Tunnel Sixers soon joined the ronda, knowing they could count on no help from the understaffed, indifferent police force in the nearby town of Paimas. Participation became almost universal by 1984, and by then a weekly turn on the trails was required of every able-bodied village man. Although patrolling was considered a man's job by the standards of gender and duty in Tunnel Six, female support bolstered male enthusiasm, because women were also happy about the end of theft. Still angry about a turkey stolen three years before, José's mother Margarita sometimes made soup for the ten men in her son's Thursday night group, "to keep the organization going and the thieves on the run," she once explained to me.

Successful crime-stopping emboldened villagers to expand the ronda's scope. A steering committee had been elected in 1984 to supervise the patrols, and it presided over assemblies that began to be held that year in the lunchroom of the low-slung village schoolhouse. Here villagers gathered in what they came simply to call *arreglos,* or "fix-its," to resolve among themselves disputes over land, water, honor, debt, family conflicts, and other matters. The slowness and expense of the official legal system heightened the appeal of local justice-making to villagers. The ronda became the court of first resort in Tunnel Six. By my arrival in 1986, the committee had also expanded into organizing occasional public works, including a House of the Rondero for a village meeting hall. The anniversary of the ronda founding was the year's biggest holiday in Tunnel Six. It was commemorated in high rural style, with music, dancing, speeches, and beef stew washed down with soda pop, cane liquor, and *chicha,* the sour, milky corn beer popular for centuries among Andeans, no matter that nowadays it is more often brewed in tin buckets than in the clay jars of earlier times.

What happened in Tunnel Six was by no means an isolated case. It was one of thousands of northern Peruvian villages to organize a ronda by the close of the 1980s. When they took to the trails with whips and flashlights during the rainy, pestilential winter of 1983, the founders of the Tunnel Six ronda had been inspired by the example of peasants 200 miles away in Cajamarca, whom they had learned about on the radio. The rondas were an established yet by no means ancient feature of life's topography in that department.[2] Only at the end of 1976 was the first committee formed, when the inhabitants of a Cajamarcan village, Cuyumalca, agreed in a meeting to "organize 'Night Rondas' to defend . . . the whole community in consequence of the continuous robberies that have been occurring."[3]

The 1980s would come to be known as the "lost decade" across Latin America. Although astronomical inflation, increasing unemployment, foreign debt, and political violence took a terrible toll from El Salvador to Brazil, Peru's deterioration was especially prolonged and dramatic. The years from the late 1970s to the early 1990s became the worst period of national crisis since the war against the Chileans in the late nineteenth century. Economic freefall was compounded by the rise of two Marxist insurgencies, which successive governments met with a dirty war of torture and massacres that further exacerbated violence and poverty. The government's unreliability and corruption heightened the appeal of the rondas as a means of stopping theft, resolving conflict, and grappling with other urgent problems that might otherwise have spun out of control. Colpa Matara, Yurayacu, Chororco, La Iraca, San Antonio, and many other villages in the Chota Valley followed Cuyumalca's lead, starting patrols in 1977 and 1978. The rondas went on to spread from Chota to the neighboring valleys of Cutervo and Hualgayoc, then to other provinces in Cajamarca, including Celendín, Jaén, San Miguel, Santa Cruz, and finally to Tunnel Six and hundreds of other settlements in the department of Piura, just to the north. By the end of the decade, there were ronda committees in the departments of Amazonas, Lambayeque, and Ancash, bringing the total number of villages involved to at least 3,400 spread over more than 60,000 square miles of Peru's northern Andes. This was one of the fastest-growing and biggest movements for change in Latin America during the second half of the twentieth century.[4]

Nightwatch is a chronicle of the rondas. In the United States, the movement remains virtually unknown, perhaps because it never involved car bombs, assassination, or other attacks that make for flashy headlines. The organizing in Tunnel Six and elsewhere was a matter of confusion even in Peru, because the very different patrols organized in the south-central Andes by the military to fight the larger of the two Marxist insurgencies, the Communist Party of Peru–Shining Path, came to be known by the same name of rondas campesinas.[5] I agree with historian John Berger that "never again will a single story be told as if it is the only one." [6] Others have, will, and should have their say about the rondas. I make no pretense of relating the "whole story" of the movement, as if that were even possible. At the same time, the size of the rondas and their achievements in maintaining a measure of security and order at a dangerous hour of Peruvian history seem to me to more than justify an effort at understanding. An examination of the movement's limits and ambiguities as well as its accomplishments can also enable us to think more lucidly about the Andes, the politics of organizing and protest, and even the condition of the countryside throughout Latin America and the Third World, or at least this will be my contention throughout *Nightwatch*.

Few in the northern countryside doubted the importance of the rondas. Although they debated and sometimes fought over the control and the meaning of the movement, José and others were seldom anything but enthusiastic about its existence, perhaps because victories of any kind were so hard to come by in the hardscrabble countryside. A reflection of their status as a marker of culture and identity for the peasantry, the rondas became a favorite theme for Andean musicians, who used battered tape players to record their songs and copy them onto scratchy cassettes to sell on market day in towns across the northern Andes. "You go back to bed, I'm going out to *rondar,* to patrol" went the bravado of one ballad sung to the lilting accompaniment of guitars and *quenas,* flutes made of bamboo or plastic water-pipe.[7] The motifs of loss, love, and politics came together in another song, which I heard at the 1986 ronda anniversary celebration in Tunnel Six in what for me is by now the receding yet unforgotten past of that year, the cornfields, the sultry stillness of the foothills, and the beauty and pain of Andean life. "Give me your little heart, I'll pack it away, if I lose it on my journey, I'll search for it with the rondas." [8]

AN ARRIVAL STORY

In writing this book I have confronted questions as thorny as the gorse of the puna. What led me in the first place to South America, Peru, and then the rondas? How was I to go about understanding the meaning of the mobilization in the northern Andes? How would I write a history of the rondas, and by what right could I and to what ends did I even want to do so? What exactly could the rondas teach about life in the Andes? About the challenges of organizing for change? About the predicament of the rural backlands of the Third World? From the recent crisis of confidence in my chosen profession of anthropology, to the turmoil in Peru, the end of the Cold War, and the advent of the digital age, the state of flux at this millennial turn forces an accounting at many levels, however tentative and incomplete.

In a way my involvement with the rondas began in a movie theater in 1981. As a junior at the University of Chicago, I saw a Brazilian film called *Bye-Bye Brazil.* In the arctic gray of winter by Lake Michigan, this tale of a traveling circus's journey across the desperate yet colorful and sensuous landscape of modern Brazil made me want to leave for South America right away. I had met and fallen in love with Robin Kirk in our cockroach-infested dorm on the corner of Greenwood and Fifty-third Streets. After graduating, we set out from Ecuador across South America, with a stop in São Paulo to teach English to finance the trip. As it happened, far from being solitary adventurers, we were following the well-trodden "gringo trail" of greasy young backpackers from the United States and Europe. We thrived on the all-night bus trips, fleabag hotels, and sour-smelling cantinas en route to Machu Picchu, Iguaçú Falls, and the Amazon jungle, and on contact with the peoples and cultures of a world less familiar and, so we supposed, more alive than our own middle-class neighborhoods in the north. It has now been almost twenty years since that first trip. While I puff harder now up mountain trails and lurch to the ball with less agility in village soccer games, I am also aware that my attraction as a twenty-year-old was sparked by travel brochure stereotypes about the mystery and exoticism of South America and by the privileges of race, class, and nationality that enabled us to travel in the first place. Even now, however, I confess to amazement and pleasure at the view from an Andean peak of the endless green of the Amazon, or the intimacy of drunkenness and friendship in dancing until dawn to huaynos in a homestead on the altiplano,[9] perhaps a residual romanticism of my own that I am unable or unwilling to put aside. Sometimes Robin and I speak of a sensation of greater intensity when we are in Peru, a feeling of life lived more fully. In some ways we remain the gringo backpackers, finding or thinking they find in another place what seems to be missing at home.

My attraction to South America also derived from the politics of growing up in Berkeley down the street from People's Park. During the turmoil of the late 1960s and early 1970s, I went to bed on some nights to the chants of "Ho, Ho, Ho Chi Minh, NLF is Going to Win" and "Hey, Hey LBJ, How Many Kids Did You Kill Today?" "To Hell with Society and All Its Followers" was etched into the wet concrete of the walkway to our house. I am not sure whether this was meant as a general observation or a specific message for our conventional academic family. Some of the time's passion rubbed off on me, however, and by the time I went off to college in 1978, I liked to think of myself as "socially conscious" and even as an "activist." I refused to sign up for the draft when Jimmy Carter reinstituted registration that year, and later I left school for a year to volunteer at a reservation high school in New Mexico for Navajo dropouts.

When I returned to college, anthropology appeared to be an avenue for further involvement in social change, the discipline most concerned with the predicament of Indians, peasants, the urban poor, and the rest of a global society's dispossessed majorities. As a graduate student in the anthropology department at Stanford University, I found that many other students wanted to transcend what critics of the 1960s and 1970s had begun to charge was a disciplinary legacy of apathy and sometimes complicity with imperialism, even more so in the atmosphere of peril and possibility of the Reagan years with the advances of feminism, the onset of AIDS, and global upheaval from South Africa to Central America.[10] We covered the "Left-Wing Lounge" of the anthropology department with posters of Mandela and Sandino and a silk screen of Karl Marx that I had bought in San Francisco's Chinatown. The ideal of an anthropology of change underwrote friends' choices about what to study: feminist organizing in India and Nepal, squatter settlements in Mexico City, the struggle over Indian rights in Nicaragua, the U.S. sanctuary movement for war refugees from Central America.[11] The traditional focus on "the primitive" and "the native" had led anthropologists earlier in the twentieth century to search out for study the most "untouched" villages and tribes in the South Seas, Africa, the Amazon, and Native North America. We were motivated by a self-conscious and sometimes self-righteous wish to reverse this history by researching upheaval and mobilization in the Third World and the United States. As part of this vision, the anthropologist would not just study but seek to support the struggle for change, and it seemed to us complicit with power to claim the Olympian remove of scientific objectivity.[12] Our hope was to reinvent anthropology by embracing values of accountability, activism, and engagement.

I turned to Peru. As I knew from my first trip to South America, this was the largest, most diverse, and most conflicted of the Andean nations. It was hard for even a would-be radical student to sympathize with the Shining Path.[13] This fiercest of the movements for change in Peru of the 1980s was led by an ex-philosophy professor named Abimael Guzmán in the Andean town of Ayacucho 200 miles southeast of the national capital, Lima. The bulk of his followers were young students at the university or even high schools. They believed that Guzmán was the "greatest living Marxist-Leninist" and the "Fourth Sword of Marxism" after Marx, Lenin, and Mao. Their absolute commitment to revolution made them ready to kill and die to cross what Guzmán announced would be "a river of blood" to the promised land of a Communist utopia. As part of the "people's war" it launched in 1980, the Shining Path murdered mayors, policemen, villagers, and priests, while justifying and even reveling in violence as the means of toppling the old order. "The people's blood has a rich perfume, like jasmine, daisies, geraniums, and violets," declared an unofficial party anthem.[14] The government responded with a campaign of torture, massacres, and "disappearances" against anyone suspected of sympathizing with the revolutionaries.[15] It was a war that in the 1980s alone cost Peru $10 billion dollars in damages and 20,000 lives. "Mother of Mercy," asked an Andean ballad, "What is happening here?"[16]

Yet the Shining Path was only one force in the turbulence of the 1980s. Although Peru was ruled by the "gentlemen's clubs" of the creole elite after independence from Spain in 1824, the vast majority of the population consisted of brown-skinned people with Indian and African as well as Spanish blood, most of them living in the extreme poverty that made the country one of the hemisphere's poorest. The restlessness of the Peruvian majorities under the old order was evident in the mushrooming of what economist Hernando de Soto dubbed the "other path" of street selling and small business, the advent of an array of Protestant sects to challenge the Catholic Church's monopoly over religion, and the transformation of Lima by the arrival of tens of thousands of migrants from the countryside of the Amazon and the Andes in search of a better life.[17] The United Left (IU), a national coalition of parties committed to socialism through ballot box politics, attempted to weld the grassroots into a force to fight poverty and discrimination. The crisis of the economy and the war heightened the feeling that the country was on the edge. For those on the left before the fall of the Berlin Wall and the decline of socialism almost everywhere, it was possible to imagine that a better society would emerge out of the chaos and upheaval of the 1980s.

The atmosphere of danger and promise attracted me. When I was in Lima in 1986 to explore possibilities for research, a North American friend told me about the rondas. She put me in touch with a rural advocacy group in Piura, the capital of the northern department of the same name and an old colonial city famous for its palm-lined streets, whitewashed mansions, cotton mills, and spicy seafood from the nearby Pacific. They told me about a ronda meeting the next weekend in the town of Ayabaca. It was twelve hours from Piura to Ayabaca across the desert and then up the switchbacks into the mountains, riding in the flatbed of one of the trucks that snake between the Andes and the city under the weight of passengers, goats, chickens, sugar candy, fertilizer, kerosene, and other cargo. Roadside crosses marked the spots where brakes had failed or tires had blown to send a truck off the road thousands of feet into a gorge. "Guide me, Lord Jesus of Miracles," beseeched a message painted onto the flatbed just above the cab. I prayed He would. Our driver had chugged three big bottles of beer during a stop at a cantina in the middle of the desert.

Ayabaca, population about 2,000, elevation 9,000 feet, had a drab cement cathedral and the usual statue in the plaza to a hero of the Independence War, sporadic electricity, a couple of stores, and an air of semiabandonment except on Sundays, when people flocked in from the countryside for the market. I tracked down a young priest whose name I had been given in Piura. A friendly, handsome young man born in the town, Gerardo Calle told me that the ronda meeting would be held in the cockfighting arena near the plaza. About 150 *ronderos,* the name for those active in the movement, showed up as delegates from villages across the blue-gray mountains of the province. Compact, brown men with bad teeth and faces weather-creased by the Andean wind and sun, they wore ponchos, rubber tire sandals, cheap tennis shoes, frayed polyester sweaters, and tractor caps with John Deere or International Harvester logos, not that any of these peasants could dream of buying so expensive a machine. Like the majority of villagers in Piura and Cajamarca, none owned more than a couple of acres, and it marked a relative prosperity in this part of the world just to own a team of oxen.

The Ayabaca meeting immediately exposed problems of the rondas. Although I had read enough to know the Andes were hardly some feminist utopia of gender equity, it was striking nonetheless that not a single woman was there, a warning sign of patriarchy and exclusion in a movement supposed to be of and for the entire peasantry. Evidencing the entanglement of the rondas with nongovernmental organizations (NGOs) and the international development establishment, the meeting was organized by the Agrarian League of Ayabaca with a grant from the Lima office of New York–based Catholic Relief Services (CRS). An association of villagers headquartered in a rattrap of a building around the corner from the cockfighting arena, the Agrarian League was in theory nonpartisan, but the president was connected to the United Left, which controlled Ayabaca's municipality. The mayor, a regional beer distributor, nicknamed "The Ceibo" for a large belly like the balloon-trunked trees typical of the Piuran foothills, inaugurated the meeting by attacking the rival and more centrist American Popular Revolutionary Alliance (APRA) and urging a vote for the United Left in upcoming elections. The campaigning underscored the way the rondas were drawn into the hurly-burly of parties chasing after peasant votes.

At the same time, however, the independence of the rondas was just as obvious in the meeting. Although most villagers there sympathized with the IU, they had no intention of letting the event become a campaign rally. The remainder of the two days was dominated by the delegates. They marched down to the table in the center of the arena, taking the microphone with calloused hands to report on the rondas in their villages, to whistles and applause from the crowd. The movement was just three years old, thus still a novelty in Ayabaca, and satisfaction about stamping out thievery was a recurring theme in these spitfire speeches in the rural slang of the northern Andes. So was denunciation of the police and judges for seeking to put down the rondas. "The authorities know we're taking the tit away by ending bribery and corruption," opined one villager, speaking no doubt for many. When the twenty-three-year-old ronda president from the village of Ambulco spoke about a police patrol beating him almost to death with kicks and rifle butts, a hush fell upon the crowd, an acknowledgment of sympathy for the purple and yellow bruises on his face. The young leader explained to the crowd that the attack had been retaliation for disobeying an order to disband the Ambulco ronda.

Víctor Córdova was one of the villagers there. A thin-faced man with a straggly moustache and wearing a cheap polyester shirt, he did not cut an impressive figure and headed the ronda from a village with the odd name of Tunnel Six. Nevertheless, I was impressed by the eloquence of his speech about the rondas and peasant empowerment. During a break, I introduced myself to Víctor and his companion, Martín Llacsahuache, another leader in Tunnel Six, and handed them a letter of introduction from the priest explaining that I was an anthropologist looking for a place to study the rondas. Víctor perused it, although I later learned that he barely knew how to read—the landowner on the hacienda where he had grown up refused to build a school for the children of his serfs. After some awkward conversation, Víctor and Martín agreed that I could visit the following week. They told me it was just a half-hour walk to their village from the town of Paimas in the Andean foothills back down the road toward Piura and the Pacific Coast.

I jumped off the truck in Paimas two days later. The path to Tunnel Six ran beside a canal of brown water snaking between cement banks. During the 1950s, the Peruvian government had contracted an American company to dig the one-hundred-mile waterway from the Quiroz River across the foothills to commercial farms in the San Lorenzo Valley. The founding of the humble village of Tunnel Six was an unplanned result of this grand project to modernize agriculture in northern Peru. Having always depended on the rains, ever at the mercy of drought and flood, peasants back up in the Andes had recognized and seized the opportunity for the security of year-round water. A stream of settlers flowed down from the higher mountains in the early 1960s, building farmhouses and using iron pipes to siphon water for fields that they hacked from the chaparral amidst a population of scorpions, buzzards, and bush vipers. A truckload of police arrived in 1970 to shut off the water, only to come against a crowd of villagers blockading the road. To avoid confrontation with the peasantry, the reform-minded government of General Juan Velasco (1968–75) ordered the police to withdraw, and a year later it recognized the settlers' rights to the water. By then, the settlement was known as Tunnel Six, the number bestowed by the American engineering company to the tunnel of the canal through a ridge near the new village.

I knew none of this history as I walked into Tunnel Six for the first time on that afternoon. The village was empty, with most people away in the fields. If I harbored illusions of research in the kind of hamlet depicted in specials about the Andes on PBS or in National Geographic, Tunnel Six shattered them straightaway. There was no colorful and exotic scenery of llamas, ponchoed Indians, thatched huts, mountain meadows, or snowy glaciers. As for animals, a couple of starved dogs and pigs were rooting for scraps in a garbage pile. Far from picturesque, the farmhouses had walls of unlovely gray mud, and their tin roofs glared in the merciless sun. The sandy, eroded paths down to the fields were littered with bottle caps, rusted tin cans, and scraps of plastic bags and used toilet paper. It was so hot that my shirt was soaked in sweat by the short walk from Paimas. I felt close to desperation at the prospect of living a year alone in such a place.

It turned out that many Tunnel Sixers did not want me there anyway. As anthropologist Charles Hale underlines, the day is long past when an anthropologist can traipse into a Third World village to gather genealogies, myths, and oral histories for the greater good of knowledge and science.[18] When I tracked down Víctor in his farmhouse on a ridgetop, he was noncommittal about my moving into Tunnel Six. The matter would have to be put before the village. At an assembly the next afternoon, a group of about sixty Tunnel Sixers gathered in the lunchroom, and most of them were unsmiling under their straw hats. I rose to explain that I wanted to live in Tunnel Six for a year to research the rondas. As part of my work in the village, I would do whatever I could to serve, listing some of the possibilities: starting a medicine chest, tutoring in the village school, writing a popular history of the Tunnel Six ronda. I doubt the vote would have gone in my favor if activism had not been part of my agenda. What I proposed was not even enough. One man pointed to the need for a small library for village school-children. Only this addition to my list brought a majority to raise their hands for permission to stay. "If you don't fulfill your promises, you'll get a flogging," warned one man, referring to the standard ronda method for disciplining the devious and the dishonest.

The first weeks in Tunnel Six were hard. When I moved the next week into the storeroom in the farmhouse of Víctor and his wife, Francisca, many villagers remained suspicious about my intentions. The rumors flew thick that I was actually a United Left organizer, a CIA agent, or a Shining Path guerrilla. One woman went to the police in Paimas to say I had buried guns in the dirt floor of the storeroom. Another man confirmed spying me with six other gringos trying to dynamite the canal. The arrival of a jeepload of armed soldiers to investigate did nothing to quell the rumors. Although the Shining Path never operated as far north as Ayabaca, the stories about me reflected the nervousness throughout Peru about the war, which Tunnel Sixers knew about from reports in newspapers and on the radio. The tales were spread further by the feeling that a tall, pale North American was out of place in Tunnel Six. Just once before had a gringo lived in the Quiroz Valley. A German shopkeeper remembered only as "Mister Otto," he was a kind of Promethean culture hero in Tunnel Six, for having taught villagers the trick of siphoning water from the canal. Yet Mister Otto made his home in the town of Paimas. Unlike him, I was living in the country-side, violating the expectation that Tunnel Six should be peasant turf. It was less than two decades since the breakup in the Andes of the centuries-old system of haciendas ruled mostly by landlords of European descent. The possibility that I might be an advance scout for a campaign by the white and the privileged to retake the land sharpened uneasiness about my arrival.

The rest of my year in Tunnel Six was not just a tale of the eventual triumph of mutual respect and understanding. As critic James Clifford observes, it has been common for the anthropologist to portray his or her fieldwork as a journey from "early ignorance, misunderstanding, lack of contact" to "adult confident, disabused knowledge."[19] Such a depiction of fieldwork can ignore the persistence to the very end of ignorance and miscommunication. I still remember the shock of the first picture I saw of myself with Tunnel Sixers. At six foot three, I looked like the World's Tallest Man from the *Guinness Book of World Records* next to villagers, none of whom topped five foot six. I was an object of curiosity anyway as an American. Not many villagers had ever met a gringo in the flesh, so they came by to quiz me about foods of choice in the United States, farming methods, airline ticket prices, and other matters. An assumption in the Andes is that gringos are all rich. It was impossible to say yes to every one of the dozens of loan requests, which sometimes caused resentment and hard feelings. As for my own understanding of Tunnel Six, it was always partial, and sometimes less than that. When Andrea Domínguez shrugged evasively when I asked if it was true she was a *bruja,* a sorceress, a secret was concealed, and I failed to record even the obvious in forgetting ever to write down the names of the first settlers of Tunnel Six. There were plenty of skips, silences, and gaps in the "data record" I compiled in those many months in Piura's sweltering foothills.

Yet I did learn a great deal in Tunnel Six. Anthropologist Sherry Ortner points out that "the attempt to view other systems from ground level is the basis, perhaps, the only basis, of anthropology's distinctive contribution to the human sciences."[20] Despite the many paradoxes and limitations of fieldwork, the fact of living in a place for a long stretch can provide an intimacy and depth of perspective unlike any other method for understanding a human society—or so at least I continue to believe. Once the tension of the first weeks diminished, I interviewed villagers about the ronda, joined patrols, and went to the lunchroom assemblies. By the end of the year, two boxes had filled with the notes I tapped out every night on a portable Olivetti typewriter, in that era between the pencil and the computer. As I sought to fulfill the commitments I had made at the start, activism and anthropology proved complementary, for working with Tunnel Sixers on the library and other projects became another source of insight into history, personality, and belief in the small world of village society.[21] I missed hot water, flush toilets, television, and ice cream enough to hop a truck across the desert to the city of Piura for a weekend once a month or so. Yet I learned to appreciate the beauty of the star-studded night sky in the Andean foothills, the buttery flutter of gray moths after a rainstorm, and other flashes of beauty in the ugliness of Tunnel Six's almost postapocalyptic landscape. More than anything I came to cherish the intimacy of friendships with Víctor, Francisca, José, and many others, even if I remained for Tunnel Sixers a "stranger and friend," as anthropologist Hortense Powdermaker once said of her research in New Guinea.[22] When I carried my backpack and boxes down the path to Paimas in 1987, the village felt as much like home as my native city of Berkeley, and more so than North Carolina, where I eventually landed a job as an anthropology professor at Duke University.

FIELDWORK AND THE PROBLEM OF WRITING

It would have been impossible to write a history of a movement as large as the rondas from research in a single village. After finishing my dissertation at Stanford, I returned to northern Peru in 1990. This time I headed down the Andes from Tunnel Six to Cajamarca. It was there in the hamlet of Cuyumalca on the mountainside of the Chota Valley that the rondas had started in 1976. By contrast to Tunnel Six, the Chota Valley was a picture of loveliness at 9,000 feet, a green and gold patchwork quilt of fields and pastures stretching up toward the turquoise sky of the Andes. I stayed for four months to study the rondas. As part of the research, I interviewed policemen, judges, and prosecutors in the town of Chota, and I went out to Cuyumalca and other parts of the countryside. Although it sometimes meant bribing clerks, I copied documents from government offices that showed the worried, sometimes violent, response of the town authorities to the birth of the rondas in the late 1970s and early 1980s. Ronda committee record books kept by villagers themselves further complemented what I saw and heard. When Robin came to Peru to work as a journalist, I joined her in Lima and from there in 1991 made several more trips back into the northern Andes, journeying by bus, truck, and sometimes on foot or mule to parts of Cutervo, Huancabamba, Hualgayoc, Morropón, and Santa Cruz.

A risk of what anthropologist George Marcus has called "multi-locale fieldwork" is spreading oneself too thin, and never gaining the close understanding that can come from staying a long time in one neighborhood, tribe, factory, or village.[23] What I learned in those trips of one or two weeks in 1991 was doubtless superficial in many ways, and I missed whole areas of ronda activity, such as Celendín and San Ignacio. The advantage was a wide-angled view of many faces of the rondas in the northern Andes. As a combination of village ethnography in Tunnel Six in 1986 and 1987 with multilocale fieldwork in 1990 and 1991, the research for *Nightwatch* was hybrid, with aspects of narrowness and breadth, closeness and distance, detail and generality.

The reader will find the book organized chronologically and by broad themes. I begin in chapter 1 with the reasons for the rise of the rondas in 1976 in the Chota Valley and with the angry, sometimes comic, battle to claim credit for founding the movement. The second chapter follows the development of the patrols against rustlers in the late 1970s and early 1980s, a drama of violence and reform. I go on in the third chapter to examine the expansion from patrolling to assemblies, and the quest during the 1980s to turn the rondas into a tribunal for resolving disputes between villagers in a faster, cheaper, and fairer fashion than the police and courts could manage. Each of the last three chapters takes up a theme of importance during the heyday of the rondas in the 1980s—the role of women, the influence of NGOs from Lima and as far afield as Europe and the United States, and the struggle over leadership. The book concludes with a discussion of ronda decline and survival in the late 1990s, and my own bittersweet return at the decade's end to Tunnel Six and the Chota Valley.

The result is not a record of Andean "voices." A red flag always goes up in my mind when an anthropologist announces that his or her ethnography will "give voice" to the marginalized. *Nightwatch* contains many direct quotations from villagers, but to claim to be the mouthpiece through which the natives speak is to ignore the anthropologist's central role in selecting and orchestrating just who and what will be heard.[24] The peasantry of the Andes has for too long been shut out of debates about the region's future. Unless paired with a commitment to let villagers have their own say in forums from newspapers to conferences, writing anthropology about the Andes risks perpetuating the history of privilege, here of the social scientist to define the truth of the lives of the peasantry.[25] A danger also exists of misunderstanding or misappropriating information. When Abimael Guzmán was captured by police in Lima on September 12, 1992, an anthology of essays by anthropologists and historians lay on his nightstand. Was the chieftain of the Shining Path reading up on the Andes to formulate his war plans?[26] This would confirm the worry of critic bell hooks about anthropologists and other scholars acting, albeit inadvertently, as "informers" on the downtrodden.[27]

It will come as little surprise that I think writing about the rondas is worthwhile despite the risks. These last decades have been a time of "anthro(a)pology," in the neologism of one pundit.[28] As part of the self-pillorying, we have spilled gallons of ink dissecting the missteps and abuses in the endeavor of writing about people in out-of-the-way places, sometimes sounding much like a committee of Maoists intent on purging rivals to chart the politically correct line. Recognition of the dangers of exoticism and silencing has hastened anthropology's transformation from the study of "primitives" to what it is today, namely, the examination of life "here" in the United States as well as "there" in the Third World—zoos, nightclubs, restaurants, biotechnology labs, museums, and just about every other imaginable form of human organization. The turn to "bring it back home" is a welcome broadening of focus. Nevertheless, the persistence of Western ignorance and miscomprehension means that a role still exists for an anthropology of places like Burundi, New Guinea, Indonesia, or, in this case, Peru. A recent piece in the *New York Times,* for example, serves up a sorry mishmash of exaggeration and stereotype about Africa as "an incomprehensible dystopia of random murder, tribal depravity, and political corruption.[29] This sort of coverage makes me thankful for studies from the likes of John and Jean Comaroff, Donald Moore, and Charles Piot, which show the ambiguity, complexity, and humanity of African life, as well as the ways in which the destinies of non-Western and Western societies have been bound together by the facts of conquest, colonialism, migration, trade, and the mutual exchange of technology, values, and ideas. Surely anthropology can contribute to combating the frightening parochialism that dismisses those who live outside the United States and Europe as unworthy of attention, understanding, or sometimes even acknowledgment.

Yet anthropology must be read to do any good. In recent years, reliance on and at times reveling in arcane and often unnecessary jargon have risked turning our discipline into a secret society, a clubhouse closed to everyone but the graduate student and professor. To advocate accessibility is not to deny the value of specialized terminology and debate in anthropology any more than in literary studies, biology, physics, or other fields. It does mean recognizing that anthropologists can do more to reach broad audiences, as did our totems such as Franz Boas, Ruth Benedict, and Margaret Mead (even if what they wrote about the Samoans, Japanese, and others has not always held up in retrospect).[30] As part of an attempt to resuscitate a more public, perhaps even colloquial, anthropology, I have written *Nightwatch* in what I remember of plain English, and have tried to blend anecdote, analysis, and reflection so as to interest the nonspecialist as well as the specialist. A movement as major as the rondas deserves recognition from more than just the odd, obscure tribe of anthropology to which I have now belonged for many years.

THE RONDAS, THE SHINING PATH, AND
THE CHALLENGES OF THEORY

So much has been written on the Shining Path that pundits have coined the label of "Senderology." Although enough journalists and scholars have focused on the rondas to talk also about "ronderology," the quantity is minuscule in comparison to the body of work on the followers of Guzmán. This economy of scholarship unfortunately gives the impression that the Shining Path was the only meaningful recent mobilization in the Peruvian Andes. Devastating as the war was in Ayacucho and other parts of the central and southern mountains of Peru—more than 20,000 villagers were killed and 500,000 others forced to flee—the number of cadres in the Shining Path never exceeded 10,000, and the revolution all but died in the early 1990s amid expanding opposition in the Andes to the Maoists' war, followed by the arrest of Guzmán and other leaders.[31] In contrast, more than 400,000 villagers were active in ronda committees well into the 1990s. This means the larger, longer-lasting Andean movement of the late twentieth century was not the Shining Path, but actually the rondas. In writing this first full-length book about them (and the only one in English), I hope to underscore the heterogeneity that marks recent history in the Peruvian Andes and in particular to show a rural mobilization that preferred democracy to hierarchy, reconciliation to hatred, and renewal to destruction.[32]

The debates of recent decades within and about poststructuralism, postmodernism, Marxism, nationalism, and feminism inevitably color my portrait of the movement, for these conversations and arguments have in one way or another shaped the ways those of us in anthropology and cultural studies understand and misunderstand what we do. Like the "-ologies" of Peruvian studies, the "-isms" of social theory are shells that enclose living matter and vital issues. It has become painfully clear of late how quickly these academic categories can empty out in the shell games of theoretical reductionism, sectarianism, and not infrequent posturing. Yet the hypertrophy of theory has surely been necessary if the hard questions that matter are not to have complacently routine answers. No consensus will emerge, of course, because theories in the humanities and social sciences are never, and never should be, formulated in anything other than the rough-and-tumble of assertion and challenge. How can we speak about the role of the individual yet recognize the weight of structures of economy and meaning?[33] What is the connection between culture, power, and history?[34] Is the concept of culture itself a dead letter, premised as it has been in anthropology on a view of the world as a mosaic of separate pieces with well-defined edges that appears evermore implausible in an age of pervasive mixture and mobility?[35] Is power a matter of guns and money, the regulation of thought and desire or perhaps neither or both?[36] Has history ended in the triumph of capitalism? If not, what are its destinations, and the futures of gender and sexual relations, poverty and economic inequality, ethnicity, nationalism, and cultural difference and sameness? Any would-be analyst of human experience must acknowledge and grapple with these issues as the ground of received truths shifts beneath us.

Because this book is meant first, and above all, as an account of an agrarian movement in northern Peru, it will not be for readers looking for universal truths or extended theoretical exegesis. *Nightwatch* pauses along the way to explain and sometimes disagree with the theories that inform the analysis, often using notes to direct interested readers to the fuller ins-and-outs of the relevant academic debates. The product is an ethnography neither against theory nor so consumed by it as to obstruct a reckoning with the luminous particularity of the rondas—or such was my intention in embarking on the odyssey of writing it almost three years ago.

BEYOND ANDEANISM

But what about now? I have learned as well as puzzled and doubted through writing this book, and, at the end, an examination of the rondas strikes me as worthwhile for at least three reasons. Perhaps the most obvious is to explode stereotypes about the Andes, the tallest and longest of mountain ranges in the Western Hemisphere and the home to 8 million people in Peru alone. "In our newest Andean escapade . . . you will encounter splendidly dressed Quechua Indians, herds of llamas, and alpaca decorated with brightly colored ribbons grazing in idyllic meadows. . . . [L]ocal inhabitants speak no Spanish . . . and maintain a mystical attachment to the land," promises Wilderness Travel Company in my own hometown of Berkeley.[37] The advertisement exemplifies what can be called "Andeanism," a way of seeing in which the highlands of Bolivia, Colombia, Chile, Ecuador, and Peru appear as an alien, fascinating land untouched by the West and modernity, in this particular case to entice stressed-out professionals with the promise of an encounter with a more pristine, natural world. As it figures in the travel brochure, the Hollywood movie, and the adventure novel, the logic of Andeanism focuses on llamas, snowy peaks, breathy panpipes, Inca ruins, savage guerrillas, and picturesque villagers, while airbrushing out the radios, tennis shoes, Coleman lamps, plastic buckets, and anything else that would crack the illusion of the primordialness of highland South America. The stock imagery telescopes the region into an island of Otherness removed from the world.

As an impatient young Ph.D., I argued almost a decade ago that Andeanism's distortions reappeared in the anthropology of the Andes, as late as the 1960s and 1970s.[38] It is clearer to me now that I was wrong as well as right. Not all of the many studies were as guilty of the sins of stereotyping and exoticism as I had assumed. Yet many anthropologists indeed failed to reckon with the full extent of flux and mixture in the Andes. Going at least as far back as the first decades of the twentieth century, there had long been an impulse in anthropology to take the side of the native and the non-Western. It peaked amidst the increasing disenchantment with the West in the turmoil of the sixties with student protest and the civil rights and women's movements at home and decolonization and revolution abroad. If a negative view had coded the culture of the Andes as a drag on development and progress, anthropologists inverted the equation to present it as a storehouse of strength and dignity, and especially of values of reciprocity, kinship, and harmony with the land presumed to have been lost in the West. Such scholarship countered the stigmatization of the peasantry as backward and savage, but left intact and even furthered the presumption of a radical split between the rural and the urban, the United States and Latin America, and the Andes and the West. It recoded highland lifeways from bad to good, yet did not do enough to question the premises of the region's isolation and traditionalism. Little attention went to evangelical Protestantism, radical political ideologies, education, social movements, migration, mass media, and the other great twentieth-century transformations of the Andes, a missing of not one but many revolutions in village society. In this way, an anthropologist could conclude that "the Indians have survived in provincial aloofness, rarely affected by the vicissitudes of time, politics, society, and technological innovations which have so stirred Western civilization."[39]

It is rare to speak this way in anthropology any longer. Although calls for studying contact and colonialism's impact were sounded even in the early and mid-twentieth century, it took Eric Wolf and other Marxist anthropologists in the 1960s and 1970s to drive home the point that Western expansion and capitalism had made the world into a "totality of interconnected processes."[40] The postmodern turn of the 1980s encouraged the fuller exploration of the centrality of mimicry, mixture, and imposition in the making of meaning and culture. If it once placed the science's stamp on the myth of the Timeless Primitive, anthropology has surely repented and reversed itself with a vengeance. Sometimes in the 1990s it felt like every one of the hundreds of panels at our annual national conference had "transnationalism" or "globalization" in the title.

The anthropology of the Andes has changed with the discipline as a whole. As part of the widening of the lens of what the writer and folklorist Zora Neale Hurston once dubbed the "spyglass of anthropology," the study of highland South America no longer focuses only on the peasantry and the village. A scan of the journals reveals that Andeanist anthropology is nowadays as often as not about Lima street clowns, Cuzcan photographers, Medellín drug lords, or La Paz maids.[41] Those who still study the rural Andes have exposed the flimsiness of the fiction of the proverbial "isolated" and "remote" hamlet. Here the task becomes to explore what it would mean to understand culture and identity as the result of the continuous interplay between the village, the region, and the world since pre-Columbian times.[42] After all, already under Chavín, Moche, the Incas, and other ethnic kingdoms before the Spanish, the traffic was heavy across the lines of local politics and state policy, provincial custom and official religion, village barter and regional commerce.[43] The Spanish conquest in 1532 changed the Andes forever by bringing the plow, the wheel, cattle, horses, sheep, and a new language, not to mention the doctrine of Christian and European supremacy.[44] Since then, the connections have only tightened; and today Tunnel Sixers and other villages listen to news from Lima on the radio, vote in national elections, and sell whatever they can spare of their flocks and crops to buy rubber boots, polyester sweaters, school notebooks, and other goods manufactured as far away as China and Indonesia. Far from fitting into the classic imagery of peasants as rooted to the land, most villagers have at one time or another labored on farms in the Amazon jungle, the cities on the Pacific Coast to the west, or even Canada and the United States.[45] The tortuous dirt roads rumble twenty-four hours a day with an armada of decrepit trucks and buses that shuttle people and cargo between the countryside and the cities. One Peruvian anthropologist even speaks of villagers as "commuters" in the search for survival and livelihood.[46]

The rondas were themselves a direct result of migration's quickening. Régulo Oblitas, a cane cutter in the coastal Chiclayo Valley during the early 1960s and a Cuyumalca native, served in the plantation nightwatch organized by his employers. Later, his own vivid memory prompted Oblitas to propose to fellow villagers back home in the Andes that they start patrols of their own against the mounting crime wave of the late 1970s. As an Andean tradition imported from another region, the rondas confirm anthropologist Ulf Hannerz's dictum that "the autonomy and boundedness of cultures must nowadays be understood as a matter of degree." [47] When a Coke bottle or Simpsons T-shirt turns up in a village of thatch-roofed farmhouses with no electricity or running water at 12,000 feet on the Bolivian altiplano, it is no longer, or at least should not be, cause for amusement, much less surprise, the chuckle at the incongruity of the appearance of the modern in the primitive. It measures to the contrary the reality of a world in which there are no truly out-of-the-way places, and perhaps never have been.

Western expansion spelled the end for many Andean customs and beliefs. More than 10 million people were killed by war, disease, and forced labor in the mines after the coming of Pizarro and his men, and with them a vast storehouse of memories, stories, and experiences of the world as it had been before conquest. The Iberians forced the natives to abandon dispersed settlements for European-style settlements, Quechua and Aymara for Spanish, and native religion for Christianity, for colonialism was a project of domination at the level of culture as well as politics and economics. After independence from Spain in the early nineteenth century, the stigmatization of things Andean persisted in a land now ruled by the landowners and businessmen of the white elite, who looked to Britain and the United States as a model. Of course, there was resistance and sometimes rebellion at every step of the way. What natives accepted was also very often "Andeanized," as in the way that Bolivian village women made the bowler hat of British railroad engineers into part of their traditional garb together with sandals and skirt. The scale of destruction and abandonment was enormous just the same. Quechua was spoken by the ancestors of Tunnel Six's José Paz and other villagers who started the rondas in Cajamarca and Piura, and they themselves had only accepted it after Inca conquest pressed north from Cuzco in the fifteenth century. Only in place-names, a few words such as *chacra* for field and *huishqu* for buzzard, and in the incantations of the legendary shamans of Huancabamba, as they heal and bewitch in the altiplano's midnight cold, does the language of the Empire of the Sun survive today.

Nonetheless the specter of homogenization is only one dimension of modernity's advance. In the century's last decades, we have witnessed the spread of shared technology and values to the farthest corners of the planet, and yet also the persistence and even expansion of diversity and the politics of identity and heritage. At the same time, it is ever clearer that culture and tradition are never fixed or pure, but always fluid and mixed, the distillation of the old and the new, the familiar and the unfamiliar, and the nearby and the faraway into ways of thinking and acting no less distinctive for their impure origins. Ajino-Moto MSG flavors the ancient fiesta favorite of *cuy,* or roast guinea pig, at a village baptism. A woman of Japanese descent takes the stage name "The Little Princess of Yungay" and becomes one of the great divas of Andean country music. Quechua continues to be spoken by more than 12 million people in Peru, Bolivia, and Ecuador, albeit spiced with Spanish borrowings. The great Peruvian activist and intellectual José Carlos Mariátegui had it right in 1927. "Tradition is alive and mobile," he wryly noted: "quite the opposite of what the traditionalists would like to think."[48]

The making and remaking of culture in the Andes pose still more questions for the anthropologist. What can be done to avoid losing sight of dimensions of continuity and stability in the rush to fashionable postmodern ruminations about "bricolage" and "hybridity" in the region? How do the injuries of poverty and racism manifest themselves in the outlook of the peasantry? How may the outbreak of feuding and schism belie stereotypes of the Rousseauian solidarity of the Andean village? What will further tightening of the global economy mean for habits and traditions of Tunnel Sixers, Cuyumalcans, and others? The next generation of anthropologists will struggle with these and other questions into the twenty-first century (and doubtless find as much to criticize in our present-day understanding of the Andes as we have with those that came before us). All that can be said with certainty is that there are no signs yet of the Andes turning into a carbon copy of the United States or anyplace else. As elsewhere around the world, history moves in more than one direction in highland South America.

The rondas prove a case in point. The models and motivations for patrolling spanned from the example of the coastal plantations to the history of vigilantism in the Andes of Cajamarca and Piura to the tradition of cooperation and mutual aid in village society. The rondas' expansion into justice-making and other duties built upon local knowledge of personal history and reputation as well as being influenced by Marxism, Christianity, Peruvian nationalism, and cherished standards of official bureaucracy and protocol. It was a mistake to think that the rondas were some sort of Incan system of justice handed down through the ages, although this did not prevent some Lima observers from insisting just that, perhaps a testament to the grip on city minds of Andeanism's tropes about the primevalness of village life. Nevertheless, the rondas were a system of justice and a movement unlike any other, a new tradition forged of the mixed codes and forced compromises of what literary theorist Mary Pratt calls the "contact zones," where cultures meet and grapple with each other.[49] It was telling that the poncho and the straw hat became the sine qua non of the rondero's unofficial uniform. This garb measured the feeling of distinctiveness as villagers and peasants that lay at the heart of the rondas. "I'm a rondero from Alfombrilla, with my poncho and straw hat . . . a peasant of big heart, patrolling the night, until dawn breaks," went a ballad by musician José Santos Díaz from this tiny hamlet in the heights of the Chota Valley.[50]

The rondas organized in a part of the Andes often presumed to have been assimilated into the national mainstream. Warming up on learning that this tall gringo came from the part of the United States, California, where his brother had immigrated to work as car mechanic, a bus driver I met at a truck stop in Piura offered advice: "You should go to Cuzco, Machu Picchu, Lake Titicaca, the south. These peasants around here don't have any culture to study." A people without culture? An assumption about the highlands of northern Peru as less indigenous and thus less interesting has certainly conditioned the traditional focus of anthropologists on the south-central Andes, the region in which the Incas had risen, Quechua was still spoken, and village life seemed to be more intact. By then I had lived in Tunnel Six for six months, and I replied to the bus driver that, at least to me, the matter was not so simple. Did not the rondas indicate the invention and renewal of a feeling of identity as villagers and Andeans that suggested it was premature to declare the death by assimilation of the northern highlands, I asked? The bus driver shrugged, whether in doubt or agreement I could not tell. He hailed the owner to order a beer and plate of goat stew, and he turned our conversation to what for him was the more pressing matter of Peru's chances in the next World Cup.

THE ANTHROPOLOGY OF SOCIAL MOVEMENTS

The topic of protest and mobilization in the Third World has been a matter of much debate in recent decades, and here, too, the rondas are revealing.[51] As a departure from the rule of Maoist warlords, party bosses, dictatorial generals, or corporate technocrats, the existence of women's organizations, ecological movements, indigenous federations, Christian base communities, and peasant unions can appear to offer hope for social change. One sociologist declares that they are "more endogenous, more participatory, and more authentic experiments of an alternative society."[52] This view would have us understand the movements of the downtrodden as a "third way," between Marxism and revolution and capitalism and the market. My first wish back in the 1980s to work with and write about the rondas was motivated by the mystique of the movement, namely, the conviction that the organizing of peasants and other marginalized groups may remake a better world.

The rondas have forced me to reexamine articles of faith about mobilization. It is revealing in the first place that I and so many other leftist scholars chose to study movements that appeared congenial to our own vision of the right kind of activism. We tended in Latin America to research the Mothers of the Disappeared in Argentina, gay and lesbian politics in Brazil, ecological protest in Venezuela, and indigenous mobilization in Ecuador, and to ignore soccer hooligans in Lima, conservative civic movements in Colombia, and neo-Nazi skinheads in Chile, even though these seemingly ignoble initiatives were just as much a part of a panorama of dissent and protest. These conscious and unconscious choices made it possible to maintain a distorted, idealized view of the downtrodden as a fountainhead of goodness and hope, a kind of Insurrectionary Other always imagined as in feisty opposition to the state and the ruling classes.

We will find the rondas to be more and less than a case of the disenfranchised struggling for justice denied by a repressive government. A distrust of officialdom was a fundamental motivation, and Ambulco's Francisco Chuquihuanga was just one among dozens of ronda leaders to be harassed, arrested, and tortured by the police. This was a willingness to suffer for the cause beyond even what I had expected or imagined. At the same time, however, there were also ways in which state officials supported and even incited the rondas, and various points when villagers sought out their approval. It will turn out that Régulo Oblitas went to Chota's subprefect in 1977 to ask his endorsement for the first committee in Cuyumalca. The government's provincial chief agreed, and, in the following years, the attitude of the authorities zigzagged from that initial authorization to a ban on rondas to a presidential decree legalizing the movement to new arrests of ronda activists. If the state's policy was seldom consistent or unified, the same was true of peasant responses, which went from the respectful Oblitas request to the burning of a police station to gratitude for the ronda legalization to anger and apathy at repression by the government of Alberto Fujimori (1990–   ). As far as the relation between movements for change and the state, the rondas suggest the possibility and perhaps even likelihood of manipulation as well as confrontation, interdependence as well as mistrust, and cooperation as well as conflict, in some cases at the very same time.

The rondas also highlighted imperfections in even the noblest initiatives. Against the sound of consensus implied in the concept of "social movement," it was easy enough to find squabbling and worse in the northern Andes. Grudges, jealousy and mistrust, and cliques always threatened to tear apart village committees. Sometimes they did. The intervention of political parties, Catholic and Protestant Churches, NGOs and other outsiders was just as prominent a part of ronda history. While spreading the gospel of peasant organizing, these groups introduced still more dilemmas and divisions, and they made maintaining a semblance of ronda unity all the more daunting. Even so committed a ronda booster as Eladio Idrogo, the young president of the ronda committee in the originating village of Cuyumalca, admitted to me one afternoon in 1990 that "division and hatred are everywhere."

Yet a reexamination does not have to mean dismissing protest's significance. As many scholars have shown, it has been part of Andean history since the Spanish conquest (and even before, such as in the anti-Inca uprising of the Chankas and the Pocras in the fourteenth century). The revolts of Tomás Katari and Túpac Amaru II came close to restoring native rule in the 1780s.[53] In the twentieth century, the rondas were just part of the story of highland upheaval. There were occupations of haciendas in Junín and Cuzco in the 1950s and early 1960s, strikes against the conservative military government in the late 1970s, and highway blockades for better corn prices in San Martín in the 1980s.[54] Even in times of apparent tranquility, villagers have very often nursed grievances, and in subtle ways challenged what they believe to be abusive authority—evading the tax collector, pilfering from the landlord, dodging the draft. Dissent powers up to mobilization and protest in the public defiance of the march, the strike, or even the armed revolt. In the Andes, these actions have often been met by guns and bullets, such as the slaughter by police of five unarmed villagers during the highway blockade in San Martín. The readiness of many villagers to fight and even die for their convictions underscores the absurdity of worn stereotypes about a "mañana attitude" throughout Latin America.[55]

What is there to show for these sacrifices? The decision of some young villagers in the early 1980s to join the Shining Path reminds us that mobilization's pathways have not always been productive, much less benign, in that case fueling a war in which there were no winners. In the rondas, however, the rewards were tangible: the eradication of thievery, the cheaper, faster justice of the assemblies, the public works. The pressure of protest throughout the Andes was one reason behind the end of serfdom, the better access to water and roads, free schools, and other twentieth-century improvements. In this way, the initiatives of villagers were more than what poet Czeslaw Milosz has called the "glory of slaves." There were not just struggles, but also conquests, even if hardship remained the rule in the countryside.

The battles of the rondas extended onto the terrain of culture and meaning. Tunnel Six's Víctor Córdova and many other movement protagonists were old enough to remember the humiliation of haciendas—the flogging of their parents for disobeying the mayordomo (the administrator), the denial of the right to vote, the torching of the farmhouses of villagers who failed to pay the rent. An assumption of the peasantry's ignorance, laziness, and lack of breeding ran through Peruvian society. "As social movements develop a struggle around a particular program," writes the British theorist Stuart Hall, "meanings which appear to have been fixed in place forever begin to lose their moorings."[56] The point suggests the inadequacy of accounts that would see protest as only a struggle over goods and property. It foregrounds the inseparability of the symbolic and the concrete, the cultural and the economic, and the meaningful and the material in the making of protest anywhere in the world. The rondas formed to defend property. Yet they involved a challenge to the assumption of the supremacy of the city over countryside, rich over poor, strong over weak. By way of the movement, explained Eladio Idrogo back on that same afternoon in 1990, "peasants were learning to demand to be treated as equals in our country." We will see that there were successes as well in this search for recognition and respect. Increased confidence developed among villagers, and a growing sense of the need to treat peasants with respect among town officials in the northern Andes, if only because they feared being beaten up and ridden out of town as several crooked policemen and judges were in the rondas' early days. "We're no longer anybody's hicks" went the new rural saying.

Protest had many faces in Peru of the 1980s. Even if those of us on the left may sometimes have overestimated the strength and ability of the rondas and other movements to bring change, there can be no denying the vitality of the rondas, shantytown associations, tribal councils, women's groups, human rights organizations, and trade unions of those years. The persistence of want and injustice underscored that it was wrong to cast even these most admirable movements of the 1980s as part of a lockstep march to social justice in Peru. Yet the organizing was a key element in the eventual decline in the human rights violations by the government, the advance of the cause of equality for women, the protection of rainforest land belonging to Amazonian tribes, and other steps toward a more genuine democracy. If Peru remained a divided and impoverished society, neither was it any longer what the acerbic nineteenth-century critic Manuel González Prada called a country of "gentlemen and serfs." The epilogue to *Nightwatch* discusses the decline of the rondas and other Peruvian movements in the 1990s. Still, this decade has witnessed the Landless Workers' Movement in Brazil, garment unions in the Philippines, and the Zapatistas in Mexico, to name but a few of the most visible movements. The facile view of the 1990s as the "Bland Decade" ignores that organizing by the downtrodden against the status quo is as much as ever a force to be reckoned with in many parts of the world. I have revised yet not abandoned my faith in the power of people acting together for change that brought me to the rondas in the first place more than a decade ago.

The changes in Peru were visible even in the chance encounter. One afternoon in 1987, a matron from the town of Paimas arrived in Tunnel Six. As Francisca Paz, Víctor's wife, recounted it, the woman had asked if Francisca had a daughter who would work as her maid, for twenty-five dollars a month. No one was kinder or more generous than Francisca, but the rise of the rondas and other developments in Tunnel Six had resulted in a growing prickliness about the condescension and the slights of the higher classes. The visitor's boldness was too much for Francisca. "I said no," she told me later, "and asked the señora if she had a daughter to help me with my washing and cooking." From my little house on the ridge, I saw the chunky woman head on to try at another farmhouse, and I could not help but admire her persistence in the face of the flies and the heat if not her quest to get a girl to work almost for nothing. She left at sunset without having found a recruit in Tunnel Six, and the episode struck me as a sign at the very least that the days of forced humility and subservience were fading into the past.

RECONCEPTUALIZING THE PEASANTRY[57]

A last and broadest contribution of the rondas may be to force us to consider the predicament of the countryside of the Third

World. About a third of the world's population lives in the backlands of Africa, Asia, and Latin America. Yet in the United States we hear little about these more than a billion people, and much of what we do hear amounts to clichés that depict them as costumed exotics rather than as fellow citizens of a shrinking planet. When villagers make the headlines, it is invariably because of famine, war, or natural disaster, a pattern of coverage that doubtless reenforces the familiar reflex to regard the Third World as a scary place best avoided by the prudent Westerner. Mainly, it seems to me that most of us in this country are simply not very interested in peasants like those in northern Peru. These small farmers do not have computers, pagers, or direct TV or in any other way seem on what we take to be modernity's cutting edge. Does a person become invisible if he or she does not have a Web page? This appears to be increasingly the case in the world today.

The work of scholars offers one starting point for trying to understand the condition of these least remembered members of global society. As anthropologists broadened their focus beyond the primitive in the 1950s and 1960s, they turned in increasing numbers to the peasantry, and to the economics and beliefs in villages in Afghanistan, Mexico, India, and elsewhere around the world.[58] The war in Vietnam led many anthropologists as well as political scientists, historians, and sociologists to examine the part of villagers in what one scholar called the "peasant wars of the 20th century," which for him included not just Vietnam but also Mexico, Russia, Cuba, and Algeria.[59] The debates about these and other topics no longer draw so much attention as when I was in graduate school in the mid-1980s or at least not in anthropology amidst the fascination with new objects of study such as cyberspace and biotechnology. Even so, a number of anthropologists continue to study the countryside, and their research ranges from the reasons for rural poverty to the experience of refugees, the influence of television, and the impact of relief organizations.

A key trend has been to rethink the much abused category of "the peasantry." As anthropologist Michael Kearney has argued, this label can do as much to obscure as illuminate the lives of poor farmers in the Third World.[60] He wants us to understand that the canonical view of peasants' attachment to tradition and the land fails to capture the experience of those who one day will stoop over their cornfield in Chihuahua, and who a week later will be hundreds of miles in Mexico City or dishwashing in a Los Angeles bistro. I share Kearney's suspiciousness about the category of "the peasant." I am less certain about his call to ditch the category entirely. Although José Paz, Eladio Idrogo, and many others scattered at various times across Peru in the quest for survival, crops and animals were still the primary subsistence for most families in the ronda heartland of Cajamarca and Piura; and many spent most of their lives in the countryside, in this sense true to the etymology of "peasant" as "people of the fields." It was just as clear that many people continued to describe themselves with the word. The rondas were not just rondas; they were rondas campesinas. The self-identification of poor farmers as peasants occurred as of the mid-1990s not just in northern Peru, but in other parts of Latin America, a fact underlined by the vitality of organizations such as the Peasant Federation of Paraguay, the Coordinating Council of Peasant Organizations of Honduras, and the Association of Central American Peasant Organizations. It may be a new kind of academic imperialism to advocate abolishing a category meaningful to so many people.

An explanation for the peasantry's existence lies in the global economy. As sociologist Manuel Castells reminds us, the distribution of money and capital remains uneven around the world, with much of the countryside of the Third World almost entirely bypassed by investment, technology, and prosperity.[61] What Castells terms the "obsolescence" of the hinterlands of Africa, Asia, and Latin America prompts the departure of hundreds of thousands of daughters and sons of villages. Yet scarcity of opportunity in the overtaxed cities of the Third World and obstacles to getting to the United States and Europe lead many others to stay behind. A downturn in the economy can even trigger "repeasantization," exactly the opposite of the "depeasantization" so often assumed to be the countryside's fate. After Alberto Fujimori in 1990 dictated the draconian austerity measures known as the "Fujishock," many young people returned to their native villages across the northern Andes, because they no longer had jobs or money even to eat in Lima and other cities. To be sure, Peru has followed the twentieth-century trend of urbanization, and two-thirds of Peruvians today live in cities. Still, the rural population has actually increased in absolute numbers. It was less than 2 million in 1900, and 7 million by 1990.[62] The growth reflects the failures of industrialization and development to provide an alternative to the meager income of farming a tiny plot in the Andes. In this way, the existence of a peasantry in Peru is not an anachronism, but a sign of the times, especially of the pattern of development and exclusion that has maintained and even multiplied the numbers of poor farmers in many corners of the planet. The villagers of the Third World are just as much a part of modernity's mix as computer programmers, university professors, or anyone else.

But why do people call themselves peasants? Part of the answer in Peru lies with the pressure from Marxist and populist parties as well as Juan Velasco Alvarado's leftist military government. These forces broadcast the word *campesino,* or peasant, as they encouraged villagers to identify as part of an exploited yet hardworking and virtuous class of small farmers. A legacy of colonialism was the association of "Indian" with inferiority and torpor. The stigma made many in the Andean countryside happy to shed what had previously been the most common label for the highland poor. As a result of these shifting winds of identity politics, "Indians" became "peasants," so much so that most Peruvian villagers would have been confused or insulted to be called by the old name. The abandonment of "Indian" did not simply or necessarily amount to an abnegation of tradition and heritage. On the contrary, a vision of shared history and culture was part of what it meant to belong to the peasantry, and in this sense the category marked ethnicity as much as class for the millions of Peruvians who made it theirs in the mid–twentieth century. It has become more common lately for people in parts of Latin America to foreground once again their real and imagined ties to the pre-Columbian past, a development sometimes measured in a preference for "indigenous" or "native." What anthropologist Xavier Albó describes as the "return of the Indian" has been much less pronounced in Peru, and at any rate "peasant" remains a standard self-designation for many villagers throughout the hemisphere.[63] Yet the changes underscore that there is nothing natural or self-evident about the choice and meaning of "peasant" in Latin America or anywhere else. As with any other kind of identity, it can vanish, reappear, and lose or accrue meanings with time's march.

I do think the case of peasants suggests the need for caution about the call to honor diversity that has become a platitude of our times. A will to celebrate can ignore the complexity of identity, which is always mixed and multistranded no matter what purity's ideologues would have us believe. An affiliation by village, region, religion, age, gender, and other factors mattered in Tunnel Six and the rest of the northern Andes, and a feeling of peasantness was just part of the package of personhood of each villager. It was not even self-evident to me or to villagers themselves that belonging to the peasantry was or should be considered a reason for pride and enthusiasm. To be a peasant is to be poor. In Tunnel Six, the majority of families owned between one and three hectares, a plot smaller than the parking lot at an average suburban shopping mall in the United States. The common wish among parents for their children to become engineers, teachers, or doctors reflected the frank knowledge of the hardships of small farmer life—the death of women in childbirth for the lack of a doctor, no money to buy a coffin for a grandfather carried away by cholera, starvation in drought and flood. A realism on the part of northern villagers about the grimness of their predicament coexisted with independence and pride about the rondas and other accomplishments in their ambivalent thinking about being peasants. As I consider it now even after the many years since I came to Tunnel Six, it strikes me more than ever as incredible and almost foolhardy that villagers were able to develop a sense of worth and dignity at all, given the doubt and hardship that they faced as part of the poorest class of people on earth.

I hope to convey a sense of uncertainty and ambivalence in this book. Individualist or communalist? Innovative or traditionalist? Revolutionary or reactionary? An examination of the rondas will disclose falseness as well as truth in all of these extremes in characterizations of the peasantry. We can only abandon the conceit that the aspirations and consciousness of people anywhere in the countryside can somehow be boiled down to a single dimension. These were lives different and more difficult yet no less full of paradox, shadings, and secrets than our own.

THE PONGO'S DREAM

A vision of redemption and utopia emerges in a rural tale from Cuzco told sometime in the 1940s to the writer José María Arguedas. In "The Pongo's Dream," a *pongo,* serf, recounts his dream of the afterlife to the landlord of the hacienda.[64] "That's how it should be," crows the landlord, upon hearing that, on Judgment Day, Saint Francis ordered a shimmering angel to cover him with honey until he shone like gold, while a "worthless old angel with scaly feet" smeared the serf with shit from a gasoline can. But, finished the serf, "our father Saint Francis took another look at us, first at you, then at me, a long time. . . . Then he said: 'Whatever the angels had to do with you is done. Now, lick each other's body slowly, for all eternity.' " Is it possible that the world will turn upside down, and the meek inherit the earth? This was the tale's forecast.

The prediction of anything like a complete reversal of the status quo does not appear destined for fulfillment. It may be wise to be wary about such transpositional dreams in any event. After all, they are not exactly, or even at all, about equality and common humanity, for their promise is not the abolition but inversion of hierarchy and humiliation—crudely put, a world where someone still has to lick shit. The inversionary model certainly does not work any better as a sociological paradigm, oversimplifying history as it does into a struggle between oppressors and oppressed with a fixed end-point, in this case the underdog's revenge "for all eternity."

The dream of a world upside down was not much on the minds of most villagers in the northern Andes anyway. In Tunnel Six, they had witnessed serfdom's end, and yet been freed into a new world that offered little in the way of comfort and opportunity. If there remained a willingness to endure and fight, it was tempered by a pragmatism about the unlikelihood of salvation and redemption and mixed with other and sometimes unexpected musings about fortune's turns. One late afternoon in 1987 I sat with Víctor and a few neighbors on the saddle blankets in front of his farmhouse. The ronda leader's little boys, Jorge and Edwin, and their precocious cousin, María Socorro, romped after an indignant chicken in the dirt clearing speckled with goat droppings, and the sun hung over the razor-backed hills toward the San Lorenzo Valley in a blaze of blood orange. As it often did, talk turned to the rondas, and the disputes to be heard that night in the school lunchroom. It did not stop there, however. Víctor segued into a story about a knife fight up in Cacaturo, and then to tales of gold and the ancients, "the gentiles," as Tunnel Sixers referred to the original inhabitants of pre-Columbian Peru. Víctor half-smiled, and I could not tell whether he was joking or serious.

"How about if we go up there tonight with the ronda, just to find out?"

ONE

Origin Stories

I lived in the gray city of Lima in 1991. My wife, Robin, was the correspondent for magazines and newspapers in the United States. There were all too many stories to cover in that year, Peru on the brink of collapse amidst guerrilla bombings, army massacres, corruption scandals, drug trafficking, and recession. I scratched every morning on yellow legal pads in the little rooftop office I was assigned as a visiting researcher at the Institute of Peruvian Studies. Through the mist down in the park below, I could sometimes make out a street sweeper in orange overalls or an urchin trying to slingshot a bony dove. I loved the city's hard edge, the street soccer, seafood, tabloids, and the faded colonial splendor of the downtown. But Lima, I had to admit, deserved its reputation as the ugliest and most depressing Latin American capital, with a misery belt of shantytowns, quick-fingered thieves, septic tap water, and the feeling of hunger and sometimes desperation on the rainless streets. I wondered whether simultaneous attraction and repulsion inspired a famous line of poet Carmen Ollé. "In Lima," she wrote, "beauty is a steel corset." [1]

I was not far removed from my anthropologist's "field" in that year in Lima. The mountains of northern Peru where I had researched the rondas were just an overnight bus ride away. I went back for meetings of ronderos in 1991 in the towns of Cutervo and Bambamarca. Since I had given friends and "informants" from the Andes our address in the capital, they appeared now and then to spend the night, report on news, or sometimes to ask for the bus fare back to the countryside after failing to find a job as a watchman or gardener in the big city.

We sent money to Tunnel Six so Víctor could come visit us with his two boys, Jorge and Edwin. Our landlady was not happy about the arrival of the Córdovas, or any of our other short, work-worn, brown-skinned houseguests from the Andes. To her they were dirty and uneducated, and fit to enter only through the servant's entrance as garbagemen, housecleaners, or peddlers. Perhaps it was predictable that we as would-be progressive North Americans felt an enjoyable edge of transgression and moral superiority in having villagers in the apartment. Mainly, however, we just had fun when Víctor and the boys came to Lima, touring such sights as the down-at-the-heels national capital had to offer. At the zoo, they tarried longest not in front of the lions, tigers, or elephants, but a pair of foxes. Foxes were common in the Andean foothills. However, few villagers ever glimpsed anything more than the flash of tail in the brush. In the grimy cage, there was no place to hide, so Víctor and the boys enjoyed the novelty of a full view of these animals, familiar yet magical for their ability to escape detection in the wild.

I started to think about how to write a history of the rondas during those gray mornings. It was not the most imaginative way to plan the task, but I began with the matter of origin, and how it was that the movement had come into existence. I had gone to Chota in 1990 to learn more about how the committees started in this high valley that in 1976 was the birthplace of the movement. Why had the rondas grown so fast into a rallying point for peasant pride throughout the northern Andes? Did a single person dream up the plan of patrolling against thieves? If so, who? Did the plan originate in the countryside? Or somewhere else? Why did the rondas start when they did? What was it anyway that led villagers to take to the trails from dusk to dawn? What did the "origin stories" I heard in Chota and elsewhere reveal about the convictions of the tellers, and about what was remembered and forgotten in the Andes? These were the questions I puzzled over in the long months of 1991.

This opening chapter of *Nightwatch* seeks to address them. As I have come to understand it, the genealogy of the rondas is complex, in places uncertain, and recorded in sometimes unexpected lines of necessity, ambition, and alliance. Village suffering in the face of want and crime was the most basic reason for the decision to patrol against thieves. But poverty alone cannot explain the rondas, and there was much more to the story. When the Cuyumalca schoolhouse was looted in a series of break-ins in 1976, the values of villagers came under attack, and patrolling meant protecting the dream of progress that had gripped the Peruvian Andes in the twentieth century. Even then, Cuyumalcans had to be urged and even bullied to sign the agreement to start a "Night Ronda," and in this sense it was the result of pressure "from above" as well as initiative "from below." As I review the welter of forces, figures, and coincidences, it should not perhaps be so surprising that I have pulped a forest of legal pads since 1991 in writing my account of the start of the rondas.

It used to be that anthropologists were only accountable to a handful of other specialists in the confines of the university. Nowadays it is just as common for "the natives" to talk back, and for "participant-observers" to feel uncomfortable in the mantle of vicarious understanding and detached analyses. After I wrote an article in 1991 on the rondas for a Peruvian magazine, I returned to Chota.[2] One villager, Segundo Edguén, confronted me with a copy in the bus station. Sunday was the day for drinking in Chota, and the cane-liquor-emboldened Edguén to complain and even shout to the confused passengers in the waiting room that I failed to credit his father as the ronda founder. A year later I got a letter from a Peruvian graduate student reporting that Edguén was saying that I had been a spy for the United States and the Peruvian government, on a mission to sabotage the rondas. On returning to Chota in the summer of 1993, I climbed the mountainside to his farmhouse to see if reconciliation was possible. Edguén was not home, so I left a note. Later, I ran into him in Chota. He thanked me for searching him out, yet claimed with a smile that "Orin" was now rural slang for traitor.

Perhaps. But most villagers seem weary about jockeying for credit for the rondas. "It took everyone to get on the trails every night, not any single person," as one Cuyumalcan explained to me in 1992. Many Cuyumalcans told me that Segundo Edguén's father was a good man and an early ronda supporter, but I found no evidence that he was the prime mover. What is certain is that the debate over the title of ronda originator will not end anytime soon. A force to be reckoned with in village society, Edguén is the current president of the Cuyumalcan ronda committee, and not shy about advancing his views, whether drunk or sober. As we shall see, however, there are others, all still living, one in Cuyumalca, two in the town of Chota, and one in Lima, each of whom believes that he is the true ronda founder. The fight for credit is tangled, contradictory, and perhaps unresolvable. As the saying goes in the Andean countryside, "success has many fathers." The rondas grew from small beginnings in Cuyumalca into a massive movement unlike any other in the recent history of the Peruvian Andes. Only about achievements of the initiative against theft and lawlessness did just about everyone agree.

"After God and the Virgin come the rondas," declared one old man in Cuyumalca I met on that trip in 1993.[3]

SCARCITY AND SURVIVAL

The most common explanation for the birth of the rondas in Cajamarca and Piura is theft. Thievery was common in the Andes in the early and middle part of the twentieth century.[4] The problem worsened in the late 1970s and early 1980s in many northern provinces. Skirts, shirts, shovels, shoes, crowbars, buckets, chickens, ducks, pigs, goats, sheep, cattle, horses, burros, and mules "did not see the dawn," as Angélica Jara in Tunnel Six put it: "It was pure sadness in the time before the rondas. You couldn't even leave a shirt out to dry on the bushes overnight. We lost five ducks one night, then a cow the next month, and there was just nothing to do about it." Some families locked horses and cattle into iron hobbles at night. Others slept outside with stones and machetes or brought stock into their houses. Jara and others remember nights filled with the sounds of barking dogs, panicked shouts, and the echo of shotguns. In 1987, I went house to house in Tunnel Six to ask what families lost. My survey showed that some 762 animals disappeared in Tunnel Six between 1980 and 1983, more than six animals per family. Everything I was told suggested the same scale of loss in Cuyumalca. The imagery of fear and impoverishment in later memories of the "days before the rondas" may have been exaggerated, but I had little doubt that theft had been rampant.

But this was not some immemorial fact of peasant existence. The rise in theft followed upon land reform in the Peruvian countryside. Until the government of General Juan Velasco Alvarado (1968–75) abolished the haciendas in 1969, the greater part of Andean land belonged to estates, many of them enormous, that were run as quasi fiefdoms by the landowner or his mayordomo.[5] The

Angélica Jara and son Manuelito, 1986

imperatives of "development" and "modernization" in the years
after World War II made the haciendas seem an obstacle to for-
ward-looking politicians in Lima, and a number of development
planners from the United States promoted their abolition to make
way for progress.[6] What the writer and anthropologist José María
Arguedas had called "the serf's dream" propelled a wave of protest
in the central highlands in the late 1950s and early 1960s.[7] Velasco
went on national television to "end forever the unjust social order
that impoverished and oppressed millions of landless peasants who
have always been forced to work the lands of others."[8] His motto
was "Land to the tiller." The 1969 reform handed over almost
600,000 hectares to ex-serfs and the landless.[9] Two million more
hectares were converted into cooperatives to be administered by
the government. Velasco, the son of a humble Piuran family, is
remembered even today by many villagers in northern Peru as
an emancipator. "Juan Velasco Alvarado, Teacher President, your
name will be remembered by peasants of every region," one ballad
gushed after the break-up of the estates.[10]

The reform did not meet expectations. Cooperatives fell into
mismanagement and corruption. There was not enough land in the
Andes for everyone, and the loans and technology promised to vil-

General Juan Velasco Alvarado promulgating agrarian reform, 1969
(courtesy of Quehacer)

lagers did not materialize. The inhabitants of the countryside got
by with sparse flocks of animals and steep plots of just a few hectares cultivated with shovels and horse- or oxen-drawn plows. Most
villagers did not have electricity, running water, or health care of
any kind. They were free of the landlords, but not of poverty. By
the middle of the 1970s, Velasco's "new Peru" seemed as distant
as ever.

A tailspin in the Peruvian economy compounded hardship. The
1980s was a period of crisis and recession throughout Latin America
and nowhere did the trouble strike earlier or harder than in
Peru. As debt and inflation mounted, conservative generals ousted
Velasco in 1975.[11] At the urging of the World Bank and other foreign lenders, the new president—General Francisco Morales Bermúdez—implemented austerity measures that included a tripling
of the price of basic goods such as flour, sugar, rice, and gas. These
steps did not ease inflation, which reached almost 70 percent in
1979. They did trigger a recession and a 15 percent decline in the
gross national product between 1976 and 1978.[12] There were spurts
of recovery in the next decade during the cycle of growth and collapse that economists Efraín Gonzales and Lilian Samamé called

Milking a goat,
Tunnel Six, 1986

Irrigating a field,
Tunnel Six, 1986

the "Peruvian pendulum." But the overall balance of the period between 1975 and 1990 was disastrous.[13] While the gross national product declined by one-third and real wages by one-quarter, the percentage of Peruvians below the line of extreme poverty grew from one-half to two-thirds of the population.

The crisis in Lima would not have affected villagers had they lived by farming alone. But they did not. Almost every rural family was involved in weaving, trading, brick making, carpentry, masonry, liquor making, or mule driving. Money earned by cutting cane or picking cotton on coastal plantations was already a crucial part of the income of many inhabitants of the northern mountains by the second half of the nineteenth century. This mobility belies what anthropologist Liisa Malkki labels the "sedentarist metaphysics" of villagers ever "tied" and "rooted" to the land.[14] Rhythms of seasonal and permanent migration speeded up in subsequent decades. By the 1970s, villagers from Cuyumalca and Tunnel Six worked on plantations of coca and palm in the Amazon jungle as well as the coastal plain. They were maids, ditchdiggers, cooks, street sweepers, gardeners, and watchmen in the big cities of Chiclayo, Piura, Trujillo, and Lima. The cash from these off-farm activities paid for kerosene, rubber boots, salt, matches, polyester shirts, tennis shoes, school notebooks, and even noodles and rice to supplement what they grew for themselves. Inflation pushed the prices of these goods upward, and the recession shrank the already miserable wages paid to migrants from the mountains for long days of labor on plantations or in the cities. It was not easy to survive in the best of times in the countryside. The crisis of the middle 1970s and into the 1980s pushed thousands of families to the edge.

What was the connection between hunger and theft? I think about Pastor Guaygua and Margarita Livia in Tunnel Six.[15] The couple and their three children lived in a little farmhouse in a clearing in a brushy canyon behind the canal. There were no furnishings besides a broken table and a straw mattress in the dirt-floored hovel. The skin of a bush viper that Margarita found curled in the eaves was nailed to the broken wall of adobe brick. With just a sliver of land by the road to Piura, Pastor and Margarita ranked among the poorest of the 100 families in Tunnel Six.

Only the few dollars Pastor made from occasional ditchdigging in nearby Paimas kept the family from going hungry. Although Robin and I became the godparents of their fourth child, we never broached the touchy topic of theft, even with the gregarious Margarita, who loved trading gossip about the peccadilloes of wild teenagers and errant husbands. Yet I knew that the couple had the reputation as "fruit birds," pilferers, before the beginning of the rondas in 1984. With a shoe size of ten, Pastor had the biggest feet in the village. The widower Luciano Alvarado once told me that the footprints he had found in his muddy corral in the morning after a night in 1983, when two of his goats had disappeared, could only have been Pastor's. That year, flooding from the El Niño tropical current had combined with economic freefall to leave many families in Tunnel Six facing starvation. Perhaps not everything that Pastor took went to maintain the family. At twenty-eight, Pastor was still something of a wayward spirit. He liked to buy a pack of cigarettes or join the penny-ante card games in Eduardo's back storeroom. The best player on the ragtag soccer squad from Tunnel Six, he even bought a used pair of cleats and a leather ball that had to be restitched before every pickup game on the rocky clearing in back of the schoolhouse. It may have been that Pastor sold a stolen animal now and then to finance these modest pleasures, or perhaps a bright polyester sweater for Margarita or the children's school notebooks. But I suspected the soup pot mattered most in that especially hard year when floodwaters washed away corn seedlings and swarms of rats spread the bubonic plague in the Quiroz Valley. Once during a conversation on the bench in front of my little adobe house, Margarita seemed to acknowledge what had gone on during that time. "It was pure hardship in those times, and just about all of us fell into bad habits out of necessity."

I was not always able to pin down the "facts" of theft. Although everywhere I went in the northern mountains villagers admitted in the abstract that "just about everyone" was involved, I did not find anyone who wanted to talk about his or her own role. Too many people believed such admissions would expose them to damaging gossip and perhaps even sorcery, if not prosecution. I think Pastor and a number of others who became my friends in Tunnel Six would have talked about thieving if I had insisted. Because these were matters of which I knew they preferred not to speak, I never

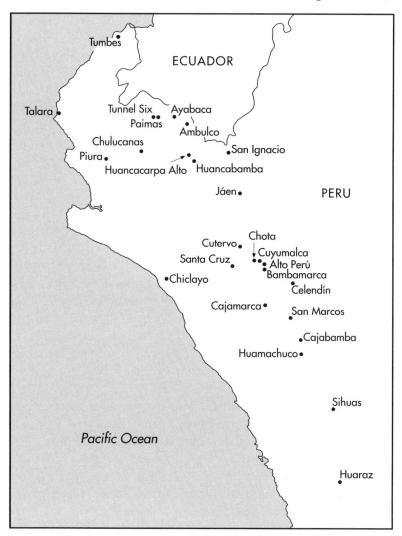

Map 1. Detail of Northern Peru

did press them. This was one of those instances where friendship mattered more than research.

Once a helpful Chotan barber said he could get a reformed rustler in the village of Colpa Matara to talk to me about his past. On the prearranged day, I walked up to his house on the country highway out of Chota. He only stared at the floor and mumbled about having to go to pasture a horse. Another time I told villagers in La Iraca about wanting to speak with someone who had robbed in the days before the rondas. They promised to help, their way of repaying me for helping them get money for potable water from a Lima development group. A few days later, a delegation of villagers knocked on the door of my hotel room. They said the person they had in mind had refused to come. One villager obligingly volunteered to pretend that he was a rustler so that I could interview him. Although I had read the fashionable ruminations about the unstable boundary between truth and fiction in ethnography, it seemed a stretch to start recording interviews with pretend thieves. I declined the offer. Perhaps it was in punishment for this literalism that I never got another chance to talk with either a "fake" or "real" rustler.

Beyond question, though, thievery had been epidemic. The threat bred an atmosphere of distrust in villages where just about everyone was a "fruit bird," a pilferer. It was compounded by the nighttime raids of rustler bands. Sometimes "fruit birds" collaborated with the "big thieves" in chains of complicity through truckers and traders and slaughterhouses in cities such as Piura, Sullana, Chiclayo, and Trujillo. Donicio Núñez lost three of his four cattle one night in 1983: "Some nights you could hear a truck coming down the road by the canal. It would have the headlights off. I think they had dealings with someone or the other here, who would have a couple of stolen cows ready to go, and maybe get a few dollars for them. Then you'd hear the truck drive away, straight to the slaughterhouse on the coast. Nobody wanted to get shot. They'd just stay in their houses." Many rustlers' identities were widely suspected or known. Some people looked the other way lest their own secrets be exposed. Others feared retaliation. "Nobody wanted to risk it," Núñez explained.

The result was spiraling lawlessness, though rustling could not have made much of a profit except for the most active offenders. Snatching a turkey rarely outweighed the price of living in a Hobbesian world where herds shrank and even crops could be stripped from the fields at night. The departure of the hacendados meant that even the "wealthiest" families in Tunnel Six and elsewhere in the northern countryside seldom had more than five or

Rustlers stealing a cow, by village artist José Espíritu Pérez Tafur from Cumbe-Chontabamba in the Bambamarca Valley, 1986 ("Go, Go, Fast. Careful the owner doesn't hear us.")

six hectares; eight or ten head of cattle; and perhaps a small store to sell pop, kerosene, and a few other dry goods. Pervasive poverty made theft a threat to everyone's survival in the countryside. Everyone was vulnerable to the trauma of loss.

This was true of Pastor and Margarita. One morning in 1982, Pastor headed down the trail to begin the rice harvest, while Margarita stayed behind to boil yucca for lunch, tend to the children, and wash clothes in the dirty creek that cut through the canyon. On arriving at their plot above the Quiroz River, Pastor discovered that thieves had descended the night before to cut, thresh, and sack the rice with the thoroughness of locusts.

It was sometimes hard for me to understand just how people in Tunnel Six patched together a living in good years. I could not imagine how Pastor and Margarita had fed themselves and their kids after losing the crop that year.

The answer was that sometimes they had not.

"We went hungry a lot," replied Margarita when I asked how they survived the rest of 1982.

DEEP PERU?

The historian Jorge Basadre drew a distinction between "official Peru" and "deep Peru." His premise was that Andean villagers lived in "deep Peru" beyond and outside the "official" Peruvian nation. The bureaucracy was seated in the coastal capital of Lima founded by the Spanish as the seat of the viceroyalty. For this reason, according to Basadre, the peasantry had never been truly incorporated into either the Iberian empire or the new nation of Peru; it was so "given to the soil, organically tied to it" as to ignore the "Nation and State." In line with the way of seeing that can be called "Andeanism," he concluded that village remoteness and government indifference had shielded ancestral ways from the outside world, making peasants into the preservers of the "primitive" and "anachronistic" traditions of the past. Basadre was not oblivious to the suffering of the rural poor, but he felt Peru's future depended on assimilation into the national mainstream. Only in this way could Peru overcome "rudimentary and fragmentary localism" to make way for "technology, dynamism, and progress."[16]

An obvious problem with the theory of "two Perus" is that Andean villagers were never cut off from government rule. Countless settlements with Iberian-style plazas, churches, and *cabildos,* or municipalities, testify to forced relocation in the wake of conquest. There was a colonial administrator in many villages throughout the three centuries of the Iberian empire. Archives from colonial times and the first decades of the new republic show that rural people came often to the seats of government to make petitions and lodge complaints.[17] In the twentieth century, the district governor appointed a man in each village to represent the central government. Even the most godforsaken hamlet usually had a school, and the teacher was named and paid by the Ministry of Education. The people of Tunnel Six, Cuyumalca, and elsewhere voted in municipal and national elections; went to the town or city to seek loans from the Agrarian Bank; and dealt often with policemen, judges, bureaucrats, and other government representatives. They sang the national anthem at Independence Day celebrations in front of the schoolhouse, and they certainly did not think of themselves as anything less than fully Peruvian. It is misleading to think that villagers were ever outside what historians Philip Corrigan and Derek Sayer call the "great arch" of the national state.[18]

This is not to say that the presence of the government was uniform in the Andes. The majority of the population was rural, yet the offices of the police, prosecutors, courts, municipalities, and ministries could be found only in town. Although lodging a complaint about theft with the police or petitioning the subprefect for a highway was very much a part of village experience, anyone with business to transact had to walk, ride, or hop a truck to town. If the matter was urgent, a villager might scrape together a few dollars for the journey to the departmental offices of the government in Chiclayo, Trujillo, Piura, or Cajamarca—even all the way to Lima.

The absence of policemen is another explanation for theft. There were offices of the regular police, prison and border police, and plainclothes investigators in Chota and other larger towns. Paimas and other seats of a district government usually had a Civil Guard (GC) station manned by one or two officers. This meant that the nearest policemen was a several-hours' hike away from many villages. Thieves were free to roam the icy punas, and a villager had to take a day or even two away from the fields to report the theft of a cow or horse. "There was nobody to stop the thieves from coming and going as they pleased," a woman in Cuyumalca reported.

Not that villagers believed more policemen were the answer. In a Hualgayoc village, over the pass from Cuyumalca, I heard the tale of a pair of thieves dressing a stolen sheep in a straw hat and poncho. According to the story, they propped it up on two legs between them to get past a police checkpoint. When the unhappy animal let out a loud bleat, one of the thieves said, "Be quiet, you're drunk, my friend." The policeman on duty waved by the men and the sheep. This merciless parable of obtuseness was one of the most generous I heard over the years in the northern Andes. Most talk centered on outright corruption: "The police were the biggest thieves around here. They just supported the bad elements. A rustler would come through town with somebody's cows, and the sergeant would just say, 'Give me a few dollars' or 'Go steal some more.'" The opinion of Donicio Núñez in Tunnel Six found expression in a skit that villagers put on in 1986 for the third anniversary of the founding of the rondas. To play a policeman conspiring with rustlers to rob an elderly couple's cows, one man donned a green cap and penned "GC" for "Civil Guard" onto his T-shirt. "Really great, compadre," crowed the policeman as he and the rustlers shared a case of beer from the profits.

It is impossible to measure the accuracy of these views. As I knew from paying "fines" of a few dollars to come back across the border from Ecuador, corruption was common among the police. A Civil Guard officer earned only $100 a month in 1975 and a judge or prosecutor in the provinces just $150. As inflation cut the value of wages, money from bribery and graft became a way to buy a dress for a daughter's confirmation in Chiclayo, or a case of beer to toast the patron saint of the police, Saint Rose of Lima. Headlines reveled in scandal: "Band of Republic Guards Carried Out Six Kidnappings"; "Drug Godfather Chose Judges"; "Police Chief Charged with Theft of Checks."[19] Peruvian president Alan García (1985–90) was accused of funneling public money to his personal account in a Miami bank, and the normality of corruption in the 1970s and through the 1980s heightened the feeling of impunity and opportunity for policemen and the rest of the bureaucracy throughout the northern Andes.

The resentment of Núñez and others was exacerbated by attempting to use official channels. It was true that distinctions between villagers and middle-class officials in town were less coded by race and ethnicity than in many provinces in the southern Andes. Historians believe the north was especially hard hit by death and disease in the aftermath of the conquest, and one reason for the predominance of mixed race and occasionally even light-skinned villagers in the mountains of Cajamarca and Piura.[20] The history of mestizaje meant that northern villagers were no "darker" in complexion than town officials, since these provincial bureaucrats themselves often had Indian as well as European blood (the holders of higher offices were more likely to be white in the Peruvian hierarchy of race and power). The fact that northern villagers spoke Spanish, not Quechua, also made them less "different" from the local authorities than were the inhabitants of the Andean countryside a few hundred miles to the south. Yet a peasant and a policeman were hardly social equals. The police and other civil servants belonged to the middle or at least the lower middle-classes, and they earned a living in offices in town. Officials conveyed their condescending superiority toward peasants in their officiously hurried or distracted manner. They addressed them like children with the informal *tú*. A lawyer from Chiclayo, Benjamín Vílchez, the district attorney in Chota, told me: "These Indians are uncivilized and uneducated. It's true that they have a hard life, but they're stoned on coca and cane liquor, and they don't work to advance themselves or even keep themselves clean."

Anthropologist Marisol de la Cadena has observed that "money whitens" in Peru.[21] By this calculus of race and class, poverty "darkens," so in the northern Andes mestizo and Spanish-speaking villagers appeared to the prosecutor and other townspeople to be "Indians" and thus less than fully civilized. The vehemence of rural tales I heard about "abuses," "criminality," and "extortion" reflected the reality of the corruption. Perception of the authorities' discrimination sharpened bad feelings. "There's never justice for the poor, for the people of the countryside," as another villager in Tunnel Six asserted on a hot afternoon in 1986.

The obstacles in official channels did not stop many villagers from pressing for action. Archives in the municipality in Chota show that people from the countryside had come to the Civil Guard between 1970 and 1975 with more than 350 reports of the disappearance of cattle, mules, horses, and shovels and plows. Although mistrusted and ineffective, the police remained the only option for recovering stolen property. Some villagers came forward even when it meant bringing a turkey as a "present" and addressing the commander as "boss." Still, chances for success were small.

Of the cases I reviewed in Chota's archives, only two of seventy-five resulted in thieves being caught.

A QUEST IN CUYUMALCA

The need for protection against theft drove Régulo Oblitas in 1976 to think about a nightwatch. Like many others in the Chota Valley, the thirty-four-year-old Cuyumalcan left the Andes as a teenager to cut cane at Tumán, a plantation just a few miles from the spot where the splendid golden tomb of the Lord of Sipán, a ruler in the ancient Moche culture, would be discovered three decades later to international fanfare. Oblitas returned to Cuyumalca in 1960 to farm a two-hectare plot inherited from his parents. After marrying Berbelina Irigoín in 1962, he built a farmhouse with a view across the valley to the mountains of Cutervo. Irigoín raised guinea pigs by the thatched kitchen to the side of the house, and saw to the needs of a family that grew to include nine children. Since their harvest was seldom enough to feed everyone, Irigoín wove saddle-bags with peacock and dragon designs to sell in the Sunday Chota market.[22] Oblitas saw to the planting and harvest, and he pastured a herd of a half-dozen cattle in the moors lying an hour's walk above the farmhouse.

Oblitas and Irigoín told me they were disappointed that there was not land enough to keep their grown children in Cuyumalca. A son went away to the Huallaga Valley coca fields in 1985. A daughter left the next year to work as a maid in Chiclayo. The children's departure was standard in the Andean countryside.[23] Every bit of land was already planted. Cornfields already clung to the most impossibly vertiginous mountainsides. "My parents have two hectares. There are four of us children. So I had to go," one nineteen-year-old in Tunnel Six explained to me. He worked for a dollar a day as a farmhand on palm plantations in the tick-infested swamps near the Amazonian city of Pucallpa. Other young villagers were attracted by the opportunity for work in a factory or opening a business. For girls, there was even the attraction of escaping the tyranny of obedience to husbands and fathers in what remained the patriarchal order of village society. Most villagers were well aware of how hard it was to be poor and Andean in Lima or Chiclayo. However, poverty's push weighed more than the city's pull in the decision to leave for these young people. They were "travelers" less by choice than necessity. "Sad is the life of the poor scattered to the ends of the earth," Berbelina Irigoín once said of her children's peregrinations to the jungle and the city.

Oblitas was appointed as Cuyumalca's lieutenant governor in 1971. The position was the bottom rung in the Peruvian system of government authority. A lieutenant governor received no salary. He was an Andean villager with work-worn hands and country Spanish, who removed his hat before the subprefect and addressed him as "Mr. Sub-Prefect." Nevertheless this was an important position in the small world of village society. As the government representative, the lieutenant governor was the "maximum authority" in the village, and organized meetings about trail maintenance and ditch cleaning. He also headed delegations to town to petition for roads, schools, and clinics. In this sense, the lieutenant governor had a double identity as a "villager" and an "authority," what anthropologist Alonso Zarzar would call a "hinge" between state and society.[24] In Peru the subprefect appointed the lieutenant governor, usually picking a literate villager who supported the government. Oblitas fit the bill. He had backed the Velasco government reforms. Unlike many villagers of his generation, he could read and write, having stayed in school until the fourth grade. Oblitas served as the lieutenant governor in Cuyumalca until 1973. The subprefect reappointed him to the position in 1975, just a year before the founding of the rondas.

I knew about Oblitas from an essay on the rondas coauthored by Telmo Rojas.[25] On the way to Chota for the first time in 1990, I stopped in the city of Cajamarca to visit the burly sociologist. He told me how to find Oblitas in Cuyumalca. When I climbed the trail from Chota, I was struck by the contrast between Cuyumalca and Tunnel Six. Cuyumalca was lovely, the opposite of the sullen foothills where I had lived in 1986 and 1987. As in many villages in the Andes, there was no real center to Cuyumalca. The homesteads of adobe and terracotta spread across a landscape of green pastures, golden cornfields, fast brooks, stone fences, patches of wildflowers under the bright blue of the Andean sky. As I climbed, I exchanged the requisite "Buenos días" with a woman in a peasant skirt and straw hat milking a cow by her farmhouse, and then with a man in rubber tire sandals and a bright purple poncho driving a herd of

Régulo Oblitas, the ronda founder? 1990

sheep down the trail to Chota. Despite the beautiful setting, scarcity and poverty in Cuyumalca were no different from Tunnel Six. These villagers also struggled to make a living from small herds and tiny plots. The average income of each household was about $500 a year.

The imagery of bucolic isolation was just as deceptive. Like Tunnel Six and other Andean villages, Cuyumalca was a crossing in the web of diaspora and necessity that connected the Andes to the rest of the world, and a hub of comings and goings to markets in towns across the mountains, the jungles and the coast, and even the United States. On learning I was from the United States, one man dived into his farmhouse to dig out a picture of his brother with his Honduran wife next to a flocked Christmas tree in their house in a Los Angeles subdivision. The brother had found a job as a janitor at the John Wayne International Airport in Orange County.

I found Oblitas building a wattle-and-daub cooking shed next to the farmhouse. The fifty-three-year-old villager looked to me like a smaller, brown-skinned version of my father back in California. He was slender, with strong yet handsome features. Despite the unexpected arrival of an oversized American, Oblitas greeted me with his gold-toothed smile. He sent a son to fetch a saddle blanket for the wood bench in front of the farmhouse. As I explained I had been given his name as a founder of the ronda, Oblitas perused my passport and a letter of introduction I had obtained from the Chota subprefect. "Thanks, Doctor," he said after copying my name into a notebook with a picture of the British royal wedding on the cover.

The conundrum of my name and title was complicated. Since "Orin" means urine in Spanish, I introduced myself by my middle name, "Raymond" in Tunnel Six. I was a student then, but even the Tunnel Sixers I knew best addressed me as "Don Raimundo." After graduating from Stanford, I became "Doctor." Nobody would ever use the intimate *tú* form for "you." In reaction to the obeisance due to the authorities and landlords, there was a premium on courtesy in the Andean countryside, and just about every older man could expect to be addressed with the respectful "Don." The fact that I was accorded this honorific as a twenty-six-year-old in Tunnel Six had less to do with me than with the persistence of a history of deference to whiteness and money. Even villagers in Tunnel Six I have known for more than a decade would never call me by the formal *usted,* and I must do likewise because informality would be an imposition rather than a sign of friendship. I supposed I should just accept this practice as a reminder of divides of class and nationality between us even in friendship's intimacy. Yet now and then it feels strange to me as a would-be relaxed American when old friends address each other in so formal a way.

Over the years, Oblitas had grown unhappy and even obsessed with what he felt was the lack of recognition in Cuyumalca and beyond for his part in starting the rondas. He and Segundo Edguén, whose farmhouse was only a ten-minute walk down the hill, hated each other for reasons I never understood. It was the opinion of Oblitas that Edguén only campaigned for his dead father to be viewed as the ronda founder from "malevolence and hatred toward" him. The wish to validate his own claim to the title made Oblitas happy to give me his account of the movement:

Doctor, the thieves took everything in those days. Somebody even cleaned out the house of my old grandparents. Cows, calves, sheep, pots—they left them without anything. . . . And there was no place to complain, because the authorities were more than anything on the side of those who were doing the theft. I remembered from Tumán that the owners organized the workers in a watch system. So when I saw so much crime on my return to the Andes, I thought it would be simple for us to do the same. We'd defend each other. While one slept, the other would patrol. So the idea came to me that we could defend ourselves organizing into ronda groups.

The plan came to fruition in December 1976:

I proposed a patrol earlier in the year, but a majority was against it. So many people were robbers themselves that they were afraid they might get caught, or that rustlers might take revenge against a patroller. . . . Then in December someone broke into the school to steal a bunch of books, desks, clothes, and a soccer ball. It was the fifth or sixth time the school was robbed that year, and people started to feel it was just getting to be too much. So on December 29, we had a meeting outside the school.

Oblitas rummaged from a shelf in the farmhouse a notebook of loose papers, recordbooks, and law statutes. Perhaps because they seemed a guarantee of entitlement and certainty, most villagers placed a premium on preserving written records such as meeting minutes and land titles. I was shown a page near the end in Oblitas's own plain handwriting:

In the village of Cuyumalca, at 2:00 p.m. on the day of December 29, nineteen hundred and seventy-six, with the citizenry of said community gathered together, and after exchanging ideas the agreement was reached to organize "Night Rondas" to defend the interests of the school and the whole community in consequence of the continuous robberies that have been occurring in violation of said school and some of the people around it. This agreement is for the purpose of organizing the community and applying for the appropriate license to the end that it will be possible for it to purchase guns. The person in charge of organizing the rondas will be the lieutenant governor, who after registering the citizenry, will distribute the personnel, the same will also be in charge of following the proper procedures for the good fulfillment of its functions.

The names of 310 Cuyumalcans were crowded onto the following pages. A number of villagers did not know how to sign their names. They put an *X* in the column of signatories. "That was the beginning, Doctor," said Oblitas.

It is revealing that the catalyst was a break-in at the school. The nineteenth-century folklorist Ricardo Palma related a tale in which a Spaniard gives his Indians a box of cantaloupe to carry across the desert with a letter to a friend in Lima. He warns the Indians not to eat any melons, threatening that the letter will give them away. Halfway to Lima, they are tempted by hunger and the sweet-smelling fruit. They hide the letter, and eat some melons. The tale ends with their astonishment, when the recipient opens the letter, tells them exactly how many melons they ate, and orders them flogged. Literacy was power in this view of hierarchy and knowledge, and it underwrote the domination of Spaniards over Indians in colonial Peru.

The opportunity to go to school became part of the succession of redemptive "myths" described by the Peruvian anthropologist Carlos Iván Degregori.[26] Degregori explains that the trauma of conquest and colonialism spurred the "myth of Inkarrí" that anticipated redemption through the restoration of the Inca empire. This gave way by the twentieth century to a dream of "development" and progress through highways, education, medical posts, commerce, bridges, electricity, and the rest of the package of Western-style modernity. Despite pressure from the Peruvian government and even from abroad to "modernize" the countryside, the embrace of the "myth of progress" in the Andes had not meant the erasure of a distinctive sense of culture and identity. Villagers in Cuyumalca and elsewhere maintained and reworked an array of traditions from wearing ponchos to labor exchanges. At the same time, according to Degregori, the quest for redemption was reframed: "Andean villagers no longer wait for the Inca . . . casting themselves instead with unexpected vitality to the conquest of the future and of 'progress.' "[27]

The school was a "black box" of advancement and opportunity in the myth of progress.[28] Many villagers believe the landlords had purposefully not allowed schools in order to "keep us ignorant and from progressing."[29] The crusade for schools was mounted in the twentieth century, and hundreds of villages in the Andes from Puno to Piura sent delegations to the authorities for benches, blackboards, and teachers. In 1939, Cuyumalca became the first village in the Chota Valley to have a school. As in the rest of the countryside, the villagers built and maintained the building as part of what they hoped would be an opening for their children to opportunities they themselves had been denied. The number of schools in Cajamarca and Piura more than quadrupled from 558 in 1920 to 2,432 in 1964.[30]

It was bad enough for a family to lose a horse or cow to thieves. When someone pried open the doors of the schoolhouse to make off with chairs, musical instruments, blackboards, and soccer balls, the plague of theft endangered an institution that villagers saw as the best hope for a better life for the next generation. The disappearance of an animal was a problem for a family to confront, but everyone had a stake in the school. "Nobody wanted it to have to close," Oblitas explained to me that afternoon.

I had not noticed how fast the sun was plunging toward the mountains of Cutervo across the immense green valley. The nearness of the equator makes the sunset much quicker in the Andes than in the United States, and afternoon gives way to night in little more than an hour. Oblitas invited me to stay the night so I would not have to walk the trail to town in the dark. Later, after a dinner of corn, cheese, and sugary coffee from the Marañon Valley, he pulled out a pile of sheepskins and ponchos for my bed, and wished me a good night. I pulled my shortwave radio from a backpack, and fell asleep to a broadcast on Armed Forces Radio of the Braves versus the Dodgers from Fulton County Stadium.

THE SUBPREFECT, THE TEACHER, AND THE POLICEMAN

Town bureaucrats and government officials would come to figure in the countryside as the enemies of the rondas. I heard a ballad in 1990 by a group called The Little Workers of Santa Rosa at a meeting of ronderos in the town of Bambamarca:

> The authorities in town refused to support us.
> So we peasants said, "We have to get organized."[31]

It was a village corollary about police collusion with thieves that the police and other authorities would not want the peasantry to organize the rondas. "They just wanted the problems of us peasants to continue, and they did everything they could to repress and dis-organize us," said Angélica Jara, expressing a common view. As evi-denced by such well-known novels of the mid-twentieth century as *Broad and Alien Is the World* and *Yawar Fiesta*, a view of mestizos as greedy, hard-hearted, and bent on exploiting Indians has circulated for decades and even centuries among Peruvian intellectuals and activists.[32] The premise of official opposition fit with the picture of the sergeant, the judge, and the subprefect as bought off or simply part of the cabal of landlords, mineowners, and merchants. "The authorities have opposed this peasant movement that threatens the traditional elite," asserts a 1986 article in a leftist Lima newspaper.[33]

I knew this was an oversimplification. Did the government oper-ate only as an agent of repression and domination? Such a view failed to fit the history of the Andean countryside in the years lead-ing up to the creation of the rondas. Far from just seeking to keep peasants in bondage, the government had in the late 1960s and early 1970s incited the hacienda workers to see themselves not as "serfs" or "Indians" but "peasants." As such, they were supposed to be instrumental for what Velasco called "social justice and real participation of the people in the wealth and future of the mother-land."[34] "The workers of the countryside and Rural Communities should meet and organize," said a flyer distributed by the Educa-tion Ministry and by agrarian leagues and federations formed in those years throughout rural provinces at the urging of the govern-ment. To be sure, Velasco viewed the organization and mobilization of the peasantry as part of the construction of a state under the au-thority of his "Revolutionary Government of the Armed Forces." Later, the generals who ousted him ignored and even tried to dis-band peasant unions that opposed their policies. However, the government had raised expectations among villagers and had even encouraged them to see the right and duty to demand a better life. In this sense, the government had a hand in producing "the peas-antry" as a meaningful category of personhood in Peru, fostering a feeling among the rural poor of identity and entitlement to pros-perity and a place in the nation.[35]

My visit to Cuyumalca suggested that government involvement in the rondas was quite direct. The nightwatch started at the ini-tiative of Oblitas, a lieutenant governor, and it was in this ca-pacity that he had urged Cuyumalcans to organize the "Nocturnal

Rounds." As I would learn from travels across Chota and Hual-gayoc, the leadership of the local lieutenant governors was key in the founding of rondas in most villages in these provinces during the late 1970s. These men used their position of responsibility for public welfare to press fellow villagers to follow Cuyumalca in organizing. In that they were part of "the state" as well as "the village," the activism of lieutenant governors already unsettled the premise of official antagonism to the rondas.

The rest of the story appeared to turn it upside down. As Oblitas had described it to me, the subprefect of Chota Province had endorsed and even encouraged the nightwatch plan. Oblitas had kept a copy of the authorization issued by Agusto Yngar Garay on January 7, 1977: "IT IS RESOLVED: to give all necessary support to the lieutenant governor of the village of Cuyumalca, Mr. José Régulo Oblitas Herrera, so that he may use it as convenient to organize groups of "Night Rondas" to control the robbery of stock and other belongings of the locals, as well as the school of said village." A storekeeper in Chota gave me Yngar's address in Lima. On a trip to the capital a few weeks later, I took a taxi out to a dilapidated suburb to visit the retired civil servant. By now an old man with the courtly formality of the provincial aristocracy, Yngar ushered me into a living room with fake gilt chairs, a glass coffee table, and a stereo with plastic dustcover. He was happy to talk about the rondas: "I knew of the problem of thievery in Chota, and I wanted to do something to prevent crime in the countryside. Since I always tried to help peasants, I decided to call my lieutenant governors together to tell them to start patrols in their villages. In reality, I was the founder of the rondas." I wondered what Régulo Oblitas was going to say when I told him that Yngar was claiming to be "the founder." Still, the account confirmed that the highest provincial official had backed the initiative. Yngar told me that he had made a recent trip to Chota to explore the possibility of running for the national Congress. It was the first time the widower had returned in more than a decade. In the solitude of retirement in Lima, he had constructed a scenario in which villagers would acclaim him for starting the rondas and then draft him as the people's choice for the House of Representatives. From the edge of disappointment I heard in his story about the trip, I inferred that nobody had shown much interest in a candidacy, or perhaps even remembered the old man.

Oblitas had also told me about a schoolteacher who had supported the ronda. It turned out that Jorge Caro Acuña lived in a little flat just off the plaza in Chota. Caro was a cheerful, teddy-bear-faced man in pressed pants and tan sweater. Like Yngar, he was retired, but he explained that he was one of eight schoolteachers posted in Cuyumalca in 1976. None of the schoolteachers had actually resided there. They chose instead to make the daily trek up and down the trail between Chota and the schoolhouse, enabling them to live in town with the amenities of restaurants, bars, stores, a church, running water, toilets, and electricity:

But I was concerned about robbery in the countryside. Many of the things stolen in the sacking of the school in December belonged to me and other teachers—shoes, raincoats, a pump for the soccer ball. That night, I went with some villagers back down to Chota to the judge's house. He was a school friend of mine, and I persuaded him to write a search warrant. We took the warrant to the station. The next morning five or six policemen went up to Cuyumalca. We divided into groups of one policeman, several peasants, and one teacher. The search turned up nothing, even though we tapped floors and looked in eaves. In the meeting that afternoon in front of the schoolhouse, I proposed to villagers that they start a patrol. That's how it began.

It was apparent that Caro believed he deserved to be recognized for his part in starting the rondas. But he lacked Yngar's broader ambition, and to me at least never pressed his claim. I saw him sometimes with his wife on the nightly promenade that brought the plaza of the Andean town to life with the whistles of teenagers and the bustle of vendors. Caro seemed happy enough with the polite greeting of "Good evening, teacher" from other Chotans that signified a reputation of honesty and respect in town society.

What about the policemen that Oblitas had also told me were at the meeting in Cuyumalca to start the rondas? The next day, I walked from my hotel to the police station, a cement block building with pea-green walls. It had been built in the early 1980s to house the seventy policemen of the Sixty-fifth Division of the Civil Guard. The size reflected the militarization of Peru in the

Schoolteacher Jorge Caro Acuña, 1990

war against the guerrillas of the Communist Party of Peru—Shining Path and the smaller, Túpac Amaru Revolutionary Movement (MRTA). A mural of a young officer from Chota on the station wall commemorated his death in "the service of the motherland" in the Ayacuchan mountains to the south that were the Shining Path's stronghold. The policemen at the entrance wore flak jackets, and carried AK-47s. Although the insurgencies never extended into most of Cajamarca and Piura, the feeling of being on the edge of danger was reflected in everything from reports of the arrival in the Chotan countryside of a guerrilla column to the stories on the television news of the latest army massacre in the jungle valley of the Huallaga River. Uncertainty and anxiety made what anthropologist Michael Taussig might call a "nervous system" of the whole country.[36]

I asked to speak with the commander. Each of the machine-gun-toting guards suspiciously inspected my passport. Since the counterinsurgency was in such disarray that there was no centralized list of Shining Path suspects to match names against, the mania for ID checking seemed to me more than anything else a way to manufacture the illusion of control, and in this case perhaps just a chance to see what a U.S. passport looked like. An officer went into the station. He returned a few moments later to lead me to a moldy office. The police commander sat behind a fake wood desk in front of a portrait of the Peruvian president and a calendar featuring cocker spaniel puppies in an Easter basket. I told the young lieutenant, with his moustache and Raybans, that I was looking for any one of the four policemen who I knew had been at the meeting to start the rondas in 1976. He told me to come back the next day. On my return, the police commander was smiling. He had found the name of one of the policemen. He could arrange a meeting for me with the man at three o'clock that afternoon. "Maybe the information is worth something?" he inquired. I pushed ten dollars across the desk. After checking the denomination, he pocketed the bill with a sad shrug that seemed to suggest a wish for a kinder world in which information could be given to a foreign anthropologist without the unpleasantry of a payoff.

That afternoon I met the policeman in a coffee shop. "Ah, it's you," I said, surprised. I had met Juan Aguirre in Cutervo a few months before.[37] He was part of the Police Intelligence Service, and as such had been assigned to monitor the meetings of a ronda federation with ties to a Marxist party. To disguise himself as a villager, Aguirre had worn an old straw hat and a poncho. But the fiction had not struck me as very effective. This forty-two-year-old had smooth skin, well-manicured fingers, and prematurely gray hair. He looked more like a surgeon or soap opera star than a policeman, and at any rate nothing at all like a villager. Just about everybody at the meeting had seemed to know that Aguirre was a policeman, so I had not been sure why he bothered with the disguise in the first place.

At that first meeting, I had gone up to introduce myself to Aguirre in the plaza during a break. He asked what I was doing at the meeting. I said I was an anthropologist studying the rondas, but I lost my nerve when it came to asking why he was dressed up like a villager and what he was doing in Cutervo. The next morning the policeman knocked on the door of our hotel room. Robin had sprained her ankle. Aguirre brought a bundle of comfrey that he assured us would reduce the swelling. We were puzzled about his motives. Was it kindness? Did he want to peek into our room to see if there was anything suspicious about it? Or maybe both?

Now Aguirre was in soccer sweats after a lunchtime game. As

we sipped watery coffee, he provided yet another account of the events of 1976:

I've been stationed in Cutervo, Celendín, Bambamarca, and Cajamarca, but I was in Chota that year. There were many break-ins and stolen animals in Cuyumalca. The lieutenant governor and a schoolteacher reported a robbery at the school. We went up to investigate two different times. The village parents didn't help us much. They'd say, "We don't know. We haven't seen anything," even though some must have known more than they let on. Since we weren't getting anywhere, we decided to organize the villagers into seven or eight groups, with each of them taking a turn on watch once a week. We held a meeting in front of the school, and asked if each parent was willing to spend a week to guard the school. The villagers shouted, "Yes, yes." Once they started, the robbery stopped. . . . The idea of the rondas was ours.

Aguirre told the tale with the intensity of a man who thought he was setting the record straight. Yet he spoke in half-whisper, with an occasional glance to see if anyone was listening. The rondas had become a thorn in the authorities' side. Aguirre did not want it spread about that he had helped to start them. I have respected his parting request, made outside the coffee shop on a cobblestone street just slicked by an Andean cloudburst: "You can write about the story, but please don't print my real name."

CONTRADICTORY WORLDS

Many critics have pointed out that the journey of the Western anthropologist to find the truth about cultures in the Third World can have the plot of a voyage of conquest and discovery.[38] I left Chota in 1991 without any illusion about having discovered the truth of the origins of the rondas—or that this was even possible. "No, no, Doctor," Régulo Oblitas had said when I went back to tell him about the stories of Yngar, Franco, and Caro. He went into the farmhouse to find a notebook with the minutes of a meeting of Cuyumalcans to discuss repairing the wall of the village cemetery. It was dated December 3, 1976: "The lieutenant governor made it known to the community that some night rondas should be formed, to make it safe for the stock raisers of our village against those who are stealing things that do not belong to them, and committing a series of abuses against our people, like break-ins and stock rustling, and also against the Cuyumalca school." Although the vote in favor was not to come until after the sacking of the school, the proposal from Oblitas came three weeks before the assembly that Caro and Franco attended, when the ronda was chartered. Could this be proof of the Cuyumalcan's claim to being the first to think of the idea? No. A pair of villagers later told me they had suggested a patrol to Oblitas before even the cemetery meeting. In yet another talk with Caro, the schoolteacher asserted that he had talked about it to the lieutenant governor in November. And so it went. There was no way to get beyond the discordant versions. I felt that Oblitas had a better claim than anyone to the honorific of "founder." In this sense, the rondas were a peasant product, the vision of a hardworking farmer with just a few animals and a sliver of land. At the same time, it was hard to fix this history's truth once and for all. A number of people could and did claim to have had a hand. If we think about history as a process, it becomes tricky, for that matter, to determine an originating moment or person for any turn of events. "Origin is an eddy in the stream of becoming," the German thinker Walter Benjamin once wrote.[39]

I do not mean to cast the ronda beginning as a postmodern parable of indeterminacy, however. History may never have singular explanations, and yet it can be a murky relativism to deny altogether the role of individual decisions and motivating forces, or the value of searching the past for lessons about the present and future. An obvious lesson of the encounter with Yngar, Caro, and Aguirre was that the government was not monolithic. Aguirre omitted mention of Caro's speech at the Cuyumalca meeting, and vice versa. Neither the policeman nor the teacher credited Yngar's claim to being "the founder." The discrepancy in these stories was emblematic of the diversity of interests and institutions within a government made up of everything from Marxist schoolteachers to apathetic clerks and right-wing generals. Sociologist Philip Abrams observes that a state is always "a mask . . . an ideological artefact attributing unity, morality and independence to the disunited, amoral and dependent workings of the practice of government."[40] As Abrams emphasizes, the mask of unity can slip in times of danger and trouble. This would certainly be true in Peru later on, during the crisis of the late 1980s. Amidst scandal and ineptitude, the government became rudderless, and infighting and self-interest dominated. A firefight in 1989 between the police and military over spoils from a drug bust in the Huallaga Valley was only the most obvious example during those years of the breakdown of the illusion of the state's wholeness.[41]

Another lesson was to show the authorities' role in starting the rondas. Wishing to stay out of trouble, Aguirre stayed silent about his part in the events of 1976 in Cuyumalca. When the government did, indeed, begin trying to disband the rondas in 1979, it was easy for villagers to imagine that the authorities had always opposed the initiative against theft, all the more so in light of the widely shared view that the town and government were hostile to the poor's welfare. A picture of a peasantry in opposition to the state appealed to the desire of radical intellectuals in Lima and abroad to imagine the dedication of the downtrodden to overthrowing the status quo. As the good leftist, I wanted to believe it. The painstaking reader will find no mention of Yngar, Caro, or Aguirre in my 1989 dissertation. Initially, in other words, I was a coconspirator in manufacturing the mythology of the rondas as a purely antiofficial village product.

I gained a deeper appreciation in Cuyumalca of how urgent poverty and violence made organizing the rondas. It became just as apparent to me that the endorsement of town officials was crucial in starting the nightwatch. When I had asked Oblitas about Aguirre's claim to having thought up the plan, he filled out his story of the schoolyard meeting:

Well, I'd been thinking of the rondas for a long time. But it was hard to get anyone to listen to me, because people were afraid of the rustlers and also whether they would get in trouble with the authorities. I thought they might pay more attention to the policemen. So I pulled them aside right before the meeting, and said, "Listen, boss, why don't you propose a ronda? And say everybody has to do it, or else they must be thieves themselves? And that's what they did, and everybody said, "Yes, Yes" to the proposal of the ronda. The teacher, Caro, spoke at the meeting too, and told villagers they must start patrolling.

The Cuyumalcan remained the prime mover in this account. Yet he acknowledged the role of Chotan officialdom. Dislike for bureaucratic corruption and arrogance coexisted in complicated and sometimes contradictory rural thinking with fear, obedience, and even respect toward government officials. The urging and even bullying by the policeman and teacher encouraged wavering Cuyumalcans to start a ronda. The seal of approval from subprefect Yngar just days later lent further impetus to patrolling, and Oblitas and other village leaders went so far as to photocopy and distribute the document to persuade still more of their fellow peasants about the new organization. In this way, it can be said that the authorities were doubly part of the explanation for the ronda founding. Their failure to stop theft made necessary the peasant initiative. Then the backing of the police, schoolteacher, and subprefect cemented the initiative to begin the patrol. As a coproducer of the rondas, the government had helped to manufacture a peasant movement, one whose independence and rebelliousness would soon become difficult for the authorities to control.

Anthropologist Irene Silverblatt points out the failures of scholars of the Andes to grapple with "the real limits, the unintended consequences, the missed chances, the unrecognized complicities, and the just unknowables." She argues that "our theoretical biases" and "well-known penchants for oppositional thinking" have led to portrayals that "swing from noble savage to murderous savage, from shattered victim to heroic resister." An unwillingness to endure crime and poverty any longer certainly had set the stage for the beginning of the nightwatch. Yet I was forced to see much more to ronda origins than the union of the peasantry in the defense of livelihood. Complications included mistrust and doubt among villagers; the myth of progress; encouragement by the Velasco government for organizing; and the urging of the schoolteacher, policemen, and subprefect. Everything about the start of the rondas underscores that Andean villagers are no less than any of us "contradictory selves, part of contradictory worlds." [42]

GUNSHOTS IN THE HILLS

Foundation myths often conceal mixed origins. But stories of the rondas as the villagers' creation told a kind of truth after all, for it remained for them to set the rondas into motion.

On the night after the signing in the schoolyard of the agreement to start the "Night Rondas," ten Cuyumalcans gathered by the dim light of a kerosene lamp in the Oblitas farmhouse. The lieutenant

The first ronderos, 1990: (from left to right) Régulo Oblitas Herrera, Arturo Díaz Campos, Aladino Burga Huanambal, Israel Idrogo Marín, José Vásquez Gálvez (not pictured: Gilberto Benavides Mejía, Artidoro Huanambal Guevara, Lino Mejía Ruiz, José Santos Saldaña Gálvez)

governor showed me yet another notebook with the checklist in blue ballpoint ink of the villagers who on that night became the first ronderos: Israel Idrogo Marín, Arturo Díaz Campos, Aladino Burga Huanambal, Artidoro Huanambal Guevara, José Vásquez Gálvez, Lino Mejía Ruiz, Gilberto Benavides Mejía, José Santos Saldaña Gálvez, and José Severino Oblitas Colunche. Since the lieutenant governor was supposed to "set an example," Oblitas joined the other men as they started toward the schoolhouse in the chill of the Andean night. All of them carried a cane or bullwhip. Vásquez had an old Mauser of World War I vintage. This did not diminish feelings of doubt and fear. To stay out in the "bad hours" risked a "cold" with cramping or fever, not to mention getting shot by the thieves and rustlers that had the run of Cuyumalca.

I asked Oblitas if he could get the ten Cuyumalcans from the first night together for a picture. One had left Cuyumalca to start a trucking business in Chiclayo. Another was working on a coffee plantation in the jungle. Three others did not show up. The remaining five assembled on Sunday in the backyard of a run-down farmhouse on Chota's edge that belonged to a relative of Oblitas. I snapped the picture of these slender and, by now, middle-aged men in dark pants and shirts newly pressed for the reunion picture and the Sunday market. Some of them stayed around to chat. I asked Vásquez what he had been thinking that first night. "I thought we were going to get shot" was his reply.

The night of December 29 passed without incident, to everyone's relief. The patrol circled the trails around the schoolhouse in the darkness. As the sun's first rays caught the peaks of Cutervo, the ronderos headed to their farmhouses to ready for the new day. Oblitas divided the rest of the village men into other groups to take a night round. The ronderos started to range away from the school across the streams and fields of the mountainsides of Cuyumalca. Rumor of unrest trickled down to Chota. A trucker was said to have been stopped on the highway over the Bambamarca pass by a posse of armed Cuyumalcans checking for stolen cattle. On some nights, the echo of gunshots could be heard from the mountains above the town. As many villagers remembered it when I asked about the first weeks of the new year, a feeling of euphoria and even aggressiveness had gripped them. "We were shooting off our guns in celebration, because the fear was gone," Lino Oblitas recalled when we talked outside his farmhouse next to a grove of eucalyptus on the mountainside by the schoolhouse.

The final lines of a ballad conveyed the exuberance of villagers at the start of the rondas, and even the dream of organizing as the salvation of the whole country:

> With our sandals caked with mud
> We race through the darkness
> Struggling on behalf of everyone
> One night a week.
> The ronda will be the example
> To obtain the solution
> Heaving selfishness
> From our unhappy nation.[43]

TWO

Nightwatch

"MACHETE JUSTICE—80,000 PEASANTS PATROL
THE COUNTRYSIDE!"

This headline topped a Lima newspaper in early 1984. Reporter
Marcos Roncagliolo covered the story from Chota: "The peasants are pacifying lands where masked bandits once murdered and
robbed with impunity . . . the jails are empty because there are no
inmates; there's no work for lawyers—even the sorcerers, specialists in spells and danger, have had to take up the shovel and hoe
to earn their bread." [1] If quaint and perhaps dangerous with their
ponchos, straw hats, country slang, coca, cane liquor, cockfighting, and machetes, the villagers of Chota came across as the heroes
of a struggle against injustice and poverty. Enthusiasm about local
movements was common in Peru in those years. The rondas appeared to the Lima journalist from the left-center paper as a heroic
epic of villagers "claiming their rights."

Photographer Hugo Váldez shot the pictures for the "exclusive."
In one a crowd of villagers on a mountaintop brandish machetes and thick sticks. They cane cringing rustlers in others. When
I went to the same part of Chota in 1991, villagers were happy to
admit they had staged the shots for the Lima reporters to show
"how our justice works." I knew from Tunnel Six in 1986 about the
pleasure many took in picture taking. Sometimes those who had
not brought ponchos and whips ran to get them to play the part
of the rondero. The men would put on their most menacing look
for the camera. Nobody wanted a smile to spoil the dramatization
of danger and purpose in what one ballad declared the struggle "to
search for liberty with honor and courage." [2]

It is no wonder the rondas were beginning to attract attention.

I described in chapter 1 how Cuyumalcans started a nightwatch against thieves at the end of 1976. Many villages in the Chota Valley followed their example in 1977 and 1978. By 1979, the concept of patrolling spread into the neighboring valleys of Bambamarca and Cutervo, and then in 1983 to the mountains of Huancabamba, Morropón, and Ayabaca farther to the north. When Roncagliolo and Váldez journeyed to Chota in 1984, 2,000 villages had ronda committees over a swath of the northern Andes the size of the state of Maryland, and effectively far more than that given the lack of roads and the jagged topography.[3] Every man took a regular turn on patrol. This meant that more than 300,000 villagers had become ronderos. The Peruvian sociologist Nora Bonifaz has reason to assert that the rondas were "perhaps the most significant social phenomenon of the 1980s on the panorama of rural Peru."[4]

I examine the rise of the rondas in this chapter. A view of villagers as chained to the past led some reporters in the 1980s to presume that the nightwatch must be "ancestral" and "traditional." The truth is that the inhabitants of the countryside had no experience at keeping the peace on their own. It turns out that the haciendas' and military's systems of patrolling were prototypes for the rondas. But villagers adopted and amended these models to forge a system of discipline and punishment that was much more than just a copy of anything that came before. These patrols were run by villagers for the purpose of defending their own animals, fields, and lives. The feeling of ownership led the nightwatch to become a vessel for the hope for survival and security, and even the demand for accountability from the government. What started in Cuyumalca in 1976 culminated in 1980 with the assaults of ronderos on officials accused of corruption and conspiring with criminals to oppress the peasantry.

Ronda pride was evident in Tunnel Six on an afternoon in August 1986. On foot and horseback from the foothills around the Quiroz Valley, a crowd arrived for the fourth anniversary of the Central Committee of the Rondas Campesinas of Tunnel Six. The injuries of poverty and violence were on display in a drunk's gashed head and the ragged clothes of many children. Yet the ritual commemoration of victory over crime brought the villagers together to celebrate with ballads, speeches, skits, stew, beer, Inka Cola, cockfights, a soccer tournament, and even the crowning of a Queen of the Ronda. "Welcome to the anniversary of our glorious organization," gushed the Tunnel Six ronda president into the scratchy loudspeaker jerry-rigged to a car battery for the lack of electricity in Tunnel Six. The drinking and dancing went to dawn to the blaring of huaynos and San Juanitos.[5]

A NIGHT IN TUNNEL SIX

I had moved into Tunnel Six just a month before the anniversary. To begin to learn more about the rondas, I joined the group of ten villagers who took their turn on patrol every Thursday night. A trickle of men climbed the ridge to the farmhouse of the group leader, José Paz, the former soldier who had returned from the city for the moment to farm in Tunnel Six. José checked off names in a notebook in a careful hand. Then the eleven of us headed out on a big loop. It was about eight miles down through the farmhouses on the ridge, along the highway, and up a trail back to Tunnel Six. Only a dog's bark and a truck rumbling on the way to Sullana broke the silence.

A couple of miles down the highway, we heard voices. Paz gestured for us to move into the trees. Just out of the cantina down the road, a trio of men lurched arm-in-arm in a boozy stupor, slurring promises of friendship and boasts of manhood. We stepped onto the road. It was scary even for the sober to be surprised in the middle of the night by a line of figures with whips and sticks. The shock was stranger when one of the patrollers was a gringo a freakish foot or so taller than any known villager in the valley. One of the drunks peed in his pants. Paz advised the men to stay out of trouble. Our group continued down the highway, until stopping to chat and catnap under the canopy of the Southern Cross. About four in the morning, one man yawned that it was time to head home. "You're lucky, Don Raimundo. This wasn't always such an easy job," another said.

What had inspired these patrols in Tunnel Six and hundreds of other villages? The most obvious model was the hacienda. It was the memory of Tumán that led Régulo Oblitas to think in 1976 of the possibility of patrolling against theft in Cuyumalca. As a field hand in the 1960s, he remembered being assigned to guard the tractors, bulldozers, and farm machinery on the sugar plantation.

Heading out on patrol, Cuyumalca, 1990

Service in patrols known as *rondas de hacienda* was expected from serfs on many Andean estates. Just over the moors from Cuyumalca, those living on the Santa Clara estate had to take a turn on the ronda de hacienda, in their case a week or so a year on the punas to guard the flocks of sheep and cattle of the Acuña family. Santos Cruz, Manuel Jara, Gerónimo Carhuapoma, and many others in Tunnel Six's older generation patrolled a night a week to protect fields and flocks on the Pillo estate in the Ayabacan mountains.

The patrols took their main instruments of discipline and punishment from the haciendas. A flogging was punishment for serfs on Pillo and many other haciendas for pilfering, rape, brawling, assault, or not paying the rent. The whip became a prominent part of the rondas. Most ronderos carried the long braided leather thong to patrol and to administer "firecrackings" to thieves. It appeared as a symbol of the rondas on pamphlets and in the banners that villagers made for anniversaries and marches. The ronderos even resurrected the stocks in some areas. Many haciendas had locked criminals for two or three days in the splintery boards before the estate house in a demonstration of landlord power. A thief in Lagunas or Pillo could find himself bolted by the ronderos between the same boards that the departed hacendado had used two decades earlier. As villagers launched the struggle against crime in the 1970s and 1980s, they retrieved the whip and the stocks from the earlier age of the landlords to make them into the instruments of ronda discipline.

The army was another, more contemporary influence. As I was reminded on a Sunday in 1987, many young men in Andean villages served in the military. The circus had come to the ugly mudhole of a district capital, Paimas. A bus with bears and jugglers painted on the side bumped up the track to Tunnel Six with a loudspeaker blaring the promise of an amazing spectacle. It came to a stop in a clearing by the canal. Forty or so villagers gathered around in hope of getting a peek at a magician or maybe the bear. Nobody recognized the trap until it was too late. A platoon of policemen jumped out of the bus to grab the teenaged boys from the crowd. They hustled the young men back onto the bus, and it clunked back to Paimas.

Angélica Jara stopped by my house on the hilltop a little later. "It was the conscription," explained the mother of ten. Peruvian law required a year of military service from men over seventeen. Most families of any means paid off a doctor for a medical excuse or a lieutenant for a deferment. This meant the children of slum dwellers and peasants filled the ranks. The mother of Eladio Gómez brought a goat to the Paimas commander for the release of her son. Other families had nothing to spare for a payoff. Their sons stayed in the jail of the Paimas station, a one-room tank reeking of mold and vomit. After a few days, a truck arrived to take the Tunnel Sixers across the scrub brush to the Suyo base near the Ecuadoran border.

More than a quarter of the men in northern villages had served in the army or, in a couple of cases, the navy, and this experience showed in the rondas. The description of the nightwatch as "service" and "patrolling" came from the military. At the start in Cuyumalca, when the danger was great from rustlers, those who had them brought old revolvers or rifles on the nightwatch. A few men in Tunnel Six still took guns on patrol. They had learned in the military how to handle weapons as well as other combat tactics, such as frisking the surrendered. José Paz was a truck driver as a private in the Fourteenth Army Battalion in the city of Sullana. When we had stopped the two drunks on that night on patrol in

1987, he patted them down for knives or guns, a routine he learned in basic training.

COPYING AND BORROWING

Were the patrols just mimicry, then? No. As historian Michel de Certeau emphasized more than two decades ago, borrowing does not have to mean copying:

The spectacular victory of Spanish colonization over the indigenous cultures was diverted from its intended ends by the uses made of it; even when they were subjected, indeed even when they accepted their subjection, the Indians often used the laws, practices, and representations that were imposed upon them by force or fascination to ends other than those of their conquerors; they made something else out of them; they subverted them from within—not by rejecting them or transforming them (though that occurred as well), but by many different ways of using them in the service of rules, customs, or convictions foreign to the colonization they could not escape. They metamorphized the dominant order; they made it function in another register.[6]

This breathless celebration of "diversion" and "metamorphosis" underestimated Spanish successes. Yet it made the key point that the targets of colonialism did not always abjectly or passively internalize or copy the worldview of the colonizers. Already on the parapets of Ollantaytambo in 1539, Pizarro and his men had found their technology thrown back at them as the young Manco Inca rallied his troops on a stolen stallion.[7] The Lucanas chief Guamán Poma de Ayala in 1613 used the novel tool of writing to pen a 1,300-page letter to King Philip III reporting Spanish abuses in Peru.[8] Just a few years later in Copacabana by Lake Titicaca, villagers placed *huacas*, Andean idols, behind the Virgin to join mountain worship with Catholicism, horrifying the Spanish inquisitor who discovered the ploy.[9] It was de Certeau's insight that the exercise of power should never be presumed to be smooth or unchallenged. As in the Andes under colonialism, the weak may turn the "laws, practices, and representations" of the strong to unexpected and sometimes oppositional ends.

This was true of the rondas. The outbreak of thievery in the 1970s provoked some nostalgia for the order of the estates. "Everyone was kept in line by the whip" was a line I sometimes heard in the northern countryside. Yet memories of the haciendas were overwhelmingly negative. Dalinda Aguilar in Tunnel Six told me this story:

Dad was a *peón* [serf] on Pillo just above here. One year there was a drought. He couldn't pay two bushels of corn to Don Leigh that was expected. So Leigh had the mayordomo lock him in the stock in front of the manor. They kept him in them for a day. The landlords in those days rode around on a big horse, and you had to address them as "Master" or "Boss." Women had to weave blankets for the landlord, and the serfs had to bring the first part of their harvest.

The work of anthropologists and historians suggests that the control of the hacendados was not always so absolute or one-sided. Many serfs left when they wanted to work on the coast. While serfs had to pay tribute to the landlord in labor, crops, and sometimes cash, the master was expected to hear requests for small loans, sponsor baptism parties as a godparent, bring in a band for saint's days, and otherwise look out for "his" serfs according to the protocol of patronage and obligation. Nevertheless, a villager was a *peón,* and the landowner was the *señor,* the lord. The villagers in Llaucán in the Bambamarca Valley had to strew flowers in the path before the path of the landlord as if he were a God. Aguilar and many others in the northern Andes spoke of the epoch before the breakup of the haciendas as the "time of slavery."

Villagers' standing in the military was not much better. It is true that the Peruvian army has been an avenue of social mobility, with a sprinkling of generals from humble origins. Velasco's leadership in dividing the estates gave the military a better reputation than the police and the rest of the civilian bureaucracy. Some young men saw attractions in soldiering. Just a week after the raid in Tunnel Six, two conscripts deserted Suyo and trekked back across the cactus hills to Tunnel Six. One appeared later at my house to ask me to snap his picture for a keepsake. Orlando posed with pride on a flea-bitten white stallion borrowed from a relative. He wore the regalia of boots, a revolver, and a uniform taken from the army. On a visit a few months later, I noticed he had tacked the picture to the mud wall of his farmhouse.

I did not have the heart to remind Orlando that he was a deserter. Although the aura of masculinity and patriotism about soldiering may have been heightened for this eighteen-year-old by Rambo and Chuck Norris movies watched on trips to town, even he viewed the reality of military service as "pure suffering." The veterans I talked with were just about unanimous in depicting the barracks as a hell, with cockroaches in the food or sometimes no food at all, rampant theft of clothes and money, and tyrannical officers. An attraction of service for some teenagers was learning to drive and repair a truck. Yet Suyo was little more than a collection of shacks within a mud wall. A pair of rusted jeeps were the sum of the heavy machinery at the "base." Even those lucky enough to be sent to barracks in the less godforsaken areas complained of doing little more than hours of sentry duty, menial janitorial work, or road building. Although the possibility for advancement existed, it was limited. Most officers were graduates of the Lima training academy and from light-skinned and middle-class urban families.[10] Boys from the village families were the grunts and in some cases targets of teasing and abuse as "llama lovers" and "mountain hicks." As Angélica Jara and many others emphasized, forcing military service only on peasant children reflected and reenforced the hierarchy of race and class in Peruvian society. Three of her boys had spent a year in the barracks: "They suffered, and it's unjust that only the poor have to serve."

The bitterness did not stop villagers from basing their rondas on the military and the hacienda. These two institutions had given them their only firsthand experience of securing order by patrolling. In keeping with what de Certeau called "the reuse of products" and "the arts of manipulation," the villagers of Cuyumalca and then other Andean settlements thus recycled the whip, the stocks, and the "Halt, Who Goes There?"[11] The weak took over the disciplinary strategies of their superiors to stop the theft that threatened survival in the postlandlord world.

What distinguished the rondas from the haciendas or the military? An obvious difference lay in the rondero's ability to use local knowledge. A village recruit seldom knew anything about the lay of the land around the base, the border with Ecuador, or anywhere else his unit might be deployed.[12] By contrast, just about everyone on a ronda patrol knew the topography of the village, down to the location of the farms and the number and kinds of animals owned by every family. When out with the ronderos in Tunnel Six on

Thursday nights, I stumbled and tripped over pathways so familiar to villagers that they glided across them through the darkness with the easy confidence of accomplished ice-skaters. What was the quickest way to cut off a rustler? Was the teenager on the road with a bay mare the owner or a thief? Who had dogs to avoid? A villager knew. Many ronderos cited familiarity with the turf as a reason for what they considered the superiority of the rondas to the police. "Because we know the people and land in the countryside, a rondero can do a better job than any policeman from town," as José Paz put it to me on another night on patrol in Tunnel Six.

The most important contrast, however, was that these villagers were acting in their own interest. It was not to guard the flocks of the landlord or the abstraction of the fatherland that Paz and others took to the trails across the northern Andes. These patrols were not rondas de hacienda but rondas campesinas, run by and for the inhabitants of the countryside. For example, José Paz had a single heifer that was his prize and only possession of any value. It was his hope to build a herd of four or five to sell for a few hundred dollars to set up a clothing stall in the marketplace in the city of Sullana.[13] To patrol a night a week was to protect the animals and fields that embodied the hope for survival and even advancement of Paz and thousands of other villagers throughout the northern Andes. A ditty from the village of La Alfombrilla in the heights of the Chota Valley proclaims the payoff for the peasantry: "Through the night's cold I battle, to protect my cattle."[14]

It was a sign of village powerlessness to have served the hacienda and the military. "I did the ronda de hacienda because I didn't want to get flogged or kicked off the land," an old man told me in the dry mountains above Tunnel Six. By contrast, the rondas campesinas protected peasant livelihood and fostered feelings of rural independence. Every man between sixteen and sixty-five took a turn on the nightwatch by the terms of the agreements villagers signed in Cuyumalca and elsewhere. Those "yellows" who dodged service could be expected to be roused out of bed by the wives of other villagers, fined, or even whipped. Yet once they could band together themselves to make the countryside safe again, the majority of men were eager and even enthusiastic about taking on obligations that still had their onerous aspects. They choose in assemblies the president, vice-president, and secretary of the ronda

A rondero with a cow recovered from rustlers, Lingán Pata, 1989 (courtesy of ILLA)

committees organized to oversee the operation of the patrols, and the men who led were villagers like them. Many Tunnel Sixers saw spiraling theft as threatening their just-won independence from the hacienda regime. As Angélica Jara put it, "the chaos and crime were bringing us back to the same misery and suffering as in the time of the landlords." In this view, the rondas asserted a refusal to give in to poverty and crime. "Now that the rondas have begun, we're not so alone . . . using our forces to confront the problems that we feel" went another of the many songs in praise of the patrols.[15]

I think with embarrassment about a visit I made more than a decade ago to one of the most distinguished specialists in pre-Columbian history in the United States. I had returned in 1986 to Berkeley after my first six months in Tunnel Six to visit Robin and my family. It had occurred to me that the rondas might have a precedent in the Incan empire, a view still voiced by some Lima observers. The meeting with John Rowe in his cramped office in Kroeber Hall at the University of California crushed that illusion. With an edge of impatience at the naïveté of a know-nothing graduate student, Rowe said it was unlikely the Incas even ruled the sierra of Piura and Cajamarca for more than a couple of decades. He doubted the rondas were a "survival" from the Incas or any other civilization from the pre-Columbian past almost five centuries before.

The old professor was right. There are certainly vestiges of pre-Columbian culture in the northern Andes. The bony greasy meat of the cuy, guinea pig, remains a favorite dish, even if spiced with packets of Ajino-Moto MSG. Singing the aching melody of a *yaraví,* a kind of dirge popular for centuries in the highlands, is still the custom in the final drunken hours of a good-bye party. The native crop of the potato has remained the staple in the chilly upper reaches of Chota and other Andean valleys. At the same time, the rondas had no ancient pedigree. They had started only in 1976 in Cuyumalca, modeled on the postconquest institutions of the haciendas and the military. Villagers had reworked these prototypes into a form of organizing they saw as their own. "The rondas are ours," was how one Cuyumalcan summed up this feat of institutional alchemy by a social movement.

RUSTLING AND THE POLITICS OF MEMORY

One afternoon in 1991, Lino Oblitas, cousin of Régulo Oblitas, stopped by my room in the Hostal Chota to talk about the rondas. "The danger of assault and robbery was horrible. To save our animals, we slept inside with them, the cows and sheep bleating, snorting, and farting in the bedroom," began the fifty-year-old Cuyumalcan, a born storyteller. Between bites of a Mars Bar from a box I brought from California, Oblitas launched into tales about confronting rustlers. The moral was the same: "With the rondas, we rose like a single man to master the thieves." Although few could match Oblitas's theatrical flair and humor, dozens of northern villagers painted the same picture of chaos, rupture, and renovation: a voyage from the darkness of thievery and fear to the light of order and discipline. "Everything changed with the rondas," said José Paz, concluding his account of how Tunnel Sixers in 1983 dunked rustler Ramón Lima upside down by a rope in the murky canal in the early morning hours before chasing him from the village for good.

What can be made of this cornucopia of tales, of the relation between people's memory of the rondas and past events? The topic of memory and history has turned into a major object of inquiry for scholars in recent years.[16] An obvious point made by many critics is that memory is never a straightforward record. Historians Natalie Zemon Davis and Randolph Starn underline that it is always in the form of "constructed narrative . . . under the pressure of challenges and alternatives."[17] These and other scholars press for inquiry into the politics of remembering and forgetting, and what it reveals about agendas and ideologies. When it came to Lino Oblitas's account about Cuyumalcan rondas, the omission of any mention of Régulo Oblitas indexed bad blood between the cousins over a plot of land. The masculinization of memory to depict the "rising as a single man" to "master the thieves" effaced what I will show in chapter 4 was the key role of wives and daughters in the struggle against theft.

It may be true that memory never offers unvarnished truth. Nor do even the most avowedly "objective" and "neutral" accounts of the past.[18] Selectivity and reworking are routine and unavoidable in the most colorless monograph or textbook. It will not do, then, to presume automatically the greater reliability of history over memory, the institutional over the informal, the written over the oral. As in Walter Benjamin's famous injunction to "seize hold of a memory as it flashes up in a moment of danger," personal memory sometimes provides key records of violence and repression that official histories suppress.[19]

The memories of Lino Oblitas and many other villagers contained valuable testimony that sometimes corroborated and sometimes filled in the blanks of more formal records. The advent of the rondas had indeed brought a remarkable decline in theft. Court archives in Chota contain seventy reports of the robbery of cows or horses between 1970 and 1976 in the time before the nightwatch. I did not hear of a single case of rustling in the valley in 1990 or 1991. The household census I performed in Tunnel Six told the same story. Thieves took 762 animals between 1980 and 1983, including more than 40 cattle, 282 goats, and 190 chickens. In 1986 and 1987, after the ronda started, just 8 animals disappeared: 3 chickens, 4 ducks, and a pig.[20] There was no mention of this transformation in the official records of police commanders or subprefects, or any official archive. The recorded memory of Lino Oblitas and others documented ronda accomplishment that might otherwise have been lost or forgotten in what historian Pierre Nora has called the "eradication of memory by history." [21]

What about memory's gaps and silences, however? I found these also existed, especially when it came to the sometimes fierce methods employed to bring peace to the countryside. To understand the occasional brutality of the rondas, it should be recognized that lore in Cajamarca and Piura had long acclaimed those prepared to use bravado and even violence to tame a treacherous world. Lino Oblitas and other Chotan raconteurs loved to tell about the exploits of Eleodoro Benel and the other bandit chieftains who turned the mountains of Hualgayoc, Chota, and Cutervo into Peru's most violent region between 1870 and 1930.[22] A readiness to seize a machete or shotgun to have one's way was memorialized, even across the gender divide. Ballads in the Piuran foothills recalled the exploits of Rosa "the Macho Woman" Palma as well as Froilán "The Black Man" Alama. The expected submissiveness from women and blacks heightened the fascination of stories about these outlaws who died in a firefight with the Civil Guard in 1928 in the Chulucanas desert.[23] In the country Spanish of northern Peru, the word for "tough" and "beautiful" was identical: *guapo*.

The tradition of toughness carried into the rondas. To a point, villagers had to be firm and uncompromising in the first years, especially when it came to facing down rustling gangs who were prepared to shoot and kill. On occasion, however, the ronda fight to defend land and livelihood veered into extremes. Perhaps the starkest example came with the killing of five men from the village of Lanchibamba in April 1978. Manuel Acuña Peralta and his brother Segundo Acuña Peralta, Israel Muñoz Cieza, Marcos Peña, and Juan Peña were returning from Bambamarca to Chota over the moor of Samangay.[24] In the desolation of a village called Alto Peru at 10,000 feet just before the pass, the lieutenant governor and a group of patrollers stopped the Lanchibambans. Manuel Acuña was the reputed head of a rustling gang. Yet fear had prevented anyone from confronting him or any of the others associated with him. In these months the climate was changing with the spread of the rondas across Chota and Bambamarca. The patrollers accused the Lanchibambans of stealing the four cattle they were driving. Two of the Lanchibambans pulled guns to try to escape, only to

Whipping a rustler, José Espíritu Tafur, 1988 ("Don't punish me anymore, Boys. From today on, I won't steal anymore.")

find themselves surrounded and tied up by the patrollers. More than 1,000 villagers from homesteads on either sides of the pass converged that night on the bone-chilling barren of Alto Peru. Perhaps fueled by cane liquor, the crowd's anger at the misery and violence of years of theft boiled over in the lynching of the Lanchibambans. The five were beaten and stabbed to death in the schoolhouse patio even as they pled for mercy.

Three days later, a truck bearing thirty policemen from Chota headed up the rural highway to investigate. By the time it arrived at Alto Peru, the police found the way blocked by a crowd of at least 3,000 villagers. One of the policemen was Julio Franco, the same officer who had encouraged Cuyumalcans to start the first ronda in 1976: "We were terrified, and tried to talk our way out of it. We started to walk back from Alto Peru toward the highway, but the peasants followed us. They yelled they'd kill us if we came back. Up on a ridge, some peasants threw rocks, and shot guns into the air, and we had to dodge some of the rocks. One of the investigative policemen with us was a black guy. He turned white as a sheet." The commander confessed failure in his official report: "about 5,000 patrollers blocked a Joint Operation of the Police Forces of Chota, with guns and blunt objects such as bottles and rocks, preventing in this way an effective investigation and leaving their execrable crime unpunished."[25]

The lynching of the Lanchibambans became legend in Chota and Hualgayoc in the intervening years. I never met anybody who would admit to being in Alto Peru on that night. At the time, just about everyone was happy to tell the tale of killing the rustlers and facing down the police. Other stories from those early days still circulated about forcing rustlers to spend a sleepless week on patrol or dunking them in glacial lakes. Nor did songsters shy away from the theme of physical punishment. A ditty about the ronderos of Lingán Grande in the Chota Valley boasted that

When they catch a thief
They hang him by the teeth.[26]

Another Chotan song goes:

Long live the ronderos
Blows to traitors
Beat the crap out of them
Until they change their ways.[27]

The unsubtle moral was that it was unwise for anyone to revert to the "bad habits" of pilfering and theft. As a number of scholars have suggested, the rumor as well as the reality of torture and violence by repressive regimes in Latin America can discourage political mobilization.[28] Fear's power was deployed differently in the rondas. It was manipulated by villagers for the purposes of stopping crime and empowering the peasantry.

Yet I came across limits to just how much villagers wanted to remember about ronda violence. In the case of Alto Peru, it turned out that one of those hacked to death, Juan Peña, was just a high school student. "He was a boy," as his uncle, a Chotan policeman, told me, even showing me a copy of the birth certificate proving Juan was only sixteen at the time of his death. No villager had ever mentioned that a teenager had been among those lynched. I am not sure to what degree the silence was intentional to keep me as an outsider in the dark, and to what extent villagers had genuinely forgotten or never known this especially unheroic part of the story. After all, more than a decade had passed; not even those who had been part of the great, angry crowd at Alto Peru necessarily knew many details about those killed that night. It did seem to me that the surprise of Régulo Oblitas and several others I knew best in Cuyumalca was real when I told them what I had learned about Juan's age. If memory recorded what history omitted in some ways, it appeared to have preempted it in others, in this case eliding the ugliest side of ronda history. Do the stories we tell about the past always both evade and report truth? They did in the case of Alto Peru.

It remains true that the killing of the Lanchibambans marked the emergence of the rondas as a force to be reckoned with in the northern countryside. "Maybe the violence went too far," one Cuyumalcan admitted to me in 1991, "but that was the night people lost their fear of the rustlers and the police." An internal Chotan Investigative Police report worried that the rural uprising against theft and corruption was starting to threaten "the Internal Security of the Nation." [29]

COMPLICITY AND THE ANTHROPOLOGIST

I chuckled along with villagers at their tales of the police's turning tail, especially before having learned the full details of what happened at Alto Peru. The ethics of violence had not been so easy for me to avoid on a night in 1987 in Tunnel Six. At two in the morning, I woke to the shadow and light thrown off by a kerosene torch and the sound of feet tramping to the lunchroom. A group of patrollers from Tunnel Six and Guir Guir had captured a suspected thief named Claudio Reyes. [30] Trying to escape, Reyes gouged the head of the ronda president of Guir Guir with an ax handle. After living in Tunnel Six for almost a year, I was free to come and go even in the tensest moments. So I pulled on pants and poncho to see what would happen. A young man in tennis shoes and a windbreaker, Reyes denied the charges of stealing a gelding and cane press. The wounding of the ronda president left the patrollers in no mood for verbal sparring. They led him outside to an acacia tree in back of the school. One man bound his arms behind his back. Another threw the loose end over the sturdiest branch. The rope cracked under the weight of the body. Reyes was suspended in midair, twisting in a lazy circle with chest parallel to the ground. A minute passed. Reyes moaned. The rope stretched his arms back from the shoulder sockets. I looked around at the ronderos, all of them men that I knew and in most cases counted as friends. One nudged me and smiled that I should go get my camera to take a picture of the hanging for my book. Most were stone-faced. I did not know what they were thinking in the deep shadows of the moonlight. Reyes groaned louder and faster, until the ronderos lowered and released the trembling man. They warned him to show up the next day to meet with the owner of the cane press and gelding.

For me the hanging of Reyes was a low. I had been an organizer for Amnesty International just the year before in San Francisco. When faced in person by a case of torture in Tunnel Six, I froze. As I will explain in a moment, a number of villagers believed violence by the rondas was no longer justified as theft declined. An argument from me against the torture of Reyes might have catalyzed opposition to the hanging. I cannot even present the failure to intervene as a parable of relativism gone awry. It was true that I tried in Tunnel Six to avoid the sermonizing of the colonizer or the missionary. Yet I was not so stupid about the doctrine of respect for diversity as to think that villagers had the right to torture. It was a simple lack of courage that made me into just another spectator of the hanging. Michael Taussig describes how anthropologists may find themselves made into knowing or unwitting accomplices of "terror's talk and terror's silence."[31] This happened to me on that night in Tunnel Six.

VIOLENCE AND FORGIVENESS

Brutality and intimidation were hardly unique to northern villagers. A founding act in the conquest was the garroting of the Inca Atahualpa in 1533 in Cajamarca, just seventy miles south of Chota. Even more so with the Inquisition in the seventeenth century, torture and public execution were common in colonial society. The socialist critic José Carlos Mariátegui wrote in 1928 that government repression often "drowned in blood . . . the desperate demands for justice of the Indians."[32] Torture remains commonplace in interrogations of common criminals throughout the Peruvian Andes. I taped an interview with the police sergeant in the town of Paimas, just up the canal from Tunnel Six. "When we catch a thief, we dunk their head in the toilet bowl until they almost drown. That makes them talk." The willingness to speak this way on the record reflects just how commonly the police employed what the sergeant euphemized as "pressure" to force confessions.

The actions of the authorities encouraged views of violence as necessary to maintain order. "We know from what happens in the station that hard methods are sometimes the best way to get a thief to confess," one Tunnel Sixer told me, a few days after the brutalization of Reyes. Police behavior could even provide a blueprint for interrogation. The *periquito,* the "little bird," the hanging by the arms inflicted on Reyes, had not been autochthonous in Tunnel Six or elsewhere in the northern Andes. To the contrary, it was learned from the Investigative Police in the town of Ayabaca, who employed it along with underwater submersion and electric shocks from a car battery in the backroom of their moldy headquarters on July 24th Street. It remained common in twentieth-century Peru for town officials to see the government as an agent of enlightenment and development, and of civilizing a peasantry presumed to be brutish, childlike, and in need of guidance. The case of the "little bird" underlined that the reality was another matter. Far from a force for moderation and humanity, the government had educated villagers about a technology of torture.

It would be wrong to minimize ronda abuses. The killings at Alto Peru alone belie the romantic claim of one scholar about Andean villagers' adherence to an ethic of "punish, not kill."[33] I do want to point out that the government was by any measure far more terrible and indiscriminate in using violence, a further warning against painting peasants as the only or even the main culprits for terror in the Andes. The spread of the patrols in Cajamarca and Piura in the early 1980s coincided with the intensification in Ayacucho to the south of the counterinsurgency against the Shining Path. There the police and military used torture that included the "little bird" on those suspected of involvement in the insurgency. I spoke in Lima with survivors who reported their interrogators' hanging them for days by steel handcuffs, and sometimes rubbing their bleeding wrists in salt water or chili pepper to increase a terrible agony. As with Reyes, villagers seldom suspended a suspect longer than fifteen minutes, and they wrapped his arms in a poncho to prevent permanent injury. More than 5,000 people were massacred by the police and military in the interiors of the south-central Andes between 1980 and 1990. The majority were Quechua-speaking villagers with little or scant involvement in the Shining Path. I documented just six murders by the rondas besides the Lanchibambans between 1976 and 1992. This meant that the overwhelming majority of the more than 500,000 ronderos were never involved in killing. The adoption of tortures such as the "little bird" was an unappealing side of peasant borrowing from officialdom. Yet villagers did not simply copy even in this case. The exercise of intimidation and violence were tempered.

Why? One inhibition against ronda abuses lay in the state structure of immunity and sanction. Most prosecutors and judges regarded the rondas as illegal and misbegotten. They were happy to jail the upstart villagers. Except in Alto Peru, patrollers went to prison for every killing of suspected thieves, seventeen of them in 1985 for beating to death two rustlers near Milpo Lake in Cajamarca province. The thought of rotting in the hellhole of a Peruvian jail was a deterrent against lynching by the ronda. The punishment of villagers contrasted with the almost complete immunity for soldiers and policemen. A sergeant could shoot a suspected guerrilla in a field or canyon without fear of prosecution. This lack of constraint was justified by the government as the defense of democracy, and encouraged by superiors as the best way to deal with "terrorists." President Alberto Fujimori codified the denial and forgetting of these crimes by declaring an amnesty in 1995 for anyone in the police and military accused of atrocities during the counterinsurgency.[34]

An ideology of forgiveness was the other restraint on ronda violence. Luciano Alvarado in Tunnel Six described this economy of punishment and absolution: "We're all peasants, all poor. Why punish someone so bad they can't work? Or send them to rot in jail? How will their family survive? In the nightwatch, you take your whip strokes, and then correct yourself, and go back to your life. All of us make mistakes, and with the patrols we learn to live better amongst ourselves, without the bad habits that corrupted everyone in the past." Underlying this view was a belief in the possibility of reform. Many in Cajamarca and Piura liked to point to the cases of dangerous rustlers who turned into ronda leaders, among them Manuel Burga in Lingán Pata and Aurelio López in La Iraca. In such stories individuals were remade, from evil to good, corrupt to moral, and damned to saved.

The imagery of conversion has Christian overtones. It was a mission of the Spanish colonizers to turn pagans into believers by extirpating Andean deities. Although blending mountain worship and other aspects of native religion into Christianity, the overwhelming majority of Andean villagers came to see themselves as Catholic. Even the neo-Incan rebel Túpac Amaru insisted that he fought the Spanish in the name of "Jesus Christ and Our Holy Father." By the middle of the twentieth century, the struggle for the peasantry's soul took a new turn with Protestant missionaries from the United States and Europe taking advantage of rural resentment of hierarchy and corruption in the Catholic Church. Evangelicals rose from less than 1 percent of Latin America's population in 1920 to more than 8 percent in 1990, including Jehovah's Witnesses, Mormons, Methodists, Baptists, and countless Pentecostal sects.[35] Protestant expansion provoked Catholic response. Priests distributed thousands of stickers saying "This Home is Catholic" for parishioners to put in their windows to discourage Jehovah's Witnesses and other door-to-door missionaries. The activity of the Catholic Church also increased in the countryside in response to the Protestant threat and to the Second Vatican's call in 1963 for encouraging lay involvement. While most priests in the Andes lived in town just like the rest of officialdom, pastoral visits to villages became more frequent, promoting chapel building and forming catechism groups. The work of some priests was propelled by an idealistic commitment to the poor and social transformation. I became friends with a tall young priest in Ayabaca who professed what came to be called "liberation theology."[36] He motorcycled into Tunnel Six on a hot Sunday afternoon in 1986 to give a sermon that included an impassioned call to "bring justice for you peasants and to our country" as well as a potshot at Pentecostals as a "tool of those who want to confuse you about religion and Jesus Christ." The inroads of Protestantism and changes in the Catholic Church combined to give issues of religion and faith in village society increased visibility in the 1970s and 1980s.

Ronda principles dovetailed with the demand by many Protestant churches for an end to dishonesty, theft, drinking, adultery, and other offenses. Leaders among the Assembly of God, Seventh Day Adventists, Israelites, and other groups supported village participation in the movement. The Catholic Church also backed the rondas in parts of the northern Andes, particularly in Bambamarca.[37] The valley belonged to the diocese of the bishop of Cajamarca, José Dammert Bellido, a scion of a wealthy Lima family and a leader of the left in the Peruvian Catholic Church. In the 1960s and 1970s, his priests worked to mobilize the peasantry against police brutality, mine pollution, and other abuses. When the people of San Antonio de la Camaca founded the first rondas in the valley on January 26, 1978, these priests supported the initiative, and Dammert himself became a prominent advocate of the rondas. "The government offers no protection, so it seems to us legitimate for peasants to join together to defend themselves," he explained to the *Latinamerica Press* newsweekly in 1989.[38]

It was not hard to see the impress of Christianity on the rondas. On the day after the hanging of Reyes, I stopped by the farmhouse of Barbara Castillo and Florencio Jiménez, organizers of a prayer group that met on Sunday in the lunchroom to sing hymns and read the Bible. This couple, with their threadbare clothes and narrow strip of land, was among the poorer families in Tunnel Six. Barbara Castillo had almost died of bubonic plague a year before. Only a shot of antibiotic from a Paimas storekeeper saved Barbara from the agony of exploding lymph nodes and bleeding through the mouth. Despite their hardships, Barbara and Florencio shared a sunny disposition. The night Reyes was caught, Florencio was somber: "Maybe we needed to be tough with the rustlers at first. But now we in the rondas have the upper hand, and it's not right to use those tortures. It goes against the faith, and God's Word. The others ignored me when I said we shouldn't mistreat Reyes, although I think maybe what I said kept them from hanging him longer." The disagreement between Florencio and the other ronderos was a reminder that opinion in Tunnel Six and elsewhere in the northern countryside was far less homogeneous than scholars sometimes seem to suggest with generalizations about "the village worldview" and "the peasant mind." As Florencio, Barbara, and a number of others saw it, charity and forgiveness needed to be in-

Eladio Idrogo with parents and son, Cuyumalca, 1990

corporated into a fight against theft so that it would not stray into the sin of cruelty, and in this case the intervention of Florencio had contributed at least to a measure of mercy in dealing with a suspect.

I discovered that many ronda leaders doubled as Catholic catechists or Protestant pastors. This was the case of Eladio Idrogo. With his confident walk and sturdy build, Eladio was a peasant version of the type of smart, handsome, generous, athletic, and popular figure I had admired and envied in high school. Like so many others in the Chota Valley, he was obligated by land scarcity to go to the jungle in search of work, in his case harvesting palm for fifty dollars a month on an isolated plantation near the Madre de Dios River. When a firefight between guerrillas and the military broke out in the area, Idrogo returned to Cuyumalca to make a go of a small plot and a pair of cows. A Chota priest spurred him to organize a prayer group that met on Sundays in an adobe chapel next to the dirt highway to Santa Rosa. Then he was elected ronda president in 1990. To make up for time lost to the duties of leadership, Idrogo arose at four in the morning to head up into the moors to bend over a plot of olluco and potatoes with hoe and pick.[39]

I am not religious, but this did not keep me from admiring Eladio's faith. Unlike Bambamarca, Chota belonged to the diocese of a bishop indifferent to the rondas, a Spaniard from the conservative Opus Dei order born of Franco's Spain. Nonetheless, Eladio saw a connection between Christianity and the rondas. As the wind shrieked across the barrens under a tungsten sky, he preached to an outdoor assembly in 1991:

Why don't the police or the judge ever investigate with fairness? Isn't the life of a poor man worth as much as that of a rich one? Doesn't the death of a villager matter as much as that of a doctor or lawyer? We have lived for too many years with these injustices. The rondas must give an example of justice, and respect to our fellow villagers. Yes, we punish criminals and rustlers, but not from hate but from love. All of us by our nature make mistakes, and we must correct ourselves to live better and to progress as peasants, Christians, and Peruvians.

The language of "love" and "charity" came from the mimeographed manuals from the Chotan Diocese that Idrogo parsed by lamplight in his farmhouse. So did the vision of imperfection, atonement, and forgiveness as the pathway to the promised land of redemption and salvation. As they appeared in Eladio's exegesis, the rondas realized the Christian ideal in a melding of religion and politics. A homemade pamphlet put together by ronderos in Tunnel Six claimed Jesus as a totem along with a neo-Incan rebel and the land reform president: "Patrollers, you are continuing the liberation work of Túpac Amaru, Juan Velasco Alvarado, and Jesus Christ."

The ethic of Christian forgiveness further explains the ronderos' success in stopping theft. To discourage anyone who might want to continue to steal, there was also the rondero toughness, displayed in an extravagant vocabulary specific to whipping: "lashes," "whoppers," "stingers," "strokes," and "firecrackers."[40] "The ronda scares people, yet it also allows us to change our ways without going to jail or suffering the abuses of the authorities," as Angélica Jara explained the push and pull of fear and forgiveness.

The matter of violence remained a point of tension as late as 1991. A roomful of ronderos gathered one night to deal with the theft of a radio. The teenage thief did not deny guilt. When it came to the matter of punishment, the owner of the radio demanded that the eighteen-year-old receive a whipping to "teach him a lesson." One villager rose to say that it was time for the rondas to punish "a little less." Eladio proposed that the boy just be fined a day of making bricks for the new village health clinic. As a majority of the Cuyumalcans in the crowded meeting hall agreed to the warning and fine, it was moderation that prevailed on this night on the mountainside of the Chota Valley.

SUFFERING AND THE PROMISE OF ORDER

The commonest answer to questions about ronda benefits revolved around survival and livelihood. Teresa Córdova was a slender woman of twenty-eight with a face prematurely aged by the hardship of bearing seven children and working under the fierce Piuran sun. We talked one afternoon on the wood bench in front of her farmhouse in Tunnel Six just above the canal: "It was getting impossible to raise animals or crops before the rondas. Some people just sold their goats or sheep because they were afraid they would be stolen first. Others let their fields go to seed because they knew the crop would be taken. Now you see fields more productive. It's possible to raise animals again, and for us to survive." As a teenager, Teresa had worked for four years as a maid for an oil company executive in the city of Talara. Yet time away from Tunnel Six did not make her any less attuned to the rhythms of farming that were second nature to villagers throughout Cajamarca and Piura—plowing in September and October, planting with the first thundershowers in November and December, harvesting corn and potatoes in May and June. The disruption of agriculture conditioned Teresa and many others to view thievery as "unnatural." It violated the order of planting and breeding that was the foundation of survival in the northern countryside.

The difficulty of the struggle for livelihood would be hard to overstate. Even when I felt able to understand a great deal about the lives of villagers across the divides of culture, race, and nationality, it always remained a mystery to me as a middle-class American just how people were able to muster daily the courage and energy to face the world with so little. The villagers of the northern Andes practiced arts of scrimping and recycling beyond the imagination of most of us in a throwaway culture of Pampers and Bic Tracers. Eladio Idrogo left the Ray-O-Vacs to his aluminum flashlight in the dewy pasture overnight to coax out the last bit of charge. Kids in Tunnel Six made kites from yarn and plastic bags. Rubber from discarded tires makes sandals for villagers throughout the Peruvian mountains. Despite such ingenuity, the consequences of malnutrition, poor sanitation, and bad health care emerged in the statistics of misery. One of every six babies born to a mother in the Andean countryside died within the first year.[41] Not that surviving to adulthood guaranteed a long life, given the threat of tuberculosis, malaria, typhoid, dysentery, and even cholera. The life expectancy of just over fifty for men and women in villages in Cajamarca and Piura was more than two decades less than for members of the middle class in Lima or the United States.

Statistics cannot convey the human cost. At three in the morning in Tunnel Six on November 1986, the eleven-year-old sister of our neighbor Francisca Paz roused us from bed. She whispered that the baby had just died. We found Francisca in the dirt-floored bedroom that smelled of wool, sweat, pee, kerosene, and smoke. A soft-spoken woman of twenty-seven, Francisca was a rock of humor and stability. Now grief overwhelmed speech. She moaned and sobbed clutching the emaciated body of her baby boy. Marco was the second of her seven children to die of dysentery. The next day, relatives filled his small coffin with pink flowers, and placed upon his head the crown of gold construction paper that Tunnel Sixers made for the "little angels" that perished in infancy. We carried the tiny pine box along the empty highway to bury in the Paimas cemetery. I helped to dig a hole in the powdery dust under a hot sun. On the way down, we came upon the tiny skeleton of another baby in what must have been an unmarked grave.

Anthropologist Nancy Scheper-Hughes shows that women do not always mourn the death of infants in the shantytowns of northeastern Brazil.[42] The high rate of child mortality in Alto do Cruzeiro shapes a "delayed attachment" to infants and a propensity to face "death without weeping." It was different in Tunnel Six. There mothers also faced a catastrophically high likelihood of watching a baby die. Yet I found no emotional defense mechanism of "delayed attachment" in this ramshackle village in the Piuran foothills. Francisca adored Marco even though she knew that he might not survive. She and her husband Víctor spent what for them was a fortune on pills and home remedies for the baby. The close attachment

Francisca with Marco shortly before his death, Tunnel Six, 1986

gave their grief at his death an almost earth-shattering intensity. The couple huddled for the next week in an inconsolable sorrow in the windowless bedroom of the dirt-floored farmhouse. Two of the ten children of Victor's mother, Graciela, had died before the age of five. "A piece of your heart is lost forever," she told me one night by the lamplight while I was helping her strip dried corncobs.

The rondas made survival just a bit easier for thousands of families. What I learned from my 1987 survey in Tunnel Six was that each family gained an average of five animals because of the decline in theft. The number was seven in Cuyumalca. These were small yet significant gains in lands where the holdings of a family seldom exceeded a dozen animals. It meant there was a little more meat in a predominantly starchy diet. Milk from goats and cows became a bit more plentiful for children and cheese-making. There were a few more chickens and ducks to sell on market day to buy kerosene, matches, clothes, salt, school notebooks, and other necessities. Graciela Domador and others could breed stock with new confidence. The addition of a litter of pigs or flock of turkeys multiplied the dividend from the end of robbery.

The struggle for livelihood extended to a longing for order. Colonialism figured in many villagers' stories as a cause of greed and division. These tales passed through generations in Piura and Cajamarca, encouraged by the anticolonial nationalism of the Peruvian educational system. The Velasco government had revised the curriculum to celebrate the Incas and show Pizarro as a miser and brute. Carlos Gómez in Tunnel Six pointed out to me a cartoon of a gold-bedecked Atahualpa as a buffed superhero in his daughter's schoolbook to illustrate his view of the conquest as the original sin in Andean history: "Everything was order and prosperity in the Inca time. The Spanish brought only laziness and ruin, and left a legacy of stealing and vice. They tricked the Incas, broke up communities, and took all the land for haciendas, leaving everyone with a legacy of disorder, greed, and misery."

Religion encouraged a vision linking the disorder of stealing and drunkenness to the propagation of division and misery. Thus some Pentecostal villagers claimed that "vice" represented a temptation of the devil as well as a tool of the powerful to keep down the poor. "I've noticed," related Hermelinda Chávez in Tunnel Six, "you don't see rich people lying dead drunk on the highway or slicing each other like meat in knife fights." Since many women saw a connection among the drinking, fighting, and wife beating, they proved just as insistent as men about the danger of disorder.

The rondas stood for salvation from the dystopia of lawlessness. "We're living more peacefully, better between campesinos," as Carlos Gómez put the common view. There had been violence and perhaps even cruelty at points along the way, yet it had been largely brought under control by peasants themselves once the victory against crime had been won. As they evolved, the patrols came to mean more to most villagers than just the basic yet limited function of protecting livelihood. A society ripped apart by mistrust, jealousy, robbery, fighting, misery, and corruption was being recomposed. Periodization of history into the hell of "before the ronda" and the redemption of "after the ronda" equated order with a politics of emancipation. "Imposing discipline frees us from injustice and self-destruction," said Eladio Idrogo.

It strikes me that the rondas go against the grain of a good deal of recent thinking in social theory. Michel Foucault led the way to a common view among a new generation of scholars that "discipline" and "order" are inevitably something negative. Such a position may apply to fascist police states, or perhaps even to the prisons, mental health clinics, and other modern institutions that Foucault accused of subjecting us to control and surveillance in the name of reason and progress.[43] At the same time, it is a mistake to ignore the multiplicity of meaning and motives that can attach to the will to create order. Any social institution, no matter how benign, imposes forms of regulation and standardization. The rondas were no exception, with their demand for participation, punishment of thievery, and an internal system of leadership and authority. Yet the committees developed at the initiative of poor farmers to meet pressing needs. Their example suggests the need to avoid an automatic equation of a quest for order with the exercise of domination. In northern Peru, disorder had served the status quo, guaranteeing continued poverty and suffering. It was order that seemed to hold out the promise of some betterment of rural life, and it was no wonder Eladio Idrogo and so many others saw the rondas in so positive a way.

REVOLUTION OR REFORM?

The rondas had stamped out theft in the Chota Valley by 1978. A bigger and enduring question was whether they would turn into more than a defensive action to restore order. The article by Marcos Roncagliolo from which I quoted at the beginning of this chapter cited a pair of incidents as evidence of a movement with more militant aims. "When the ronderos get mad, they're fearsome," the Lima journalist concluded from the beating of a judge and torching of a police station.[44]

Roncagliolo's story was sketchy about these ronda actions. Visiting the Chotan mountains for the first time in 1990, I hoped to learn more about what had happened a decade before. On a bright blue mountain morning in Eladio Idrogo's farmhouse, I asked the young leader if he knew anything about the episode with the judge, which was supposed to have occurred in Chota. Roncagliolo had related only that the magistrate's name was Manuel Calvay and that his demands for bribes had earned him the nickname of Dr. Cuánto Hay, or "Dr. How Much." The ronderos were credited with sending him packing for his abuses. Eladio blinked under his broad-brimmed straw hat. "You know, Doctor, the man who knows is out back." A villager from farther down the Chota Valley, Máximo Ortiz Torres was on a municipal crew laying pipe to bring running water to Cuyumalca. The crew was at that moment on break in the pasture just behind the farmhouse. I reflected that this was unlikely to go down as an episode in the romance of the anthropologist as hero, an odyssey into the unknown to discover the secrets of other cultures. Luck had placed the "native" I was after in the backyard.

Ortiz was a square-shouldered man with a moustache and big sideburns. I explained that I was writing a book about the rondas and showed him my letters of introduction from Stanford University and the Chotan subprefect. Ortiz invited me to come to talk to him that Saturday. I followed his directions to make the hour walk from my hotel in Chota down the sunny valley to his farmhouse in the village of Chororco.

The family awaited the gringo in the cavelike cool of the farmhouse. I had brought some Ninja Turtle sticker books for the seven children of Ortiz and his wife. They listened to their father between glances at the turtles Michelangelo, Raphael, and Donatello:

I was the president of the ronda committee then. One of the things we did was maintain order at parties, to prevent fights and disorder. There was a young guy causing trouble. We gave him a couple of lashes to calm him down. The next day he went to the courthouse. He accused me and two others of kidnapping and attempted murder. . . . Calvay called us in. He said, "My children, I need fifty dollars from each of you." I refused to pay, I said, "Doctor, I'm just a peasant, a poncho wearer. I don't have that kind of money." He called a policeman to handcuff me. I pushed them out of the way and ran out the door back to the countryside. We sent out an urgent call to the other rondas to mobilize to Chota the next day. . . . We went into town, dragged him out of his office with blows. We wanted to take him to the countryside to make him do the ronda barefoot, to see how we lived. But the PIP [Investigative Police] were just around the corner. They came out firing, and saved the judge by pulling him into the station. . . . Later we prepared petitions for the president and the Supreme Court asking for him to be removed for good.

A copy of the official report I bribed later from a policeman gave a similar account without painting villagers in quite so favorable a light:

Máximo Ortiz, leader of the uprising against Judge Calvay, Chororco, 1990

The peasant mob . . . insulted [Calvay] with filthy and improper words, calling him a thief. . . . [T]hey prevented him from entering and began to attack him. Various members of the rondas knocked him down and dragged him along the ground, while the other threw rocks, hit him with sticks, and punched and kicked him on different parts of his body, yelling that they were going to take him to the countryside, and kill him. . . . [T]he officers of PIP intervened in an energetic and decisive fashion, shooting their guns in the air to scatter the peasant mob . . . employing force, but without causing any injury or damage, they succeeded in rescuing the aforementioned Judge, Dr. Manuel Calvay Solano.

Even the Investigative Police agreed that the action may have been justified. A section of the report stamped "Confidential" explained: "It has come to our attention that the judge charged bribes, and earned hatred. We recommended that he leave for his own good." Calvay took a bus to Lima never to return.

Ortiz wanted recognition for his role in this triumph over corruption. The forty-year-old villager had stepped down from the ronda presidency to devote himself to his fields, day labor, and tailoring piecework. This and his awkward and withdrawn manner meant that few recalled his leadership in expelling Calvay. I left the farmhouse on that afternoon in 1990, promising to do what I could to set the record straight. I wrote a magazine article on the rondas a few months later with a sidebar on "Forgotten Heroes" with a picture of Ortiz. He came up to me one evening on a cobble-stoned Chota street to say that a cousin in Chiclayo had sent him the piece. Somehow I had inverted matronymic and patronymic so that his name appeared as "Torres Ortiz." Although mentioning the mistake, Ortiz seemed happy enough with the piece after years of anonymity. We talked about his oldest daughter starting high school before we said good-bye under a dim street lamp.

The other episode of ronda fury was the station burning in Cutervo. I journeyed by truck in 1991 to this town of about 4,000 under the Ilucán Volcano, the capital of the province of the same name. A friend from Chota gave me the name of a schoolteacher there. He directed me to a house at the town's edge to talk to Cirilo Muñoz and Rosalía Montenegro. No one was home. A neighbor said the couple lived in the village of La Succha, only coming into town for Sunday market.

I returned then to find the house bustling with family unloading sacks of corn and coffee packed in by mule. Muñoz and Montenegro were a pale, heavyset couple in their fifties. They and a sister of Montenegro looked at my letters of introduction. Muñoz let the sisters do the talking:

There were some cattle rustlers near La Succha. My husband was part of the ronda that had just started there. It was a rainy night. He and the others surrounded the house where they were having a party. They told the rustlers to come out. They came out shooting. A couple of them were PIP. They were with the rustlers, splitting the take. My husband was shot in the leg. He crawled into a ditch, and one of the ronderos went to get me. He was just unconscious from losing the blood. I loaded him onto a burro to try to take him to town.

Muñoz nodded agreement. His sister-in-law continued the tale:

The morning after the shooting, about 250 ronderos came together in La Succha, Salín, Yatún, and other villages to demand justice. Rosalía said to the PIP station, "Who ordered you to kill ronderos? Who gave you permission?" Then the PIP pointed his machine gun at her, and threatened her. She picked up a bunch of manure and threw it in his face.

Rosalía Montenegro (with husband, Cirilo Muñoz), leader of the burning of the police station, Cutervo, 1991

Then she charged into the station, everyone followed. The other fled out the back. We made a bonfire with their things in the street.

Rosalía concluded: "I never imagined doing anything like that, but there was no justice from PIP. Not like the GC [Civil Guard]. They treated us with more respect. We were careful not to put the Peruvian flag or the shield in the bonfire. We turned everything else to dust." I thanked the family for the story. On the way back to the plaza, I went by the PIP station. It had stayed boarded shut ever since the attack of the ronderos.

The tales of Ortiz and the Montenegros reveal much about the status of the rondas in 1980. I show in the next chapter how Marxist activists encouraged villagers to see the movement as a step in a march to socialism. It does not appear that they had any direct involvement in either of the episodes of 1980, however. Neither Ortiz nor the Montenegros belonged to any party. They did not regard themselves as revolutionaries. Ortiz and the Chotan villagers only wanted a bad judge removed. The Cutervan ronderos demanded a stop to one police branch's malfeasance. All the protestors maintained a measure of respect for the structure of law and authority. This attitude came across in the appeal of the Chotan ronderos to the Superior Court and the president for removing Calvay. It was just as evident in the cooperation of the Montenegros with the Civil Guard in protecting the national emblems of honor. There can be no question about village participation in Mexico, Cuba, Vietnam, and a number of other countries in what the anthropologist Eric Wolf calls the "peasant wars of the 20th century."[45] But nothing suggests that the ronderos had come to the point of fighting to overthrow the government.

The events of 1980 did indicate an evolution in the rondas. It took a push from the police and other officials in 1976 just to get cautious Cuyumalcans to guard the school. Much had changed locally and nationally four years later. The rondas were squashing crime. A cluster of teacher and worker walkouts and regional autonomy movements culminated in 1977 and 1978 in the first truly national strikes in Peru's history. The military was giving up the presidential palace to a civilian government. It was an atmosphere of flux that had paved the way for the demand for a minimum standard of accountability and honesty from the government. The movement started to stop local thieves. It expanded its purview by 1980 to punish town authorities who were thought to be or support criminals.

Lenin drew the distinction between reform and revolution in a famous manifesto just after the October Revolution. The Bolshevik leader contrasted the "ridiculous" view of those seeking "nothing more than concessions on the part of the ruling class" against the righteousness of advocates of its overthrow.[46] The stories of Ortiz and the Montenegros suggest the difficulty of tidy categories in struggles for change. It may not have been much to demand honesty by the criterion that sets toppling the state as the standard of success. Yet villagers' flinging manure and even beating up corrupt officials was unprecedented in northern Peru. Nobody in Chota and Cutervo could recall a case of any such challenge by the *gente humilde,* humble people, from the Andean countryside.[47] The rondas were revolutionary in breaking from the traditional deference of the villager to the town, the better educated, and those in power.

It was enough to worry the government. An order from Lima removed Agusto Yngar Garay from the subprefecture of Chota in

1978. He was reassigned to a post in the malarial jungles of Puno in southern Peru. This was his punishment for endorsing the rondas in the first place. A high-ranking general told a Lima newspaper that "The rondas are a double-edged sword. They end rustling, but I have reliable reports that there are zones in Cajamarca that no one can enter, not even the Police Forces, because the patrollers are the only ones to control those areas."[48] The interior minister telegrammed a secret order to the prefect of Cajamarca. He emphasized that "the existence of the so-called night rondas in the provinces of Chota, Hualgayoc, Cutervo, and Jaén, particularly in the first, has generated an alarming situation. . . . [T]hey cannot be allowed to continue."[49]

FACING THE FUTURE

It was too late for the government to decree the rondas out of existence. A change had occurred in the countryside with their advent. To be a villager was no longer just to be poor, dirty, ignorant, backward, pitiable, oppressed, or any of the other usual adjectives. It was to be one of those rural stalwarts braving the mud and the evil night hours for justice and reform. As a rondero, a villager was a newsmaker, a hero, and even a legend, whipping rustlers and even the bureaucrats into line. The telling and retelling of the tales of Dr. How Much and the Cutervo PIP cemented the prestige of the committees.

Andean history abounds in movements that went down to defeat. Apathy, infighting, fear, and repression set the odds against village initiatives for change. I had planned in 1985 to do my dissertation on a rural union in the jungle foothills that organized for higher corn prices. When I arrived in San Martín the next year, the union had dissolved with the switchover of farmers to coca. Guerrillas and narcotraffickers ruled the region.

The odds against organizing may explain the surprise that many villagers seemed to feel about the rondas. Oscar Berrú lived by a creek in Tunnel Six. The forty-two-year-old villager was born without ears, only fleshy stubs, as if the rest had been chewed off by some wild animal. This along with his deep voice and thick forearms made Oscar an intimidating figure. Equipped with whip and poncho in the moonlight, he was the prototype of the tough patroller, never missing his turn with the Wednesday night group. When I stopped by one afternoon in 1986, Oscar explained that "no one dreamed the rondas would ever work. . . . [T]his is the clean justice we have never had." He paused. The heat of the tropical afternoon pounded through the tin roof. A guinea pig rustled in a pile of hay in the corner.

"Will it last? No one can say."

THREE

Nightcourt

I took a break from Chota to visit Cajamarca for a few days in 1991. A night by bus across the altiplano, from the heartland of the rondas to the north, the city of 150,000 sits at 8,000 feet in a lovely valley. It was in the plaza of Cajamarca in 1532 that Francisco Pizarro and his band of 150 Spanish adventurers ambushed the Incan emperor Atahualpa to launch the conquest of Peru. The beauty of the mountain setting and red-tiled roofs and colonial churches made the city a favorite destination for tourists from the rest of Peru and abroad. Under the turquoise sky on the cobblestone streets of the department capital, the parade of Arequipan high school kids and Brazilian and German tourists with Nikons and backpacks gave the streets an atmosphere almost as uproarious as the Lenten carnival that is part of the city's fame.

Tourism was down in this year of crisis and upheaval in Peru. As recession deepened, it was hard even for members of the Lima middle class to vacation in the provinces. The outbreak of cholera and the Shining Path bombings scared away foreigners. Restaurateurs, hotel keepers, and shopkeepers had time to chat when I introduced myself as an American anthropologist researching the rondas. Some Cajamarcans expressed admiration for village success in stamping out crime. Others were less positive. One said she heard ronderos poked the eyes out of rustlers. Another reported that they torched policemen with gasoline. The geography of imagination made it easy for unsympathetic city dwellers to sensationalize or dismiss the rondas as a sign of the ignorance and brutality of the Andean peasantry.

It was another matter in the countryside. There the rondas enjoyed an almost universal popularity for stopping crime. Most villagers even seemed to take pleasure in their reputation for toughness. Just about every village had its own stories about punishing thieves by immersion in glacial lakes, whipping, or a day in the stocks. One Chotan villager told me about meting out ronda justice to a pair of unexpected victims: "Some of us stopped a bus on the highway to check for contraband. There were two French tourists. They were mad. They said, 'Who are these dirty peasants? Who do they think they are?' So we ronderos made them get off the bus. They were terrified. We made them do the ronda that night barefoot, until we let them go." The days of scraping and bowing were over in this parable of new rural boldness. Serfs had turned into ronderos. They demanded respect even from gringo tourists. The Chotan villager could not resist a coda. "You know, Doctor, they were really tall and white, just like you."

Ronderos taming both rustlers and tourists made for great storytelling. Yet it failed to capture a fundamental change in the rondas. Because the patrols had largely ended thievery, there was no longer as urgent a need to take to the trails every night. The nightwatch was sporadic or ceased altogether in many villages in Cajamarca and Piura by the mid-1980s. Energy shifted to the less dramatic, but just as urgent, task of resolving conflicts over inheritance, slander, assault, domestic violence, damages caused by loose animals, and land and water rights. The instrument of justice was the assembly. Here villagers crowded into the local meeting halls to adjudicate disputes under the supervision of the ronda steering committee. One-hundred and fifty-six cases came before ronda assemblies in Tunnel Six in 1986 and 1987. The villagers in Lingán Pata near the top of the Chota Valley dealt with more than 300 cases in 1900 and 1991. The volume was just as great in hundreds of other villagers in the mountains of Cajamarca and Piura. "We're making a new, better justice with the ronda assemblies," or such was the explanation of Pascual Ruiz from Lingán Pata, with his boyish face and at six feet by far the tallest peasant I ever met in the northern Andes.

This chapter examines the assemblies. It shows how discontent with policemen, lawyers, and judges led villagers to widen the ronda purview from patrolling to justice-making. The assemblies incorporated protocol from the police station and courtroom. Yet they made it part of a way of dealing with discord that placed a premium on consensus and reconciliation. While failing to end or

Pascual Ruiz speaking at a ronda assembly, Samangay Pass, 1990

perhaps even diminish conflict in the northern countryside, the assemblies provided faster, fairer, and cheaper justice than the government bureaucracy. As so much else in Peru was unraveling, the assemblies increased for villagers a feeling of control over their lives, and elevated the status of the rondas as a rallying point for peasant pride in northern Andes.

It was hard for me simply to keep up with the pace of the villagers. I was then in my mid-twenties and fancied myself an athlete, and yet I still could not match villagers on the trails or in the fields. They had a capacity for endurance belying the meagerness of bodies fueled on corn and potatoes in a countryside without the luxury of a "balanced" diet. As I discovered on a July night in Tunnel Six, it was the same with the assemblies. The rays of a Coleman lantern flickered across faces of the fifty villagers who gathered in the lunchroom to listen and have their say about a pair of brawlers, a disagreement over rights to pasture, and a marital dispute. I knew it would take until close to dawn to come to closure in the three cases. I am not much of a night person anyway, and by midnight my duty of "data collection" lost out to the lazy pull of sleepiness. I slipped out with a nod to Oscar Berrú, the earless Tunnel Sixer who as the "delegate of discipline" always scowlingly policed the

After a ronda assembly, Cuyumalca, 1990

door with his whip, flashlight, and poncho. The murmur of voices and the hissing of the kerosene lamp followed me as I walked up to my little house just above the school.

MAOISM IN THE ANDES

I did stay long enough to watch one case be resolved that night. It concerned a brawl between a pair of men from the nearby village of Algodonal. The Algodonal lieutenant governor, a young man in a T-shirt and tractor cap, described what had happened. At a cockfight, Elías Jiménez accused Lucas Domínguez of failing to pay up on a lost bet. Domínguez had replied that Jiménez was an "asswipe," and his mother a "whore." These insults to honor and masculinity were serious business given the usual courtliness of rural manners. As several witnesses now told the assembly, Domínguez had jumped Jiménez, and they fought and rolled in the dust until separated by men in the crowd. Since no one was hurt, the consensus of villagers was that the two men should simply be warned, and fined a day's work on the school. There was a look of relief on their faces about escaping the humiliation of the whip. Each came forward to sign an agreement, consenting to the fine and promising "not to cause such problems of Social Disorder in the future."

Many scholars have documented village justice-making in the altiplanos of Bolivia and central and southern Peru.[1] What they call "customary," "indigenous," "folk," or "peasant" law resembles the rondas in that the local assembly serves as a tribunal. Yet communal judgment went as far back as pre-Columbian times in these areas to the south of Cajamarca and Piura. The lack of a history of local autonomy in northern Peru meant villagers there had no comparable experience at making justice for themselves. So the ronda assembly I witnessed was not traditional or ancestral.[2] It is hard to overemphasize what a novelty it was for villages to administer justice as they did through the rondas in the late 1970s and 1980s.

It might not have happened without Daniel Idrogo. The second of eleven children of a poor family, Idrogo was born in 1954 in Cuyumalca, the hamlet in which the ronda would begin two decades later. He worked his way through high school to the University of Chiclayo, where he took the graveyard shift in a pool hall to support himself. This was the heyday of campus radicalism around the world, and Idrogo became a leader in the Federation of Revolutionary Students (FER), a Maoist organization.[3] In Peru, Maoism was an especially influential force in the 1960s and 1970s, partly because the Chinese leader's emphasis on the peasantry's role in revolution fit with Peruvian radicals' long-standing conviction about the potential of the Andean majority as a force for change and renovation.[4] The most notorious Maoist organization to form during this time was the Communist Party of Peru–Shining Path, which went to war in 1980 to encircle the cities from the countryside as Mao had done in China. Yet the Shining Path was by no means the only party inspired by the Chinese leader's brand of Marxism. Among the other pretenders, the largest group was the Communist Party of Peru–Red Homeland. Red Homeland did not advocate armed revolution at least in the short term, and it even entered elections in the 1980s. The Shining Path scorned Red Homeland as "sewer-rat revisionists" for "selling out to parliamentary cretinism, while Red Homeland derided the Shining Path as "anarcho-infantile-terrorists."[5] Idrogo's Federation of Revolutionary Students was controlled by Red Homeland, and the young law student became a party member. In 1976, he won the leadership's

Daniel Idrogo with daughter Daniela,
Cuyumalca, 1993

blessing to drop out of school to go back to his native Chota Valley
to organize the peasantry.

It was only a few weeks after returning that Idrogo heard from
relatives about the nightwatch just starting in Cuyumalca. The
young activist recognized an opportunity to gain a foothold in
the countryside. During the next several years, he became a figure
of legend and controversy, organizing rondas in dozens of villages
across the northern mountains. It was rumored that Investigative
Police had a price of $1,000 on his head. Another story depicted
Idrogo traveling the mountain trails dressed as a woman to escape
rustlers and policemen. When the military gave up power to civil-
ians in 1980, Idrogo ran for national Congress on the Red Homeland ticket, which had decided to enter the elections in spite of the

minority within the party who believed armed revolution was the only solution.[6] He won the highest vote total of any Cajamarcan candidate and thus became one of Peru's first congressmen from a peasant family.

I met what the newspapers called the "rondero congressman" for the first time in 1987 in the Lima office he shared with seven other deputies. Still slender and fresh-faced in his mid-thirties, Idrogo appeared in a politician's pinstriped suit. He was handsome with the pale olive skin, roman nose, and ink-black hair typical of many Cajamarcans. The manifestos of Red Homeland displayed the same didacticism and intolerance as a Red Guard wall poster, even if the party never went so far as to adopt the methods of violence and terror that characterized the Chinese Cultural Revolution. "Obey the Eight Warnings and Three Cardinal Rules of Chairman Mao," demanded a broadsheet at a Red Homeland congress.[7] Idrogo was every bit the party loyalist, but he answered my questions without preachiness or jargon. He recalled organizing a meeting in Cuyumalca for January 29, 1977, just a month after the founding of the ronda, crisscrossing Cuyumalca to spread the word. Over 150 Cuyumalcans had shown up for this gathering held in a village pasture. Idrogo hoped it would be a first step toward turning villagers to revolution.

I found the agreement made at that assembly on a subsequent trip to Cuyumalca. Idrogo had written it in a clear hand.[8] It reveals his attempt to bring the rondas under Red Homeland control. To build support for the party, Idrogo had founded a "Neighborhood Committee" to demand water and electricity from the municipal government. He stipulated that Cuyumalcans should "be in constant contact with the Steering Committee of the Neighborhood Committee." At the same time, it was incumbent for villagers to "organize aggressively, and demand solutions . . . from the political and judicial authorities." Idrogo did not even refer to "Night Rounds," as the name appeared in the original ronda charter of a month before. As part of pressing villagers to see themselves through a Marxist prism as a class with a common identity and interests, he described them as "rondas de campesinos," an organization built by and for the peasantry under the stewardship of Red Homeland.

It was to further radicalize the rondas that Idrogo proposed an

El Rondero, a newsletter published by Red Homeland, 1980

expansion into conflict resolution. Before then, nobody imagined that the organization was anything more than a crime patrol. Yet Idrogo put into the agreement that villagers should begin to "resolve among themselves problems of feuds, damages, and threats." He explained to me a decade later over the clattering typewriters and street noise from Abancay Avenue: "I thought the rondas could be more than just cowcatchers. They could be a vehicle for resolving problems amongst peasants, for an alternative to the official corruption. I knew that Mao had encouraged people's justice on the Long March, and I believed the ronda assemblies could follow the model." A newsletter distributed in Chota by Red Homeland in 1980 reaffirmed that "disputes over boundaries, marriage, and other . . . contradictions should be resolved through criticism and self-criticism with the support of the steering committee of the Rondas." This was part of how "the ronderos raise the torch of revolutionary triumph to achieve National Liberation and Popular Democracy on the road to Socialism."[9] The justice-making of the assemblies was to become a custom specific to northern villagers. Yet the concept came from Idrogo, who had drawn it from his embrace of a dream of revolution that arrived to Peru by way of Red Homeland, China, and Europe. It was a genealogy that underscored historian Arif Dirlik's injunction to see the "global in the local."[10]

FROM PATROLS TO ASSEMBLIES

Idrogo planted the seed for the ronda assembly's justice making. But why did it take root? As many scholars of culture and globalization have observed, the acceptance of outside ideas often depends on their fit with the mood and the moment in local society. To take an example from the Andes south of the Chota Valley, the rate of village conversion to Protestant sects promoted by U.S. missionaries mushroomed in the 1980s. Historian Ponciano del Pino shows that the war between the Shining Path and the government was the key factor in increasing openness to the Assembly of God and other Pentecostal groups.[11] The religious vision of apocalypse and the Last Judgement at the heart of these sects resonated with the lived realities of fear and terror in the countryside.

The reasons for openness to justice making began with the need for a forum to deal with bickering and infighting. It would be silly to view villages in the Andes or anywhere else as more prone to jealousy and conflict than any other human society.[12] Any academic will confirm that no village outdoes university and professional politics for envy, factionalism, character assassination, and status anxiety. Still most northern villagers acknowledged that conflict and hatred were a fact of life in rural society. The explosiveness of love and betrayal contributed to the oft-repeated view of their world as "full of envy." So did matters of property, their urgency heightened by the precariousness of survival. Was the rock or the eucalyptus the border between plots? How would three siblings split the property of deceased parents? Who was allowed to divert water from a stream? Tunnel Six's Martín Llacsahuache had a scar across his forehead from a machete blow received in a battle over land by the Quiroz River. Another Tunnel Sixer was hacked to death in the same 1980 confrontation. Even if few villagers wanted to give an inch when it came to their dispute, they could agree at least in the abstract that the sorcery, slander, and even murder triggered by infighting damaged peasant welfare. Martín expressed it to me this way in 1987: "How are we going to work together for the good of our community so long as we're fighting over every little thing?"

It was just as plain to most villagers that the judicial system was not going to resolve these fights. Dissatisfaction with the administration of justice was long standing throughout the Peruvian Andes. Already in 1613 in his letter to King Philip II, the Lucanas chief Guamán Poma de Ayala denounced Spanish magistrates for adoring "gold, silver, and property as their idols." [13] The eighteenth-century rebel José Gabriel Condorcanqui, who took the name of Túpac Amaru II after the last Inca killed by the Spaniards, protested the sale of "justice by auction to whoever bids the highest or gives the most." [14] So did one of the most popular of twentieth-century Andean balladeers, Ernesto Sánchez Gallardo, "the Troubadour of Huascarán":

> They free the guilty
> And punish the innocent
> Jail the petty thief
> And adore the rich who steal millions. [15]

Such accusations were not completely fair. Even the angriest villagers would admit that there were honest judges. One Bambamarca Valley judge suggested to me that "those who lose trials always blame it on corruption no matter how much they were in the wrong." Yet he acknowledged that demands were made for bribes and payoffs by such as Manuel Calvay, the infamous "Dr. How Much" who was run out off Chota by ronderos in 1980. The poor service did not stop many villagers from going to court to seek punishment of an assailant or win land. It was the only chance for redress. Nevertheless, doing so meant putting up with the condescension and disregard for rural people. Money had to be found for notaries, lawyers, and bribes for the clerks and judges. The process was not just costly, but slow. In Peru, judges hear and rule on cases without juries, for the legal system there derives from the Napoleonic Code. Most northern towns had only one judge. Short-staffing contributed to a backlog that stacked up further with holidays and strikes. In looking at 105 cases in Chota's District Court between 1970 and 1976, I found that the average time from the lodging of charges to a verdict was four years.[16] There was a reason why villagers were convinced that the legal system did not work.

Therefore Idrogo's plan for ronda justice fell on fertile ground. Yet the fact that the plan originated with this young Marxist made it controversial. In 1978, Idrogo and other Red Homeland activists had led a march on Chota to protest the sugar hoarding by town merchants.[17] Looting occurred. The military government sent in troops, which arrested and in several cases tortured those suspected of organizing the protest. The events of 1978 made many villagers cautious about Idrogo and his party. Memory endured throughout the region of government repression of radical protest, as far back as the 1914 gunning down by police of 300 villagers who had occupied the Hacienda Llaucán in the Bambamarca Valley.[18] As it would prove again in the counterinsurgency against the Shining Path in the 1980s, the government could be especially brutal in the Andean countryside, because the region was out of the eye of the media and a poor villager's life counted for less anyway by the calculus of class and race in Peruvian society. Would attending meetings organized by Idrogo and Red Homeland get them into trouble? The fear of reprisal led at least some peasants to shy away from anything to do with the Marxists.

It was not just fear that created difficulty for Red Homeland, however. Many villagers already had prior allegiances to other political parties. Though the stereotype in Peru had it that the peasantry was so isolated and parochial as to be "prepolitical," the truth was that many villagers had strong views about the news from Lima and about the right and wrong direction for their country. The American Popular Revolutionary Alliance (APRA) was the party of choice for many inhabitants of the northern Andes during the 1970s and 1980s.[19] Founded in 1931 by the shrewd, mercurial Víctor Raúl Haya de la Torre, APRA was populist; it wooed the poor and middle classes with vague promises of social justice yet proving willing to compromise with conservative governments, including the Manuel A. Odría dictatorship of the 1950s. During the mid-twentieth century in northern Peru, APRA was a powerful political machine that operated through patronage and handouts, a quasi-religious faith in Haya and the party, and the occasional use of "buffalos," thugs, to club recalcitrants into line. When Haya's young protegé Alan García won the Peruvian presidency and brought APRA to national power for the first time in 1985, he garnered over 60 percent of the vote in Chota, Bambamarca, Huancabamba, Ayabaca, and the other northern provinces.[20]

Pedro Risco was the party leader in Chota. The short and jowly Risco had the brillantined hair and pugnacious eye of an aging prizefighter. The APRA leader resembled Chicago's Mayor Richard J. Daley, not just in physical appearance but also in a political style grounded in patronage and bossism, albeit on Chota's far smaller stage. As subprefect and then a member of the city council, he had channeled money to villages that supported APRA and sought to cut off anyone who opposed the party. A former schoolteacher, Risco owned a rustic store just off the Chota plaza, which doubled as party headquarters papered with APRA campaign posters. Many evenings, villagers loyal to the party stopped by to report on goings-on in their part of the valley, and to listen to "Don Pedro" hold forth about politics in his slow, raspy voice.

Risco had many eyes and ears in the countryside. He heard about Daniel Idrogo's meeting in Cuyumalca, and quite rightly guessed that Idrogo wanted to use the rondas to build up Red Homeland. APRA was anti-Communist, not to mention jealous of any political rival. So Risco went on the attack, spreading stories that Idrogo was an atheist and a terrorist and that he only wanted to "disorient the Peasantry or psychologically terrorize them."[21] At the same time, however, Risco understood the popularity of the rondas and their potential for growth. Thus, the APRA boss did not oppose the organizations themselves. To the contrary, he decided to try to outmaneuver Red Homeland by supporting and seeking to control the rondas, and to turn them into a dependency and stronghold of his own party. During the next few years, Risco traveled across

The APRA's Pedro Risco in his store, Chota, 1990

the Chota Valley and to other parts of the northern Andes to organize ronda committees, which he instructed his village followers to call "Pacific Peasant Rondas" to distinguish themselves from the more radical view of the movement favored by Red Homeland. Risco rode the ronda expansion of the 1980s and by the end of the decade had named himself the "President of the Presidents of the Pacific Rondas." Infighting between APRA and Red Homeland in the Chota Valley was constant and dirty, with Idrogo and Red Homeland giving as good as they got. They derided Risco, crippled from an old soccer injury, as "the old gimp," and seldom lost a chance to blast him and his party as "servants of the old order and the poor's enemies." Red Homeland encouraged its village supporters to adopt the name of "Independent Peasant Rondas" as the battle between APRA and the left made controversial even the naming of the rondas.

"WHO DO YOU FUCKING PEASANTS THINK YOU ARE?"

APRA opposed the rondas' entry into justice making. In the 1930s, the party was much more radical than it had became in the 1970s. It had led a famous 1932 insurrection against the quasi-fascist government of military strongman Luis Sánchez Cerro. Although the bloody uprising remained a part of party mythology, APRA had turned into a force for the status quo in the northern Andes by the middle of the twentieth century. Many shopkeepers and civil servants belonged, and there was certainly no longer talk of armed revolution. As a result, Risco and his party encouraged the rondas, yet they also wanted to restrict their independence and scope. The statute of the "Pacific Rondas" instructed villagers to turn over captured thieves to the police and otherwise "collaborate with Political, Police, Judicial and Municipal authorities," though I found that even die-hard village apristas often ignored the provision to punish rustlers on the spot.[22] To do more than patrol was discouraged. The organizations were "exclusively to combat robbery," read the statute, which Risco had mimeographed as handouts for his rural followers.[23]

APRA opposition to justice making sparked conflict in Cuyumalca. Almost ten miles across, the village was subdivided into twelve sectors: Cañafisto, Conga Blanca, Actotambo, Huacarcocha, Capilla Pampa, Cuchupachán, Nuevo Oriente, Alto Cuyumalca, Chaupelanche, Samangay, Progresopampa, and Quichpé. Although the sectors had come together to form the ronda in 1976, they were semiautonomous, with their own soccer teams, catechism groups, and fiestas. The distinctions carried into politics, at least in part. Daniel Idrogo grew up in Cañafisto, where his father, one brother, two sisters, and countless cousins still reside today. These links of kinship and friendship enabled the young activist to turn this part of Cuyumalca into a stronghold. By contrast, Alto Cuyumalca teemed with APRA supporters, among them the early ronda activist Régulo Oblitas, along with Artidoro Huanambal, Gilberto Benavides, and others among the very first patrollers. Like Oblitas, many of these men had worked on the coastal sugar plantations of Tumán, La Colpa, Casa Grande, or Roma, and several of them had become loyalists through their involvement in APRA-controlled workers' unions there. Moreover, Oblitas and others in Alto Cuyumalca were growing resentful of the younger Idrogo for seeming to take over the movement, and for moving the center of ronda activity from Alto Cuyumalca to Cañafisto. This made the Alto Cuyumalcans all the readier to undertake a common cause with Risco. Oblitas told me in 1990 that he had been a frequent visitor to Risco's store in the late 1970s and had voted for the APRA ticket in the 1980 election.[24]

I visited Alto Cuyumalca's single biggest APRA booster in 1991. A fast talker with a long face and lopsided grin, Fredesvindo Huanambal lived with his wife and daughter in a mud-walled farmhouse near the schoolhouse. At the start in 1977, Huanambal was friendly with Daniel Idrogo, and even helped him organize the January meeting. Yet it was not long before he grew resentful of the spotlight on his distant cousin. He had broken with Idrogo by 1978 to become Risco's point man in Alto Cuyumalca, and a fierce enemy of Red Homeland. The election of APRA's own Alan García in 1985 to the Peruvian presidency was the highwater mark for Risco and his party in the Chota Valley. For allegiance to the party, Risco arranged for Huanambal to receive an Andean Peace Fellowship, a prize awarded by the U.S. Agency for International Development to bring promising village leaders to the United States. By lamplight in his farmhouse, Huanambal showed me trophies of his month in Wyoming—a dollar bill, a postcard of Old Faithful, a doll of the University of Wyoming Cowboy. In one snapshot, Huanambal stood in front of the Cheyenne McDonald's, holding up a dirty gob of snow like a gold nugget. This was the first time the Cuyumalcan had ever seen snow; proximity to the equator and warming mist from the Amazon jungle means it never goes beyond frosting in the northern Andes, though the mountains reach to 17,000 feet as part of the world's second highest mountain range.[25] It was a measure of villagers' desperation for a pathway from poverty that dozens quizzed me about the possibility of going to the United States. Although Huanambal raved about the hormone-injected Herefords the size of small elephants and other sights in Wyoming, he told me he had refused an offer to stay behind to work as a farmhand for what by Andean standards was the astronomical sum of five dollars an hour. Later I learned why. As a further reward from APRA, Risco had gotten him a part-time post as a "technician" in a Chota government office, a further cementing of his loyalty.

Alto Cuyumalca elected Huanambal president of its ronda steering committee in 1978. By that time, the villagers just down the mountain in Cañafisto were acting upon Idrogo's suggestion to expand the movement into justice-making, and ronda assemblies had already resolved several long-standing land disputes. The com-

bination of APRA ties and dislike for Idrogo led Huanambal and
other Alto Cuyumalcans to oppose a similar extension of ronda authority in their sector. It was agreed in a meeting in 1978 that "Our
Peasant Night Rounds are exclusively to control the continual Robberies of cattle, crops, break-ins, and armed murders."[26] Alto Cuyumalca wanted nothing to do with any proposal by Idrogo and
Red Homeland, clarified the minutes of a subsequent gathering:
"We reject Extremist Politics . . . brought from other nations, because they do not help the peasant resolve anything."[27] A common assumption of otherwise dissimilar Latin American Marxists
such as Idrogo, Abimael Guzmán, and the famous Argentine guerrilla leader Ernesto "Che" Guevara was that poverty made peasants
into natural revolutionaries. Alto Cuyumalcans certainly qualified
as poor, but they were far from ready for revolution. Although villagers in parts of Peru and Latin America would join the fight to
overthrow capitalism, at least as many others turned out to be un-
interested or even actively opposed to talk of revolution, whether
for fear of reprisal, local rivalry, preexisting partisan ties, or some
combination of these and other factors. The politics of ideology
and allegiance were much more sticky and fractured than recognized by those Marxist leaders who expected the exploited of the
countryside to flock as one to the uplifted hammer and sickle.

Government officials encouraged peasant rejection of Red
Homeland and any extension of ronda jurisdiction. At the end of
the 1970s the conservative military government of General Francisco Morales Bermúdez was still in power, and it banned the rondas in 1979. The Chotan subprefect, Víctor Goycochea Bazán, a
retired military officer, did not try to carry out the order, perhaps
in part because he knew the patrols saved money and personnel for
the government as well as because of the difficulty of trying to suppress them. At the same time, the visit of Augusto Yngar Garay's
successor to Alto Cuyumalca on October 14, 1978, did show that
the authorities wanted to rein in the rondas.[28] The minutes of the
ronda meeting record that the subprefect enjoined villagers "not
to be deceived or induced by political elements that want to get
them in trouble."[29] A police commander who had accompanied
Bazán expanded on this point: "Mr. Police Commander made rec-
ommendations about the rondas, that this activity is only and exclusively for providing security for their property such as houses,

plants, and animals; but that they should not entangle themselves in other matters because it is not their job." To borrow a distinction from the great Italian activist and theorist Antonio Gramsci, the subprefect and policeman were not mounting a "war of position" to wipe out the rondas, but a "war of maneuver" to prevent them from becoming a touchstone for rebellion against the state.[30] The rondas would be allowed so long as they did nothing more than patrol. Alto Cuyumalca's APRA majority had little use for the military government, whose national approval rating had by that time shrunk to single digits. Yet the injunction from the Chotan authorities not to hold assemblies and to keep out the Communists fit with what these villagers wanted to do anyway. As the ronda president, Fredesvindo Huanambal closed the meeting by assuring the visitors that Alto Cuyumalcans "would not entangle ourselves in matters other than protecting ourselves from thievery."[31]

The promise proved to be true and false. Alto Cuyumalca never opened up to Red Homeland or any other Marxist party, and at first it did not use the ronda to mediate conflict. Yet the determination only to patrol began to weaken by the beginning of the 1980s. For example, on March 21, 1980, the first day of a winter in the Southern Hemisphere, Alfredo Días Medina asked the ronda to do something about "young Alejandro Benabides Huamán, who belongs to our sector . . . and is grazing his cattle in my pasture, causing fights between neighbors."[32] The ronda assembly warned Benabides to keep better track of his cows, and the records show that this was only the first in a number of interventions beyond the sphere of patrolling. When Régulo Oblitas took me to a ronda assembly in Alto Cuyumalca in 1991, I found it little different from gatherings in Cañafisto, with the villagers meeting to hear and judge disputes from brawling to water rights. The origin of the justice-making plan with the Marxists of Red Homeland ensured rejection at the start, but the thirst for an alternative to the police and courts prevailed in the end. "The corruption's so bad that the rondas are best for taking care of village problems," acknowledged Fredesvindo Huanambal to me in 1991, even though he and other Alto Cuyumalcans would never admit that the hated Daniel Idrogo and Red Homeland were the first to have recognized the possibility for enlarging the movement's purview.

Those charged with law enforcement would remain mostly opposed to ronda justice throughout the 1980s. A rare compromise between the left and APRA led President Alan García to legalize the rondas in 1986.[33] Many villagers believed that the law authorized justice making, since it broadly recognized the rondas as an "organization at the service of the community." Like many other town authorities, the police sergeant in the little town of Paimas disagreed. The thin-lipped young Cajamarcan summoned Víctor, Martín Llacsahuache, and other Tunnel Six ronda leaders time after time to berate them for daring to administer justice. During one tense time, I went with Víctor, in the hope that the presence of a North American observer might make the policeman more cautious about mistreating the village leader. I waited at the little cement-block station along with Víctor's wife, Francisca, and several other friends and relatives. The sergeant did not jail Víctor. He did yell so loudly that we could hear every word from the street outside. What he said gushed with contempt for peasants and resentment at the ronda challenge to police turf and was sharpened by a few too many beers that afternoon at the nearby cantina. "You piece of shit! You fucking hick! Who do you fucking peasants think you are? I'll rip your balls off the next time I have to call you."

Sometimes the threats were effective. One night at a meeting in Tunnel Six, I met Marcelino Guaygua, president of the ronda committee in the nearby village of Culqui.[34] I asked how the ronda there was going. "Badly," he said. He pulled a paper from a plastic binder: "In Culqui at 8:30 in the evening of Saturday September 20 of 1986 gathered in the house of Mr. President of the Committee of Ronda Campesina of Culqui . . . it was agreed to Reorganize the Service of the Ronda Campesina. . . . Mr. President of the Ronda Committee will be charged only with seeing to matters of rustling and theft. . . . [T]he resolution of houses [i.e., domestic disputes] water damages and fences [i.e., boundary disputes] will be turned over to the political authorities." Guaygua was a radical who kept a copy of Mao's *Little Red Book* in his farmhouse. He wanted to hold assemblies in spite of police warnings. As he explained, however, signing the agreement to stop justice-making had been forced upon him by villagers who did not want to get thrown in jail, or who were encouraged by APRA leaders to restrict the ronda to patrolling. The legitimacy of ronda justice depended on the participation and backing of the entire village. "We can't hold assemblies anymore because people won't come," said the ronda leader.

Culqui remained the exception. It was far more common for the rondas to turn into tribunals throughout the northern Andes. Even after the scare with the sergeant, Víctor refused to shut down the assemblies, and instead he mounted a counterattack by lodging a complaint against the policemen with his superiors in Sullana. The parade of villagers wanting their cases heard by the ronda continued day and night. "Don Víctor, Don Víctor," would come the whispering from the outside at four or five in the morning. The shoeless Córdova would get up to listen to the outpouring about a pilfering neighbor or abusive husband. Then he would promise to schedule the problem for a hearing at the next assembly. Volume was just as heavy at the farmhouse of Eladio Idrogo and the ronda presidents in hundreds of other villages. I asked an old clerk in Chota's courthouse whether the number of cases brought to the official system had declined as a result. "It's true, Doctor," he replied, "we get just half as many cases as a few years ago."

The advent of ronda justice-making was a transnational tale. It arrived by way of Mao's China. Yet the expansion of committee scope was also a story of what scholars of globalization and transnationalism call "transculturation," namely the reshaping and the redefinition of influences from abroad as they find their way into a new culture.[35] The rondas became more than "cowcatchers"; yet they never became the instrument of peasant revolution hoped for by Idrogo. Partly because of APRA's influence and the fear of repression, the vast majority of committees advocated a measure of coordination with police and judges, a falling off from the radical autonomy of the masses envisioned in Maoism. Nor did the assemblies become a greenhouse for a revolutionary consciousness among the peasantry. Even in Cañafisto and other Red Homeland strongholds, rondas were dominated by the back and forth of disputes, personality, responsibility, and behavior, not talk of dialectical materialism and class struggle. Idrogo himself recognized that Mao's blueprint for popular justice had been transformed as it had become part of ronda society. "The assemblies don't have the political edge that I had wanted," he lamented to me in 1991, still vainly hoping that Marxism and the revolution were on their way.

Robin and I had become close friends with Idrogo in 1990. Then living in Lima, he was in love with his secretary's sparkling-eyed younger sister, Betty. We often made the long bus ride across the haunting gray decay of Lima for parties at the half-finished house they shared with other relatives in an outlying neighborhood of Andean migrants. Do Marxists make the best partiers? A video captured in 1991 recorded a social event attended by the chubby Shining Path chief Abimael Guzmán and other top guerrilla leaders at a Lima safe house. It seemed incongruous to see this Stalinist band of killers dancing the night away to music from Zorba the Greek with goofy smiles and raised glasses like high schoolers on prom night; but perhaps their high spirits should not have appeared strange as much as an extension of the intensity about life and politics that characterized so many of those attracted to Marxism in the twentieth century. If Daniel and other comrades in Red Homeland had not chosen war and revolution as their route to the promised land of Communism, they were no less insistent in getting the most from life's pleasures. Betty also belonged to Red Homeland. She and Daniel twirled around the living room at our parties in 1990 with flirtatious elegance to the beat of marineras and huaynos, which Betty's brother Willy sang on an old guitar.[36] I remember those gatherings as an island of warmth and refuge from Peru's mean and troubled streets.

The good times were not to last for Daniel. The fall of the Berlin Wall hastened the decline of Red Homeland and other leftist parties in Peru. Idrogo's term in Congress expired, leaving him unemployed. Betty left him in 1992 for a job in Sweden, marrying a Colombian engineer there. Although Idrogo talked vaguely of returning to the Chota Valley to start an organization to help peasants, it was hard for him to go home again. He had not maintained ties to his native Cuyumalca or the rest of the countryside. Many Chotan villagers now mistrusted the once legendary figure, and their doubts were augmented by stories spread by APRA about his supposedly using government money to buy a sports car.

Last year, in 1996, an acquaintance told me that Daniel was living in Trujillo. I got the address to send him a Christmas card and a picture of our three-year-old, Frances. A fax came back just a few weeks ago. It must have cost Daniel more than he could spare to send it from a copy store. The one-time congressman reported he was working nights as a desk clerk in a downtown hotel. By day, he went to university classes, resuming the law studies he had left twenty years before to devote himself to the rondas and the revolution. Daniel retained his peasant origins in the formalism of his letter writing. Yet the warmth of his personality and of our friendship was there, too. "Your Letter is a moral support of much value, and I do not lose hope that in Trujillo, the Capital of International Festival of Spring and the Marinera, the four of us will meet again. I reiterate my thanks and say good-bye with a strong embrace. Happiness to you all."

THE LETTERED VILLAGE

In 1986, I lived for my first three months in Tunnel Six in the storeroom of the farmhouse of Víctor Córdova and his wife, Francisca Paz. Víctor, the ronda president, had shoved aside black polyester sacks of rice and a plastic bag of chemical fertilizer to make a space for the folding cot I had lugged from the United States. Stacks of papers were piled onto the rickety bamboo shelves on one wall of the dirt-floored room. They included record books, invitations, memos, pamphlets, and flyers. I was surprised. Nothing I had read said much about writing having a place in village life. These were supposed to be oral, even preliterate, cultures. Víctor referred to the shelves as the *archivo,* or the archive, using the bureaucratic parlance for the records of ronda justice-making.

The Mexican novelist Carlos Fuentes has said that an obsession with the formalities of law and writing is "one of the strongest components of Latin American culture."[37] He goes on to declare that "we only believe what is written down and recorded." It may be questionable to speak of "Latin American culture" in the singular in light of the stunning diversity of a region inhabited by everyone from Amazonian Indians to Afro-Brazilian housewives to Argentine businessmen. At the very least, however, anyone who has dealt with the Peruvian bureaucracy knows that the preoccupation with paperwork is extraordinary. On the sidewalks and in small offices close to government offices one can see assembled an army of typists, stamped paper vendors, rubber stamp manufacturers, notaries, lawyers, and fixers known as *tinterillos,* or "ink men." As seat of the viceroyalty for three centuries, Lima was the center of Spanish bu-

The ronda secretary taking minutes, Cuyumalca, 1990

reaucracy in South America. Thus the Peruvian capital was from the start a city of the scribe, the notary, the bureaucrat, and the lawyer. Each of the main cities of Peru's twenty-eight departments has archives so stuffed with official papers that they defy the underpaid employees to organize them enough to be useful for the historian.

Víctor's archive underscores that the preoccupation with record keeping was not limited to city bureaucrats. No ronda assembly in Tunnel Six or anywhere in the northern Andes went forward without someone taking minutes. No document was considered complete without signatures and thumbprints. Every member of the ronda steering committee had a rubber stamp to affix a seal on every piece of paper. For the three centuries of Spanish rule and then in the new nations born from the Independence Wars of the early nineteenth century, the inhabitants of the Andes had lived under governments that placed a premium on record keeping, rules, and regulations. Enchantment with the seal, the law, and the memo testified that administrative ritual had carried over to become an integral part of rural tradition.

It should be emphasized that observing administrative formality was a source of pride for villagers. The matter of signatures was revealing. Most villagers, even those otherwise unable to write, signed with baroque exuberance, complete with dots, loops, and curlicues. Víctor could read a bit, but he did not know how to write. Late at night, he would practice his signature in his daughter's school notebook. When I added my name to the row of signatures in the record book at the end of an assembly in Tunnel Six, there was surprise and even disbelief. "Is that really your signature?" one man in poncho and blue jeans asked me by the lamplight. The hurried scrawl of a white, middle-class American reflects a lack of interest in displaying education and status in penmanship. By contrast, an elaborate signature for villagers to whom the power of writing had so long been denied was an achievement. The management of rubber stamps, memos, and minutes was a matter of self-respect for villagers who for centuries had been cast into what anthropologist Michel-Rolph Trouillot calls the "savage slot" and dismissed as backward and uncivilized.[38] Víctor was proud of being the master of the small bureaucracy of the Central Committee of Rondas Campesinas of Tunnel Six: "We're learning to follow proper procedure, and maybe better than the town authorities."

The town authorities' reaction to ronda assemblies was displeasure at the unraveling of the old order of things. A thin man of about fifty in a gray suit, Napoleón Díaz was the judge in Chota's First District Court, the provincial level in a national judiciary system under the final authority of the Supreme Court. Díaz admitted that villagers had reason to complain of the slowness and sometimes the corruption of the official system. "How can we do our job when sometimes the government doesn't even pay us, and in these conditions?" he asked with a sweep across an office with case documents piled on the floor and plaster falling in chunks from the ceiling. Yet the state of things did not convert the judge into a supporter of ronda assemblies: "It's ok for them to defend their animals. But they don't have the preparation to administer justice. They just think they know the law, and this leads into mistakes and abuse. It's wrong for them to act like authorities with the little education they have."

What struck Díaz and many other policemen, prosecutors, and judges as out of place was villagers' daring to think themselves knowledgeable enough to make justice without town guidance. It was acceptable for the uneducated rural poor to fight rustlers, but not to "act like lawyers" and "think they know the law." The Uruguayan literary critic Angel Rama speaks of the supremacy of "the lettered city" in colonial Latin America. As Rama observes in a book written just before his death in a 1983 plane crash, the monopoly of officialdom on writing broke apart with the spread of literacy, newspapers and magazines, urbanization, and mass politics.[39] Now the town authorities were facing villagers gone beyond the seizure of "lettered culture" to interpret and administer the law. The Paimas sergeant who had threatened Víctor was one of the many officials to react violently to this silent peasant insurgency. The worldly Napoleón Díaz was more philosophical. "Things are changing, and there's nothing I can do about it," he shrugged to me over a bowl of soup at a restaurant near the decaying municipal court.

THE JUSTICE OF THE ASSEMBLIES

The ronda assemblies exhibited the rural enchantment with official protocol. In addition to the seals, the thumbprints, and the minutes, it was common to hear flowery honorifics such as "Mr. Ronda Vice-President" and "Mr. Ronda President," the same decorum and preoccupation with rank and titles found in the town courthouse. I argued in the previous chapter that villagers reshaped procedures borrowed from the haciendas and the military to develop their own distinctive system of patrolling. The dynamics that went into the creation of assemblies were similar. Although the justice-making system used in the rondas poached procedure and protocol from the police and courts, it was more than a copy of the official system, and in particular it placed a far greater emphasis on participation and reconciliation. Borrowing from the legal bureaucracy was just part of the process of invention and creation by which an original way of resolving conflict came into existence in the northern Andes.

The premium on participation was the most immediate contrast between the ronda assembly and the official system. One had to have a law degree and be a lawyer, prosecutor, or judge to speak with authority in the official system. Everyone had the right to intervene in the village assembly. Francisco Chuquihuanga was the lanky young president of the ronda committee in Ambulco near the Ecuadoran border: "Everybody participates. This is a place where no one is better than anyone else, where everyone has a voice. We know the problems better than the people in town, and we can resolve them more effectively." The concept of a forum run by and for the rural poor ran through the talk of dozens of villagers about the assemblies. "We want to be able to decide for ourselves," Cuyumalca's Eladio Idrogo explained.

Many factors contributed to the thirst for participation. If the decades after independence in Peru saw the domination of politics by the gentlemen's clubs of the creole elite, the twentieth century was marked by the increasing demand of villagers for a voice in national life. The advent of APRA and other mass parties, the experience of migration to the cities, and the implementation of universal suffrage contributed to the combativeness in the countryside. For example, Agustín Sánchez from the village of Colpa Matara just above Chota, an albino with the nickname of "the Gringo," headed for Lima as a twenty-one-year-old in 1971. There "the Gringo" experienced an epiphany: "I found a job in construction. We slept in the shell of the building we were building. One night I went to a movie theater in the La Victoria district. There was a movie about the Cuban Revolution. It gave me the idea about revolution, and change. And I was learning from the insults and poverty that a peasant suffers in Lima that change was necessary, that my Peru had to be transformed."

Sánchez returned to Colpa Matara to buy a plot with money saved in Lima. He joined Red Homeland, and later became president of a ronda federation it controlled. Not everyone turned as radical as Sánchez. A culture of servility survived in everything from hat doffing to engineers and doctors to addressing a white anthropologist as "Don." But most villagers were no longer either confined to the village nor inclined to be subservient. An old radical priest in Cajamarca told me this story: "A store owner asked a peasant why he hadn't come to the Sunday market for the last few weeks. 'I've been traveling.' 'Oh, did you go to another village, my son?,' asked the store owner. 'No,' said the peasant, 'I was in Brazil for a meeting of rural catechists. And don't call me son.'" "I don't know whether this tale is really true," admitted the priest: "I do know from working here for thirty years that peasants are far less parochial and passive than ever before."

Agustín "the Gringo" Sánchez, Colpa Matara, 1990

The demand to participate pervaded the assemblies. More than half the village showed up for most meetings in Tunnel Six and Cuyumalca.[40] They sat or stood in a circle so that it was easy for anyone to get in a word. The ronda steering committee, lieutenant governor, and any visiting dignitaries sat at a table, but it was positioned along the arc of the circle. Typically, an assembly heard three or four disputes in a night. The ronda president introduced each case; next, the accuser and accused stood to have a say. Then anyone could jump in with an opinion. The insistence on speaking resounded throughout the night in calls of "*Pido la palabra, pido la palabra,*" literally, "I want the word." At one 1990 assembly in La Iraca in the Chota Valley, I charted the number of speakers. Forty-two of the fifty villagers in attendance had spoken by the meeting's end. It was an outpouring of charges, countercharges, interruptions, and opinions bearing little resemblance to any standard courtroom procedure.

Silencing has been a modality of power in Peru as far back as Spanish rule. The villager was to listen and defer to the priest, the bureaucrat, or the landlord. The cliché about "Andean melancholy" even depicted voicelessness as if it were an inbred characteristic of

Having a say, Cuyumalca, 1990

the rural poor. The cacophony in Tunnel Six or Cuyumalcan assembly burst the stereotype in debates about the loss of a chicken or the theft of shoes. These were people ready to speak and be heard.

Although the ronda president ran the assembly, his job was not to control, but to facilitate. Any leader who appeared to be trying to make or impose a decision risked heavy criticism for being an "egotist" and "prideful." Some presidents lost reelection just for appearing to have pressed for outcomes out of line with the majority's will. "What does the assembly think?" or "What does the community say?" Eladio Idrogo would ask, eyes glinting in the lamplight. These formal queries prompted any number of proposals from around the room for how to solve the controversy at hand. A payment of three or five dollars by the owner of the pig to the owner of the eaten corn? A strip of land to which of two brothers who claimed it? A warning or a flogging for a wife beater? The ronda committee president's task was to sum up village opinion. Others could suggest modifications. When an assembly seemed in agreement, the secretary wrote out an Acta de Arreglo, or "Resolution Agreement," in the record book or on a loose sheet of paper. Everyone involved in the dispute came forward to sign their willingness to what one Tunnel Six acta emphasized was "fulfillment of this agreement."

The circle of participation extended beyond the local village. Frequently, conflict involved three or four rondas: a burro stolen in one place turning up in another, a marital discord involving relatives and in-laws from a cluster of nearby villages, a land controversy over a plot purchased by an outsider. When a case involved people from another village, representatives of the ronda steering committee from that settlement sometimes walked or rode as many as eight or nine hours to be at the assembly. Víctor Córdova explained: "There are rondas in every village from here to Cajamarca. It's a system of justice that means we don't always have to go to town; we work between villages in the rondas." The government forced villagers in search of justice to go to town and to the city. To borrow the terminology of French theorists Gilles Deleuze and Félix Guattari, the rondas drew a "line of flight" that undercut the urban primacy of the official geography of authority and power.[41] The trails of the Andes buzzed with villagers bypassing town to carry memos between rondas or go to assemblies in other villages. "This justice ties together the countryside," Francisco Chuquihuanga recognized.

An emphasis on reconciliation was the other big contrast between the rondas and the official system. The police and courts were to enforce law regardless of the consequences of a decision for the rest of society. It was different with the rondas. The aim was ending disputes by repairing relations between villagers. An assembly was not referred to as a trial, and the language of guilt or innocence did not appear in the vast majority of ronda agreements. It was an *arreglo*, literally a "repair job." As it was put in an agreement obligating Angélica Córdova in Tunnel Six to pay a fine of three dollars for corn eaten by her pig in Asunción Savedra's field, the assemblies were supposed to enable villagers to "live better with their neighbors."

The explanation for the value placed on reconciliation lies in a number of factors. One goes back to Christianity. From Sunday meetings of Catholic groups or services in the local evangelical church, the villagers of the northern Andes heard about Christ forgiving and even dying for the sinner, and the equality of humankind in God's eyes. The teaching carried over into speech making by Eladio Idrogo and others about the imperative of putting hatred aside to "live more united" in "love for one another." Marxism was not so widely influential as Christianity, but it also advocated and encouraged reconciliation between villagers. The peasantry should put aside divisions to unite in the struggle for the revolution. "It only serves the rich and the powerful for us to continue fighting among ourselves" went the claim of one Tunnel Six sympathizer of the United Mariateguista Party (PUM), which along with Red Homeland was one of numerous small Marxist groups that coexisted uneasily in the United Left coalition. The intimacy of the ronda assembly made the premium on mediation into a matter of pragmatism as well as ideology. It was common for the anger of the aggrieved to be fierce. One man in Cuyumalca was livid in spitting out a demand for a son who had struck him in an argument to be beaten with *an arroba de beta,* a "bushel of lashes." [42] Because villagers knew they had to live with those punished in the days and years to follow, to press for harsh punishment unqualified by forgiveness was to increase the chances of becoming a target of hatred and sorcery. Finally, a ronda president had additional incentive for decisions that would enable everyone to leave the meeting hall without excessive resentment and bitterness. When the anger of those who felt mistreated by the rondas was fierce enough to lead them to complain to the police, he faced summons to the station, and sometimes jail, as the titular head of the committee. Government hostility to ronda assemblies had the consequence of fortifying the emphasis on mediation over judgment in the new village justice system.

The process of justice-making prioritized reconciliation. After the ronda president gave villagers the details of the case at hand, the accuser was first to speak. The testimony of any witnesses who came forward was recorded by the ronda secretary, much in the way police took a statement. Then the accused would respond. As often as not outraged by the charges, the accused would accuse the accusers of lying, sometimes turning the tables by bringing up their past offenses. Counterattacks contributed to the atmosphere of anger that prevailed during the first hour or so in the discussion of the case. As argument dragged on without apparent hope of solution, the tide would begin to shift toward resolution. Those less invested in the dispute would have their say, and press the protagonists to compromise. "Recognize your error, Don Concepción" someone said to Concepción García when it became clear that this Tunnel Sixer had set out poisoned grain to kill a neighbor's chickens for straying into his yard. A Cañafistan suggested that a brother who accused a brother of stealing part of his inheritance ought to be "more understanding, more respectful of family." As pressure mounted on those involved in the fight to give ground, there would be calls from around the room of "*¡Qué arreglen!*" or "Resolve it!" This is not to say that an assembly would not take a side. When a man was to blame for picking a fight or a woman for stealing the shoes of a neighbor, the majority of villagers would call for punishment. Still, it was unusual for an assembly ever to impose as stiff a sanction as that demanded by an accuser. This helped dissipate resentment that could fester after the assembly was finished. Although unhappy about being forced to pay a fine for failing to return a plow borrowed from a man in another village, Oscar Llacsahuache of Tunnel Six knew he had escaped the whipping demanded by the lender. The agreement he had signed forced him to acknowledge having taken the plow, but it was an acta de arreglo and not a verdict or sentence against him. This further diminished the humiliation of the assembly's disbelief at his dubious claim of having intended to return it on his own even after keeping it for more than a year. "We all make mistakes, and need to be able to live together," concluded Eladio Idrogo.

The theme of forgiveness and reincorporation stood out even in the harshest punishment. Only those who repeated the same offense or committed what seemed an especially egregious crime found themselves subjected to a whipping. It was physically painful. By contrast to reports of flayings in the days of the haciendas, I never saw the rondas administer more than four lashes. Yet I discovered once by thwacking myself on the back that even a single blow was shockingly painful, putting a fast end to my experiment in self-flagellation. To be whipped was just as hurtful symbolically. It was the indignity of being disciplined as a serf or child in front

Ronda assembly, José Espíritu Tafur, 1988

of the entire village. Even when they could ill afford the money for a two-dollar fine, most villagers preferred any other punishment to the lash.

Whipping punctuated ronda power and seriousness. It sent the message that the assembly's will would be enforced by any means necessary. But the punishment was also less about retribution and more about forgiveness and reconciliation. A relative was often picked to administer the whipping. This lessened the chance of assault charges later being lodged with the police, and yet the relative had to hit hard because holding back was itself punished by a whipping for not enforcing the assembly's will. As the villager to be whipped came forward to the center of the hall, he received a few words of *consejo*, or advice, from the person about to administer the lash: "Learn to live better from now on!"; "Respect your neighbors!"; "Don't create more problems for yourself in the future." The lash came next. The hush of the assembly made the crack of rawhide on flesh sound like an exploding cherry bomb.

Afterward, tension lessened, and smiles and chatter again returned to the meeting hall. It was hoped that life would return to normal with the offender having paid the price. "I'm sorry about this, but we need to learn to understand each another," said Víctor to a man given four lashes for abandoning his wife and two small children for a woman in the jungles of San Ignacio. Although bitterness about the outcome was evident on the tight-lipped faces of some of those whipped, many took it with good grace. It was common to say "Thanks, brothers" just after the whipping; this signaled acceptance of the punishment and gratitude for being received back into village society.

It should be more than evident that the ronda assembly was very different from the town courthouse. However, the relation between the two systems of justice was a classic example of the ironies, intertwinings, and ambivalences of what literary critic Mary Pratt has described as "the mirror-dance of postcolonial meaning-making." [43] Villagers borrowed heavily from official procedure. At the same time, they made it part of a more open and forgiving system that challenged the state's traditional monopoly on the administration of justice. Most villagers believed that deciding cases on their own did not make them lawbreakers. To the contrary, they felt that they and not the town authorities were truest to the Peruvian Constitution and other codes. "The laws are good," went the saying in the 1980s. "The problem is that those that enforce them are crooks." The rondas were a force not against but for the rule of law from this point of view, not to mention simply faster and fairer. "Don't you understand now, Don Raimundo?" Víctor asked me on the morning after one assembly in Tunnel Six. "This is the best justice there is."

IMPERFECTION AND ACHIEVEMENT

But was it? A 1986 commission headed by Nobel Peace Prize winner Adolfo Pérez Esquivel certainly concluded that ronda justice was exemplary. It published a report that focused on torture and killing in the raging war between the government and the Shining Path. The commission cited the northern rondas as a counterexample of hope in the face of terror. The assemblies received special praise: "In their meetings the ronderos look for favorable results in legal matters concerning the community: material losses, fights between neighbors. Land Problems and even some personal problems are discussed by all. In a fraternal way, they identify the responsible and apply justice with the consent of all, without losing time or money to official trials and lawyers." The rondas, according to the report, were "rich and pure" and "put into practice voluntary and conscious participation."[44]

It was hard to find discussion of ronda flaws in the 1980s. Among Peruvian scholars, who were overwhelmingly tied to the political left, a hopefulness prevailed about the poor mobilizing for change. Anything "from below" and the "grassroots" was equated with the good, just, and progressive for many. The wish to view the peasantry as "rich and pure" led Esquivel's group to overlook cases of lynching, torture, and whipping that made the rondas less than a paragon of the protection of human rights. As sociologist Luis Pásara points out in reassessing social movements in Peru, it is always easy to miss "the other side of the moon" in the rush to praise grassroots movements, and to ignore inconvenient "ambiguity, contradiction, and uncertainty."[45]

I do not want to idealize the assemblies, or at least not so unconditionally as Esquivel. I will not forget, for example, one night in Lingán Pata, where I was visiting Pascual Ruiz. A mist swirled around the mud-walled meeting hall of this hundred-family settlement that clung along the upper heights of the Chota Valley. Most of the forty villagers arrived for the assembly in ponchos and rubber boots, some chewing coca against the bone-chilling damp at 11,000 feet. One case that night involved wife beating. A young man in a polyester shirt with unkempt hair and an angry look, Marcelino Sánchez had come home drunk from a bar two weeks before to club Berbelina Llacsahuache with a shovel, screaming that she had slept with a distant cousin of his. Although muttering that the blows amounted to just "a touch or two," Sánchez did not deny "disciplining" his nineteen-year-old wife. The purple bruises on her arms and legs testified to the vicious assault. One man asserted that this was the first time for Sánchez. Two others added that wives were to blame for "being disobedient." Sánchez got off with a warning. The light punishment troubled me. Tolerance of violence against women led to a decision that slighted what I considered to be a serious problem in village society. Perhaps too swept up by my own desire that such behavior be punished, I remember being disappointed that Sánchez escaped the lash.

There will be much more to say about ronda imperfections in the next chapters. Failure to give women equal rights was one way the assemblies did not live up to the promise of democracy and participation. Yet what movement does not have skeletons in the closet? The African National Congress tortured suspected informers in the fight against apartheid. A streak of anti-Semitism ran through Poland's Solidarity Movement. Acknowledging imperfection should not lessen appreciation for the courage and achievement of these initiatives for change. It does mean moving beyond romanticism that strips away humanity to present the poor and the oppressed as simply icons of innocence and dignity.

I remain convinced that the assemblies were an improvement over the official system. Speed was the most obvious advantage. When someone complained about a marauding burro or an unpaid debt, it was seldom more than a couple of weeks before the next assembly, as they were held at least monthly in Tunnel Six, Cuyumalca, Ambulco, Lagunas, Aragoto, and most other northern villages. To be sure, the need to hear from additional witnesses led some cases to be carried over to a future meeting. At other times, one or the other party's refusal to accept any agreement led an exasperated assembly to turn the case over to the town police, a threat that sometimes induced the recalcitrant to compromise. Yet assemblies reached a decision right away in more than three-quarters of the cases in Tunnel Six and Cañafisto. No dispute dragged on for years as it could in the official system. There a villager could be jailed for three or four years just waiting for trial. Lingán Pata's Pascual Ruiz hardly exaggerated in telling me that "we solve in a night what takes the judges years."

This justice system was also free. I heard about a few cases of ronda presidents' demanding money to bring a case to the assembly or even to influence the decision. The overwhelming majority of these men, though, served in the pressure-packed post out of commitment to the village. They embraced the honesty that was part of the official ronda creed. If not, they could be removed if proven or even thought to be corrupt. The poorest villagers were less likely to go to the courts because of the fees, bribes, notaries, and lawyers. Everyone could take complaints to the rondas. For instance, Margarita Lima, a widow with only a lean-to and a pair of sheep to her name, went to an assembly to claim rights to a piece of land from a dead relative. "Since I don't have a cent for a lawyer, I couldn't have protested without the rondas," she noted in contrasting the ronda assembly and the official system.

Another benefit lay in the quality of justice. The police did not have the personnel or interest for on-site investigation of a battle over a strip of land in a village far up in the Andes. Nor were judges able or enthusiastic about going out to get a firsthand view of rural disputes. Francisca Paz explained the advantage of local knowledge: "The police and judges live in town. They don't know anything about what's going on in the countryside. Here nothing can be hidden since everybody knows everybody else. It means that we make a better justice." Little was left to the imagination in the hours of debate that laid bare idiosyncracies, histories, and relations. A knowledge of "what's going on" meant that a prosperous store-owner could not plead poverty to escape a fine for missing patrol for a month. A woman known for letting her pigs stray into neighboring fields could not claim never to have allowed the animals to roam free. As history and personality informed decisions, the assembly experimented in what law professor Jennifer Nedelsky calls "justice that highlights, not suppresses[,] the pattern of relationships behind it." [46]

I remember a 1987 assembly in Tunnel Six. As rain drummed on the tin roof, fifty villagers gathered in the lunchroom to deal with a pilfering case. Bernabé García was accused of stealing rice seedlings, and his accuser wanted him whipped. A young girl testified to seeing the forty-five-year-old villager making off with a bundle of plants. Yet everyone knew García as a regular on patrol. He and his wife had just lost a baby to typhoid fever, furthering sympathy for him. The assembly allowed García to escape the lash by agreeing to replace the seedlings. Since villagers knew of his decent reputation, they moderated punishment, as attention to context and character figured into the administration of justice.

A sense of accomplishment about the assemblies prevailed across the countryside in the late 1980s and early 1990s. Two German anthropologists carried out a survey in Piura that showed an overwhelming majority of villagers preferred taking conflicts to the rondas rather than police station or courthouse.[47] A Peruvian researcher obtained similar results in 1991 in the province of Sihuas, two hundred miles to the south.[48] By the criterion of satisfying those they served, the assemblies were a success, a system of justice that in just a few short years had gained a credibility far greater than the government's.

It struck me that the attraction of the assemblies went beyond just the chance to end strife. The deeper promise was the establishment of community. I think about the book of minutes once shown to me by Máximo Ortiz, a former ronda president there and the organizer of the revolt against Manuel Calvay in Chota. The entry for August 7, 1985, said that the ronda assembly decided everyone should contribute to pay for an operation to reset the leg of Demetrio González Regalado, who had broken it "falling from a tree while working in Amazonas."[49] It was agreed on December 1 of the same year to "collaborate with money for Medicine and an operation to remove a tumor from the neck of Alberto Barboza." Here the quest to heal pain and division manifested itself in providing assistance to the neediest among fellow villagers. I heard of other cases of the ronda assembly becoming the instrument of this kind of generosity and mutual assistance in many parts of the northern Andes.

It has been commonly assumed that modernity spells doom for the Andean community. "The Indians . . . are apparently following an open road to a skeptical individualism," asserted José María Arguedas in 1964.[50] He presumed that village community was a primordial marker of the Otherness of the Andes. Arguedas was one of many to believe that traditions of collectivity would probably be destroyed by urbanization, migration, mass culture, and other tectonic shifts of the twentieth century. The city would triumph over the countryside, reason over custom, individualism over collectivity. As a lover of Andean ways and a critic of Western modernity, Arguedas lamented a "loosening of the ties to the Gods who have regulated their social conduct . . . and removing the Indians from the foundation on which their Indian culture rests."[51]

There can be no doubt that many established forms of Andean community disappeared in the twentieth century. A prime example is the system of organization for running local fiestas called the *varayoc* in the Ayacucho region.[52] As many villagers became Protestants in the 1950s, they no longer wanted to invest time and money in rituals associated with the worship of Catholic saints. At the same time, however, the rise of the ronda assemblies evidenced the opposite side of the story, namely, the emergence of new forms of highland collectivity. This tale of creation is particularly striking considering the absence of a history of self-rule in the northern Andes. Although forms of reciprocity and cooperation existed in the countryside going back to pre-Columbian times, many of the region's villagers had lived on haciendas until 1969. They took their orders from the mayordomo and the landlord. The inhabitants of Cuyumalca and other areas of the Chota Valley had long been independent smallholders, but they had neither the strong informal system of self-government nor the juridical rights of self-rule ceded to officially registered "peasant communities" in the central and southern Andes. As a settlement dating only to the building of the canal in the late 1960s, Tunnel Six was even less the model of the primordial Andean community. Political scientist Benedict Anderson emphasizes that nations are "cultural artifacts" that must be "imagined" and "created."[53] This is no less true of villages. By contrast to a nation, everyone in a village knows everyone else. Yet familiarity can just as easily breed rivalry as commonality, contempt as cooperation, and schism as unity in a local society. The ties of community were by no means a received tradition in northern Andean villages. They had to be created.

This was part of what the assemblies were about. At least in theory, most villagers saw their justice-making as a way to put a "skeptical individualism" behind them, and, as Víctor Córdova so often said, "to learn to live better amongst ourselves." The gatherings in Tunnel Six, Cuyumalca, Lingán Pata, and so many other places established and strengthened forms of cooperation and obligation that had not existed in the past. This was not the triumph of fragmentation or atomization. It was a bid to bring the village together to confront a hard world.

Even Arguedas might not have been altogether surprised at this late twentieth-century story of the genesis of collectivism. The great writer did hedge his bet about the disappearance of Andean community. "Inkarrí will return, and we cannot help fearing he may be powerless to reassemble the individualisms that have developed" was his guess about the prophesied return of the Inka. Unless he can detain the Sun, once more binding him with iron bands to Osk'onta Peak, and change man; all is possible where such a wise and resistant creature is concerned." [54]

A BARRIER AGAINST THE SHINING PATH?

A number of observers went so far as to credit ronda organizing with turning back the Shining Path in the northern Andes.[55] I heard anecdotes that seemed to confirm the point. Eusebio Chávez was the ronda president in the Bambamarcan village of Churuyacu, and a member of the Assembly of God.[56] As Chávez recounted it, a young man claiming to have been sent by the Lima office of this Pentecostal sect arrived at his farmhouse in 1989, requesting lodging for a few weeks while he spread God's word in the countryside. Chávez agreed. On a Sunday, however, he returned from the town market to find a pig digging up a cache of Shining Path propaganda, which his guest had apparently buried. Chávez threatened to turn the young man over to the ronda if he did not leave by dark. The young man fled. "I felt sorry because I knew the boy would get in trouble with his commanders for failing in his mission," Chávez confessed to me. "But allowing in the Shining Path would have been the beginning of war, and the end for us."

However, other tales suggested that ronda opposition to the rebels was far from absolute. One story involved the arrival of a trio of young *senderistas,* Shining Path members, arriving at a nighttime assembly in a village just an hour from the town of Cutervo. They demanded that the locals join the battle to "smash the rotten old order." The villagers decided to lock the revolutionaries in the schoolhouse. A group of four went to town to get the police. When they returned with the policeman, the school was empty. The villagers on guard said armed guerrillas had descended on the village, forcing them to free the prisoners. It came out later that the prisoners got away by promising their guards a payoff of thirty dollars each from party coffers. The chance at a few dollars trumped any commitment to prevent the spread of the revolution.

More deeply, evidence existed of attraction to the Shining Path in parts of the northern countryside. Many young men had been exposed to the guerrillas from having worked in the coca fields in the Huallaga Valley, which was largely controlled by Guzmán's followers in the late 1980s. Bad wages and seasonal migration led at least some of these villagers open to the message of revolution. On an overnight trip in 1990 to the village of Chororco in 1990, I woke up to find the standard slogans painted on the mud wall of the schoolhouse: "Long Live the People's War! Long Live President Gonzalo!" "It's some of those boys back from the jungle," shrugged my host, a ronda committee leader. "They're not really organized for now, but that could change."

I also found a measure of interest and even support among a scattering of northern villagers who had no direct contact with the Shining Path. "Aren't they for the poor?" an old man in Tunnel Six once asked me as we sat together in 1987 discussing politics in his smoky farmhouse. At the start in the late 1970s and early 1980s, the hardship of rural life and the discontent with the government had allowed the Shining Path to win the sympathy of many villagers as it executed the Maoist blueprint by moving in to seize control of the countryside.[57] It was possible that the guerrillas might have tapped disenchantment with the status quo in parts of the northern Andes, and perhaps even taken over rondas in the process. This appeared to be the hope of the revolutionaries. "The rondas are not bad organizations," a young organizer for the Shining Path informed Robin in a 1990 prison interview in the northern city of Chiclayo. "All they need is the direction of a party like ours."

Yet ronda relations with the Shining Path were never put to the full test. Contrary to breathless, uninformed exaggerations from think tanks and policymakers in Washington and Lima, the actual membership of the Shining Path was never large, even if it was true that members fought with a deadly precision and passion to lead Peru to the promised land of a classless utopia. Seizing the northern Andes was doubtless not a top priority for a party already stretched thin as it expanded from Ayacucho to battle for coca dollars in the Huallaga Valley, the breadbasket of the Mantaro Valley, and Lima. Perhaps the factor of intimidation associated with the rondas contributed to the decision never to mount anything like a full-scale offensive in the northern Andes. So may have the knowledge of the influence in the region of Red Homeland, the United Mariateguista Party, and APRA, all fierce opponents of the Shining Path. The decline and virtual disappearance of the guerrillas in the mid-1990s meant that questions about their chances in the northern Andes would forever go unanswered.

The inhabitants of the southern and central highlands were not so lucky. Once villagers there had begun to see the violence and authoritarianism of the Shining Path and the costs of reprisals by the military for allowing the guerrillas into the countryside, disenchantment mounted.[58] By then, however, it was too late. The countryside had been sucked into the war. The Shining Path and the military took turns in massacres, killings, and forced disappearances to keep villagers in line. When the military at last began to move to a less violent policy of seeking cooperation with the countryside, the bulk of the peasantry proved willing to oppose the Shining Path, even taking up arms in a rural counterrevolution against the Maoists. Their militias came to be known as rondas after the original and very different patrols in the northern Andes. The rise of these militias and Guzmán's capture in 1992 hastened the demise of the Shining Path. Peace was restored to the countryside. Yet thousands had been killed and many more forced to flee, and the survivors were left even poorer than before. There were no winners in what would go down as one of Latin America's cruelest twentieth-century wars.

I visited the altiplanos of Ayacucho in 1993. In Quechua, Ayacucho means "Corner of the Dead," and the devastation was terrible: the ruins of countless villages razed in the war, the stories of rape by troops and babies hacked to death by the Shining Path. Liberating the peasantry, Abimael Guzmán declared in 1980, was the "heroic destiny" of "our brilliant revolution."[59] It had turned out instead that the poor of the countryside had been the Peruvians to suffer most from the revolution waged in their name.

PEASANT AND NATION[60]

Not only the south-central Andes seemed to be falling apart in the late 1980s and early 1990s. The deterioration infected Lima, the once-proud "City of Kings," so named after the Magi by Francisco Pizarro when he founded it on Epiphany in 1535. When I made the twenty-four-hour bus ride there from Chota to visit Robin in 1990, streets stank of garbage and urine. Hyperinflation meant that a million intis bought one carton of milk. The Peruvian currency was as valueless as Confederate bills or Weimar marks, carted around in wheelbarrows. Hunger was rampant in the "misery belt" of poor neighborhoods ringing the national capital. Even members of the middle class felt the pinch. Our own neighborhood of Jesús María went without water and electricity for days at a time. The apartment we rented was fortified with barred windows and a spiked iron fence, but we woke some nights to the rooftop footsteps of prowlers, prying around for a way to enter. Several government ministries were nearby, and shockwaves of occasional guerrilla bombs rattled our apartment windows. When President Alberto Fujimori took office in 1990, the veteran journalist Patricio Ricketts wrote that Peru was in the middle of the "deepest and most widespread crisis since Independence."[61]

The ronda story was one of rare achievement during those years. Far from crumbling, they expanded from patrolling into justice-making, enlarging their organizational structure to answer crisis. While life in the northern Andes was far from utopian, the sense of security and solidarity was much greater in the mountains of Cajamarca and Piura than just about anywhere else in Peru, partly because hopelessness and mistrust were so rampant in the rest of the country. "We're proving that we can take care of ourselves," Tunnel Six's Martín Llacsahuache opined one night over a beer in my little house on the ridgetop.

A result of the movement was to fortify village loyalties. The actual level of cooperation may sometimes have been small in northern settlements, and there were plenty of villagers who stayed put only for the lack of opportunity anywhere else. Yet an attachment to community of origin had remained a feature of Andean life, perhaps even strengthened as part of what geographer David Harvey would call the "intensification of localism" that has been one by-product of twentieth-century flux and upheaval.[62] Support for the soccer team, ballads about the landscape's beauties, and celebration of the patron saint's day were just the most obvious manifestations of local pride. Since the village committee was the building block of the rondas, the movement deepened connection to place, a readiness to declare oneself a Tunnel Sixer, Cuyumalcan, or Ambulcan. The stories about the ronda committee's exploits added a new layer of color and feeling to the commemoration of village tradition. The songs to the rondas further memorialized community accomplishment. "I sing with all my heart on this lucky day, for our Ronda Campesina turns five years old," pro-

Map 2. Areas of rondas campesinas in Northern Peru, 1990

claimed a huayno from the village of Alfombrilla in the Chota Valley. "We're here with emotion for you beloved Alfombrilla, land of my dreams."⁶³

This enthusiasm about the rondas connected to pride about belonging to the peasantry. Colonialism had transformed identity in the Americas by compacting indigenous populations into the monolithic category of "Indian." Yet many leftist parties began in the mid-twentieth century to push "peasant" over "Indian" as the best word for villagers in a Marxism that ranked class over ethnicity in the struggle for revolution. The non-Marxist APRA also encouraged the rural poor to see themselves as peasants, even if Haya's party was never so militant as the faithful of Marx and Mao. A vision of villagers as peasants became official under General Velasco's government. June 24 was the "Day of the Indian" in Peru. The flamboyant Velasco proclaimed agrarian reform on that date in 1969, and announced that it would henceforth be known as the "Day of the Peasant." Villagers were to become "free citizens," with "the right to the fruits of the land they work."[64] Centuries of the equation of Indianness with servility and bondage made the Andean poor quick to embrace the new label of peasant. I remember the small party on June 24 for schoolchildren and parents held in Tunnel Six in 1986. An old schoolteacher absently referred to the holiday by the prior designation of the "Day of the Indian." The feisty Angélica Jara was just one of the Tunnel Sixers who did not take kindly to the mistake. "We're peasants, not Indians. He'd better get it right next time," she said to me afterward.

The rondas fortified a sense of peasant identity. By insisting the rondas were "of peasants" back in 1977, Daniel Idrogo had catalyzed patrolling as the mark of membership in the peasantry. Together with poncho and straw hat, taking to the trail defined a kind of commonality, and fast turned into a way peasants distinguished themselves from the rest of the country. Justice-making furthered a feeling of rural fellowship. Villagers spoke about their "fix-its" as "peasant justice" to distinguish them from the government system. From Cañafisto to Tunnel Six, as an experiment in mediation the assemblies made visible a dream of cooperation and possibility and of rural capacity to reorder the world. Ambiguity persisted in village thinking, a self-perception of inferiority derived from the stigmas of poverty and lack of education. "It's needed," announced one Tunnel Sixer at a ronda meeting about starting a community library, "because we peasants are sometimes backward and uneducated." Yet there was more than ever a feeling of ability and even distinction connected to rural identity.

> We are no longer so divided
> It's the turn of us poor peasants
> To deal with the problems that we feel

declared a song from the Bambamarca Valley.[65]

The vigor of peasant identity distinguished Peru from many other Latin American countries. Even if millions in the region continued to see themselves as peasants, it became more common by the 1990s for villagers to identify as indigenous, and in this sense to foreground ethnicity over class. Guatemala's Mayans, Bolivia's Aymara, and Ecuador's Quechua were part of the surge of heritage politics that recoded "Indian" from a mark of subordination to an emblem of pride. Although often speaking languages and maintaining customs dating back to the Incas and even before, the inhabitants of Peru's mountains have in this century displayed a notable disinterest in laying claim to indigenousness. Does this tendency stem from the ferocity of the stigmatization of Indians in colonial Peru? The success of the nineteenth-century campaigns to assimilate Andeans into the national mainstream? The strength of the promotion of peasantness by the left, APRA, and Velasco? A number of anthropologists and historians have begun to speculate about the reasons for Indianism's weakness in the Peruvian Andes.[66]

The topic merits the attention it is likely to receive in the next few years. I do hope that scholars and activists will avoid simply depicting the absence of Indian solidarity among Peru's peasants as a failing, a blindness of villagers to their real roots. Such a view has recurred in recent studies, as in Mexican anthropologist Rodolfo Stavenhagen's opinion that Peru is "behind" in the "rise of the indigenous peoples of Latin America as social and political actors."[67] The downgrading of Peru assumes that only an explicit ethnic identification can be pure and true to blood and tradition. I admire the fight of Mayan organizations and other groups for rights of land and life so brutally denied to native peoples since the Europeans landed more than five centuries ago. Yet the will to embrace one's Indianness is as much a product of choice, mixture, and power as with any other brand of personhood. Far from ancestral anywhere in the Americas, the category of Indian was imposed by Columbus in a geographical mistake, and the new revaluation of it has been at least partly encouraged and sometimes incited by nonnatives, among them human rights and environmental groups, New Agers, and even moviemakers and the music industry. More important, Indianness as a measure of correctness can obscure a fuller understanding of the meaning of other and nonethnic forms of identity. When Peruvian villagers said they were peasants, they were defining themselves, partly, by economics, and by their predicament in farming a small plot of land for a living. Yet this was a cultural statement, too. To identify oneself as a peasant in the northern Andes was to declare a liking for chicha, huaynos, straw hats, house baptism parties, ritual first haircutting for toddlers, and other customs distinctive to the rural way of life. It did not necessarily signify the denial of heritage or the desire to assimilate, as some critics have charged in equating adopted peasantness with "stripping the Indian population of its cultural identity."[68]

Yet it is certainly true that being a peasant implied some measure of acceptance of membership in the larger nation. Like any kind of ethnicity, a claim to be Indian connotes a common culture and descent. The politics of Indianism has very often underlain the dream of secession to restore native autonomy lost to white conquest. By contrast, the self-perception of distinctiveness was not so great for Peruvian peasants, who considered themselves a group with common interests and traditions without going so far as to assert to be a people apart. These villagers very much felt and wanted to be recognized as Peruvian, albeit with their own special concerns and customs. Their patriotism was on display from enthusiastic commemoration of Independence Day on July 24 to purchasing a Peruvian flag to raise before just about every major event. The declaration of national allegiance appeared everywhere in ronda culture. "Hurray, hurray for the Rondas / Long live our Peru" went a song by Augustín "the Gringo" Sánchez from Colpa Matara. One by José Santos of La Alfombrilla echoed that

> We are Peruvians, we are ronderos
> We are hicks of brave heart
> Through good and bad
> We will defend our nation.[69]

The theory of the two Perus has imagined the Andes as an indigenous, tradition-bound world beyond the modern country governed from Lima. In the opinion of novelist Mario Vargas Llosa,

Peruvian citizenship was for mountain villagers little more than an "incomprehensible abstraction."[70] This theory was undone by the practice of a flourishing patriotism in Cajamarca and Piura.

It can be argued, of course, that this nationalism was misguided.[71] Why should villagers have felt attached to a country that had given them so little? There can be no doubt that the apparatus of the state had long encouraged the Andean poor to consider themselves Peruvians. The message of love and duty to Peru was inculcated through the schools, the army, and even the speeches by the president broadcast on Independence Day and other national holidays. Every Sunday when villagers came to town for market, the local authorities held a flag-raising ceremony in the plaza, complete with a parade and anthem singing. It was as if the government felt it needed to refresh villagers about patriotic duties and symbols that they somehow might have forgotten during the week in rural isolation. The possibility of Andean villagers rising up in rebellion had long been the worst nightmare of Peru's white elite. It became the premise of Manuel González Prada and other turn-of-the-century intellectuals that Peru could only prosper if the peasantry was fully incorporated into the nation. If the nationalism on display in the rondas and elsewhere in the countryside was any measure, the project of making peasants into Peruvians had been successful.

I wondered. Although Peruvianness had come to be felt by villagers as part of their identity, their vision of and for Peru was not exactly what was thrust upon them from Lima and the seat of government. The patriotism taught in the early and mid-twentieth century emphasized the heroism of creoles from Bolívar and San Martín to Cáceres, Grau, Bolognesi, and Ugarte.[72] It was implicit that Andean villagers had stunted Peru's modernization. Even Velasco's populism represented the peasantry as a noble yet still childlike and backward class. In this view, only the tutelage of the armed forces could make the countryside more productive. As historians Florencia Mallon and Nelson Manrique have shown, the experience of guerrilla fighting against the Chileans in the War of the Pacific (1879–83) had already led many villagers in the central highlands to see themselves as Peru's truest defenders, by contrast to local landowners who collaborated with the invaders.[73]

A conviction about peasant primacy in defending national sovereignty resurfaced in the rondas a century later.

The rondas will be the example
To obtain the solution
Heaving selfishness
From our unhappy nation

concluded the same song from the Bambamarca Valley that asserted the ronda role in healing peasant divisions. The lyric captured Víctor Córdova's belief that "we're defending the Constitution and the country far better than the judges and the police." To be a rondero was not just to strengthen the village and the peasantry; it was to protect the nation at a dangerous hour. This nationalism was orthodox in that villagers respected the flag, the Constitution, and Bolívar and the rest of the pantheon of official heroes. It was unorthodox in foregrounding the peasant contribution to Peru. Historian Partha Chatterjee reminds us of the inevitability of struggle over "trajectories and rhythms" in the "imagining of nationhood."[74] The peasant nationalism connected to the rondas was a case in point. It challenged the view of Peru's past and the present that had for so long dismissed the Andes as the *mancha india,* or "Indian stain," on an otherwise progressive country.

Yet the future was at stake as well in the struggle over the peasantry's role. When villagers insisted on their loyalty to Peru, it was a corollary that the nation owed them in return. "We grow food for the cities, we protect the countryside with the rondas," Cuyumalca's Eladio Idrogo expostulated: "So there needs to be more support for peasants." The demands most often listed by Idrogo and others were modest—the right to a measure of control over local affairs; the wish to be treated as equals; the government's responsibility for schools, electricity, water, roads, and other basic infrastructure. It was only the harshness of discrimination and poverty that made these aspirations seem radical and threatening. The conservative Lima tabloid *Expreso* worried about ronda legalization in 1986: "The rondas campesinas should not be promoted . . . for they may be turned against the democratic system and its legally constituted civilian and military authorities . . . provoking dangers, distortions, abuse, and arbitrariness . . . and becoming an object of terrorist infiltration.[75] Dissenting from the status quo made the rondas into targets of the discourse of suspicion and fear then so pervasive in Peru at the intersection of the real threat of the Shining Path, the anti-Communism of the Cold War, and the persistence of apprehension about the "insurgent," "primitive" Andes.

The clamor of the peasantry was not altogether in vain. It was no longer so easy by the 1980s to ignore the rural poor. Any politician aspiring to national office was starting to be expected to don a poncho at campaign appearances in the Andes, declare respect for highland tradition, promise aid and make other gestures toward recognizing the realities of multiculturalism and poverty. Even if they were by turns inept, corrupt, and violent, the governments of Fernando Belaúnde (1980–85) and Alan García (1985–90) were beginning to get around to providing for basic needs such as schools, running water, and electricity. Yet change was limited. While Lima politicians incorporated dimensions of peasant nationalism into their program, Peru remained marked by a gigantic gap between the rich and the poor, and the money of the tiny elite still gave that minority first say in running the country. Land in the Andes was divided with relative evenness in the wake of the land reform, but the minuscule size of the average plot made it impossible to hope for prosperity through farming. The travails of the 1980s scared away foreign investors who might have pumped money into the Peruvian economy. By refusing to renegotiate Peru's enormous foreign debt, the World Bank and other international financial bodies further deepened the country's crisis, and sharply limited the possibilities for social spending by the government in those years.

This did not keep many villagers from viewing the rondas as a pathway to a better society. A snapshot given to me by a store owner in the town of Huancabamba captures the movement's spirit in the late 1980s. As a supporter of the rondas and a provincial councilman, the store owner had been invited in 1989 to the sixth anniversary of the ronda committee in Huancacarpa Alto, and he brought his old Kodak Instamatic. Huancacarpa Alto perches high above Huancabamba close to the glacial lakes of the Huaringas, which are famous in Peru for local sorcerers who cure the sick, the lost, and the unhappy with midnight baths in the freezing waters. A thick line of villagers marches around the edge of a soccer field in the picture. Their straw hats and ponchos declare identity as vil-

The sixth anniversary of the ronda, Huancacarpa Alto, 1989 (courtesy of Domingo Guerrero)

lagers and peasants, but they also carry a Peruvian flag, embodying their claim to national citizenship. In that moment a sensation of resolution and solidarity came across undiminished by the puna's threatening gray sky.

THE UNCERTAINTY OF JUSTICE MAKING

It was sometimes hard to maintain enthusiasm. In 1991 Eladio Idrogo got back home after dark from a long day weeding his plot on the *jalca,* the high moors of the Andes. It was the start of the rainy season. A hailstorm had drenched the young ronda leader on the way down the big mountain. He pulled off his soaked poncho at the doorway shivering from cold and exhaustion. A model of service who was well liked throughout Cuyumalca, Eladio did not lack for energy. Besides serving as president of the Central Committee of Rondas Campesinas of Cuyumalca, he led a Catholic prayer group and starred on the village soccer team. Yet it was obvious from his slow step that Eladio needed a good night's sleep. The problem was the Monday assembly of the ronda. Eladio had to run it. There were five cases on the docket. It was likely that the meeting would close at dawn in the nearby "House of the Rondero."

I thought about studies of Africa. As it appeared to anthropologists in midcentury, the local resolution of disputes was a given for tribes there. The South African Max Gluckman wrote that they did not need "officers with established powers to judge on quarrels and to enforce their decisions."[76] The force of custom and kinship in local society meant that feuds over cattle, witchcraft, and land ended in the reestablishment of the social order. E. E. Evans-Pritchard's *The Nuer* deduced that "within a village differences between persons are discussed by the elders of the village and agreement is generally and easily reached and compensation paid, or promised[,] for all are related by kinship and common interests."[77] It sounded so easy. Settling conflict was as certain as the laws of physics in this view.

It would be impossible to see the northern Andes this way.[78] A fight over land could spark years of hatred and violence in the days before the rondas. The assembly offered a mechanism to restore peace. Yet nothing guaranteed it would survive, much less continue to be so successful. Eladio's exhaustion suggested the strain on leaders that could lead to disillusionment and withdrawal. A fight could divide a village so deeply that it could no longer come together to hear cases. The government might renew the campaign to shut down the rondas. So sudden had been the rise of the assemblies that they could surely collapse just as fast.

But not that night. Eladio lay down on his bed for a moment to gather his energy. Then he pulled on dry clothes and ate a bowl of corn soup made by his wife, Sefelmira. A light flickered in the House of the Rondero across from the pasture. It was the signal to villagers that an assembly was about to begin. Eladio shut off the battered shortwave that was reporting the latest bombing from Lima, then gestured to me.

"Shall we go?"

FOUR

Women and the Rondas

The cloudbursts began after Christmas in the year I made my home in Tunnel Six in 1986 and 1987. Every afternoon, the sky darkened and exploded with rain, thunder, and lightning, a cause for apprehension and unpleasant memory among many villagers. Just three years before, the storms of El Niño raised the creeks into muddy rivers, washing away fields, rotting crops, and cutting off Tunnel Six from the coast. The flooding multiplied armies of rats, which not only ate precious stored grain but carried fleas bearing the bubonic plague. The rodents nested in the soggy straw roofs of the cooking sheds attached to many farmhouses, and the fleas jumped down onto the guinea pigs raised for food in these peasant kitchens and then onto the human inhabitants of the farmhouse. Nowadays a shot of tetracycline stops the bubonic plague. One young woman died in the agony of searing fever and vomiting blood, but dozens of other Tunnel Sixers made it to the little health clinic in the nearby town of Paimas in time to be saved by an injection. The unhappy necessity of coping with pain in a doctorless world meant that many survivors dismissed the Black Death as if it were little more than a bad cold. "Malaria was worse," shrugged the ronda leader Martín Llacsahuache.

The catastrophe of 1983 was not repeated that year. Some afternoons in February and March saw no storms, and yet it still rained enough to turn the hills green with weedy pasture for goats and cattle and to water kitchen gardens of squash and beans in the backyards of farmhouses above the canal. When a cloudburst raised the canal into a mad torrent tumbling down from the Andes, there were even prizes to be lassoed from the cement bank—logs to dry out for firewood, a half-drowned sheep to sell or eat. Even so reserved a man as the widower Luciano Alvarado admitted that the weather had been *regular,* not bad, when I met him driving his bleating flock of goats into the hills on a path gooey with gray mud.

There was a ronda assembly one night during the rainy season. Since a House of the Rondero had not yet been built, the assembly was held as usual in the school lunchroom, which was empty except for the adobe bricks stacked in one corner and the beer caps from the last village party scattered across the unswept cement floor. A couple of chairs and a table were brought over from the nearest farmhouse for the lieutenant governor and ronda steering committee. The rest of the crowd made do. A majority of the villagers there were men, and they commandeered adobe bricks for benches. A small cluster of women huddled together on the floor in blankets to ward off the night's chill. I had just returned late from a few days away in the city of Piura to pick up my mail. By that time, I was no longer fazed by the six-hour trip across the Sechura Desert in the flatbed of a rickety truck crammed with goats, sacks of penny candy and insecticide, and peddlers and peasant families. After washing in the irrigation ditch below my house and making a quick dinner of canned tuna and noodles, I headed down through the darkness to the lunchroom, which buzzed with the conversation and laughter of the fifty or so villagers there for the assembly.

One of the four disputes that night was between women. Hermelinda Chávez, a precocious teenager in white tennis shoes, gold earrings, and a bright red dress, said Chavela Ramírez had insulted her as *metida,* a meddler. Hermelinda's mother, Agustina, backed up the charge with a tirade against Chavela for "jealousy and ugly hatred." The problem was a man. Childhood was short in Tunnel Six and throughout the Peruvian Andes. Although just fourteen, Hermelinda was involved with Ercoles Castillo, a former lover of Chavela. Chavela was twenty-two, a single mother who waitressed at the truck stop in Paimas and kept to herself in the little farmhouse she shared with her two toddlers and aging father. Hermelinda had threatened to "beat the shit out of me," countered the indignant Chavela to the assembly. When called forward to testify next, Ercoles was sheepish, disclaiming any knowledge about the matter. A number of men and women contributed their views, variously blaming Hermelinda, Chavela, and Ercoles for the trouble. At one point, Gerónimo Carhuapoma, the lieutenant governor, advised Hermelinda's mother, Agustina, to "do a better job controlling your children." "Oh really, Mr. Lieutenant Governor, like you do with yours?" retorted the señora, an older woman in a skirt and straw hat. Gerónimo's fifteen-year-old had recently run off with a married villager from Culqui just down the Quiroz Valley from Tunnel Six. The crowd snickered, Gerónimo turned red, and Agustina sat back down with a triumphant smirk. By the time the lieutenant governor could think up a retort, it was too late, because other villagers had already jumped in with new opinions in the usual winding and heated debate about innocence and guilt.

The feud between Hermelinda and Chavela raised a series of basic questions about women and the rondas across the northern Andes. Had the daughters and wives of the countryside played a part in the committees in Tunnel Six and elsewhere? Was it common for a woman to bring a dispute before the assembly? What did the fact of the conflict's setting a pair of young women against each other say about solidarity and division by gender in the countryside? Did the ronda movement reenforce what was, in so many ways, the second-class citizenship for women in village society? Could a woman even be a rondero? These issues had concerned and sometimes confused me from the start in the northern Andes, all the way back to the meeting of ronda committees in 1986 in the cockfighting coliseum in Ayabaca. When I met ronderos for the first time there, women were completely absent.

This chapter focuses on women's role in the rondas. I want to document the contribution of Omelia López, Ersila Cabrera, Juana Vásquez, and dozens of others. Thus far, their part has been discussed only peripherally or not at all by scholars and journalists. It has remained invisible as well in standard storytelling in the countryside. As we shall see, however, female enthusiasm about stopping theft and crime was vital to the quick and resounding success of patrolling. Already in 1977, a women's committee was organized in Cuyumalca to roust from bed with whips and shouts men shirking their nightwatch service, and women even headed marches to town to defend the existence of the rondas. Many women went on to take cases before ronda assemblies as the movement broadened beyond patrolling in the 1980s. These complaints often involved wife beating and in this way forced the rondas to

confront the serious and potentially deadly matter of domestic violence in village society, which at that time was almost completely
dismissed and ignored by Peru's national authorities.

An examination of the involvement of Omelia and her companions will shatter the easy stereotypes of submissiveness and passivity
of peasant and non-Western women. At the same time, their story
hardly reduces to an inspirational parable of unity and struggle.
Many peasant women chose not to get involved in the rondas,
and the thinking even of the most active señoras was bound up
with spoken and unspoken assumptions about sexuality and gender, particularly with the mythology and reality of patriarchy in
village society that drastically restricted the rights and movements
of wives and daughters. Although the refusal of many women to
stay on the sidelines violated the strictest interpretation of a doctrine of female submissiveness, it left intact the first principles of
male rule in the rondas and the village, at least as late as the early
1990s. Were women ronderos? The answer in the end was yes and
no, an issue that remained unresolved in the northern Andes.

The punishment of Chavela and Hermelinda said much about
participation by women in the movement. It was not just that
forty-five of the fifty villagers in attendance were men, and that
not a single woman sat among the village authorities at the table—
belying the claim of one manifesto from a Cajamarca ronda federation about the movement as "a true democracy." In this case,
the meting out of justice reflected a common view in Tunnel Six,
that women were tied by nature to the pettiness of jealousy and
scandal, and less able than men to see what was best for the family
and village. "This is a problem of women's rivalry and scandal,"
as Ercoles's widowed mother told the assembly, an invocation of
the supposed weakness of her own sex in order to get her boy off
the hook. The majority of the Tunnel Sixers agreed that Chavela
and Hermelinda were the main culprits. It was decided that the
two girls should get a lash each. Hermelinda came out to sit on an
empty gasoline drum placed in the center of the lunchroom. After
prefacing the punishment with the advice to "stop gossiping and
other troublemaking," her brother, Justo, reached back to give her
the lash, and the whoosh and a crack echoed through the dimly lit
room. A similar admonition was issued by Chavela's father Teofilo
before he brought down the rawhide across her back, which was

protected only by a polyester blouse. The man of the family had executed the will of the ronda assembly, and if only for the moment forced the unruly young women back into their place.

Omelia López lived in Cuyumalca with her husband, Armando Quintana. Their farmhouse was on a hillside dotted with eucalyptuses in the lower part of the village, with a beautiful view down to the town of Chota and the mountains rising up beyond at the other side of the high valley. When I had asked around on arriving in the Chota Valley for the first time in 1990, a number of people had mentioned the women's committees of the rondas, the first having been established in Cuyumalca, the village where the movement had begun. Eladio Idrogo, the young Cuyumalcan ronda leader, told me that Omelia was the first president of the women's committee, and he directed me to her farmhouse, not far across a meadow from his. The usual mangy dogs raced out to attack in a snarling fury as I came up to the yard, but I had learned by this time to carry a stout bamboo cane, and took an admitted pleasure in trying to land a solid blow across the nose of my persecutors. Before the confrontation escalated in this case, Omelia scurried out of the farmhouse. A short and handsome woman of about fifty in a straw hat, blue sweater, and rubber tire sandals, she yelled at the dogs to be quiet as I came up to the door.

Anthropologist Catherine Allen describes being treated as an "honorary man" in the Andean countryside.[1] As a North American, educated, and wealthy by village standards, she seemed too powerful to be classified with other village women, and her pants-wearing furthered the tendency for the visiting researcher to be seated with men at ceremonies and in other ways be treated as male. I was never exactly an "honorary woman." When Robin arrived in Tunnel Six for a six-month stay, she received a stream of visitors; many were women quizzing her about birth control, sex and marriage in the United States, and other delicate topics they would never have broached with me. At the same time, I was not generally viewed as much of a threat to seduce daughters or steal wives, whether because I was assumed to be above having interest in peasant women, known to be with Robin, or viewed as too gaunt and homely to

be a Romeo. This meant I could visit a woman like Omelia even
when she was alone at home without it being taken as a threat or
insult to the husband in this rural world where adultery and honor
could turn explosive.

The sudden visit of a North American was not a common event
in the Andes, however. My arrival to a farmhouse for the first time
was very often greeted by a mix of courtesy, warmth, and nervousness no matter who was at home, and such was the case with
Omelia, the leader of the first ronda women's committee. After
seating me on a poncho spread over a bench, she retreated to the
kitchen for fifteen minutes to make me a plate of toasted corn
and salty cheese and a cup of sugary coffee, and then at last she
sat down across from me at the splintery table along with her ten-
year-old daughter, a miniature of her mother in the same peasant
outfit of skirt, straw hat, and long black hair. I asked her to tell me
the story of the woman's committee in Cuyumalca:

That was a long time ago, Doctor. It was tough at the start of the rondas,
because some men didn't want to do their service, and the authorities
were trying to stop the rondas, persecuting the ronderos. We wanted
to help, and started to go with men to meetings, and especially to the
farmhouses of men who didn't want to patrol. We'd force them out of
bed, shouting at them to get on the trail or to the assembly. I got other
señoras to participate here in Cuyumalca, and I went to La Iraca and
other villages to organize them there.

Unlike so many other villagers who took an obvious pleasure in
recalling for me the early days of the rondas, Omelia told her story
in a flat and almost distant way, as if the events somehow remained
a bit painful for her.

Many centuries before, it might not have been unusual for
a woman to have a strong role in Andean society. Anthropologist Irene Silverblatt has argued that ancient Peruvian kingdoms
granted equal recognition to women. Until the expansion of the
Inca empire in the fourteenth century, women in Huarochirí and
other societies "perceived kinship and descent to follow lines of
women" going back to ancestor-heroines, while men saw themselves as descending from ancestor-heroes to create lines of men.[2]
The children of the Moon and the Sun figured as different yet equal
and complementary in this system of what Silverblatt calls "gender

Omelia López, the leader of the first women's committee, Cuyumalca, 1990

parallelism."[3] It is questionable just how far equality went in states such as Chavín and Moche in which the highest leaders remained men; and at any rate the Andes were certainly not the matriarchy that some feminist writers have sought to find in ancient history to prove patriarchy is not necessarily natural or inevitable in human society.[4] All the same, there can be no doubt about women having occupied a visible, active role in many ancient Andean societies. Pachamama, the Earth Mother—perhaps the single most important deity in pre-Columbian cosmology—was female.

A generation of feminist scholarship has taught us that gender roles can always change over time.[5] In the Andes, as Silverblatt shows, the position of women had worsened even before the Spanish conquest, since the empire building of the Incas had come to mean a much more androcentric order, which was manifest in the creation of the *acllas,* or chosen women, under the male aristocracy in Cuzco. The conquest of Peru by Pizarro and his men imposed Spanish laws that further restricted female access to property and political office. It meant as well the advent of the Catholic faith, which excluded women from positions of

Víctor Córdova and Francisca Paz, Tunnel Six, 1987

religious authority while restricting their autonomy and regulating their sexuality. The eighteenth-century rebel leader Micaela Bastidas, the nineteenth-century novelist and pro-Indian activist Clorinda Matto de Turner, and the early twentieth-century painter Julia Codesido were notable figures in a society where discrimination and exclusion of women still persisted. Illiteracy rates as of the start of the rondas in 1976 were almost three times higher for women than men, abortion was illegal, and not a single woman was to be found in the top ranks of business and government.[6] Women were not granted the vote until 1965.

When I went to visit a family during the day in Cuyumalca and other villages, the husband was unlikely to be there, perhaps planting potatoes up in the *jalca,* the moors, or even away for a few months cutting cane in the plains of Chiclayo. The wife stayed behind to cook, care for the children, wash clothes in a plastic tub, and tend to chickens and pigs. Despite the increasing migration of young women to the cities for jobs as maids and cooks, a man remained far more likely than a woman to have ranged far from the village in search of work and adventure and to the jungles of the Amazon and the cities of Piura, Chiclayo, and even Lima. In the case of Francisca Paz and Víctor Córdova in Tunnel Six, Francisca had never even been to the city of Sullana just forty miles away. It was exciting for her to make the half-hour walk to the little town of Paimas to buy a pound of noodles and perhaps fabric for a dress. Víctor, on the other hand, had left home in the mountains of Pillo for a job in the San Lorenzo Valley, and had later spent five years in jail in the city of Piura. As ronda leader, he traveled to peasant congresses as far away as Chota and Lima, not to mention trips across the desert to Sullana to sell the ten or twenty sacks of rice harvested from the family plot.

The very different lives of the sexes were reflected in their talk. In Tunnel Six, the favorite subject of women was the minidrama of village life. Was the newborn of Fidencio Neyra and Josefina Malacatos healthy? Why did Concepción Jara put out pellets of rat poison to kill the chickens of Maximo Piñín? Did Víctor Jara contract a sorcerer to bewitch Adriano Jiménez after a run-in at a Paimas cockfight? Men kept up with these topics, but they would also talk about sports, corn prices, national politics, and other issues from the larger world. When Dalinda Aguilar asked me about the United States, she was most interested in stories about my parents and other relatives. A man was much more likely to quiz me about the plane fare, wages, skyscrapers, and farming methods.

The exclusion of women from posts of official authority in village society was complete. I never heard of a single instance across the vast region of a woman's becoming the lieutenant governor, justice of the peace, or even parent-teacher association president. The standards of propriety made it risky for women to attend a village meeting on their own—especially at night when rumors might arise about their inattention to domestic duties and perhaps infidelity. Undoubtedly, a wife could exert what historian James McPherson has called a "domestic feminism," shaping the opinions and actions of her husband as well as her children.[7] Even in the private world of the household, however, the power of women was restricted, and the man supposed to have the final say. Francisca Paz's mother, Margarita García, was a hardworking woman in her forties, who had given birth to fourteen children, five of whom had perished in infancy as was so common in the northern countryside. She expressed her opinion with an earnestness that suggested

Margarita García and daughter Santos,
Tunnel Six, 1987

it was more than just a matter of telling the male anthropologist what she thought he wanted to hear. "The man is the *jefe,* the boss, and he should decide about the money, the kids, and everything."

The women's committee had begun in Cuyumalca in 1977. Because they had suffered the theft of pigs and chickens fattened for months with kitchen scraps, the vanishing of shirts and pants from the clothesline, and break-ins and shootings by marauding rustlers, the majority of women there wanted the rondas to survive. Yet there was little or no precedent for collective female organizing in the northern countryside. As Omelia explained to me in 1991, it had taken a push for her and others to start the women's committee, in this case from Daniel Idrogo, the charismatic young organizer for the Communist Party of Peru–Red Homeland. "Daniel talked to me about the idea and brought it up first at a ronda meeting. That's when I was elected the president, and the committee started." What had prompted Daniel's intervention in the first place? It was Maoism. The Chinese leader had often repeated that "[w]ithout the participation of women there can be no victory against imperialism," and Daniel later explained to me that Mao's teaching inspired his belief that women were necessary in making the rondas an instrument of peasant power and revolution (even though he followed Mao as well in believing class struggle should be the first priority).[8] A native son related to many villagers, Daniel was popular in the lower sector of Cuyumalca called Cañafisto. This made Omelia and other women receptive to his suggestion to organize behind the rondas. At the same time, Daniel's advocacy made the concept more palatable to skeptical village men. "He told us the rondas would be stronger if everybody participated," remembered one Cañafistan in 1990.

A number of feminist scholars have cautioned us recently against presuming the spontaneity and independence of women's organizing in Latin America or anywhere around the world. Especially in the last few decades, as one political scientist puts it, "feminist practices have gone global," which means that local organizing of women in shantytowns and the countryside is often closely linked to and sometimes even dependent on national feminist groups and international funders.[9] There was as yet only one small women's rights group in Peru in the late 1970s, formed by middle-class women in Lima, and the impact of the global feminist movement was minimal.[10] Yet Daniel's role underscores that forces beyond the village were pivotal to the birth of the women's committees, albeit in the form of Marxism, not feminism, and in the person of a man, not a woman. We have seen that a simple image of grassroots origins did not apply to the founding of the rondas in 1976, nor the expansion of the movement into justice making, the latter a development that involved Daniel at the same time that he was trying to organize women. Like the rondas themselves, the women's committees had mixed origins, embodying the interest of women in ending theft and the influence of Maoism via Daniel and Red Homeland.

The committees gave women a formal role in the rondas. Yet the scope and power of the organizations were restricted from the start by the premise of subservience and even physical weakness. As far as anyone could remember, actual patrolling by women was never considered in Cuyumalca or elsewhere. It was simply assumed that taking on the thieves was a male job. The nightwatch was a drama

Women's Committee, Tunnel Six, 1987

of masculinity and violence in which the man defended the honor of family and village by taking on rustlers, policemen, and other forces of evil with the phallic whip dangling from his hand. It required what were supposed to be the male qualities of courage and strength, or, in a word, *huevos,* balls, as some men declared. As Omelia and others saw it, they were not protagonists, but auxiliaries, whose main task was to "accompany" and "support" their men. The women's committees did not keep record books, have meeting halls, or even gather on their own. In Cuyumalca and other villages, the president and vice-president were elected at ronda meetings attended by the whole village. The women's committee was only an appendage of the ronda committee, which was run exclusively by men.

The chief duty was to enforce the male obligation to take a turn on the nightwatch. Omelia explained in the course of our conversation in 1991:

It was risky for the men to go after the "yellows" [those that shirked the ronda]. A lot of people had shotguns in their farmhouses in those days, whether to rob or to protect themselves from robbers. They could fight back and even shoot the men trying to make them patrol. But not with us women. A man would be embarrassed to hit or shoot at a woman, because he knew people would laugh at him, a man attacking a bunch of señoras.

Her reasoning reminded me of the Mothers of the Plaza de Mayo in Argentina.[11] There in the 1980s women marched once a week in front of the presidential palace carrying pictures of loved ones who had been disappeared by the military dictatorship. Those activists recognized that those men would have been beaten up and taken away by the security forces, who were reluctant to use the same public brutality against them, mothers in white head scarves and black dresses. In the same way in the northern Andes, the women's committees were able to turn standards of masculinity and honor to advantage, because they allowed the women to drag unhappy skulkers from bed with little fear of violent retribution.

Even the relatively modest role of the women's committees was still a novelty in the northern Andes. At that time in the late 1970s and early 1980s even the primarily female Catholic and evangelical prayer groups were invariably headed by village men. Although the women's committees could not glory in facing down thieves, they did license women to gather as a group, and broke the taboo against a woman moving about unaccompanied at night. The fast-talking Ersila Cabrera headed the women's committee in Santa Rosa just north of Cuyumalca:

We'd go out together across the meadows under the stars and moonlight. We really showed people that they'd better do the ronda. Most everybody wanted it, but there were a few who didn't, especially the ones accustomed to the bad habits of thieving. They had to be made to do their service, too. Otherwise, others might start to complain. The organization would fall apart, which is just what the authorities wanted to happen. If a man refused to come along to join the patrol, we'd give it to him hard—with sticks, stones, and the whip.

Besides acting in their own villages, Ersila, Omelia, and other early leaders journeyed with Idrogo and other ronda leaders across the Chota Valley to form women's committees in San Antonio, La Iraca, and Lingán Grande. The trips broke the isolation of the farmhouse by linking women locally and regionally.

So did participation in marches on the town of Chota. The largest

Speaking up at ronda congress,
Bambamarca, 1991

and most remembered of these mobilizations occurred in 1979. It was just after the interior minister had telegrammed the subprefect to shut down the rondas. On July 6, a coalition of Chotan villages marched on the town. The protest was backed and perhaps even suggested by Daniel Idrogo and Red Homeland, who wanted the peasantry to confront the military government. Thirty or so women in their straw hats and puffy wool skirts pushed to the front lines. A platoon of policemen blocked the way to the main square, and threw tear gas toward the angry peasants. "I was used to smoke from cooking with green eucalyptus wood, so I and others from the women's committees just threw the canisters back at the police," said one Cuyumalcan woman, remembering what happened next. The police were surprised and even scared by the fury of the señoras. After all, an image of the ferocity of the peasant woman has a long history in Peruvian society. She was stereotypically a figure doubly irrational and dangerous as both a woman and an Indian. "Those señoras turn into savages when they're mad, Doctor, and they know how to use a machete," the owner of a Chota stationery store told me in 1990. "The boys in the police that day turned tail. The peasants went into the square to yell their slogans about the rondas."

THE LIMITS OF MOBILIZATION

Among various obstacles stunting the women's committees was a lack of female solidarity. Anthropologists Jane Collier and Sylvia Yanagisako warn against assuming that within any society there is ever "a unitary 'woman's point of view' . . . crosscut[ing] significant differences in, for example, age, household position, and social class."[12] The allegiances of northern Andean women were certainly multiple, and they undercut the feeling of commonality along gender lines. In the village of Aragoto in the mountains of Piura, religion trumped gender, and members of the Jehovah's Witnesses refused to participate in the women's committee because it was run by a Catholic. The bond of kinship was the trouble in San Antonio in the Bambamarca Valley. When a ronda assembly ruled against one woman's father in a land dispute, she withdrew from the women's committee, and persuaded her sister-in-law and several cousins to do the same. Age could be an issue as well. The leaders of the women's committees were largely in their twenties and thirties, and in general older women were more conservative than this new generation, which was more likely to have been sent to school or to have worked in the cities. Few women over fifty joined the women's committees, and, indeed, they were more prone to deprecate the endeavor, as I found when one widow in Tunnel Six informed me in a conspiratorial whisper that it was just "an excuse for lazy señoras to get together to gossip." The conflict and tension among women contributed to the difficulty of galvanizing support. Even at the high-water mark at the end of the 1970s, no more than half of the women were active in the women's committee in Cuyumalca, a figure typical of the modest level of participation throughout the northern countryside.

The larger problem was a backlash against the new activism. According to the standard organization of gender and power, a husband controlled a wife, who was "not to take a step without the boss's permission," in the conclusion of Margarita García. Fear of betrayal hung thick in the rural world. No theme was more popular in Andean ballads than the lament of the jilted man. "Ungrateful little farm girl, you left me for another, and now my heart is broken" went a favorite San Juanito in Tunnel Six.[13] The touchiness of men about being perceived to fail to measure up to expectations was extreme. To describe a man as *saco largo,* henpecked, literally a "dress-wearer," was to invite a brawl, even murder, especially in the days before the rondas.

The assurances of Idrogo and others went only so far. To many village husbands, wives' going out on their own at night was hard enough to swallow in the short run, and impossible to accept over the long term. It exposed them to rumors that they were sacos largos, spread not only by men but also by women opposed for their own reasons to the women's committees. Juana Aguilar from San Antonio in the Bambamarca Valley explained that she did not join in the first place for fear of family trouble: "It was better to avoid problems caused by the evil things people will say." In several instances in Cuyumalca, a husband permitted his wife to participate, but later ordered her to stop. In San Antonio, on the other side of the Chota Valley, a wife often decided on her own to withdraw to avoid trouble with her husband as well as to protect herself against charges of neglecting the hearth. The spectacle of women whipping men and heading marches hinted at an inversion of the principles of patriarchy, a kind of gender bending in which women suddenly seemed to be the ones with balls. "It's not right for a señora to hit a man," one Cuyumalcan man later told me. Reining in the women's committees became a matter of restoring the proper order of things in this view.

A final factor was outside opposition. "The followers of the Communist Daniel Idrogo Benavides are now trying to include women . . . a part of their abusive and amoral manipulation of the rondas," said Pedro Risco in a 1980 interview in a Piuran newspaper, reflecting the hostility to the women's committees felt by the Chota leader of the APRA party, the most powerful political machine in northern Peru.[14] At least by the measure of numbers of women in top positions in the party hierarchy as of the 1980s, APRA was better about addressing gender than Red Homeland, whose national leadership was all male in spite of talk about equality in the march to socialism. Yet the connection of the women's committees to Red Homeland ensured bitter APRA opposition by the logic of political rivalry in the Chota Valley. Risco stoked the worst fears of village men by darkly depicting the committees as part of the campaign to force property as well as women to be shared. Later, in the 1980s, APRA formed Mothers' Clubs. This act further encouraged party leaders to discourage the women's committees, since the clubs obstructed the plan to control female participation in villages and shantytowns. In the village of Culqui, just down the Quiroz Valley from Tunnel Six, talk of forming a women's committee was squelched by local *apristas,* or APRA supporters, who were encouraged to oppose the proposal by the party's district leaders. A proposal made by Idrogo and Red Homeland had taken root anyway in the case of justice-making, responding to what most villagers felt was the urgent need of alternatives to the failing police and courts. It was another story with the women's committees. Female activism was already so precarious and controversial that APRA opposition could be decisive. "Political division kept us from organizing," concluded a Culqui woman I spoke with in 1986.

The denouement of Omelia's story indexed the obstacles to activism. It was rumored that she went out at night only for orgies with the ronderos. Men walking by the farmhouse shouted insults at her husband, Armando, that he was a cuckold. As I found on meeting him on a second visit to their farmhouse, Armando was a quiet, gentle man in a rust poncho and torn straw hat, who was himself never very active in the rondas beyond normal patrolling. He was upset by the insults, a reaction that caused what they both agreed were "arguing and fighting between us," and Omelia quit in 1979. Another señora took over, but she also stepped down after less than a year. The organization never revived in Cuyumalca, fading away in the birthplace of the first committee.

It would be wrong, however, to ignore the achievements of women in those early days of the rondas. A social movement is never easy or guaranteed, a "process of becoming [or unraveling] rather than an already achieved state," as anthropologist Richard G. Fox has put it.[15] Many men themselves admitted that female enthusiasm bolstered male participation in the rondas' vulnerable infancy, when village reluctance and town opposition made the organizations anything but a sure bet to survive. "The señoras were a key," said Filiberto Estela, the one-time president of the ronda committee in San Antonio. It was limited in autonomy and purpose, but the organizing of Omelia and her companions reflected their unwillingness to be only spectators of ronda history, and in this way it unsettled male rule in village society. By the early 1990s, the women's committees did not go out anymore to get patrollers onto the trails, but they still were charged in a number of places with keeping the peace at assemblies. An unsmiling, thick-set señora would stand guard in the official capacity as "delegate of discipline" and administer a tap of the whip to men who dared to doze off as the hours stretched into the late night. Although a matter of joking as much as fear, this role for women testified to a female visibility and real power that would not be bottled back up altogether in the northern countryside.

Yet the limits of the women's committees remained just as apparent. As in Cuyumalca, the organizations had dissolved by 1990 in Santa Rosa, San Antonio, and a number of other villages in the Chota Valley, or they existed only on paper, as they did in Aragoto and Yangay in the mountains of Piura. The functions of the surviving and active committees remained limited mostly to policing the assemblies. In this sense, they never turned into a vehicle for pressing a broader agenda of female equality or even participation in the rondas and the village. Male monopoly on village leadership remained just as absolute as it had at the start of the rondas in 1976. Adjectives such as "growing," "increasing," or "mounting" appear in a good deal of writing about women's movements, a vocabulary of progress that can imply an unstoppable march toward the end of patriarchy and sexism in Latin America. The rise and decline of the women's committees warn against quite so unilinear a view. As evident in this case, activism can follow any number of pathways, and just as well end in setback as opening, disappointment as fulfillment, retreat as advance.

A feeling of discouragement ran through Omelia's account of the late 1970s. It did not mean that she had become passive about life in general, however, and she explained that every other weekend she got on the bus in Chota with boxes of cheese and fruit to sell on the coast, staying with a son who worked on a sugar cooperative near the big dam at Carhuaquero. Omelia's profits were the margin of survival for her and Armando, who was going blind from glaucoma and could not work away from their farm, which was in any case far too small to support even the modest needs of the aging couple. "Tomorrow I go to Chiclayo," she said, staring out in the direction of the Chota Valley, the mountains, and the ocean and cities beyond.

WIFE BEATING AND THE RIGHTS OF MEN

María Paz was from the hamlet of Tazajeras just above Tunnel Six. At fifteen, she had married Elías Cruz, a man of twenty-eight from a village farther down in the Quiroz Valley. The couple soon moved to San Ignacio. In the 1970s and 1980s, many northern Andean peasants were migrating eastward to that tropical valley to hack plots from the rainforest, where the new homesteaders often entered into conflict with the Aguaruna Indians who had an ancestral claim to the land. Elías had become increasingly abusive with María as they struggled to start a small coffee farm in the mud, rain, and isolation of the jungle. He would return late from the raw frontier town of El Oro in a drunken rage to beat his young wife, screaming accusations that she was unfaithful. At least once in 1994, he strung María by the arms with a rope from the rafters of the farmhouse, leaving her thin wrists raw and bloody.

The desperate María had finally fled with her baby on her back. She arrived, starving and tattered, at her parents' farmhouse in Tazajeras after a trek of more than a hundred miles across the gorges and cloud forest of the eastern Andes, among the most unforgiving landscapes anywhere in this hemisphere. Cruz had followed. He stayed with a brother in the nearby village of Culqui, and there he spread the story that María had stolen money from him. María's father, Temistocles, complained to the Tunnel Six ronda, since the committee in their own Tazajeras was divided and weak. Víctor Córdova, the ronda president, said he would put the matter on the agenda for the next assembly. And so, a week later, Cruz and his brother, María and her family, and forty Tunnel Sixers arrived at the school lunchroom as dusk fell for the *arreglo,* or "fix-it," as villagers throughout the northern Andes referred to the justice-making of the rondas.

The case of María and Elías was part of a new front in the conflict over the rights and roles of the sexes, in this case over the question of wife beating. By the mid-1980s, it had become clear that the women's committees were not going to grow or even survive. A function for women in getting men on the trails was becoming irrelevant altogether as patrolling succeeded in lessening theft. Yet the decline of the committees did not mean the end of women's involvement in the rondas. As resolving disputes in assemblies became the movement's main function, many women came forward with complaints, almost a quarter of them against their husbands. In Tunnel Six in 1986 and 1987, eight wives took abuse charges to the rondas. The Central Ronda Committee in Cuyumalca dealt with five complaints in 1990 and 1991, and there were instances as well during the late 1980s and early 1990s in San Antonio, La Iraca, Lingán Pata, and Chugur. As would occur with María and Elías in Tunnel Six, a matter of violence, rage, and gender was forced into the open in village society.

Wife beating was common in Tunnel Six and elsewhere in the northern Andes. When Leonila Neyra came by to visit on a Sunday afternoon in 1987, I asked her about the bruises on her arms. The ponytailed mother of five said that her husband, Edilberto López, had returned from the town of Paimas the night before and had struck her with an ax handle.[16] "It's what a lot of husbands do," she said matter-of-factly. As was almost always true in the northern Andes, drink had been the combustible, in this case too much of the sickly sweet anisette hawked at ten cents a bottle in Paimas as well as the two general stores in Tunnel Six. Village señoras passed the bottle on occasion at baptisms, first-haircutting ceremonies, or the ronda anniversary celebration. Yet only men ever got knock-down drunk, especially on Sundays, the single rest day from farmwork. The norm in rural society was a formal reserve. All the stronger for being repressed in everyday life, anxiety and anger welled up in drunkenness, and at least some men turned ready to settle scores with those they believed had wronged them in any way. Not only could wives be the target of violence, but also other men, over debts, grievances about land, or insults to honor. Brawls and knife fights had left many men in Tunnel Six with scars on their faces and forearms. Although few drank regularly enough to be alcoholics, the quality of the poor man's liquor was a further danger of drinking. When I returned to visit Tunnel Six in 1997, four men had died at a haircutting party. The manufacturer in the city of Chiclayo had spiked the "Royal Marquis" anisette with poisonous industrial methyl alcohol to cut costs. My friend Francisco Aguilar, who had helped me build my little adobe house, was blinded for life. "How will we live now that I can't work?" he asked, when I saw him and his family of eight in their mud shack in a rocky canyon above the canal.

It was impossible to compile anything approaching exact statistics about domestic violence. From the grapevine as well as conversations with women such as Leonila, I estimated that about half of the wives in Tunnel Six had been beaten at least once. In Cuyumalca, the incidence of wife beating was lower than in Tunnel Six, but still high, occurring in about one-quarter of village marriages. A ballad from the state of Ancash advised husbands:

> If your woman gets too loud,
> break her ribs.
> If she's jealous,
> apply hard wood.
> If she doesn't cook lunch,
> give her a black eye.[17]

As this common view of duty and punishment had it, violence was justified against any woman who violated the social standards of fidelity, domesticity, and submission, and a night of drinking at a party or in a cantina could embolden a husband to act. The force of culture and a culture of force came together to power male mastery in the northern Andes.

Until quite recently, many anthropologists had ignored or downplayed the question of power and inequality between the sexes in Andean society. As disenchantment with the West mounted during the student protest and radical upheaval of the 1960s and 1970s, a new interest and appreciation for the Third World emerged in much scholarship on the Andes of Peru and Bolivia. The enthusiasm for things Andean carried over into a benign view of gender in the region as a matter of complementarity and cooperation. Too many studies glossed over the frequency of wife beating, the reluctance of parents to educate girls, the exclusion of women from village leadership, and other obvious indications of inequity. Although the emphasis on the richness of village ritual, religion, and ecology was a valuable antidote to stereotypes of Andean inferiority, the desire to see the best in the Andes meant anthropologists simply failed to grapple fully with the serious discrimination and violence against women. This pattern of omission only began to change with rising interest in the relation between gender and power.[18]

Recent scholarship connects wife beating to conceptions of violence, love, and family across the Andean countryside. As anthropologist Penelope Harvey shows for a Cuzco village, it was generally accepted (at least among adults) that the lash could be used to discipline a disobedient child, although not against the very young or with undue severity. This meant that aggression against a wife fit with a pattern of the "use of force within kinship" to enforce "hierarchy and respect."[19] Other studies in the Andes have documented a confrontational courtship style involving hurled insults and brides dragged away from their homes by the husband's kin. I heard this riotous duet in Tunnel Six:

Young man: You're telling everyone I'm a deadbeat. You say I'm just a loser who can't find a woman.

Young woman: Get out of here, lazy peasant boy! Shut your mouth for a while! You think you can take advantage of me because I'm a peasant girl. I've got a stable of better-looking men, and I don't need you at all.

Young man: If I'm not good-looking, why did you make love to me? Let me remind you of the times when you spoke these words: "Tasty big daddy, I love you with all my heart."

Young woman: Liar, it was just one time! Nobody's going to believe your stories. Let's see some proof. You go around whining and barking like a puppy dog in the cold.

Young man: I've never noticed the cold because it's been so warm in your skirts. Maybe that's why they call you the husband-stealing girl.

Young woman: Long live women! Down with men! Dominate them like helpless lambs.

Young man: Long live men! Down with women! Kicks and punches until you tire.

Together: Nobody loses. Nobody wins. Everything ends. Long live the party!

"Kicks and punches" were a normal, even relished, part of what has been called *amor andino,* or "Andean love," in this bawdy view of violence as an avenue to union and pleasure. Once lovers married, the expectation of wifely obedience meant the woman lost license to give as good as she got. I never heard of a wife attacking a husband. Still, the concept of violence as part of the drama of sex and desire remained to be invoked by some men as a justification for wife beating. A husband in Tunnel Six once punned to me that "the stick is something women want."

It was just as apparent that government indifference exacerbated the problem. Until the late 1970s, Peru had no female police officers, and, even today, there are almost none outside Lima. The culture of the police was an archetype of machismo with the brothel and the cantina among the usual hangouts. There was little investigation of wife beating, rape, or other crimes against women. Not until 1993 was a law banning domestic violence promulgated in Peru.[20] Indifference to women's issues intersected with denigration of peasants to make it doubly difficult for a rural woman to hope for justice from the official system. "The Sergeant said a wife should just be silent and obey," recalled Santos Llacsahuache of Tunnel Six, who in 1985 had brought a complaint against her husband to the grimy little station in Paimas.[21] Lack of official intervention meant wife beaters had a virtual impunity. Thus local dynamics of gender and violence were reenforced or encouraged by the national institutions and policy, in this case a depressing example of how village society could be influenced by the forces of the wider world.

Historian Ward Stavig claims that "domestic violence was . . . a tolerated feature of marital life among Indians in the Andes."[22] It seems risky to me to reach such a categorical conclusion. Can it be said with certainty that no opposition of any kind existed to a husband's use of force? Or does it simply not appear in the archives of the Spanish colonial bureaucracy, an example of the kind of gap in the official record that leads literary critics to ruminate about whether the subaltern can speak?[23] As for more recent times in Tunnel Six and other villages in the northern Andes, it was obvious that no consensus existed about wife beating. I heard Cuyumalca's Ilarión Oblitas proclaim that "a girl won't respect you unless you whip her now and then" to assenting nods from other men in the cantina.[24] And yet, others, women and men, told me that they believed "it's wrong for the man ever to be abusive," as Teresa Córdova of Tunnel Six put it. The morality of wife beating was the kind of point of internal disagreement in peasant society that led anthropologist Edward Sapir in 1932 to complain about the "fatal fallacy" of viewing culture as an "impersonal, supeorganic whole," long before postmodern critics of the 1980s attacked the discipline for ignoring the heterogeneity of opinion and perspective that exists in any society.[25]

Christianity's influence was one reason for opposition to wife beating. In Tunnel Six, the priest, Father Tomás—a pudgy, funny, and irascible man with dark skin burned black by the desert sun— jeeped in every month to say mass in the school lunchroom. Once Robin and I went, as godparents of a child to be baptized that day. There we found ourselves the subject of a homily. "The way these gringitos, these dear little gringos, hold hands, show affection, and respect each other, should be a model for all of you," Father Tomás declared to the dozens of sweaty peasants crowded into the lunchroom on this hot, humid day. Impulsively, he grabbed a toothless old man, and forced him to hold hands with his aged wife, shouting "Jesus wants you to love your wife." Hand-holding and kissing in public were unheard of in village society, and the old couple looked as if they were about to go into shock. As white leftists wishing to be respectful toward the brown world of Tunnel Six, Robin and I were just as horrified at being set up as the standard of godliness and civilization for peasants to emulate. It seemed doubly ironic because we were atheists, and because I knew that Father Tomás had advised Tunnel Sixers to kick me out when I first arrived, probably suspecting I was a missionary for the Jehovah's Witnesses, Assembly of God, Israelites, Nazarenes, or one of the other evangelical sects springing up like weeds in his parish.

Father Tomás was no feminist. "Man is the head of Christ, and woman is His body," he would quote Ephesians, in this sense part of the Catholic Church's long history of propping up patriarchal authority. At the same time, he enjoined husbands to behave responsibly, reflecting increased clerical emphasis on family and social welfare after the Second Vatican Council in 1963. Whether a priest was radical and an advocate of liberation theology or old-fashioned and conservative (and Tomás, fiercely anti-Communist, was the latter), discouraging wife beating was part of the religious message about being a good family man, delivered to peasants in conversations and masses in their villages in addition to catechism training sessions in the town parish. No matter that Tunnel Sixers sometimes joked about his abrupt, eccentric ways, the opinion of Tomás still carried weight, especially with women who had suffered violence firsthand. "God does not want a husband to harm his wife," said Leonila, citing Tomás on the sullen gray Tunnel Six afternoon when she had come by to visit. Along with drunkenness, adultery, and even dancing, violence was frowned upon by the evangelical churches as well, extending the view of wife beating as ungodly.

The rise of the rondas further encouraged a negative view. "How nice it is with our organization, ending the injustices of the past," went a song that stated the new credo about wiping out violence and corruption as part of the pathway to the peasantry's salvation.[26] The ideology of dignity and reform emboldened a number of women to question a husband's prerogative to beat his wife. "The rondas mean respect and harmony, including in the family," Omelia had said in 1991, explaining to me why the targets of moralization should go beyond sneaky rustlers and embezzling policemen to include violent husbands. Some men saw it the same way. This was especially true of village ronda leaders, who were often calm and humane as well as religious men. Thus, the imperatives of religion and the rondas came together for Eladio Idrogo in Cuyumalca. "We need to be ronderos with the love Christ teaches. I cannot imagine He would want men to be cruel to their wives."

The assemblies became a forum for challenges to wife beating. To be sure, as a percentage of those abused, the number of women coming forward was small. Disincentives were strong—the humiliation of airing the private in public, the discouragement of women from going to meetings, the fear of further angering the husband. Nevertheless, the readiness of some women to go to the rondas reflected their desperation. I remember awakening late one night in Tunnel Six in 1987 to the sound of shouts and screams. A neighbor, Eusebio Chávez, was yelling that he would kill his wife, Florinda Paz, for sleeping around (a charge even the most shameless village gossips agreed was absurd), or else throw himself into the canal's dark waters to end "my miserable life once and for all."[27] A pitiful as well as scary sight plastered with mud from a tumble into an irrigation ditch on the way back from a Paimas cantina, Eusebio seized a kitchen knife, staggering outside after Florinda as she fled along with their four terrified children. Fortunately, the ronda patrol was out that night. The ronderos restrained Eusebio. Still, there had been recent cases in nearby Jambur and Algodonal of wives murdered by husbands driven by booze, jealousy, and frustration, not to mention the kind of extreme violence inflicted by Elías Cruz against María Paz. The police would seldom intervene, and the option of leaving the husband was fraught with complications, especially for women with children. In many cases, the wife's parents could not afford or did not want to have their daughter take refuge with them over the long term, and it was just about impossible for her to flee to work in the city if she had children, as most did. The ronda was the only option for those unwilling to endure any longer what María had explained to the Tunnel Six assembly was "a suffering too great to bear."

The process of going to the ronda testified to the continuing lack of female rights and autonomy. A key aspect of most cases was what historian Steve J. Stern calls a "pluralization of patriarchs."[28] When an abused wife at last decided to seek redress, she usually enlisted the support of at least one male authority figure, usually the father. He would set the case in motion by asking the ronda president for a hearing at the next assembly. By seeking protection from a father or sometimes a brother or uncle, a woman signaled that she was not rebelling against male authority, making it easier to gain sympathy in the predominantly male assembly. Despite new doubts, most villagers still believed a husband could use force, and for a woman to suggest otherwise in public was to invite the label of a *machona,* a "ball-breaker," a troublemaker. This climate meant it was not enough for a wife to prove she had been assaulted; the assembly needed to be convinced that the attack had been unjustified. "I always cooked and obeyed him everything," as María said, implying that what Elías had done to her would have been understandable had she not been a dutiful wife. In this way, the assemblies did not break the pattern of appeal to, and acceptance of, the primacy of men in the family and the ronda and to the principles of patriarchy in rural society.

Yet wives' willingness to come forward remained a significant development for the rondas. It should be remembered that the movement's justice making was still a fledgling endeavor in the 1980s. The character of the assemblies was a matter of experiment and struggle, not a given. Even if María and others acted from personal desperation as opposed to a collective political strategy, the presence of these women prevented the meetings from becoming an altogether men-only endeavor, as at least some men would have liked. Even woman-on-woman complaints such as those of Hermelinda against Chavela were in this sense part of an assertion of the rights of women to have a say in the new forum of the assembly. In the case of wife beating, women were not only participating, however limited their numbers, but also pressing the committees to address a problem of special concern to them, one that might otherwise have continued to be ignored. There was grumbling. "The rondas shouldn't get involved in family affairs bullshit," one Cuyumalcan told me in 1991. As of the late 1980s and early 1990s, pressure from women and the relatives they mobilized, backing of ronda committee leaders, and momentum of the rondas as agents of moralization combined to control this backlash in most places. Complaints about wife beating continued to appear on assembly agendas.

An immediate, tangible consequence was action against at least some abusive husbands. Only two of the eight cases in Tunnel Six in 1986 and 1987 were dismissed. In four others, the husband signed a promise to not abuse his wife any longer, and, in the event of further offenses, to face what the ronda secretary wrote into the agreement would be "a punishment according to the customs of our organizations." A whipping was meted out straightaway in the remaining three cases. Two husbands were absolved, two were warned, and one whipped in Cuyumalca in 1990 and 1991. The numbers indicated similar rates of admonition and punishment elsewhere in the northern countryside. It was impossible in the short run to judge the results, but a number of villagers in Tunnel Six felt the punishment was a deterrent, and in the long term would mean a decline in attacks. "Men are becoming a little less bold about what they do," concluded Teresa Córdova.

Elías got the lash. As the assembly began in Tunnel Six, there was little conviction behind the blustery assertion of innocence by the nervous, mustachioed villager, or behind his legalistic defense that María had no doctor's certificate. María's half-whispered words were far more convincing. She broke into soft sobs at several points in her story as if the memory were too much to bear. Still in her teens, she had the delicate brown features of a peasant madonna

in her straw hat and blue polyester sweater, which added to the
pathos of her account of the events that had forced her to flee Elías
and San Ignacio. As the hushed assembly watched, she rolled up
her sweater to show the scars from the night Elías had hung her
from the rafters. Elías fell silent. The assembly turned to the matter of punishment. It was decided that the accused man should
sign a statement dropping the robbery charges, and receive three
lashes. Cruz bent over on a chair in the middle of the room, and his
brother stepped forward to administer the whipping. It remained
the custom in the rondas to have the relative do the job in part to
lessen the likelihood of charges later being lodged with the police.

Historian Linda Gordon shows that the gradual establishment of
the "right not to be beaten" led to further feminist inroads in the
United States.[29] As many feminist critics have warned, however,
it can be wrongheaded to hold up this country as a standard for
the rest of the world, as if inequality and discrimination no longer
existed here, or as if pathways to change must everywhere be the
same. In the northern Andes of Peru, the future of the question
of wife beating was hard to predict. As it stood, the terms of the
struggle had remained as the right not to be beaten excessively, or
without what counted as cause by the standards of rural society.
Would a larger proportion of abused women begin to come forward? Or a smaller one? Could it be that women might begin to assert the right never to be assaulted under any circumstances? What
would happen to the struggle against wife beating should the rondas decline or even disappear later in the 1990s? The only certainty
was that individual women and their supporters had succeeded in
pressing the rondas to act against the most excessive violence. This
was a victory of no small importance given the lethal extremes to
which abuse could go. Pitted against the view of machismo as a
kind of genetic trait of Latin Americans, such visible progress was
a reminder as well that nothing was indelible about the organization of gender in the region. The rights of men and women were
a cause for maneuver and doubt, an unfinished matter that would
continue to be a point of tension.

It was the future that concerned Elías. Was reconciliation possible with María? He wanted to think so. After wincing through the
trio of lashes, the young villager was bent on atonement. "*Gracias,
hermano,*" "Thanks, brother," were his first words. Then he turned

to María: "Please, *cholita* [my little peasant girl], take me back." María refused to respond, looking away, while her father, Temistocles, glared at Elías for presuming forgiveness would come so easily, if at all. By then, it was three in the morning anyway. María and her family left to climb the switchbacked path up to Tazajeras. A few men stayed behind in the lunchroom to talk. Elías went up to one; he begged him to give María a little plastic bag with some sugar wafers for her and a sweater for the baby. At last Elías decided there was no more to be done for the moment, and with bowed head he walked out the door into the night, under a moon so bright that the squat molasses trees threw giant, spidery shadows across the eroded ridges of Tunnel Six.

THE PARADOXES OF PROTEST

Social theorist Chandra Mohanty has attacked a common portrayal in Europe and the United States of women in Africa, Asia, and Latin America. Her focus is the reduction of the category of "Third World women" to "underdevelopment, oppressive traditions, high illiteracy, rural and urban poverty, [and] religious fanaticism."[30] This view reduces the "everyday, fluid, fundamentally historical and dynamic nature of the lives of third world women into a few frozen 'indicators' of their well-being."[31] According to Mohanty, such a view ignores the range of opinion and culture among women in the Third World, and their part in struggles for dignity and justice. It can also reenforce a doctrine of Western supremacy by assuming that only Europe and the United States have made meaningful strides against sexism. Mohanty concludes that the category of "Third World women" fits with an imperial tradition of dividing the human continuum into an advanced, entrepreneurial, and modern "us" and a backward, passive, and archaic "them."

Yet the opposite kind of thinking has not always been much more satisfying. What can be labeled a "feminist orientalism" (or what performance artist Guillermo Gómez-Peña perhaps too derisively mocks as "ethnofeminism") also presumes that women in the Third World confront difficulty.[32] But it does invert the image of passivity to see heroism against racism, poverty, and sexism. "Communities of resistance," "cartographies of struggle," and "popular feminism" become the order of the day, with a reading list for

Latin America that includes *Lucha: The Struggles of Latin American Women* and *Compañeras: Voices from the Latin American Women's Movement.*[33] The aim is to dispel stereotypes of ignorance and submissiveness: the result can be reductionist and romantic and fail to grapple with the full ambiguity, contradiction, and diversity of the experience of the billions of people swept into the category of "Third World women." We hear a great deal about resistance, dignity, and mobilization, and much less about compliance, betrayal, and division. The flattening of the lives of women in Africa, Asia, and Latin America reflects would-be progressive wishes to make the indigenous, the native, the Third World, and the female into a screen for projections of purity, redemption, and perhaps even revolution.

The story of women in the rondas defied any easy formula. In my view, "heroic" describes the commitment of Omelia to the women's committee in Cuyumalca or the readiness of María to confront Elías in the assembly. Yet lethargy, infighting, or back stabbing also figured in those stories a few Tunnel Six señoras whispered about María's having fabricated her charges simply as an excuse to leave her husband for a secret lover in Tazajeras. At every turn, the marginalization of women carried over into the rondas, but the movement was still a terrain for jockeying and conflict about gender roles in village society, sometimes for small victories such as the punishment of wife beaters. Although denied full citizenship in the committees, most women spoke positively about the rondas, and in some cases were among the most articulate defenders of the cause.

The puzzle of why women may support ostensibly patriarchal movements has concerned much recent feminist scholarship. As a number of studies show, the participation of women not only in male-dominated, but also in conservative and sometimes murderous causes, has been significant in many cases. It turns out that women comprised fully a quarter of the membership of the Ku Klux Klan in the first half of this century. There were highly active, deeply committed women in Hitler's Nazi Party. More recently and closer to Peru, thousands of Chilean women clanged empty pots in 1973 to protest the democratically elected socialist government of Salvador Allende; many later formed Mothers' Clubs that actively supported the right-wing military dictatorship of General Augusto Pinochet. By insisting on recognition of "bad" examples of female activism, these studies question simplistic and idealized presumptions that women are somehow intrinsically connected to the life-giving, the just, and the peaceful. Far from programmed by biology, the politics embraced by women have always varied with the place and the moment, spanning fascist to progressive and just about everything in between.

Feminist scholars offer several explanations for women's involvement in conservative movements. The simplest revolves around the tangible rewards of participation. As sociologist Kathleen Blee shows, the Ku Klux Klan supported suffrage for white women, giving them incentive to join.[34] Historian Claudia Koonz underscores the attractions of the Nazis to female supporters, including tougher divorce laws and aid to large families.[35] More deeply, a politics of recognition can come into play. In the Chilean case, analyzed by historian Margaret Powers, not only had shortage and inflation alienated housewives from the Allende government, but also the Marxists concentrated their appeals on the male workers, whom they believed had to lead the fight for a revolutionary society.[36] This contrasted with the right-wing junta's success in mobilizing enthusiasm for Mothers' Clubs by recognizing and appealing directly to women through profoundly patriarchal yet nonetheless deeply held conceptions of family and duty.

The rondas certainly marginalized women at many levels. What they offered was nonetheless significant. Feelings of responsibility for family well-being were strong for most señoras, who took pleasure in fattening a pig for slaughter or watching a brood of ducklings hatch in a muddy backyard. In addition to protecting the animals, the rondas gave women the opportunity to air complaints about matters from somebody else's cow grazing in their cornfield to an abusive husband. Tunnel Six's Teresa Córdova was especially enthusiastic the day after an assembly ruled her neighbor would have to give back the old radio he had borrowed and had refused to return. "Thank God for the rondas," the widow told me on that hot afternoon in 1986.

Yet the rondas offered far less to women in terms of the politics of meaning and recognition. There was almost never any mention in the speech making, ballads, and poems about the role of women in the cooking and child care that made it possible for men to patrol in the first place, or even of the exploits of the women's

Poster for Red Homeland Congress, 1990

committees—a gendering of memory that wrote out women. I think back to a poster for a 1990 ronda congress organized by a federation connected to Red Homeland. It showed angry and determined peasants in march, presumably toward the battle for justice and revolution. A patroller with stick raised loomed at front in a line stretching back to the Andean horizon. Just one woman appeared. She did not carry the stick symbolizing ronda power. Instead, a baby was slung over her back, emphasizing women's primary obligation to domestic duties. For once a female face was included in public culture of the rondas, and, indeed, the activists of Red Homeland had argued for a place for women. At the same time, the habits of male authority and sexism's status as a "secondary contradiction" in Marxism meant the terms of inclusion were anything but egalitarian. The result was recognition of the woman first as a child rearer and as a camp follower literally in the movement's second rank.

Lack of recognition accounts for dimensions of alienation and uncertainty in women's thinking about the rondas. I was struck by the general disinterest of some women in Tunnel Six (if by no means the majority), who referred to the rondas as "they," as if to reciprocate the failure to acknowledge women with an indifference of their own to the committees. Even those most enthusiastic about the rondas could seem doubtful about their standing in the movement. Ersila Cabrera, the one-time president of the women's committee in Santa Rosa near Cuyumalca, described the rondas for me revealingly in 1990: "What the rondas do is good for the rest of us. We have made these organizations strong. I hope the ronderos will keep them going." Ersila began from the third-person position outside the rondas, switched to the first-person, suggesting a standpoint inside the movement, and then back again. Her syntax measured the feeling and the reality of a belonging that was partial at best.

Ersila's uncertainty underscores the diversity of interest and perspectives at the interior of just about every mobilization for change. As in the march on Chota in 1977, there were moments of cooperation and collectivity in the rondas, but also of division and conflict, whether related to religious preference, political allegiance, or any of the other cleavage lines in rural society. Gender proved to be another point of tension, belying the unifying label "social movement." Unity in protest is never completely possible, or perhaps even desirable, because diversity of opinion and concern can be a resource as well as a liability. Still, the cleavage of gender was debilitating for the rondas. It diminished participation in the assemblies, halved the pool of patrollers and committee leaders, and weakened enthusiasm for the movement. As a fight of the poorest in a poor country, the rondas from the beginning were precarious in the northern countryside, and, no matter what the bravado of the ballads, even male leaders recognized the marginalization of women damaged the peasantry's cause. An internal report in 1983 of the Provincial Ronda Federation of Bambamarca acknowledged that "women's participation is small, and more will have to be done to integrate them into the organizations," not that any action was taken to remedy the problem.[37]

A story told to me in 1990 by Juana Vásquez summed up the costs. A pale, square-shouldered woman of thirty-one from the high moors above the Chota Valley, Juana had been exposed to Marxism through schoolteachers in the village; she later married a leader of the Chota ronda federation connected to Red Homeland, Oscar Sánchez. The couple lived with their baby, Oscarcito, in a dark room just off the plaza in the town of Chota. Juana wrote ballads about the rondas and occupied the largely ceremonial position of "Secretary of Women's Affairs" in the Chota federation. Lonely in Chota with Robin far away in Lima, I visited Juana and Oscar on many evenings, sometimes bringing a bag of the carmelized peanuts street vendors hawked to nighttime strollers, sellers as well as customers bundled up in jackets, ponchos, and mufflers against the mountain cold. One night, Juana recalled the election of a new ronda president in her native village: "To lead the ronda is hard work. There's the gossip, the jealousy, the danger of being arrested by the police. Last year in Chugur, there came a point where no man wanted to take the job. So some of us women said one of us would do it. But then the men said, 'No, we're not going to be the only village with a woman as president. They'll call us hen-pecked and dress wearers.' So one of the men agreed to be the new president." The insistence on protecting masculinity and honor had hurt the ronda in Chugur, Juana explained, with Oscar nodding agreement. "The man who became president wasn't really enthusiastic about it, and the committee declined. It's now the weakest in that part of the countryside."

It was late by that time. Oscar had dozed off in front of the eleven o'clock news from Lima, which we viewed on the little black-and-white TV on the rickety table in the corner. Juana and I watched a bit of the coverage of the presidential campaign in which an unknown agronomist named Alberto Fujimori was closing fast on the early front-runner, the novelist Mario Vargas Llosa. "I don't know who would want to run this country," Juana said, referring to the hyperinflation, violence, and corruption that were peaking in that year of 1990. I agreed, said good-bye, and headed back to my little pea-green room in the Hotel Chota.

THE QUEEN OF THE RONDAS

It seemed unlikely that women's standing in the rondas would be transformed anytime soon. Nevertheless, pressures on patriarchy were mounting in the village, the nation, and the world. By the end of the 1980s, the number of girls in school had risen in the Andean countryside, and their rate of illiteracy was becoming far lower than among their mothers and grandmothers. The migration of women to jobs as maids, street vendors, and cooks was also increasing with deepening scarcity of land and opportunity in the Andes. Although many stayed in the cities, others returned to the farm for a time or for good, meaning that the new generation of women was more traveled as well as better educated. At the same time, the influence of the global feminist movement was growing in Peru. In 1995, President Fujimori established a Ministry of Women's Affairs, and asserted that he himself was "a feminist" (his wife, Susana, whom he had locked out of the Presidential Palace two years before, would not have agreed). A statute outlawing domestic violence passed in 1993, though enforcement was uneven in Lima and much less in the backlands of the Andes. The daughter of a French mother and an Arequipan aristocrat father, the nineteenth-century activist and writer Flora Tristán longed for a society where a woman would be free from "values, customs, prejudices, styles" to "enjoy her independence, and rely with confidence on that true force every being feels within."[38] As far back as the Incas, the alchemy of the local, the national, and the global had fired substantial, sometimes radical, reordering of Andean gender relations, and perhaps it would do so again in the future, even if the travails of women from Malaysian sweatshops to Afghani towns under the Taliban remind us that no simple or necessary equation yet exists between modernity, globalization, and equal rights for women.

A reordering would depend on teenagers such as Rosa Alvarado.

Rosa the First, Queen of the Ronda, Tunnel Six, 1986

A quiet, thin girl who always wore the same frayed red dress, she lived with her deaf twin brother and aged father in a farmhouse just down the ridge from me in Tunnel Six. Her mother had died of breast cancer three years before, so Rosa did the cooking, washing, and mending for the family. Somehow, in 1985, Rosa had managed to finish high school in the town of Paimas, the first girl in Tunnel Six to get her diploma. At eighteen, she had gone to live with an aunt in the shantytowns of Piura, hoping to study in a technical institute to become a nurse. It was too expensive. Rosa returned to Tunnel Six in 1986. Sometimes she would stop by the farmhouse of the committee president to make banners or send out invitations for ronda events. It was a mark of appreciation that she was chosen Queen of the Ronda for the 1986 anniversary celebration, although it was also partly because nobody else could be found. It had been decided at the last minute that crowning a queen would add a cachet to the event, following the style in the cities of picking a girl bedecked in formal gown and white gloves to preside at graduations, Independence Day, and other festivities. Could being the queen possibly lead into more serious responsibilities for Rosa in the rondas? I wondered if Rosa would become the first woman to break into ronda leadership.

This was not to be. On my last visit to Tunnel Six in 1997 I came across Rosa's father, Severino, hacking brush for a corral for his chickens. Already thin a decade before, he looked fragile and old now, with a tremor in his voice and hand, and yet he inquired after Robin with the standard rural formality and politeness. I asked about Rosa. It turned out that she had left again for the city in 1987, this time finding a relatively good job as a waitress in a Chinese restaurant. She had married another migrant from the Andes, a young man from Huancabamba. The Queen of the Ronda now had two children and lived in a little house at the edge of shantytown of San José.

"Her life is there now," Seferino said, blinking for a moment in the bright sun.

FIVE

The Rondas in the Age of the NGO

GOLD DETECTORS
For finding treasure and precious metals, high sensitivity, sporting or
professional use. José Pardo Avenue, No. 620, Office 314. Miraflores.
Telephone: 441198. Fax: 474494.
—Advertisement in Lima newspaper, 1986

An index of Tunnel Six's poverty was the parade of people that
came to me to ask for loans. Most wanted the money for basic necessities. An antibiotic for a baby stricken with a urinary infection.
The textbook a daughter needed for the third grade. The coffin
to bury a grandparent. To have money to give for the most urgent
needs, I had to say no to a teenager's request for $200 for the metal
detector, even though his appeal was in some ways all the more
poignant for its expression in the age-old fantasy of buried treasure and Inca tombs. I was then just a student with what seemed
a slim chance of landing a job in anthropology back in the United
States. A doctoral fellowship for that year of $8,000 still made me
by far the richest person in a place where the annual earnings of
most families did not exceed $800. The loan requests were a re-
minder of the contrast between the relative privileges enjoyed by
a middle-class American and the privation faced by Andean villagers, and thus of the stark inequality of opportunity and income
in today's global system.

The bodies of Tunnel Sixers registered hardship. As rice and
yucca were often the only thing to eat, children grew up under-
sized, and potbellied with amoeba from drinking the foul-smelling
canal water. A number of adults shivered with malaria contracted
from labor in the jungle. Giving birth alone in a rough farmhouse,
with the nearest doctor a hundred miles away, took a special toll

on women; it showed in lines, tired eyes, and the brown splotches they ruefully called the mask of pregnancy. "It was fabulous, what the body told," the poet Rafael Campo writes about his study of anatomy and physiology.[1] It was terrible in Tunnel Six for what it said about pain and disease in the Andes.

The urgency of combating poverty has been the main rationale for the proliferation of nongovernmental organizations (NGOs) in the last few decades.[2] The category is a catchall for the vast array of privately funded groups concerned in one way or another with social welfare.[3] As government programs failed to meet basic needs, NGOs multiplied with special speed in the Third World, promising more efficient, innovative, and democratic ways of improving poor people's lives.[4] Typically, the Peruvian NGO was made up of middle- and upper-class professionals from Lima and other cities, who sought and used funding from U.S. and European foundations to implement projects connected to health care, human rights, environmental protection, credit, literacy, and other social issues. There were less than 50 NGOs in Peru in 1960. By 1994, a registry listed 897, which were among the 15,000 NGOs in operation across Latin America.[5] It was no exaggeration to call NGOs a "third sector" together with business and government.

This chapter will scrutinize the role of NGOs in the rondas. From early on in the late 1970s, a number of these groups stepped forward with advice and aid for the rondas, and more than twenty became involved over the next decade. Why were NGOs attracted to the rondas? What work did they do with the movement? How were the villagers of the rondas and the city professionals of the NGOs changed by the experience of working with one another? What does the history of this interaction contribute to rethinking debates about development in the Third World? A reckoning with the encounter between NGOs and the rondas must be a part of any understanding of the making of the movement.

It has been common simply to praise NGOs as catalysts in empowering the downtrodden. One recent observer extols the organizations as one of the most important contemporary forces in the struggle to make "available an equal opportunity for social development to each citizen of this planet."[6] An examination of NGO labors with the rondas does not support so clear-cut a view. It shows dimensions of misunderstanding, power, and control on the part of NGOs, not to mention moments of bad faith on the part of NGOs and villagers alike. At the same time, NGOs turn out to have been important in spreading and strengthening the movement in the countryside, and in defending it against hostile forces in national society. A number of scholars have begun to point to the potential for social movements, NGOs, and international foundations to weave elastic and sometimes effective webs of alliance and mobilization for social change.[7] As I have come to see it, the case of the rondas and northern Peru in the late 1970s and through the 1980s foregrounded these possibilities for constructive collaboration across geographical and economic borders, even if sometimes only in modest ways.

I remember the visit of Center for the Promotion and Research of the Peasantry (CIPCA) to Tunnel Six in 1987. This largest NGO in the city of Piura had just started Radio Cutivalú as an alternative to commercial stations that blasted out salsa and Coke ads. It was winning an audience with programming that featured music and news originating in this region famous for chicha, cotton, goat stew, and the white-hot desert sun. I was affiliated that year with CIPCA in order to have occasional use of its library on sojourns. The reporters at Radio Cutivalú were looking for features. I suggested the Tunnel Six ronda. One afternoon a month later, their jeep bumped into the village. Not many cars and trucks of any sort braved the washed-out track from the highway. A pack of kids ran behind the jeep yelling in excitement. A Peruvian economist and a German archaeologist from CIPCA had come along with the two reporters to gather material for an atlas about Piura for use in schools throughout the region.

A chasm in education and class separated the villagers and their four visitors. It did not, however, prevent anyone on either side from enjoying and even learning from the encounter. Víctor Córdova brought out stilettos requisitioned from rustlers, with evident satisfaction at displaying the evidence of ronda achievement for the city visitors. The reporters from Radio Cutivalú interviewed the committee president and others about the organizing in Tunnel Six. Then the Tunnel Sixers gave a tour of village landmarks: the pipes used to siphon canal water, the crosses marking the spots where children and drunks had drowned in it, and the spot on a ridge above where they planned to build a House of the Rondero.

Angélica Jara with Radio Cutivalú's Mercedes Ruiz Jiménez, Tunnel Six, 1987

Mercedes Ruiz Jiménez was the senior reporter and station director, an expatriate Spaniard with strong feminist convictions. After returning to Víctor's farmhouse after the tour, she realized that she had spoken only to men, and looked for women to interview. Angélica Jara had stopped by to meet the visitors from the city across the desert. It was a chance for this funny and smart mother of eleven to speak up, a moment often denied to women in village society. Her views would be part of a story broadcast to tens of thousands of listeners in northern Peru. "Let me tell you about the fight against the rustlers, Señorita," said Angélica, leaning toward the microphone to begin her story.

NGOS AND DEVELOPMENT

I was no stranger to NGOs. As a graduate student at Stanford, I wanted to find a way to connect anthropology and social activism. One possibility was to work for a development group.[8] This idea led me to set up an internship for the summer of 1984 with Catholic Relief Services (CRS). An arm of the Catholic Church in the United States then headquartered in New York, the CRS disbursed more than $2 million a year in aid to Latin America and the rest of the Third World. Their Lima field office distributed money to Peruvian NGOs for stock improvement, potable water systems, and other projects designed for Andean villagers as well as city shantytowns. When I told the personnel director in New York that I hoped to work in Peru, he talked with the Lima office. My summer task would be to observe an Andes project funded by the CRS—the Integral Development Project of Huamachuco—about fifty miles down the spine of the mountains from the city of Cajamarca. It was administered by Caritas-Huamachuco, an NGO run by the Peruvian Catholic Church. The CRS gave several hundred thousand dollars a year to Caritas-Huamachuco to fight village poverty.

The poet César Vallejo grew up in a little town to the south of Huamachuco. He could have been thinking of his homeland in a 1918 poem about the "cold tint of painful gray."[9] The bus up from Trujillo bumped through silent villages, blasted-out mining camps, and stark altiplano to reach Huamachuco. The capital of the province was a town of 3,000, with bushes in the plaza carved in the shapes of peacocks and llamas, a pair of flea-infested hotels, and a concrete bullfighting ring used for the annual fiesta. A diminutive, chain-smoking Spanish Franciscan, Juan Barcelo directed Caritas-Huamachuco and the Integral Rural Development Project of Huamachuco from a little office just off the plaza.[10] He had hired a young development team of recent graduates in social work and agronomy from universities in Trujillo and Lima. They headed out into the countryside in a Land Rover to start cooperative stores; organize "Community Development Committees"; and give talks on hygiene, neighborly cooperation, and farming techniques. Over the summer of 1984, I went out with the Caritas-Huamachuco development workers on most days to evaluate their progress for the CRS.

The project was a disaster. I had only been in town a few days when I heard a litany of complaints from the team about Father Juan. "He never goes out with us and drinks too much of that Spanish wine," griped the agronomist from Trujillo. The charges were part of jockeying to move up the ladder in Caritas-Huamachuco. A week before I was to return to the United States, the agronomist and one of the social workers approached me separately for a word in private. Each suggested I propose to the CRS that he replace Juan as the director. Although I never saw Father Juan take even a sip during the time I spent in Huamachuco, it was obvious to me that the aging Franciscan was tired of the priesthood and maybe even of life. He lacked the will to energize the project.

Overextension was another obvious problem. It sounded good for Caritas-Huamachuco to report to the CRS that seventy villages were participating. Yet the size meant that the "impact" amounted to a visit from the team every three or four months and $500 or so a year in aid for the communal stores, a loan fund, and rice and cooking oil. Naturally, the team wanted to put a good face on the project for me, the outside evaluator, because they would lose jobs should the CRS cut off funding. However, when I pressed Ana, another of the social workers, she admitted that the project was overambitious.[11] "We're trying to do too much, and I don't think people are listening."

The team had the youth and energy Juan lacked. Guillermo, Ana, and the others loved to tell corny jokes and belt out choruses of "Condor pasa," "Ojos azules," and other schmaltzy Latin favorites to pass the hours spent stuffed like sardines into the Land Rover on the way to the next village. As children of shopkeepers and bureaucrats in Huamachuco and graduates of the less prestigious public universities, they earned only $100 a month, forming part of a lower middle class in Peru that was pressed hard in the 1980s by inflation and unemployment. I did not blame them for trying to enlist me in their quest for a better job.

Yet paternalism and condescension toward villagers was the project's greatest liability. This announcement sent out by the team was typical: "We wish to communicate . . . that you should meet at the time and place indicated below, for the purpose of receiving some teachings from the CARITAS team that will be for the benefit of all of you . . . and learning new methods of farming, how to fertilize and attack the diseases that afflict your crops and to talk about loans. We desire your punctual attendance." The infantilization of villagers extended into the team's use of first-person plurals and diminutives of a kindergarten teacher. "We must learn to wash our little hands," one of the social workers instructed a group of about sixty assembled under a gray sky on the soccer field in Caramaca. It was assumed that villagers themselves had nothing to contribute to the battle against poverty and could only be rescued by the "teachings" of a team endowed by the university with the latest Western expertise. Ana summed up the project's mission: "to change the backward habits that keep them underdeveloped."

The Colombian theorist Arturo Escobar has attacked the enterprise of development.[12] In his view, increased assistance to the Third World in the aftermath of World War II was bound up with the assumption of Western superiority. He states that the expansion amounted to a "colonization of reality" by an aid bureaucracy that painted the "advanced" world's values and technology as the only possible salvation for poor counties in the Southern Hemisphere.[13] The intentions of Caritas-Huamachuco were largely noble. Yet the work of this particular NGO exemplified the dimensions of power and control in the will of Westerners to "develop" the Third World. The type of development promoted sought to make the poor into wards of the institutions and professionals of aid agencies.

This is not to say that many villagers were convinced that the Integral Rural Development Project of Huamachuco was their ticket to prosperity. As anthropologist Donald Moore emphasizes, it would be a mistake to paper over "the multiple reworkings and resistance to development across the Third World."[14] To be sure, villages in the Andes sometimes spoke of themselves as "ignorant" and "underdeveloped," a testimony to how development's argot could become a part of local thinking. At the same time, they were often proud of their own traditions and skills at farming and not simply ready to act according to the Caritas-Huamachuco blueprint. Participation in the project was unenthusiastic. It mostly amounted to congregating every few months to hear the "teachings" of the team when the Land Rover bumped into their corner of the Andes. Even the team realized that the villagers came because it was required in order to pick up a ration of rice and cooking oil. "If we didn't give out the donations, this field would be empty," acknowledged the good-natured Ilde surveying a crowd of about seventy on the soccer field of Chugolpa, most of them dressed in the *llanques* and the peaked, almost witchy, straw hats favored by both sexes in the Andes of Huamachuco.[15]

The Shining Path cemented the project's fate. It would turn out later that the insurgency's second-in-command had arrived clandestinely in the early 1980s to direct operations from a village just south of Huamachuco.[16] When I was eating dinner one night just off the plaza, the guerrillas announced their presence. An explosion boomed in the distance. The room went dark. I went to the door to see what was happening. In one of their signature tactics, the Maoist revolutionaries had dynamited the town generator, a part of their design to sow uncertainty and chaos they believed would speed the revolution. Meanwhile, they had lit the dry grass in the shape of a hammer and sickle on a hill above the darkened town, a bit of pyrotechnics to advertise Communism's imminence. Then a firefight broke out down the street between the police and guerrillas. I cowered under a plastic table with visions of being dragged out to be executed as a yankee imperialist spy. After five minutes of shooting, the guerrillas retreated back into the hills, and no one was hurt that night. A year after I left, they attacked once more, this time murdering Huamachuco's mayor in front of his wife and children.

The Shining Path detested development groups. "They give crumbs to the people to keep them from joining the people's war," explained one party leaflet. An Australian nun, two Japanese engineers, and a U.S. Agency for International Development (AID) employee were among those murdered to clear the way "to put the noose around the neck of imperialism and the reactionaries."[17] Caritas-Huamachuco started to receive threats the year after I left. Two members of the team resigned, and Father Juan took refuge in Trujillo. The project closed in 1986.

The debacle of the Integral Rural Development Project of Huamachuco forced me to rethink my own plans. I wanted to escape the world of NGOs, projects, and all of the bureaucrats and "experts" who made plans for Andean villagers without deigning to consult them. I read that summer about highway blockades and strikes organized by villagers themselves to demand fair prices for their products and other reforms. These movements sounded like a more promising pathway for the Peruvian countryside. I returned that fall to Stanford's prosperous, palmy campus with an edge of righteousness, ready to tell everyone that I planned to devote my dissertation to a peasant movement.

RETHINKING DEVELOPMENT

I was far from alone in questioning the standard model of development. The turbulence in the United States during the Vietnam War
years had triggered doubt about the desirability of Westernizing
the world. Critics charged that dams, highways, the "improved"
technology of the Green Revolution, and the rest of the regulation recipe for progress were destroying the lifeways of villages and
tribes.[18] In reaction to the premise that the West was the only
model for the Third World, the call was sounded for "participatory" and "grassroots" development, and the incorporation of "indigenous" and "local" knowledge into the work of aid agencies.[19]
The American Friends Services Committee, Ox-fam International,
and other left-leaning groups formed to finance rural cooperatives,
indigenous craft projects, women's literacy, tribal land rights, and
other locally run endeavors. Even the World Bank and IMF began
paying lip service to questions of cultural sensitivity, environmental impact, and social justice previously ignored altogether in the
rush to modernize the Third World.

The changing view of development was evident in Catholic Relief Services. Huamachuco was one of the last large-scale, top-down
projects it funded in Peru. In Lima in 1984, Robin and I became
friends with Coletta Youngers, a new program officer for the organization. At twenty-four, Coletta was funny and smart; reflecting
her political leanings, she sometimes wore the sandals and flowing
Indian print skirt of a hippie. As we did, she supported the Sandinista Revolution, the struggle against apartheid in South Africa,
and the other leftist causes of the day, and in Peru she forged close
ties with socialist leaders, human rights activists, and progressive
Catholic leaders. Her views were reflected in a commitment to
funding Afro-Peruvian and Amazonian indigenous rights organizations, shantytown women's movements, and rural health cooperatives. Coletta was not an anomaly. There were aid representatives
in Peru with similar politics from the Ford Foundation, Ox-fam,
and a number of European funders. These development workers
maintained the traditional hope that the assistance of their Western agencies could help Peruvians out of poverty. Still, they were
not the same old aid bureaucrats. Even if the word suggests a West-

ern view of history's trajectory as headed toward progress and freedom, it should not be forgotten that how "development" ought to
be achieved and what it means has always been in dispute, whether
by Marxists believing it to be the revolutionary struggle for a classless society or neoconservatives arguing it to be entrepreneurship
and the arrival of the free market and global capitalism. At least
among many aid groups working in the Third World, the 1970s
and the 1980s were a time of rethinking, and a search for forms of
engagement that would be less ethnocentric, apolitical, and hier-
archical than they had been in the past in Peru and other countries. "There's resistance to rethinking development even within
our organization," the representative of one well-established U.S.
foundation told me one night in Lima, "Yet I still think major
changes are happening."

A panoply of Peruvian NGOs stepped forward with projects for
Coletta and others of the new breed to fund. Many of these organizations were connected to the left wing of the Catholic Church.
The Second Vatican Council in 1963 and the Latin American Bish-
ops' Conference in Medellín in 1968 had encouraged church involvement in social change. What the Peruvian Dominican Gustavo Gutíerrez baptized as "liberation theology" was premised on
the imperative of a "preferential option for the poor." [20] The advocates of liberation theology were never a majority in a church filled
with middle-of-the-roaders in the vein of Father Juan and, increasingly in the 1980s, the conservative order of Opus Dei supported by
John Paul II.[21] Yet this did not prevent them from forming NGOs
with the agenda of social justice. CIPCA in Piura was started by
Jesuits in 1973 to provide loans, training, and advice to peasants; it
sought to promote preservation and appreciation for rural culture
and eventually founded Radio Cutivalú. A handful of Dominicans
started the Bartolomé de las Casas Center in Cuzco for research
and support of the peasantry in the former Incan capital. As the
dirty war between the Shining Path and the government escalated
in the 1980s, the progressives in the church formed NGOs that took
the lead in documenting and fighting against human rights abuses:
the Center for Social Action (CEAS), the Center for Action for
Peace (CEAPAZ), and the Service for Peace and Justice (SERPAJ).
Although the priests and nuns behind these and other Catholic
NGOs saw their work as a matter of faith, they hired laypeople and

received funding from secular foundations, trying to be ecumenical in spirit. The Jesuit Bruno Revesz, head of research at CIPCA, and many others wore street clothes and not the religious garb connected to the aura of priestly privilege promoted by the traditional church.

A number of middle-class and left-leaning laypeople also spearheaded Peruvian NGOs. As the military ceded power in 1980, it seemed to many urban professionals that the democratic opening offered an avenue for building institutions to support and collaborate with peasants, Indians, women, and other marginalized groups. Only the few thousand cadre of the Shining Path and the Túpac Amaru Revolutionary Movement (MRTA) insisted on war as the best avenue for change. Hope prevailed on the left of changing the system from the inside, including electing socialists to congress and the presidency. To start an NGO was a way to work on social issues, and even to make a living at it, a matter of no small urgency for all but the wealthiest Peruvians in the hard times of the 1980s. Because the Ford Foundation and other funders saw the governments of Fernando Belaúnde (1980–85) and Alan García (1985–90) as corrupt and conservative, they encouraged NGOs as better ways to channel aid to Peru. Their money bankrolled the Educational Association of Cajamarca (EDAC), the Center for Amazonian Development (CIPA), the Center for Development Research and Action (DESCO), the Association of Educational Publishers (AREA), and the dozens of other NGOs that became as much a part of Peruvian life of the 1980s as street vendors, blackouts, and the wildly popular national women's volleyball team.

These groups shared skepticism about the Green Revolution and the rest of the Western recipe for progress. Organizing among peasants, women, tribes, and shantytowns appeared to be a more democratic and endogenous option to many NGOs, in much the same way it had to me after my experience with Caritas-Huamachuco. The left-leaning and sometimes feminist urban professionals in these NGOs tried to reach out and support social movements—the Flora Tristán Center channeling advice and money to women's committees in Lima's poorest neighborhoods, the Labor Rights Association financing union organizing, the Center for Amazonian Development providing legal aid to Asháninkas to defend land from Shell Oil.[22] The reports of the NGOs always applied the adjectives of "grassroots," "autonomous," and "independent" to the social movements they supported. These labels reflected the desire of NGO staffers to imagine the spontaneity of organizing from below. It was certainly wise at any rate to play up the vigor of popular mobilization, because international funders were more likely to fund a Peruvian NGO's work on a local initiative it believed was genuinely self-generated and independent. Yet the impression of the grassroots' independence belied the depth of the involvement of the outsiders of the NGOs. They paid for the rental of offices for shantytown and peasant federations, bailed out imprisoned leaders, advised on dealing with the government, and printed posters to announce meetings. Far from operating entirely on their own, the social movements of the 1980s were directly encouraged and funded by Peruvian NGOs underwritten themselves by donors from the United States and Europe.

The rondas were no exception. As Peru's largest and most vital agrarian movement, they were an object of admiration for most urban leftists, and many NGOs decided to try to back the mobilization. EDAC, the Rural Educative Services (SER), and the Jorge Basadre Institute (IJB) held training sessions for ronda leaders in human rights, environmental conservation, and other issues. TAREA, CIPCA and the Center for Education and Communication (ILLA) published pamphlets and oral histories for and about the movement. Still other NGOs provided legal services for jailed ronda activists, among them the Association for the Defense of Human Rights (APRODEH). By the middle of the 1980s, the Department of Social Assistance (DAS), the Center for Rural Development and Research (CEPESER), and a few other NGOs were trying to channel money to committees for clinics, potable water systems, and other village development projects.

I might never have learned about the rondas had it not been for the NGOs. It was Coletta who told me about the movement for the first time in 1986, and she only knew about it because the CRS was funding a Piuran NGO that was organizing rondero meetings. I had naively imagined that the decision to work with a rural movement would transport me into a pristine realm of protest and vision beyond the world of development. The truth was that Peruvian NGOs and their funders in wealthy countries had already entered into rondas and movements like them years before me. Anthropologist

Eric Wolf pointed three decades ago to "the importance of groups which mediate between the peasant and the larger society of which he [or she] forms a part."[23] We have seen in the rondas the hand of the national government, political parties, and the Catholic and Protestant Churches. The NGOs add yet another layer to the history of a movement that was shaped by forces and institutions extending far beyond the northern countryside, though it always remained the peasantry's organizing upon which the survival and strengthening of the cause would depend in the final account.

A NEW INTERNATIONALISM?

Political scientist Sonia Alvarez has argued the case for the potential for collaboration between social movements and NGOs.[24] A professor at the University of California, Santa Cruz, Alvarez researched the women's movement in Brazil in the 1980s, and she later took a three-years' leave to work in Rio de Janeiro for the Ford Foundation. These experiences are the basis for her examination of alliances between social movements, Latin American NGOs, and international funders, around such causes as stopping domestic violence and getting water and electricity to shantytowns. Alvarez coins the label "movement webs" for these connections woven across borders of nationality and also race, class, and education through funding, meetings, conversation, and common, or at least related, conviction. It is her contention that these webs create an "alternative public sphere" for visions and voices otherwise shut out of the media and the halls of state. As evidence of their role in Brazil, she points to the protagonism of a coalition of social movements from shantytowns and the countryside along with NGOs in the 1992 mobilization to impeach the corrupt president Fernando Collor.

I am attracted to Alvarez's thinking. Her view refuses to jettison a belief in the value of mobilization by indigenous peoples, women, slum dwellers, peasants, victims of human rights abuse, and other marginalized groups. At the same time, it moves beyond the romanticism that imagines such mobilization in the Third World can by itself remake the world. Instead of insisting on the spontaneity or autonomy of politics anywhere, the concept of the "movement web" recognizes that social movements in a global world will always be tied into far-reaching networks of power and meaning, and it accepts and embraces border crossing in political activism. When Witness for Peace in North Carolina raises money for a Mexican NGO to support the return of Mayan refugees to Guatemala or the Peace Brigades from Germany and Holland "accompany" Colombian human rights activists twenty-four hours a day to deter death squads, links are forged between First World and Third World, NGOs and social movements, and middle classes and the poor. Alvarez hopes that these kinds of pluriethnic, multiclass, and transnational alliances will fortify agendas of accountability, respect, and social justice.

A closer look at NGOs and the rondas, however, forces caution about the talk of a new internationalism. An obvious problem in northern Peru was manipulation and even dishonesty on the part of some NGOs. The Manuel González Prada Institute in Chota had funding from the Danish government to do agricultural extension work through the rondas.[25] Although the director insisted to me that the institute served "all peasants regardless of their beliefs," the truth was that it was closely tied to Red Homeland. Funding for irrigation projects and other benefits only went to villagers loyal to that Maoist party. At least in this and several other cases, an NGO became a vehicle of political patronage, and exhibited what seemed to me an unsavory juxtaposition of the declaration of inclusiveness with the reality of a highly partisan agenda. Sometimes dishonesty was more direct. An NGO in the city of Cajamarca ran a so-called Peasant School with courses in farming, organizing, the environment, and other social issues. It recruited students through the rondas as part of what the director told me was a commitment "to principles of honesty and respect for popular movements." Yet I learned later that this well-known agronomist had given the father of the Peruvian vice-director of the Lima office of a major American aid group a phantom job in the school at a full salary. It was a quid pro quo for the vice-director's continued support for funding the Peasant School and the NGO. In fairness, staffer idealism and supervision of international funders prevented corruption from ever becoming pervasive or commonplace. In the poverty and turmoil of 1980s Peru, though, the commonplace that "the smart live off the stupid" was hardly an abstract proposition.[26] The most ostensibly progressive NGOs were not immune to the graft and bribery rampant in the rest of the society.

Not that villagers always acted in complete good faith toward the NGOs. I remember a trick played in Tunnel Six on the Center for Rural Issues (CAR).[27] This Piuran NGO had Dutch grant money for health clinics, meeting halls, and other public buildings in the northern Andes. Villagers had to make adobe bricks, and build the structures. Tunnel Six ronda leaders applied for a health clinic. It was agreed that Tunnel Sixers would make 1,000 bricks, at which point CAR would come to check on the brick making and survey the proposed site. A month later, CAR was about to come. No bricks had yet been made. Víctor Córdova and other ronda leaders worried they would lose the money for the roof. They hatched a plan. Manuel Guerrero was making mud bricks to extend his farmhouse. They would show these to CAR, saying they were for the health clinic. On getting back from a morning soccer game in the town of Paimas, I wondered why Víctor and other straw-hatted villagers were showing Manuel Guerrero's bricks to two CAR staffers who had arrived on motorcycle. Only later did someone explain what had happened. The two NGO staffers were fooled. "Very good, you've made excellent progress" said the project head. The tin sheeting was delivered the next week, but the clinic was never built, since Víctor and the other ronda leader were never able to get their fellow villagers to agree on a brick-making schedule. Eventually, Tunnel Sixers divvied up the rusting tin with a sheet per family, a useful supplement to plug leaky tile and straw roofs, yet nonetheless not the way they had promised CAR to put the sheeting to use.

The invitation of collaboration from an NGO could also be rebuffed altogether by the rondas. In 1986 I met a group of students, social workers, and sociologists from Lima's National Engineering University (UNI) in the town of Ayabaca. They were young leftists who liked the Kjarkas, Che Guevara, and socialist Cuba and Nicaragua; their plan was to go village by village, to talk about the reasons for discrimination and want.[28] It was a bid to put into practice Paulo Freire's concept of "conscientization." The famous Brazilian educator argued that through dialogue and self-reflection the poor could come to recognize and act against injustice. According to this model in vogue among progressives throughout Latin America in the 1980s, the NGO should not be teacher and expert, but catalyst and facilitator, encouraging what Freire called "actual experimentation with a truly liberating education."[29] Although the model was condescending in assuming villagers lacked a "critical consciousness," it was not implausible to think some good could come out of discussing common problems. The related idea of "consciousness-raising" groups was certainly an important part of other struggles, among them the women's movement in the United States. Unfortunately, however, it was the first time in the Andes for many of the young Limans from UNI. Their unfamiliarity with rural slang and the lay of the land made it hard for them to communicate with villagers, or with the ronda leaders they hoped would promote discussion sessions. Like most of Peru's universities at the time, UNI was a radical stronghold, and chiefs of the APRA party in the province suspected the project was a cover for the United Left. They spread the story that the Limans were campaigning for the left, or perhaps even that they were Shining Path terrorists. If UNI had free food or anything else to distribute, they might have persuaded villagers at least to show up for meetings, but they barely had enough from the university and a German grant to cover bus fares from Lima. Attendance was sparse, sometimes nil. The project shut down at the end of 1986. This case showed how commitment by outsiders to a more democratic view of development was no guarantee of village response.

The most disheartening outcome of NGO involvement could be to weaken the rondas. Sociologist John Gitlitz details damage in the Bambamarca Valley.[30] To improve the potato harvest, an NGO called PRODIA set up groups in 1990 to receive technical advice and guarantee the payback of the improved seed it distributed to villagers. The ronda association in the district of Frutillo saw the success in raising production among the selected groups. It demanded that PRODIA work through the association. A number of villagers in the groups set up by PRODIA resented the intrusion. The originally vigorous district ronda association was divided and weakened as a result. "Handing out aid is not support," one ronda activist told Gitlitz. "It makes people fight."[31]

The failures of NGO-ronda interaction stood out in the city of Cajamarca, home to the Federation of Rondas Campesinas of the Province of Cajamarca (FPRCC). The federation was founded and led by Gilberto Rojas.[32] He had lived in the city for many years, but still wore the peasant garb of poncho, llanques, and straw hat, a refusal to assimilate into urban ways. When Robin and I visited his little office on a dirt street at the edge of Cajamarca, he told a self-promoting but gripping story of his own journeys on foot across the Andes to organize the peasantry. "The villagers respect me," he concluded with a smile, "as the leader of the rondas everywhere in the northern Peru." It was easy to see how his persona as a villager and rap about the rondas' promoting appropriate, ecologically sound technology, fighting exploitation of the peasantry, and defending Andean culture could have attracted well-meaning leftists from Lima and abroad. Grants from a Peruvian NGO and a German aid group paid his salary and office rent.

We could see even from a brief visit that funding the FPRCC was a questionable proposition. A sign on the wall listed the price for resolving disputes. It was a dollar for a fight over land, fifty cents for a quarrel about a debt, and so forth. The office had become a paid tribunal with Rojas as judge, a mockery of the commitment to free, collective justice that was supposed to underlay the rondas. As we learned later in Cajamarca, many villagers were outraged that Rojas was pocketing money for making justice. It was at best an exaggeration for Rojas to have claimed to represent the most Cajamarcan rondas. The truth was that only a handful of the more than 200 villages in the province supported him and the FPRCC. Far from strengthening the rondas, the money from progressives in Lima and abroad bankrolled a leader regarded as illegitimate by the majority of villagers, obstructing the emergence of more representative and unified regional leadership.

A consequence of failed connection could be to reenforce mistrust between the country and the city. Among villagers in the northern Andes, a stance of suspicion toward the white, the educated, and the urban was long standing, and part of the reason for the negative reaction I had run up against when I moved into Tunnel Six in 1986. The imagined and real instances of NGO malfeasance fueled views of these organizations as just the latest in the line of evil-intentioned outsiders who were making a living off the peasantry: the conquistador, the landlord, the mineowner, the bureaucrat. Although the skepticism toward the NGOs was justified by history, it was not entirely fair, because many staffers were self-sacrificing activists genuinely dedicated to social change. Conversely, the cases of village manipulation and dishonesty led at least a handful of NGO staffers to lose their idealism about the peasantry, and to begin to echo the old stereotypes about the Andean poor as lazy, untrustworthy, and incapable. "I was wrong in thinking that peasants could ever change their lives," said one agronomist I met in the city of Cajamarca, who admitted frankly that he had kept his job in a village reforestation program only for lack of openings in the private sector. Literary critic Mary Pratt underlines that incomprehension, failed connections, and missed chances will always be perils of the "contact zones" between people divided by class, ethnicity, religion, and other social lines.[33] This was true of the meeting between villagers and NGOs in northern Peru in the 1970s and 1980s.

The denouement of the story of Gilberto Rojas did nothing to encourage a more hopeful view. I heard from friends in Cajamarca that his FPRCC had shut down less than a year after our visit. It had come out that Rojas kept wives in Cajamarca as well as in Lima and that they had joined together in a lawsuit against the putative ronda leader. To escape jail, Rojas somehow managed to get an airline ticket and visa to Sweden, and in 1991 he jetted out of Peru to make a new life in the wintery north country halfway around the world from his native Cajamarca.

RONDAS, NGOS, AND THE WEAVING OF WEBS

It would be wrong nonetheless to conclude that nothing good came from NGO engagement in the rondas. "Movement webs" will always have "snags" and "knots," acknowledges Sonia Alvarez, "exclusionary dynamics and uneven power flows."[34] What struck me as notable precisely in light of the obstacles were the positive aspects of the NGO-villager encounter. Far from justifying despair about alliances across racial, economic, and national borders, the work of NGOs made worthwhile contributions to the movement's fight against poverty and injustice in the 1980s, and perhaps even holds lessons worth remembering now more than a decade later.

One positive result was public works. When I visited a ronda assembly in 1991 in the Chotan village of Iraca Grande, many villagers rose to speak about the problem of water. Children were dying every year from worms, diarrhea, and dysentery from the polluted Chota River. Was there no way to get money to run water from a mountain spring to farmhouses below? I was asked. I knew the Lima office of an NGO funded by Lutheran World Relief gave cement, iron, and tubing for water projects in rural areas. The group agreed to give Iraca Grande $2,000. The ronda president and the lieutenant governor joined forces to organize villagers to build a concrete collection box, and to pipe the water to every farmhouse. The result was an interlinkage in which money from U.S. parishes funded a Peruvian NGO to enable a Chotan village to meet a fundamental human need.

The symmetry between compelling need and corresponding resources was rarely so strong. One sticking point was that NGO aid did not always match rural priorities. For example, television was not part of the commitment of aid groups to health, farming, and education, and yet for better or worse many villagers wanted to be able to watch *Natacha, The Simpsons,* and World Cup soccer.[35] I found myself explaining at one meeting in the village of Tazajeras in Piura that they were unlikely to find an outside funder to pay for a satellite dish. As controller of the purse strings, the NGO had the final say over what counted as "needs" and in this sense reenforced, even flaunted, the power of staffers over villagers.

Yet the success of Iraca Grande was not an isolated case. Many villagers wanted running water, latrines, clinics, assembly halls, libraries, and other initiatives that NGOs were willing to fund. Although there were plenty of tales of overambitious and failed projects, many NGOs were savvy enough to check out those who came forward to ask for money, and to maintain a system of monitoring and accountability to prevent abuse.[36] The balance of successful collaboration included construction of an assembly hall with support for the roofing from CEPESER in Piura, a trail built in Lingán Pata with cement from the Jorge Basadre Institute, a library in San José with books donated by DAS, and dozens of other projects. The villagers of the Andes had never been able to count on the government to provide basic services. As a way to get running water, sewage, and the other amenities of modernity, many villagers seized NGO funding, and completed projects to improve in a small way their quality of life.

A second and perhaps more innovative area of NGO-ronda cooperation lay in education and communication. As part of a concern on the Peruvian left fueled by the Freirian emphasis on grounding learning in the poor's experiences, a number of NGOs were formed in Lima to produce materials for workers and peasants, experimenting with children's books set in the countryside for Andean kids, oral histories of rural struggles, and pamphlets explaining new laws affecting villagers. These NGOs were staffed by smart, young, and university-educated leftists of the kind who lived in the bohemian seaside district of Barranco, and who on Saturday nights frequented the avant-garde Yuyachkani theater and underground rock clubs. By cobbling together funding from the Ford Foundation, Ox-fam International, and European charities and governments, they paid for offices, modest salaries, and printing costs, and put to use their skills in photography, video, art, graphic design, media, and education.

A pair of these NGOs jumped into the rondas in the early 1980s. By sending two young staffers to Chota in 1983, ILLA gathered material and interviews for a pamphlet about the rondas in Cajamarca. It described the movement in simple Spanish with photographs and cartoons. Two thousand copies were distributed to Chotan villagers. An NGO with ties to the Catholic Church, SER, put out a publication about the rondas by a parish priest based on his village interviews in the Bambamarca Valley. The booklet featured the drawings of the village artist José Espíritu Tafur from Cumbe-Chontabamba. SER also published features on the rondas in the free, creatively produced magazine called *Andenes* it published monthly for village readers. ILLA, SER, and later TAREA printed and distributed many other materials related to the rondas throughout the 1980s—fact sheets on laws affecting the rondas, collections of reprinted newspaper articles about the movement, pamphlets about the achievements of local committees, songbooks with ronda ballads, and posters announcing meetings. As an extension of the mission of promoting dialogue within and about the rondas, SER paid the way to Lima for dozens of ronderos for a workshop to discuss their movement's future.

The work of SER, ILLA, and TAREA posed questions: How would villagers and the rondas be portrayed in pamphlets? Which interviews would be included in histories about the movement? Which excluded? Should materials be made just for the countryside? Or ought the NGOs try to educate city audiences about the rondas,

TAREA's poster for the Piura Convention, 1986

too? The assumption of many NGO staffers that they were simply the "supporting" villagers belied the thorniness of the issues arising from media work with the rondas.

It was probably inevitable in the first place that NGOs would project their own vision of and for the peasantry into what they produced about the rondas. An example was an ILLA poster announcing a regional ronda meeting in Piura. It showed a pair of ronderos at night coming upon a stolen cow tethered to one of the thick ceibo trees typical of the region. One rondero was barefoot. The other wore sandals, and both were depicted with ponchos, saddlebags, canes, broad-brimmed hats, and exaggerated lips and eyebrows. The folk primitivism emanated from the young Liman designer's view of a peasantry tied to custom, the past, the land, and a quaint way of life no longer to be found in the city. Such an understanding did not fit the self-image of one Huancamban villager I spoke with about the poster. "I don't like it all because it makes us look like primitives—big lips, no shoes." The majority of villagers were no longer ashamed of their calloused hands, ponchos, straw hats, and other markers of belonging to the peasantry.

Yet some peasants had internalized enough of a white standard of modernity and beauty not to want their own traditionalism or non-Western features to be exaggerated. As anthropologists have learned many times over from attacks on their work by those they study, the objects of representation may rebel against the way they are portrayed. The commitment of ILLA and other groups to the rondas did not exempt them from backtalk by villagers displeased with the way they were depicted by outsiders.

This is not to say that giving peasants the power to portray themselves was a simple solution. The 1980s brought a growing U.S. and European interest in testimonial literature, or *testimonios,* the first-person accounts from the colonized and downtrodden in Latin America. These books aimed to allow the oppressed to speak directly to a global audience.[37] Yet observers note that the genre never simply expressed the "voice of the people," as one advocate too easily claimed.[38] After all, the publication of a testimonio depended on a sympathetic, middle-class collaborator taking the initiative to tape-record, transcribe, edit, and find a publisher: the Venezuelan anthropologist Elisabeth Burgos-Debray for *I, Rigoberta Menchú: An Indian Woman in Guatemala,* the Brazilian journalist Moema Viezzer in *Let Me Speak!: Testimony of Domitila, a Woman of the Bolivian Mines,* and so forth. In this sense, outsiders retained a power to choose who would be permitted to speak, as well as to decide what part of their story would be included in the final product. The promoters of testimonios were leftists. It is not surprising that these intellectuals and journalists chose to work with Indians and peasants whose radical views mirrored their own, excluding the stories of the apathetic, the middle-of-the-road, and the conservative in their quest to show a Latin America rising in rebellion.

For their part, the subjects of the books often claimed to be speaking for their entire people. "I'd like to stress that this is not only my life," said Rigoberta Menchú on her famous account's very first page, "it's also the testimony of my people." The truth was that more conservative Mayans would not have agreed with the young activist in her support for the guerrillas, backing for liberation theology, and other positions. To raise the question of representativity in testimonios is not to doubt the value of this genre that gives the marginalized a platform for their views. It does mean avoiding the assumption that any subaltern group will ever be so homogeneous that a single member can entirely represent the rest. Because Mayans and others seldom, if ever, concur about politics or anything else, the project of making available to them the means of self-representation is less likely to close debate about who will speak for whom about Latin America than to expand and enliven it still further.

The trickiness of opening a forum for ronderos to represent themselves was exemplified in the making of a film called *Los ronderos*. It was initiated by ILLA and an expatriate Norwegian staffer in that Liman NGO. Marianne Eyde had become fascinated with the rondas on a 1983 trip she made to Chota. She thought a movie ought to be made about the movement. Eyde wanted this to be a peasant film, a chance for Chotan villagers to interpret the ronda for themselves and perhaps a larger audience in the rest of Peru. At her request, the president of the Provincial Federation of Rondas Campesinas of Chota, Oscar Sánchez, wrote the screenplay. Songs written and performed by village musicians made up the soundtrack. The actors were local peasants. *Los ronderos* was filmed in two weeks, mostly in the village of Colpa Matara just above Chota. It stuck to a simple, melodramatic plot that showed ronderos overcoming the opposition of nasty policemen to triumph over rustlers. The only parts not played by villagers were those of the policemen, which fell to schoolteachers, all of them members of the Marxist-controlled teacher's union. In real life, the majority of the teachers viewed policemen as bad guys who upheld the capitalist order; in the movie, they played the roles with obvious relish, kicking dogs and torturing innocent peasants, a bit of revenge for being on the receiving end of police billy clubs at so many demonstrations. *Los ronderos* premiered in 1986 in the Chota municipal auditorium and ran for several months in theaters in Trujillo and Lima.

The film allowed a group of peasants to craft their own vision of the rondas. What they fashioned in their collaboration with Eyde talked back to the negative stereotypes of the movement as bloodthirsty and lawless. In this sense, *Los ronderos* was an "auto-ethnography" in one literary critic's definition of the term, namely, "an appropriation of idioms of the metropolis," the movie in this case, to make a statement in which villagers undertook "to describe themselves in ways that engage[d] with representations that others have made of them."[39] Yet a number of their fellow villagers gave a thumbs-down review. The man with the best claim to starting the rondas, Régulo Oblitas, disliked *Los ronderos* so much that he once brought it up on his own in his native Cuyumalca. "Doctor," he opined, "the movie was full of falsehoods, because it didn't show how the rondas began." Whereas Oblitas objected because *Los ronderos* did not say anything about what he believed to be his own role as ronda founder, Fredesvindo Huanambal, the APRA party's point man in Cuyumalca, disliked it on political grounds. Eyde was a socialist, and Oscar Sánchez and the other villagers she chose to work with were mostly members of Red Homeland, the bitter rivals of the more centrist APRA in the Chota Valley. "They only let Communist villagers be in the movie," complained Huanambal, "and not those of us who might have been better actors." Eyde's initiative was a welcome challenge to the presumption of the unilateral right of and even duty of anthropologists, politicians, and other middle-class city people to speak for villagers. At the same time, it underlined that the urgent project of democratizing the rights of representation would hardly end conflict about the rondas within the peasantry. "*Los ronderos*," concluded Huanambal, "was the worst movie I've ever seen."

I think that NGO labors in communication and education were valuable in spite of the complaints. The ILLA poster was tacked to the doors and walls of innumerable farmhouses in the Piuran mountains. Not only was the poster free, but plenty of villagers liked and even encouraged a mythologization of themselves and their rondas as connected to tradition and ancestral ties to the land; and, at any rate, the Lima designer did have ronderos carrying flashlights, a mark of modernity. If anything, the ronda drawings by Cumbe-Chontabamba's José Espíritu Tafur were more primitivist than anything done by a city NGO, a reflection of what can be called a kind of self-folklorization tied to pride in the imagined and real distinctiveness of rural life. Although *Los ronderos* was controversial, the number of villagers to object to the movie was actually limited. I met hundreds of peasants who enjoyed watching a story so closely tied to their own experience. Meanwhile, NGO fact sheets about ronda legality became a resource for local leaders defending the cause to other villagers and townspeople. NGO-produced pamphlets about local rondas, songbooks of ronda musicians, and oral histories featuring ronda activists were used by rural schoolteachers to teach children about the movement, which was never mentioned in official textbooks. A sense of the importance of being a rondero was necessary for the movement's survival. However, ronda coverage in the newspaper much less on radio and TV was minimal, and the mainstream media often ignored the Andes to focus on the latest from Lima and abroad. By making a film, distributing a booklet, or doing a radio story on a local committee as in the case of Radio Cutivalú with Tunnel Six, the NGOs recognized ronda achievement, and added to the movement's luster. What the NGOs produced heightened the aura of value and dignity that the rondas had to maintain to continue mobilizing the peasantry.

Los ronderos and other projects sometimes encouraged new ways of thinking. I discovered that although contact with Andean realities led a handful of staffers simply into cynicism, other NGO workers learned from the experience in good ways, losing their edge of romanticism about peasants while increasing their appreciation for beauty and courage in village society. "I can see villagers now as more than cardboard cutouts," one staffer reflected to me in 1991, "and this will only make the work I do in the future better." Conversely, the materials made by the NGOs could give villagers new ideas. Víctor Córdova and others in Tunnel Six got the concept of a women's committee from reading about it in a pamphlet about the Chota rondas. *Los ronderos* showed ronderos working together on communal projects, and the committee president in Huancambamba cited the movie in persuading villagers to work together to roof a sick widow's house. It seemed to me in these and other moments that NGO work sped a flow of knowledge and information between ronderos that enriched the movement.

NGO involvement in media and communication had an additional dividend, namely, in educating city people about the rondas. It had been the goal primarily to provide materials that could be used by villagers to learn more about their movement. Yet the materials found an audience beyond the countryside. Although *Los ronderos* was the closest the NGOs came to reaching a mass audience, the booklets and other publications sometimes came to be used in town high schools and even university classes as well as consulted by journalists and scholars. Little had been written about the rondas in the early 1980s, besides brief swipes in conservative tabloids at their supposed radicalism. The publications of SER,

TAREA, and ILLA gave city people their first more sympathetic and informed view of the movement.

A final and related contribution of NGOs was to defend the rondas against government suppression. Although I have argued that the role of NGOs in funding projects and producing educational materials was worthwhile, it was a form of working "down," of middle-class people going out to help the rural poor. Yet the reasons for the peasantry's plight clearly did not just rest in the village. There had to be more rural investment by the government, a willingness to include the peasantry in policymaking, and other measures to offer the opportunity and participation denied in the past. Anthropologist Kamala Visweswaran makes a useful distinction between "fieldwork" and "homework" that applies to an NGO role in influencing policies affecting the peasantry.[40] "Fieldwork" suggests a trip away from the university, the city, the middle and upper classes, and the West. In anthropology, it has gone along with the convention of "studying down," the history of making "natives" and "peasants" into the only object of study for the discipline. Visweswaran asserts that an increased emphasis on "homework" is crucial to rethinking anthropology. It demands that anthropologists expand their scope to study "across" and "up." Researching the corporation, the country club, the shopping mall, the private school, the college classroom, and other institutions of middle class, urban, and elite life becomes part of a role for anthropology in unveiling and transforming the practices of the powerful in global society. Applying Visweswaran's thinking to the NGO would mean staffers' moving beyond just "fieldwork" with the slum dweller, poor farmer, or rain forest Indian to try to educate, pressure, and transform the attitudes and policies of the bureaucrats, businesspeople, and the professional and ruling classes. As part of a flexible and wide-ranging vision of engagement that would work "up" and "across" as well as "down," the NGO would militate for change in the boardroom and the village, the suburb and the shantytown, and the United States, Europe, and Latin America.

Several NGOs did "homework" in this sense when they sought to force the government to respect ronda rights. The story of Segundo Torres exemplified the possibilities and achievements of this dimension of the NGO's work with the rondas. A jaunty, likable native of the village of La Succha in Cutervo Valley, Torres was well

Segundo Torres at the radio station, before his arrest, Cutervo, 1991.

known as the "rondero announcer" for hosting a weekly local radio program of huayno ballads, ronda activities, and national news. He was arrested by the police on the night of January 24, 1993, on his way back to town from a ronda meeting. I had met Torres in 1991. He described what happened in a letter from jail in 1993: "They held me for two weeks, interrogating me constantly to try to force me to confess to being a 'terrorist,' and beating with me sticks, iron bars, and using electric shocks from a car battery. They broke three of my ribs, and yet still I have not seen a doctor or had any medical assistance."

There was no evidence to suggest Torres had any connection to the Shining Path. The main reason for the arrest was the ronda activist's on-the-air criticism of police corruption. Although the rondas had been legalized in 1986, the government was not ready to allow the movement to become a forum for dissent and criticism, especially with the clampdown on free speech under the government of Alberto Fujimori. Guerrero and more than twenty other ronderos were jailed under a new Antiterrorism Law that restricted the access of anyone charged to legal defense and a fair trial. The government sent them to the violent, tubercular jail of Piccsi in the burning desert on the plain of Lambayeque, where they awaited trials by faceless military courts that denied the accused the right to full defense, and sentenced the majority of those who came before them to life in prison.

The intervention of NGOs secured the release of Guerrero and most of the other jailed villagers. At least a half-dozen human rights organizations had formed in Lima in the 1980s in response to escalating torture, disappearance, and massacre by the military and the Shining Path. The Association for the Protection of Human Rights (APRODEH) and the Institute for Legal Defense (IDL) led a national and international campaign to free the innocent in Piccsi and other prisons and to repeal the Antiterrorism Law. They encouraged Peruvian and foreign journalists to write stories about the plight of the imprisoned; provided the falsely accused with free legal counsel and money to support their families; and sent out information by mail, e-mail, fax, and phone to human rights groups in the United States and Europe. The Fujimori government desperately wanted to rebuild Peru's image to revive tourism and investment that had just about come to a standstill by the end of the 1980s. It did not want bad publicity through the cases of Torres and others. After more than a year in jail, Torres and almost all the other ronderos were freed in 1994. A year later, Fujimori revoked the harshest provisions of the Antiterrorism Law, even though some innocents remain in jail to this day. The partial success of pressure for the respect for human rights illustrated the value of "working up" for change, in this case APRODEH and the IDL's direct influence on the Peruvian authorities as well as transnational mobilization with North American human rights and solidarity groups to force the United States to pressure the Fujimori government.

Segundo's release showed the potential of "movement webs." Although there were protests in the Andes against the arrest and torture of Segundo and other leaders, the rondas alone did not have the regional or national organization to force the government to free the prisoners. It took the transnational, multiclass, cross-professional, and interreligious alliance of the men's families, ronda activists, leftist journalists, priests and pastors, and Peruvian and U.S. and European human rights groups. The alliance's ecumenicism could be read as an indicator of impurity by those questing for the grail of autonomy and the autochthonous in the Andean or the grassroots. It is true that the work of human rights NGOs in Peru was not always unassailable, and perhaps too often fell into overcautiousness, inefficiency, and bureaucratization, among other limitations. Nonetheless I still see the defense of ronda leaders as an example of how networks that link the local, the national, and the global can engage and sometimes even make inroads in the struggle for social justice. Once freed, Segundo and the other men returned to the Andes, in many cases reassuming leadership posts in ronda committees, and the day-to-day challenges of running patrols and administering justice. The capacity to organize locally was secured by and sometimes dependent on linkages between villages in the Andes, the offices of APRODEH in downtown Lima, and the cubicles of Human Rights Watch–Americas inside the Washington Beltway.

It should be apparent that NGOs were important to ronda survival and strength. As I look back on Peru of the 1980s, it strikes me that NGOs were part of what kept the country from going over the abyss into the devastation of absolute chaos. Their support for the rondas as well as for feminist organizing, shantytown politics, indigenous federations, and other social movements was never free of conflict and contradiction. Still the economic crisis and the bankruptcy of political parties made the NGO into one of the few functioning sectors of the country that provided a thread of resources, ideas, and hope. The "movement webs" of which NGOs and the rondas formed a part were the closest approximation in Peru of that time to a civil society with a meaningful vision of participation and change.

There was little doubt that Segundo Torres was glad for the NGOs. After his release from Piccsi, he returned to Cutervo. It was not going to be easy to rebuild an interrupted life. Gossip persisted that he was a guerrilla. His plot of land in La Succha was just a hectare, and he made only a few dollars from returning to his weekly radio show. Prison left him weak, and his ribs never properly healed from the police beating. He remained happy to be free, and grateful for what APRODEH and the IDL had done on his behalf. "I'm facing terrible circumstances," he wrote to me in 1994, "but now out of prison can at least live again like a real human being."

BACK ACROSS THE DESERT

It would be wrong to generalize about NGOs on the basis of their work with the rondas in the 1980s and early 1990s. Even then, many organizations remained wedded to a more top-down view of development, never trying to coordinate or consult with those they wanted to help. The last years of the century have accelerated NGO growth throughout Latin America. Although the great majority of NGOs in the 1980s had ties in one way or another to the political left, this is no longer the case. Conservative political parties, right-wing Catholics and evangelicals, and even drug lords and paramilitary groups have set up NGOs a decade later.[41] The bewildering mix of ideologies, objectives, working styles, social composition, and funding sources makes it wrongheaded to pronounce in the abstract "for" or "against" the NGO.

The 1990s, moreover, showed how NGOs could metamorphize into a threat to rural organizing. As the power of social movements waned in Peru, many NGOs were no longer attracted by the possibility of working with the rondas, and ignored them altogether in their work to improve Andean life. Sociologist John Gitlitz argues from research in the Bambamarca Valley that these projects sometimes made a "valuable contribution" by "providing drinking water, improving potato harvests, reforesting hillside." At the same time, he thinks they winnowed "people away from a commitment to their communities" and in particular from patrolling and assemblies. Gitlitz concludes that NGO projects posed a "serious problem for the rondas."[42]

The bypassing of the rondas points to a more recent trend toward the depoliticization of NGOs across Latin America. Although NGOs remain diverse in philosophy and purpose, the talk prevails in many organizations of "microcredit," "infrastructure improvement," and "technical training" and too seldom about the problem of justice and equity in a region where the poor's predicament remains as desperate as ever. "Development" entailed diminishing the gap between rich and poor, encouraging multiculturalism, and perhaps achieving socialism to Marianne Eyde and other NGO workers involved in the rondas. The new breed of NGOs understand their mission to be fostering entrepreneurship and the gospel of self-reliance and competition. In this sense, many NGOs are not involved in encouraging dissent as they were in the 1980s, and to the contrary in manufacturing consent to the vision of free trade and the market. The distinction between "governmental" and "nongovernmental" has even occasionally blurred, with the formation of semiofficial organizations to carry out development projects. Pundits now talk about "GONGOS" (government-organized nongovernmental organizations) and "BONGOS" (bank-organized nongovernmental organizations).

It was hard to predict the future of the relation between the rondas and NGOs. SER, TAREA, ILLA, and other NGOs prominent in the rondas survived into the mid-1990s, and continued their work with movements at the grass roots, including in northern Peru. Even though they have become a minority in the sector, other Latin American NGOs throughout Latin America remain committed to involvement in organizing for change, especially those committed to women's issues, indigenous rights, and the environmental activism. The decline of Marxism and trade unionism in the new world order of the 1990s makes it difficult and almost unfashionable for anyone to organize around economic justice and the plight of the poor. However, there are Peruvian NGOs such as the Association for Development (ADEC) that prioritize the issues of job security and wages. These NGOs link up with the U.S. activist and church groups an alliance called the Peru Peace Network that fought among other causes for the IMF and World Bank to provide debt relief, one obstacle to social welfare in Peru and other Third World countries.

It does seem beyond doubt that "movement webs" will remain a feature of today's world. As anthropologist Arjun Appadurai has underlined, the scale of "postnational" political mobilization has increased dramatically in recent years, an expansion of organizing that "transcend[s] the border of the nation-state."[43] The "post" may be misleading, in the sense that nation-states have survived and even prospered in the age of globalization. Yet instantaneous communication, jet travel, migration, and the other hallmarks of global modernity have certainly made trans-, if not post-, national types of protest mobilization into a commonplace. It is no longer realistic or possible, if it ever was, to imagine that a "movement" can be bounded and self-enclosed any more than a "culture" or "society" in an evermore interconnected world. To be sure, border crossing is never a priori a mark of the subversive, the emancipatory, or the politically progressive; to the contrary, it may be connected to any political project from the worthy to the horrifying. To take just one example, recent research shows how ultraconservative and neo-Nazi groups in the United States, Great Britain, and Germany have established connections through cyberspace and international meetings to forge a "movement web" for white supremacy and hatred. The story of U.S. and European funders, Peruvian NGOs, and the rondas is all the more important in this light. It reminds us of the possibility and the imperative to press border crossing to more ennobling ends, and the potential for far-reaching networks of solidarity and support to fortify initiatives for peace and justice that come from below.

I think back to the visit of CIPCA and Radio Cutivalú to Tunnel Six. It displayed the most encouraging and human side of the connection between NGOs and villagers, the establishment of personal and institutional ties that might strengthen the rondas. After their interview, Mercedes invited Francisca and Angélica to come to visit in Piura, and Angélica gave the Spaniard a saddle blanket as a present. Víctor, the ronda president, asked whether Radio Cutivalú could announce an upcoming meeting of village ronda committees in the Quiroz Valley, and Mercedes also promised to do this. The other reporter from the station, Pepé, pulled out a guitar. He and three Tunnel Sixers formed an impromptu quartet to sing the Ecuadorian San Juanitos that were so popular in the scrub brush hills near the border. The visitors from Piura stayed far beyond the hour of four o'clock, when they had planned to leave, until at last we said good-byes and the jeep bumped away into the dusk on the journey back across the desert.

SIX

Leaders and Followers

I met Francisco Chuquihuanga at a 1986 ronda meeting in the cockfighting arena in the town of Ayabaca. A gangly, enthusiastic man in his twenties, he had told the story of being beaten up by police who were intent on breaking up the ronda in his home village of Ambulco, of which he was the committee president. As I was then just starting to search for a place to study the rondas, I introduced myself to Chuquihuanga, and asked if I could visit him in Ambulco. It turned out that the young leader was returning to his village the next day, and he invited me to come with him.

We set out at dawn on horseback. The trail snaked up and down across the canyon of the Aragoto River, through a rain forest filled with chattering parrots and the crumbling walls of the pre-Columbian fortress of Aypate, and below gigantic peaks shrouded in mist. Literary critic Mary Pratt attacks accounts by nineteenth-century European travelers in the Andes of a breathtaking world of untamed nature and ancient mystery, a "dehistoricized celebration of primal America" that ignored the "powerful everyday realities" of exploitation and poverty.[1] Still, I could see how Alexander von Humboldt and others in Romanticism's heyday had been carried away by the Andes. The landscape really was remarkable in size, texture, and the ruins of bygone civilizations.

Ambulco was a scattering of forty or so farmhouses just below crags by the border with Ecuador. Francisco and his wife, Indolfa Llacsahuache, lived in a thatch-roofed hovel with a dirt floor patrolled by an army of guinea pigs. The couple ate for dinner on most nights the mealy potatoes they grew. In my honor, Chuquihuanga had bought a pound of rice and a can of sardines in town. We ate by the light of the unofficial lamp of the cash-strapped

Andean peasantry, a tin can filled with kerosene stuffed with rag for a wick. In the cold at 12,000 feet, after a long day, the hardscrabble meal was a feast.

Then Francisco told his saga as the ronda committee president. A part of an Ambulco hacienda was never divided in the reform of 1969. The son of the mayordomo kept fifty hectares, thirty-five above the maximum of fifteen allowed by the law. After Francisco, backed by most of the village, pressed for dividing the excess among the more needy, the landholder complained at the little station of the Republican Guard on a pass by the border.[2] Four of these policemen came to Chuquihuanga's farmhouse after midnight. They dragged him from bed, then beat him senseless with their rifle butts. They told the terrified Indolfa they would kill her husband if he pursued the land division. The beating led other Ambulcans to back away. Indolfa could not get anyone to chip in for Francisco's doctor bills. Francisco showed me the shirt he was wearing on the night of the beating, caked brown with his blood. He said he was thinking about resigning from the ronda presidency because of the lack of backing from other villagers.

I would have stayed in Ambulco. It had a lonely beauty with the crags and a sky the color of steel. I liked and admired Francisco with his sincerity and tale of sacrifice. At the same time, the ronda's disrepair seemed to make Ambulco the wrong place to study the movement, or so I thought without having read new scholarship that suggests it can be just as revealing to examine why people choose not to join or stay in a movement as why they do.[3] I left my address in Lima and the United States for Francisco and Indolfa, made them a present of my Swiss Army Knife and Mini-Mag flashlight, and rode back across the Andes to Ayabaca.

Francisco's tale fit a pattern in the northern mountains, namely, the downfall of the ronda leader. Every ronda committee had a president picked by villagers from their own ranks. The choice was usually among the most well-liked and respected of village men. Yet as often as not their tenure ended unhappily. Some were so overwhelmed by the duties of what was, after all, an unpaid job that they resigned, or refused a second term. Villages ousted others for real or imagined sins of favoritism or corruption. Sociologist John Gitlitz found that by the mid-1990s in the Bambamarca Valley many villages had trouble finding anyone to take the job.[4] "It's a thankless post that's nothing but trouble and ingratitude," one man there explained to me in 1993.

This chapter examines leadership in the rondas. Studies of rural organizing have sometimes overlooked or willfully ignored the topic of authority and command within a mobilization, perhaps in part because the impulse of outsiders to see cooperation and solidarity as a hallmark of village society can discourage the examination of cleavage and hierarchy. The label of a "peasant movement" itself can conjure a picture of union and horizontal comradeship that may overlook conflict between followers and leaders.[5] I was so intent on showing the achievement in my 1989 dissertation that I said little about the often ugly rifts about leadership—the resentment of committee presidents about lack of backing from the rest of the village, the danger of their turning into caudillos, the absence of effective regional leadership. It would be just as hard to guess at any of these tensions from those studies by Peruvian scholars that depict the rondas as a paragon of equality and democracy.[6]

I hope to make amends in this chapter. It opens by examining leadership in the village. The phenomenon of the "fallen leader" reflected the difficulty, perhaps impossibility, of reconciling opposed visions of leadership in the northern countryside. The ronda president was entrusted with a heavy burden of responsibilities that included running the patrols, receiving complaints, directing the assemblies, and representing the ronda to the government. At the same time, the experience of domination and betrayal fostered a deep suspicion of hierarchy and command of any kind. The combination of limited authority and huge responsibility was too great, even for the mostly honest and even heroic leaders. Many withdrew or were exiled from the rondas as a result. I think of the line from one of the most famous chroniclers of rural poverty and union organizing in the United States. "They were ours and we exercised the right to destroy them," wrote John Steinbeck.[7]

The chapter moves on to examine leadership regionally. Why, I ask, did no strong or unified organization develop to represent the tens of thousands of ronderos in northern Peru? The problem was not a lack of pretenders. A fricassee of federations formed and fought to represent the rondas at the provincial and departmental level. By the 1990s, however, most were inactive or had disappeared altogether. The rondas became a collection of village committees without an umbrella organization. The failure of common feeling among the region's ronderos to translate into organization underscores obstacles to "scaling up" a rural movement to fight for regional and national change.

I saw Francisco again in 1987 in Tunnel Six. On his way down from Ambulco to look for a job on the coast, he passed by to visit, hearing that I was living there to do my ronda research. He told me that it was good that I had not stayed in Ambulco. When it was clear his fellow villagers would no longer support him against the big landlord, he had resigned, frustrated and fearful of being arrested again, perhaps killed this time. In this case the leader's fall meant the ronda's demise and the dissolution of the Ambulco committee. "There's nothing there now," said Francisco before heading down the path for Paimas to catch a pickup down to the city of Sullana.

THE LIMITS OF CHARISMA

Max Weber's classic analysis distinguished three types of authority and leadership.[8] The "traditional" power of the king or emperor derived from birthright. The electricity of a leader's personality underwrote "charismatic" command, and in particular the ability to convince followers of his own privileged purchase on the divine or the sacred.[9] "Legal" authority, more prosaically, came from appointment or election, and the statute and the law defined and regulated it. According to Weber's typology, modernity was supposed to end traditional and charismatic leadership, subjecting society to legal authority. The victory of the administrator over the prophet was not cause for celebration for the German sociologist. He saw power's rationalization as part of a "disenchantment of the world" that was forging the "iron cage" of bureaucracy and centralization in the modern west.

A pair of history's most famous leaders in the Peruvian Andes claimed a "traditional" authority derived from the Incas. Juan Santos Atahualpa took his name from the Inca executed by Pizarro in Cajamarca. In the jungles of Huánuco in 1742, he launched a rebellion that kept the Spanish at bay for a decade.[10] Later, José Gabriel Condorcanqui adopted the name of the last Inca, whom the Spanish had also killed. As Túpac Amaru II, the muleteer and chieftain led a war in 1780 to drive the colonizers back across the Atlantic and reestablish native rule. After his execution by quartering in 1781 in the plaza of Cuzco, the mystique of Túpac Amaru II was heightened by the telling and retelling of the myth of Inkarrí, prophesying the recomposition of the body of the executed rebel paired with the return of the Inca empire.

The image of the messianic leader became a standby in the way the Andes were imagined from Lima in later years. The early twentieth-century thinker Luis Valcárcel foretold the arrival of an "Indian Lenin" to bring "dignity to the Indian, that lord of the land, creation of the Andes, granite symbol of an immortal culture." Others in the 1920s and 1930s painted Túpac Amaru II as a symbol of the struggle for dignity in the Andes; later, leftist and sometimes rebel groups from 1960s onward took his name. "And they will not be able to kill him," declared a melodramatic poem by the mid-twentieth-century writer Alejandro Romualdo.[11] If this view saw Lima and "official Peru" as droning to bureaucracy and law, it correspondingly assumed that "deep Peru" of the Andes stirred to the excitement of violence and charisma. The irony of the growing fascination of Limans with Túpac Amaru II was that his memory was fading in the twentieth century among villagers in the Andes. As we saw from work by Degregori discussed in chapter 1, the myth of Inkarrí was ceding to the myth of progress, and to the hope for advancement through schools, roads, credit, and clinics. The concept of salvation through the great leader had waned in the twentieth-century Andes. No one from the mountains emerged as a spokesperson or leader of the same magnitude as Condorcanqui or Juan Santos Atahualpa, much less an "Indian Lenin."

This is not to say that something like charisma was absent in the rondas. Víctor was a case in point. At thirty-seven, the ronda president of Tunnel Six did not look the part of the magnetic, celluloid-style Indian chieftain of the films *Geronimo* or *Viva Zapata!* He had slumped shoulders and stringy hair, and he complained often of exhaustion. Although he told me their liaison was consensual, Víctor at twenty was convicted of the statutory rape of a teenager. Like those of a man on guard against being jumped from behind, his eyes remained wary under their droopy lids from five years in the earthly hell of the Piura prison. He loved to tell stories about

Víctor Córdova, Tunnel Six, 1987

the prison, the haciendas, and the rondas. As part of a pride born from surviving the haciendas and prison, Víctor usually cast himself in the starring role in these tales. "I told him" or "I showed him" punctuated his endless repertoire of stories about battles with thieves, policemen, and other malefactors.

Yet there could be no doubt about Víctor's skill as a leader. At the cusp of middle age, he was old enough to get along with the older generation that shared the experience of serfdom, yet young enough to take to the soccer field with the young blades in Tunnel Six. His enthusiasm for the rondas was boundless. It was a rare day that he did not spend hours hearing complaints, going over invitations to the ronda anniversary celebration, or traveling to another village on request to help form a committee there. His reputation led less-experienced presidents from nearby Culqui, Jambur, and other villages to come to Tunnel Six for advice. The rondas were a religion for Víctor, and he was the chief priest in the Quiroz Valley.

A basis of Víctor's power was his extraordinary gift as a talker. Like most children on Pillo, he did not know how to write, and only to read a little, because the owners, the Leighs, did not think serfs needed schooling. This did not stop him from communicating with depth and complexity, a contrast to the wrongheaded assumption that illiteracy and ignorance necessarily go together. Even when tinged with self-aggrandizement, many of his stories were masterpieces of humor and subtlety. Unlike a Juan Santos Atahualpa and a Túpac Amaru, Víctor had no interest in claiming real or imagined Incan blood, and certainly he entertained no illusions about the Incas returning. To the contrary, his hopes were grounded in a pragmatic, incremental view of the future. "Through the rondas" he liked to say, "we will organize to change things little by little." As he spun speeches at assemblies, Víctor blended self-awareness about village faults with denunciation of the injustice of national society. "All men are philosophers," the Italian Marxist Antonio Gramsci insisted in his famous prison notebooks.[12] Historian Steven Feierman carries this dictum to the countryside to speak of rural leaders in Zimbabwe as "peasant intellectuals."[13] Víctor was just such a figure, unschooled yet a wordsmith and thinker. Part of the pleasure that even cynical Tunnel Sixers took in listening to Víctor stemmed from pride that an uneducated child of Pillo from their own peasant stock spoke as well as any "Doctor" or "Engineer."

What struck me remained the limits on the ronda president. Weber depicted charisma's magic as absolute. A word from the leader was supposed to be enough to compel followers to kill or die for the cause. Nothing of the sort occurred with the ronda president. While most villagers liked to listen to Víctor or other accomplished speakers, they were hardly docile followers and ceded little personal power to their leaders. Quite the opposite: it was vital to a ronda president's survival not to appear to be too independent or self-important. To come across as anything more than a first among equals was to spawn talk about "egoism" and "selfishness." When Víctor, Eladio Idrogo, and other ronda presidents asked and even pleaded "What does the majority say?" they emphasized their desire to obey village will, not wanting to come off as thinking themselves better than anyone else. Sociologist James MacGregor Burns distinguishes between "transformational" and "transactional" leadership.[14] If the Andean rebel was supposed to have transformed followers by "raising them to a higher level of morality and motivation," the latter-day ronda president had the worldly job of fining those who dodged patrol duty and taking down complaints. Called for was an effective administrator, albeit one who also spoke eloquently enough to make villagers proud of having him as their representative. Marking the expected commitment to duty and obligation, the job was labeled a *cargo,* literally, "a burden."

What explains the restrictions placed on the local leader? Part of the answer lies in history. At least as early as the extortion carried out by Spanish administrators in the aftermath of the conquest, villagers had reason to associate authority with domination, and with an order that subjected the poor and the Indian to the whims of the powerful.[15] The prevalence in government of the educated and the middle-classes into the twentieth century reenforced an association many villagers made between politicians and their marginality in national life. The disastrous presidencies of Fernando Belaúnde Terry (1980–85) and Alan García (1985–90) only heightened distrust of government. Many villagers maintained the respect for office that came across in a love of honorifics such as "Mr. Subprefect" and "Mr. Police Commander" in their letters and speeches. At the same time, however, "the authorities" remained synonymous with domination and betrayal for most northern villagers in the 1970s and 1980s. "Justice is a fugitive in the village of Pampachiri, and the judge and governor are with the thieves" was the common view that one ballad declared.[16]

The 1980 changeover to democracy in Peru was a more specific influence on attitudes toward the local leader. By the Constitution of 1979 that sent the military back to the barracks, the illiterate voted for the first time. Each party's symbol appeared on the ballot so those who could not read could mark their choice: a star for the APRA, a banner for the United Left, a shovel for the Popular Action Party, and so forth. Because more than half of Andean villagers had been excluded until then by the literacy requirement, this marked a dramatic increase in rural involvement in elections, even more so because not voting was punishable by a fine. Now that they had the ballot, villagers became a target in campaigns. Mark this way or that, urged the graffiti on the walls of thousands of Andean towns. Candidates also forayed into the countryside to woo voters. During 1986 and 1987, Tunnel Six received visits from the APRA mayor of Paimas, Raúl Chávez, and United Left senator Andrés Luna Vargas, both seeking reelection. At just the moment of ronda expansion in the late 1970s and early 1980s, the culture of democracy was spreading, with talk in every village about "the vote," "the election," and "the democratic process."

This development fortified the demand for accountability from the ronda president. Like the Peruvian president, the village leader was elected, in this case by hand vote from candidates nominated at the assembly. The 1979 Constitution limited the president to one term. Many rondas did the same to prevent the accumulation of power. The increasing disappointment with those elected to serve in Lima only strengthened watchfulness at home. Tunnel Six's José Paz told me that "we don't want our leaders to behave like the crooks in Lima." As the hollowness of campaign promises was revealed by the end of the 1980s, many villagers painted their rondas as the only organizations upholding democracy. "The rondas are real democracy, where everyone has a voice," Paz added.

Ultimately, then, the expectation for a ronda president straddled the line between "charismatic" and "legal" authority. When an assembly sat spellbound by Víctor in the shadowy lunchroom lamplight, the hush reflected pleasure in having someone who connected the rondas to a higher promise of emancipation for the peasantry, and possessed the magic of oratory so linked to charisma. Yet they never granted the ronda president free rein. As a creature beholden to the vote of the assembly, he had the attributes of "legal" authority, and the duty of accountability to those that elected him. The followers wanted a visionary and administrator rolled together in the ronda president.

It was hard to live up to the standard. Víctor was born with and reveled in his ability to captivate a crowd. When I taped interviews with him about the rondas, he asked to borrow the little Sony to listen to himself on the cassettes, doing so alone in the bedroom of the farmhouse with narcissistic pleasure. The expectation of accountability and consultation was not so easy for the Tunnel Six president to meet. I heard grumbling about Víctor for mishandling

money from NGOs, claiming credit for starting the Tunnel Six rondas, and otherwise acting out of line with village will. Still, most
Tunnel Sixers thought he was doing a good job. It seemed to me
that Víctor would continue for many years in the job he loved so
much.

I was wrong.

LEADERSHIP'S BURDENS

The problem of leadership concerned U.S. feminists at the dawn
of the women's movement in the 1960s and 1970s. As Joreen Freeman pointed out in his 1973 work, many women were suspicious
toward authority of any kind, because they associated it with male
domination of politics and society. At the same time, Freeman insisted, structures of authority and responsibility were unavoidable
in any movement. To pretend otherwise threatened a "tyranny of
structurelessness" in which tension festered over leadership but was
never addressed because of the desire to maintain the mythology
of absolute equality and collectivity.[17] Freeman argued that for
this reason the challenge for social movements was not to abolish
leadership, but to rethink it in ways that maintained and promoted
values of accountability, participation and democracy.

It might have seemed that the rondas went a long way down
this road. Suspiciousness about authority limited the chance for a
president to turn into a ruler. Yet the rondas never pretended to
abolish hierarchy and authority, maintaining the offices of president and vice-president. When I visited Tunnel Six in 1993, the
number of positions on the ronda steering committee had multiplied to fifteen, including secretaries of sports, agrarian defense,
women's affairs, human rights, and press and propaganda. If social
movements must navigate between structurelessness and hierarchy,
the rondas appeared to be on a promising course.

I found much to admire in this setup. The president received
the honor of the title, and the rights of speaking first at the assembly, directing debate, closing the meeting, and representing the
committee in other villages and before the town authorities. The
checks on his authority, however, restrained the concentration of
power. The danger of bossism was obvious in Peru in the national
political parties, many of them run for years and even decades by

the same chieftain: Haya and APRA, Jorge del Prado and the Communist Party of Peru–Unity, Fernando Belaúnde and the Popular Action Party (AP), Javier Díez Canseco and the United Mariateguista Party, Luis Bedoya and the Popular Christian Party. Alberto Fujimori manipulated the Constitution with military backing to rule Peru for the century's last decade. No wonder so many villagers were proud of enforcing accountability and democracy in the rondas.

Yet the system placed tremendous strain on the ronda president. The work demanded was endless—sending out summons, organizing and attending assemblies, overseeing patrols, organizing anniversary celebrations, going to ronda meetings in other villages and at regional conventions, responding to charges against the rondas made with the police. The roster of secretaries in places such as Tunnel Six obscured the fact that the rest of the steering committee usually did little. Just about everyone with ronda business went straightaway to the committee president.

No one had less privacy than he in a countryside where the concept hardly existed in the first place. When a villager in Tunnel Six wanted to come by to chat or ask for a loan, it did not matter if it was three in the morning and I was asleep. "Don Raimundo." Pause. "Don Raimundo." The respectful yet insistent whispering would go on until I rousted myself from bed to open the door. Although I came to like the refusal to allow people ever to cordon themselves off, it went to extremes with the ronda head. I knew from staying with Víctor and later Eladio Idrogo that they were visited at all hours by villagers wanting to report a theft or land battle. If the ronda president tried to sleep through the paging, it escalated to whistling, knocking, or pebbles thrown on the roof. This was a twenty-four-hour job.

Money was another problem. Taking so big a job without any recompense was an expression of dedication to village welfare that cost a ronda president financially in a number of ways. Most obviously, the post left less time for attending to the farm. "Doctor, do you know how you can tell who owns the worst-kept fields in a village?" riddled one peasant in the Cutervan village of Santa Cruz. "The ronda president, because he never has time to weed them." Many leaders had to shell out their own scarce funds. Although villagers might agree at an assembly to pitch in for paper and carbon paper or truck fares to town to answer charges with the authorities, it was never easy to collect. Poverty bred stinginess in the northern Andes. Nobody wanted to part with even a dollar or two for the ronda. Víctor estimated he had used more than $100 of his own money on ronda business in 1986 alone.

The ronda president also had to put up with criticism. A belief in the danger of visibility in a jealous, treacherous world led most villagers to avoid public attacks. It was another matter altogether in conversation with relatives, friends, or even the anthropologist. Did the ronda president pilfer money from beer sales at the ronda anniversary? Was he taking the side of a compadre in a land dispute? Had he colluded with the district mayor to rally votes for the APRA Party? "Women are born to gossip," Apolinar García in Cuyumalca said, typifying the common gendering of the base pleasures of character assassination. The truth was that men were every bit as responsible for spreading rumor. The tale of imagined and real malfeasance of ronda presidents raced across the countryside as fast as on any computer bulletin board.

RUMOR AND THE SACRIFICE OF THE LEADER

Political scientist James Scott describes rumor as a "weapon of the weak." His argument is that publicly attacking people with money or power carries the risk of reprisal. This predicament encourages the downtrodden to opt for surreptitious opposition by gossip, dissimulated, feigned ignorance, pilfering, evasion, and character assassination. They become what Scott calls "small-arms fire . . . intended to mitigate or deny claims by superordinate classes."[18]

It was true that rumor could be valuable in checking ronda presidents. I think of the case of Víctor's predecessor as the committee leader in Tunnel Six. Martín Llacsahuache was one of six men to organize the patrol during the year of thievery and flooding in 1983. A hooked nose and thin black moustache gave this twenty-seven-year-old the look of a bad guy in a vaudeville melodrama. The scar over the right eye from a knife fight and abrupt movements heightened his air of toughness and unpredictability. Martín advocated the liberal use of the lash. Although we became friends later, he was the villager who threatened me with flogging on my arrival if I misbehaved in Tunnel Six.

Martín Llacsahuache plowing his field, Tunnel Six, 1987

Intimidation and even violence may have been necessary to bring thieves into line in the beginning. Martín was perfect for the tough-guy role of vigilante leader. The problem was that he did not scale back the violence when thievery declined. The front room of his farmhouse was an interrogation center. There Martín, Manuel Guerrero, Efraín Llacsahuache, and a few other hard-line Tunnel Sixers sometimes employed the "little-bird," suspending accused rustlers from a beam to force confessions.[19] Although Martín and the others were hardworking, honest men, I knew how hard they could be from the night I witnessed the torture of Claudio Reyes. They were the ones to press other villagers to keep him hanging from the molasses tree until he fainted or confessed.

As the ronda turned the tide against crime, fearfulness about police retaliation, religious conviction about charity and mercy, and a diminished feeling of threat spawned a desire for moderation, putting Martín's ferocity out of line with village opinion. On the other hand, no one wanted to risk being accused of siding with thieves by the mercurial ronda president. Instead of daring to challenge Martín at a meeting, a number of villagers spread stories about what went on at his farmhouse. A widower after losing his wife to cancer, Luciano Alvarado lived alone with his forty goats in a farmhouse just below the school. He recalled: "I heard Martín was a terrorist, and that he did the most inhuman things in his farmhouse, making the rustlers scream in pain. Sometimes it was said he hung them from the beams, and then put adobe bricks on their shoulders to create a terrible agony." It was ridiculous to suggest Martín was part of the Shining Path. The nearest guerrilla front was 100 miles to the south. As far as I could tell, the tale about Martín as "terrorist" was started by APRA loyalists in Paimas, who knew the ronda president supported the United Left and wanted to discredit him for this reason. I could not even say whether Martín put adobe bricks on the backs of suspended thieves. When I asked him one night on the bench in front of my house, he denied it.

What is certain is that the rumors weakened Martín in Tunnel Six. When it came time to vote for a ronda president in 1985, he had little support. Víctor was elected as the anti-Martín, a more level-headed and older man to temper ronda rashness. A point emphasized by Scott is that rumor and the rest of the "arts of resistance" can sometimes force change: "Desertion and evasion of conscription and of corvée labor have undoubtedly limited the imperial aspirations of many a monarch in southeast Asia or, for that matter, in Europe . . . [becoming] a social avalanche of petty acts of insubordination."[20] It was the same on a smaller scale in Tunnel Six. The tales about Martín's farmhouse as a chamber of horrors spread the discontent that led to his removal from the ronda presidency.

It could be argued that rumor's function was benign in this case. The storytelling hastened the removal of a ronda president at the very least overzealous with the whip and the rope. The result of rumor was by no means always so positive, though. This was obvious from the saga of Adolfina Neyra.[21] After the 1982 death of the mother of this shy, moonfaced teenager, her father, Adriano, began to force himself on her. A grandmother and aunt encouraged Adolfina to report the incest to the police and ronda. When she did, Adriano sold the family plot. Then he fled Tunnel Six. The two hectares of lemon orchard and cornfield ended up in the hands of Eduardo Gómez, the owner of one of Tunnel Six's two small stores.[22] Although a ronda assembly voted to return the land to the girl, Gómez refused. He counterattacked against Adolfina and ronda authority. Those Tunnel Sixers known to sympathize with Adolfina had credit cut off at the store. Then the store owner complained to the Paimas police sergeant. A pale officer from the city of Cajamarca, the sergeant hated the rondas, and once told me that "they should be banned for giving these upstart peasants ideas about running their own lives." He warned the ronda committee in Tunnel Six against pressing any further to return the land to Adolfina.

Gómez and his wife, Agrippina, also spread stories about Adolfina and Víctor. "I think it's a lie when the girl said her father assaulted her," Agrippina confided to me when I stopped by the store for a lukewarm bottle of Bimbo Cola on another scorching afternoon in Tunnel Six. I heard from other Tunnel Sixers that the couple was even saying that Víctor himself was sleeping with Adolfina. They said this was the real reason for his backing her cause. In the case of the dispute over the plot, the whispered story was being used by the best-off family in Tunnel Six to keep an abused and penniless teenager from her birthright. Rumor could be a tool of the strong as well as a weapon of the weak, it was clear.

Víctor refused to be intimidated. As he related to me one night, it was a matter of defending the ronda credo of justice and honesty. "Just about everybody can see that the girl needs the land. That's why they voted that way in the assembly. We can't let fear make the ronda back away from doing what is right." Yet many other villagers were not so resolute. When Víctor called a second assembly to force Gómez to turn over the land, only ten members appeared, a sign of waning willingness to act on the matter. The wish to buy at the store and fear of trouble with the police may have counted most in the change, but the rumors about Adolfina and Víctor heightened the difficulty of keeping Tunnel Six behind returning the land. It was sympathy for Adolfina that led to the vote in her favor at the first assembly. By impugning the girl, the rumors spread by Gómez and his wife weakened her cause, providing villagers a justification to themselves and the anthropologist for jumping ship. "I'm not sure everything Adolfina says is true, and I don't think the ronda should be involved in this" was how one man explained to me his nonattendance at the second assembly. The cause of returning the land died. Adolfina left Tunnel Six for a job as a maid for the family of an American oil company executive in the city of Talara.

The rumors about malfeasance could change or ruin the life of ronda president. After losing the presidency to Víctor in 1984,

Martín was bitter. The young villager told me he was upset that he never had a chance to defend himself against the stories of mistreating suspects. "I was one of the first to organize and fight for the rondas, and yet I was brought down by gossip and envy, without any gratitude for what I did." He, his wife, Manuela, and their three adorable daughters left Tunnel Six in 1988. They built a house of adobe on the garbage-strewn edge of Paimas. On most mornings, he rode his burro to work in his fields in Tunnel Six, circling around the center by the canal to avoid the villagers he felt had been so ungrateful.

Eladio Idrogo withdrew as well. The young president of the Central Committee of Rondas Campesinas of Cuyumalca was so highly regarded for revitalizing the ronda that the sectors of Cañafisto and Alto Cuyumalca united for once to ask him to serve a second term. Eladio refused. Exhaustion was part of the reason, as he explained to me one night: "This job tires you out. The problems never end, and people are never satisfied, and talk about you behind your back." Finances also figured in his decision. A ronda president had too many duties to be gone for more than a few days. Obligation to the rondas was a liability for those like him who could only make ends meet by going away to work in the palm plantations of the Ucayali or in construction in Lima. When his term ended in 1992, Eladio left for the jungle to make enough to buy a new plow and shoes for his toddler, José.

It appeared that Víctor would avoid becoming yet another casualty. Although he remained bitter about the abandonment of Adolfina, the ronda anniversary was approaching in Tunnel Six. Finding a bull to slaughter, sending invitations to other rondas and government officials, and other preparations took up much of his time. After shying away during the land battle, a majority of villagers assembled again in the lunchroom to hear disputes. Víctor was skilled as ever in supervising conflict settlement. As a measure of his popularity in spite of the war over the land, he won reelection to a second term in 1987, just before I left Tunnel Six to return to the Bay Area to write my dissertation.

It was from Profelinda that I learned what happened next. Víctor and Francisca's eldest child had followed the route of hundreds of thousands of other daughters of peasant families in leaving for the city to labor as a maid. When in Lima in 1992, I went to see her.

Her mistress in the new suburb was at the beach with the children, so we sat in the living room trading news.

Profelinda said her parents were no longer in Tunnel Six. They were renting land a day's walk away, near the town of Las Lomas. I asked why they had left. The sixteen-year-old blushed. She explained her father was charged with theft. Someone from another village deposited $100 with him to turn over to a Tunnel Sixer in a settlement over disputed land. When the Tunnel Sixer came for the money, Víctor did not have it. The scandal forced him to resign from the ronda presidency. Whether out of embarrassment, bitterness, or both, Víctor decided to leave Tunnel Six for good, and to try to start anew somewhere else. "He devoted himself to the ronda for all those years, and now he has had to leave Tunnel Six as if he were a criminal," said Profelinda as we sat in the living room as outside the *garúa*, a mix of fog and smog, lay over Lima like a dirty wet blanket.

I remembered the French critic René Girard's recasting of the concept of ritual scapegoating and sacrifice.[23] Girard recalls that many religions depend on the figure of the man whose stigmatization and death make up for the sins of the living and who ensures the survival of society. The "generative scapegoat" is the victim whose pain and suffering resolve or at least mediate unbearable social "tensions, conflicts, and difficulties of all kinds."[24] Girard premises that this victim and redeemer, as with Jesus as Jew among the Romans, will come from the category of the "imperfectly assimilated," whether immigrants, the poor, the disabled, the sick, or, as anthropologist Nancy Scheper-Hughes shows in northeastern Brazil, infants.[25]

Was the ronda president a "generative scapegoat"? Unlike the babies mothers allowed to die in Alto do Cruzeiro, he did not undergo a physical death. Nor was he always blameless in the events that forced him out in disgrace. Notwithstanding, Martín, Víctor, and many others did suffer the social death of humiliation and exile. These men risked reputation, jail, and financial hardship to run the rondas, only to end on the outside of the movement to which they gave so much.

One president's departure meant choosing another one. An act of renewal, the election of a new leader underlined that the ronda belonged to the village. No single man owned it, no matter how much he had done for the cause. At the same time, the obviousness of leadership's burdens made it harder to find willing replacements for departed presidents, as John Gitlitz's research in the Bambamarca Valley confirmed. It very often took cajoling to persuade a pick to take the post, and many men did so at last only because of their conviction in the value of the rondas. "I didn't want the job," explained the new village president in Chota's Negropampa to me in 1991, "but I feel the rondas must survive for what they do for us as the peasantry."

Renewal occurred in Tunnel Six. When I went back to visit in 1992, the village had made Liberato Chuquihuanga the new president. Chuquihuanga was a strong and quiet man of just twenty-two. Although among the poorest in Tunnel Six, with just one hectare and a one-room farmhouse on the hill above the canal, he was a model citizen, always showing up when the call went out for villagers to repair a roof, cut beams for a chapel, clean ditches, or perform any other job in Tunnel Six. Unlike Víctor, Liberato was an awkward speaker, but he was likable and forthright. Only thirteen when patrols started in Tunnel Six in 1983, he reflected the assumption of authority of younger villagers and the ronda's ability to renew itself beyond the first generation of men who had organized it. The House of the Rondero was finished in 1991. It filled often for assemblies with Tunnel Sixers more eager than ever to maintain the ronda for the next decade.

I was happy about the ronda.

I missed Víctor.

THE PROMISES OF REGIONAL LEADERSHIP

As NGOs and political parties proliferated in the 1980s, Peru became a country of acronyms, as if their crisp abbreviations could bring the order and efficiency so lacking in a nation in shambles. The ronda federations that formed in northern Peru followed suit. Chota, a town of fewer than 10,000, seated three federations: the Federation of Rondas Campesinas of the Province of Chota (FRCH), Federation of Pacific Rondas of the Province of Chota (FRCPCH), and Federation of Rondas Campesinas of the Department of Cajamarca (FRCC). The smaller town of Bambamarca had the Unified Front of the Rondas Campesinas of Hualgayoc

Ronda Convention, Cutervo, 1990

(FURPH) and the Committee of Pacific Rondas of Bambamarca
(CRPB). As befitted a departmental capital and city of 150,000,
Cajamarca housed four federations: the Federation of Rondas
Campesinas of the Province of Cajamarca (FPRCC), Departmen-
tal Federation of Peasants and Ronderos of Cajamarca (FEDUCAR),
Provincial Committee of Pacific Rondas (CRP), and Federation of
Pacific Rondas of Cajamarca (FRPC). At least one federation could
be found in the towns of Huancabamba, Ayabaca, Celendín, San
Ignacio, Jaén, and Piura.

These regional federations were begun and controlled mostly by
a relatively small group of men. In the typology of ronda leadership
suggested by the Peruvian anthropologist Alonso Zarzar, the village
committee head was a well-respected man with limited education

and power outside his village. By contrast, the regional ronda leader was "immersed in political intrigues of his province, usually not a peasant, but a townsperson and assimilated . . . tied to political parties and savvy about the justice system."[26] The regional leader was likely to have occupied the most posts in his federation, in the process becoming a kind of peasant leader for life. We saw in chapter 5 how money from NGOs unwittingly bankrolled personal moneymaking scams of some of these men.

The need for effective regional organization and leadership was obvious regardless of the risks. As far back as Pizarro's manipulation of internal rivalry within and external hatred of the Inca empire, divisions among Andeans have made exploitation and subjection far easier. Whether the goal was stopping a mining company from polluting groundwater or forcing the government to offer loans to peasants, success depended on coordination, linking villages to advance common interests. Leaders had to inspire enthusiasm, organize protests, and otherwise prevent the powerful from trampling the inhabitants of the countryside. Many villagers understood this. "It's because of our divisions that we peasants get exploited," Tunnel Six's José Paz admitted to me in 1986.

I saw excitement about alliance-building at a convention that same year in the city of Piura. It was organized by the Regional Agrarian Federation of the Departments of Piura and Tumbes (FRADEPT). The government started FRADEPT in 1969 as part of the National System of Social Mobilization (SINAMOS) to rally the poor behind Velasco's reforms. The Gildermeisters and a handful of other families of the Piuran oligarchy had made fortunes exporting the silky cotton of the desert to Britain and the United States. To mark the breakup of the estates, Velasco seized a property at the edge of Piura once owned by their Association of Landowners of Piura. He turned over the ten hectares complete with a cockfighting coliseum and acacia grove to FRADEPT for a headquarters. When conservatives booted Velasco in 1975, the federation had survived and by the 1980s was tied to the United Left and receiving money from Ox-fam International and other left-leaning international funders.

FRADEPT maintained an office in a lowslung, rundown building by the entrance to their property. During the irregular hours in which it was open, a secretary plunked out memos on a typewriter, and the president or others on the steering committee planned marches and trips to Lima to lobby Congress. Luis Montalván, Juan Tumi, and the other FRADEPT leaders were big-bellied from the milky chicha so popular on Peru's northern coast, and burned deep brown by the sun. Although FRADEPT was supposed to represent villagers throughout Tumbes and Piura, these men came from the coast near the cities of Tumbes and Piura, measuring the lack of involvement in the federation of villagers from back up in the region's Andes.

The rondas offered FRADEPT an opportunity to reach out to the mountains. As Robin and I found after taking a truck down from Tunnel Six across the desert for the convention, the arrival of 300 delegates from villages in the interiors of Piura had brought the compound to life, a sea of short men from the Andes in jeans, tractor caps, and straw hats. A row of stables once used for the elite's horses was opened up to sleep the many villagers without relatives in Piura or money for a hotel, while a cluster of women outside stirred giant aluminum pots of rice and beans over a wood fire to feed the delegates. The delegates met in what had once been an enormous hangar for repairing farm machinery, and which FRADEPT now used as a convention hall. Speeches followed by the president and vice-president of FRADEPT, a pair of congressmen from the United Mariateguista Party (PUM), a priest, and the director of the Center for the Promotion and Research on the Peasantry (CIPCA). Agustín "the Gringo" Sánchez had even come from Chota, the president of the Federation of Rondas Campesinas of the Province of Cajamarca. Few of the villagers had ever seen an albino, much less one who wore a straw hat and spoke rural slang just like them. FRADEPT leaders' allegiance to the PUM made them hesitant to cede the microphone. They knew Sánchez belonged to Red Homeland, and Red Homeland and PUM were rivals for power in the United Left. To the dismay of Montalván and the others, the ronderos were riveted by Sánchez, who was a funny and passionate public speaker. Their refusal to let him speak once more at the closing led "the Gringo" to storm out to get on a bus back to Chota.

Nonetheless, I saw the value of the convention. It was never easy for a village to press back doubt and isolation from attack by hostile authorities. When other villagers jumped ship as in the case of Adolfina in Tunnel Six, it could be especially hard for committee

Greetings at a ronda convention, Bambamarca, 1990

leaders to maintain morale. Many of the delegates came from village steering committees. The gathering reminded them that they were not alone. Here they were told by speaker after speaker that the rondas were good for the peasantry and Peru. They stood for the national anthem and a "Hymn of the Rondero" penned by a schoolteacher from the hills of Morropón. By drawing ronderos together in the one-time getaway of the landlords, the convention allowed them to step away for two days from the grind of village life to recognize themselves as makers of history and a movement in cause with the rest of the northern peasantry. It was a bit like a party convention in the United States, drumming up a sense of purpose and esprit de corps to invigorate delegates to return to running the rondas.

The convention was also a clearinghouse for information. A congressman laid out for villagers a proposal before the national Congress to legalize the rondas, while a lawyer counseled them about dealing with the threat of arrest. The exchange of intelligence between villagers was even more important. When delegates rose to report on their committees, others learned about the state of the movement and the challenges confronting it in the rest of Piura.

Just as important, they traded ideas, sometimes with a dose of humor. A villager from Huancabamba in a corduroy overcoat and *chullo,* a knit cap with earflaps, proffered this advice about whipping, to guffaws from the crowd: "In Quispicancha, we have discovered that the body has five delicate spots. That's why we give the lash in a sixth spot that is not delicate, to avoid injuring our fellow villagers when they misbehave: the butt." Other villagers exchanged notes during breaks about which NGOs to ask for roofing for a House of the Rondero and lawyers in Piura to consult in case of trouble. Far from restricted to the rondas, the convention was a crossroads for news of every kind: where in Sullana to get the best price for a sack of lemons, what it was like to start a farm in the jungles of San Ignacio, the kind of fertilizer to buy for corn.

The broadest promise was regional and national change. Although villagers in the Andes made up 30 percent of the population of the department of Piura, they were easily the poorest and most voiceless sector of society, with less than 5 percent of the wealth and no representation in government. As the oligarchy in the oasis city of Piura vacationed in Disneyworld, village children four hours away across the desert in the Andes lived in dire poverty, literally perishing by the hundreds of bubonic plague and dysentery in mud hovels without doctors. The rondas' success had fortified a hopefulness about change on display among villagers at the convention. One villager announced a plan to run a slate of ronderos for mayor and councilmen in Morropón, and another from Ayabaca advocated that the rondas organize to force truckers to reduce rates for hauling corn to the coast. They reasoned that it was only natural for the rondas to extend from reforming the village to transforming the region and the nation. President of a ronda committee in the heights of Morropón, Emilio López was a handsome man with a muttonchop moustache and a dignified air. He explained the thinking to me during a break from a workshop: "The rondas have imposed justice in villages. Now we need to fight against other injustices, cleaning up this whole society to end injustices." As part of connecting the rondas to the cause of peasant power, FRADEPT pushed the delegates to think about changing the structure of the economy and society, and even held a workshop on "Problems and Alternatives for Development for the Piuran Sierra." The president of FRADEPT issued a call at the convention's end for villagers to "begin to organize around issues of economic justice under the leadership of this combative federation."

THE OBSTACLES TO ORGANIZING

As it happened, this was the end and not the beginning of regional organizing. Although FRADEPT held other ronda conventions in 1989 and 1990, they drew shrinking numbers of delegates, and no more were held after that. Villager participation in some of the federations in Cajamarca was minimal from the start, and even the once proud Federation of Rondas Campesinas of Cajamarca of Agustín Sánchez and Red Homeland managed to draw delegates from fewer than forty of more than 1,000 Cajamarcan villages to the "departmental convention" in Cutervo in 1991. It was part of the arc of regional organizing—the formation of federations in the late 1970s and early 1980s, a period of operation in the mid-1980s, and then decline and shutdown in the 1990s. Few federations ran activities of any kind. All that was left was the pile of acronyms pertaining to organizations that no longer existed in more than name. The rondas proved to be a movement that was strong in the village without ever becoming a force for regional and national change.

Why? Poverty was part of the explanation. It demanded time and money for many villagers to travel far from home to a ronda event. Although Víctor and other crusaders would find a way to go to anything to do with the rondas, many villagers were reluctant to shell out three dollars for truck fare, and spend days away from the fields. Froilán Pintado resembled Luke Perry of the evening soap opera *Beverly Hills 90210* and was the heartthrob of teenagers in Tunnel Six. He was a patrol stalwart, but did not go to the ronda convention of 1986: "I'd like to go, but I don't have the fare." Marx once noted the "dull compulsion of economic relations" can obstruct mobilization on a mass scale.[27] Perhaps one of the greatest paradoxes of protest is that those with the most to gain are exactly those for whom survival's grind can make it the hardest to do so.

Geography was a related barrier to regional organizing. The dispersal of villagers across the hinterlands of the Andes obstructed speedy communication, with messages passed by word of mouth in this telephoneless rural world. The countryside's remove was an asset for the rondas locally by allowing a greater freedom of operation with the nearest police station often hours away. It became a liability in regional organizing.[28] Days might pass before someone traveling to the city could be found to get word of the arrest of a ronda president in Aragoto to FRADEPT. The call of the Federation of Rondas Campesinas of Cajamarca for a march in Chota to demand subsidies for corn did not arrive in Alto Peru until three days after the fact. It was hard to maintain much less to strengthen a feeling of accountability and connection between ronderos and the federations under these circumstances.

A further obstacle was conflicting interest and opinion in the countryside. The word "peasant" sounds straightforward. We have seen throughout that the reality was anything but simple, and rural people divided by religion, politics, gender, and other factors. At the village level, the concern for ending theft encouraged inhabitants to bond, even if unity was partial and precarious in Tunnel Six and elsewhere. Finding common ground was harder regionally and nationally. The payoff from going to a convention or march was less immediate and obvious than from patrolling; and still further divisions came into play, among them rivalry between villages over land and water and competition for government funding among districts and provinces. In 1987 in the Cutervo Valley, the majority of Arenal withdrew from the provincial ronda federation, angry that the steering committee contained three officials from Tambillos, who the Arenalans felt had usurped pasture belonging to their village. A year later, villagers from the Aragoto District stopped going to meetings of the Agrarian League of Ayabaca, accusing the president of lobbying the municipality for a new high school only in his home district of Montero.[29] It was little wonder that the regional ronda federations never took off in view of the barriers of poverty, geography, and division in the way.

The feuding of political parties sealed the federations' fate. It would be wrong to regard APRA, Red Homeland, PUM, and other groups as just a source of division and weakness. As we have seen, the parties were involved in the rondas from the very start, and it was Red Homeland in the person of Daniel Idrogo that shaped the decision to go beyond patrolling to assemblies. The activism of Idrogo and others in Red Homeland and APRA chieftain Pedro Risco spread the gospel of the rondas across northern Peru in the early 1980s; they founded committees in dozens of villages. A cluster of schoolteachers and lawyers from the more conservative Popular Action Party (AP) of then president Fernando Belaúnde was involved in organizing the rondas in the province of Huancabamba in Piura.[30] Still, infighting among the parties was fatal to regional organizing in the long run. Each wanted to turn the rondas into a base of support. Their competition explained the multiplication of federations. When Red Homeland formed the Federation of Campesinos of Chota in 1979, APRA started the Federation of Pacific Rondas of the province of Chota a year later. The problem of "parallelism" recurred in Bambamarca as the Unified Front of Rondas Campesinas of the Province of Hualgayoc, which was tied to PUM, vied for support with the APRA-run Committee of Pacific Rondas of Bambamarca.[31] To visit the office of one federation was to hear a litany of horrific charges of lying and stealing about the other in town.

Robin and I found out about the rivalry's pettiness on our first visit to Chota in 1990. Searching a dusty street at the town's edge for the office of the Federation of Rondas Campesinas of the Province of Cajamarca, I asked a man in a straw hat and llanques for directions. His eyes narrowed. He did not know, he muttered. The only federation was back by the plaza, the store of "Don Pedro Risco." A few doors down, we asked again, this time a señora selling peanuts in her doorway. She pointed across the street. Chota was too small for anyone not to know that we were standing a stone's throw from the federation's doorway. As indicated by the honorific "Don" for Pedro Risco, the villager was surely an aprista, and as such had refused to direct gringos to the federation affiliated to Red Homeland.

No one exemplified partisanship more than Risco. As the squat, pugnacious APRA chief in Chota, he fought Idrogo and Red Homeland for ronda supremacy from the beginning in 1977. To villagers stopping by at the store that doubled as the APRA office and headquarters of the Federation of Pacific Rondas of Chota, Risco said Idrogo had stolen congressional money to buy a sports car. The APRA leader also began declaring himself to have been the ronda founder, undaunted by the complete lack of evidence for his claim to the title. When I visited in 1990, Risco's penchant for self-aggrandizement and paternalism came across in his talk about "my rondas." He flashed a three-toothed grin at the anthropologist from behind the store counter. "I have rondas in Sullana, also in Huancabamba, I have them in Cajamarca. I've been to Ancash, and I have them in Ancash. I have the whole north."

It was easy for me to feel snippy about Risco and APRA. The party's centrism made it an object of disdain for me and other leftist North Americans coming to Peru in the early 1980s. When Alan García of APRA won the presidency in 1985, he allowed the military to kill thousands of villagers in the war against the Shining Path, further influencing my negative view of this party whose leaders seemed driven by ambition and greed. The United Left appeared to be good guys in the story. After becoming the first socialist elected mayor of a Latin American capital in 1983, Alfonso Barrantes started social welfare programs in poor neighborhoods, and congressmen from PUM, Red Homeland, the Communist Party of Peru–Unity, and other members of the coalition spoke out against the government's trampling of human rights. The left's vigor throughout Latin America made it possible to think the United Left could seize power to make a better Peru.

It did not take me long to lose idealism about the United Left, however. When in Lima in 1984, a fellow North American graduate student told me about Alfonso Barrantes's initial receptivity to her proposal to do a magazine story on a day in the life of Lima mayor and United Left leader. Yet the older and married mayor grinned that this would mean being with him for "twenty-four hours." Sue demurred about this part of the plan. The mayor canceled the story. Although we laughed about it, the incident suggested that the United Left might be less noble than we wanted to believe, in this case at the very least evincing the boorishness that prompted feminists in Latin America to deride "Machismo-Leninism."

The flaws became more apparent to me in Tunnel Six. The beer distributor from the town of Ayabaca, the mayor of the province belonged to PUM. He was exactly the same as the apristas in handing out jobs and money only to those known to support his party. When visiting Tunnel Six in 1986, the mayor promised a clinic so long as the village voted for "our coalition for change," and he spent more time denouncing APRA than laying out a vision of his own. No different in this respect from parties of the center and right, the United Left was dominated in the provinces by lawyers, merchants, and teachers. Villagers seldom appeared on the local slates of the coalition, despite making up the majority of the population in the northern Andes. The majority of the national leadership of the United Left came from Lima's light-skinned elite in still another reflection of failure to fit the measure of the party of the downtrodden. As it came to appear to me from the angle of the countryside, the United Left resembled the other parties in dirty politics and the exclusion of villagers.

These faults carried into the ronda federations controlled by the left. A FRADEPT functionary arrived in Tunnel Six one afternoon from the town of Paimas. Because the man had come to invite villagers to a first national ronda meeting set for the next month in Lima, Víctor called Tunnel Six together for him to give them the details. One man asked if FRADEPT would pay bus fare to the capital. Unfortunately not, said the activist, a man with the slicked back hair and leather loafers of a schoolteacher or perhaps villager who had moved for good to the city. After the meeting, he motioned to Víctor for a word in private, and I tagged along around the corner of the farmhouse. "Pass the word to others who support us that there will be free buses leaving from Piura the night before the meeting." FRADEPT wanted the bus seats as a reward for Víctor and others who supported the United Left, and to obstruct apristas from getting a free ticket. As part of the jockeying of partisanship, the activist was willing to lie to the assembly. The "national meeting" ended up being little more than a campaign rally for the United Left, with speeches by Javier Díez Canseco, Rolando Ames, Henry Pease, and other honchos who had nothing to do with the rondas.

RED HOMELAND AND THE END OF THE FEDERATIONS

I found the problem of partisanship to be most poignant in Red Homeland. A product of the breakup in 1965 of the Communist Party of Peru–Red Flag, the leadership of the party came from the provinces; many were teachers in high schools and vocational schools that served the children of the poor and the peasantry. I knew about the reputation for close-mindedness and sectarianism of this party that wanted to usher Peru down the pathway of Mao's China into socialism. Yet I liked many of its leaders in Chota tremendously. It was hard in the first place not to admire the handsome yet friendly and articulate Daniel Idrogo, and what he stood for as the child of villagers who had become a congressman. When I was preparing to go to Chota for the first time in 1990, Idrogo wrote me letters of introduction for Oscar Sánchez, Diego Sánchez, and Agustín Sánchez, no relation to each other but all leaders in the federations allied to Red Homeland. These men were smart, talented, and fun to be around.

I got to know Oscar Sánchez best. After locating the doorway at last, Robin and I had found Oscar inside the office of the Chota federation, little more than a dirt-floored room with a calendar and a few posters tacked to the wall. He was tall for a Peruvian of village stock, a young man of thirty-two with a mat of curly black hair and a stern eye. After reading the letter from Daniel, he invited us to go with him to a meeting in a village that was "nearby." As many a gringo has discovered in the Andes, "nearby" turned out to be a marathon eight hours over a trail that zigzagged up and down the mountains, in this case in the misery of a hailstorm and then night's darkness. "Taxi!" I remember yelling only half in jest when my horse dumped me upside down in the mud. That Robin and I survived the trip raised our stock with Oscar. We became friends with him and his wife, Juana. After Robin returned to Lima, I used to visit them in the room they rented in a tenement off the plaza. We discussed the rondas and politics and played with their baby, Oscarcito.

The Italian political theorist Roberto Michels hypothesized in 1915 about the existence of an "Iron Law of Oligarchy." It says personal power and enrichment will always matter more to political leaders than constituent interests. Nothing about the law applied to Oscar. His father died when he was five, and his mother raised him and five siblings in the village of Cabracancha, near Chota. While a teenager in Chota getting a degree as a math teacher in the Pedagogical Institute, Oscar saw a march of ronderos on Chota in 1978 against a food price hike by the military regime. It sparked his interest in politics. He joined Red Homeland and became president of the Federation of Rondas Campesinas of the Province of Cajamarca in 1985 and again in 1990, while running the program *Rondas in Action* on Saturdays on Radio Chota. Yet Oscar was modest and quick to credit others. Far from benefiting from being a leader, he worked without pay for the party and the rondas. The

Oscar Sánchez (right), recording a speech at a ronda meeting for his radio program *Rondas in Action,* Alto Peru, 1990

family got by on Juana's earnings from the market stall. As a member of Red Homeland and an activist in the rondas, she shared a commitment to change, and was proud about Oscar's giving himself over to activism.

An article of faith was the absolute truth of Marxism. On the shelves in the room in the tenement, he kept the works of Marx, Lenin, and Mao, and for him they held laws of society as indisputable as the theorems of Pythagoras and Archimedes: the antagonism of the proletariat and the bourgeoisie, the falling rate of profit of capitalism, the inevitability of Communism. In the opinion of Oscar and Red Homeland, the Shining Path was wrong to launch war before the peasantry and workers were ready for it and PUM members were *pitucos,* spoiled kids of the Liman elite, and coffeehouse revolutionaries. He shared the faith of other cadres that Red Homeland was the only genuine upholder of Marxism in Peru, in the words of one pamphlet "the party to apply the scientific principles of dialectical materialism to the struggle in our country." Anthropologist Carlos Iván Degregori described the Shining Path as a "dwarf star" because of the smallness of size yet intensity of commitment to the cause of revolution.[32] Although no love was lost between Red Homeland and the Shining Path, Oscar and other Chotan leaders' certainty made me think of Red Homeland in the same way. The fire of their conviction gave them the energy to meet late into the night to plan strategy in Chota and to criss-cross the Andes hungry, frozen, and exhausted to deliver the gospel of socialism to the peasantry.

It was also the biggest liability of Red Homeland. The times were changing in Peru and worldwide by the end of the 1980s. With the fall of the Berlin Wall and the left's decline in Latin America, it was beginning to sound silly to speak about socialism's imminence. Yet Oscar and the others did not adjust to the times. Party publications insisted even in 1990 that capitalism would be overthrown by the "union of the peasantry and the proletariat." As if just a little more persuasion would turn the tide of history, Oscar attacked APRA and the government on *Rondas in Action* with the same brio as ever, for cheating and lying to the peasantry. He was frustrated and puzzled by charges of partisanship against Red Homeland. "People accuse us of sectarianism, but Marxism is not about politicking. It's a sci-ence," he said to me one night in his room.

The truth was that most Peruvians were sick of all the political parties by 1990. At the start in 1980, elections were a novelty, a menu of ideologies and candidates with something for everyone. The disastrous presidency of Belaúnde finished his Popular Action Party. APRA died with Alan García's presidency, which was among Peru's most corrupt and mismanaged governments in recent mem-ory. A fixture in the country for half a century, APRA vanished into air, managing to obtain less than 4 percent of the vote in the presi-dential elections of 1995. When Alfonso Barrantes broke from the United Left in 1990 to run for president, the coalition had fallen apart, and the tiny parties on the left self-destructed in corruption and bickering. As no party seemed to be able to stop the Shining Path and hyperinflation from tearing the country apart by 1990, "politician" became an epitaph of the worst kind, and cynicism and apathy mounted. A novice whose primary appeal was not be-longing to any party, Alberto Fujimori swept into the presidency in 1990, staying there for the rest of the decade.

As the parties died, so did the ronda federations that they had created and controlled. The APRA's fall meant that Pedro Risco no longer had tractors and loans to reward villages for joining his Federation of Pacific Rondas of Cajamarca. When I saw him from across the plaza in Chota in 1993, he was using a cane and his son was helping him get across the street; the once-brazen chieftain of APRA looked weak and old. Few villagers came by the store anymore, and the Federation of Pacific Rondas of Cajamarca existed only in name. The same was true for Red Homeland's Federation of Rondas Campesinas of the Department of Cajamarca. With party membership shrinking to barely 100, there was not even enough money for Oscar and others to mimeograph flyers or hold congresses. FRADEPT was paralyzed by an internal struggle between supporters of PUM and one of the tiny leftist parties formed after the collapse of the United Left. All of these federations were connected in the minds of villagers to the partisanship that even those once active in the parties had come to see as necessary to move beyond for Peru to face the future. Eladio Idrogo voted for Red Homeland in the 1980s and was a regular at meetings of the Federation of Rondas Campesinas of Chota. He had stopped going to any federation activities by 1990. "I think its time has passed," he told me one afternoon in Cuyumalca in 1991.

The end of the federations made me think about tales in Tunnel Six about struggle for freedom from the haciendas. As we climbed one afternoon in 1986 in the heat of the hills to a fiesta in the village of Tazajeras, Víctor recalled a man named Juan Retete as a hero of the fight in the dry mountains of Ayabaca. The mayordomo of what was then the hacienda of Pillo demanded days of free labor from Víctor's parents and other serfs, as well as "endearments" of cheese, dried meat, and fowl.[33] Víctor said Retete traveled the mountains to organize opposition on foot with just his poncho and a sack of corn, "like us with the ronda" he added by way of connecting past and present. I have never found the name of Retete in any history book, although Víctor thought he belonged to the Socialist Party that was organizing in Piura in the 1930s.[34] Nevertheless, his absence in official literature did not stop many older Tunnel Sixers from remembering him as a prophet, one who envisioned the end of the haciendas as a step in a march toward the emancipation of the peasantry. Pablo Jiménez, a grizzled man of sixty, conjured up Retete for me between weaving a straw hat in front of his farmhouse in Tunnel Six. "He would say, 'My children, the Law of the Rich will end. The Law of the Poor will come.' "

The failure of the federations suggests just how hard it was to fulfill the prophecy of a "Law of the Poor." Organizing by the poor in a shantytown or village has been seen again and again as sowing the "seeds of change," or "preparing the ground" for further steps toward bettering society. The label "grassroots movement" holds an assumption about the likelihood of growing taller and stronger. The examples of Brazil's Landless Workers' Movement (MST) and Central America's Association of Peasant Organizations for Co-operation and Development (ASCODC) suggest that rural organizing can achieve advances in the fight for opportunity and justice. Yet the rondas force us to recognize that there is nothing natural at all about a movement going regional, national, or global. A collection of tribes in the Amazon of Peru or neighborhood associations in the United States or any other movement may join together as a force for change, or they may not, depending on many factors, as occurred with the rondas. The French theorists Gilles Deleuze and Félix Guattari propose the concept of the rhizome as a way to model the multiplicity, inconsistency, and discontinuity of human history.[35] The failure of the rondas to grow into strong federations offers confirmation that even mobilizations for change can proceed in many ways besides up.

I wonder how much the federations could have accomplished even if they had worked far better than they did. The problem of theft and strife could be resolved through the patrols and assemblies of the rondas. Although the rondas made life better, poverty remained overwhelming and the misery of scarcity seemingly as intractable as ever in the northern Andes. The socialist critic José Carlos Mariátegui believed dividing the haciendas would unlock prosperity in the Andes. He was wrong. Almost every bit of hacienda land was parceled out after the reform of 1969. The result in the Andes was farms literally a hundred times too small to be the basis of a decent living. If the children of Tunnel Six were to prosper, it would be by going to the cities, or perhaps someday by finding a different way to rebuild the economy of the Andes.

I went to see Oscar and Juana last in 1993. They had moved to rent a store with living quarters upstairs. The store had cobwebs on the ceiling and a creaky wood floor, and little to sell besides penny candy, matches, needles and thread, and yarn. Juana was quiet and restrained as ever, but she was happy to see me again, and asked after Robin. I admired the happy and vigorous Oscarcito, a toddler using a stick as a pretend motorcycle outside on the sidewalk. Juana said the family could not survive the recession brought on by the "Fujishock" of 1990 without Oscar going back to work. He found a job for $100 a month as a teacher in Lajas, a backwater eight hours by foot from Chota whose one claim to fame was having been the home of a legendary late nineteenth-century warlord, Eleodoro Benel. Oscar was able to come back to Chota only on weekends to be with Juana and Oscarcito. As Juana explained with resignation, he was no longer active in the Federation of Rondas Campesinas of the Province of Cajamarca. The organization was just about dead for lack of interest and participation.

"All that work for nothing," she concluded.

A MEETING IN BAMBAMARCA

The experience of Francisco, Martín, Víctor, Risco, Oscar, and other local and regional leaders reminded me of a classic Peruvian novel. *Broad and Alien Is the World* was published from exile in Chile by Ciro Alegría in 1934.[36] Set in the Andes of northern Peru, it is also about the story of the downfall of a rural leader. The self-sacrificing and noble president of the village of Rumi, Rosendo Maqui, heads the fight to save Rumi from Don Alvaro Amenabar, an evil rancher and mineowner. Although backed by the bloodthirsty yet bravehearted bandit Fiero Vásquez, the villagers are betrayed by a quack lawyer, and Amenabar buys off local authorities to force the Indians into bondage. The police beat Rosendo Maqui to death in a jail cell smelling of "rotting mud, of sweat, of urine, of misery." As the novel ends, the army surrounds and guns down the last Rumians.

Literary critic Víctor Vich points out that many mid-twentieth century novels about the Andes end with violent repression.[37] This was the tragedy of the helplessness of villagers against the forces of profit taking and modernization. The story of Maqui and Rumi, read this way, allegorizes the consignment of a people and a culture to history's dustbin.

The real-life stories of ronda leaders might seem just as bleak as parables about rural society's fate. Víctor and other leaders discovered formidable obstacles in their own villages. The downfall of the federations and their chiefs showed how hard bringing villages together was on a larger scale. As Vich notes, *Broad and Alien Is the World* and similar novels of that time represented villagers in courageous and prolonged struggle, and acknowledged the nervousness of an elite long preoccupied with the threat of Andean rebellion. Yet resistance was depicted as futile. Alegría and others presumed villagers were not up against just the mineowner and the army, but history, one thought to mean the extinction of village tradition and culture by modernity's advance. By this logic, the inability of the rondas to resolve the problem of leadership could be read as practically inevitable in a world rigged against peasants and the marginalized everywhere.

Nonetheless, the stories of the ronda leaders were obviously not merely parables of powerlessness. As occurred in Tunnel Six, the downfall of a committee president did not always destroy the ronda and the village, and the changing of leaders could be reinvigorating. The results of patrols and assemblies were limited, but not futile in times even harder than usual because of the crisis of the government and the economy in the 1980s. Nor had it proved to be correct to assume the death of the village. Although hundreds of thousands left to seek their fortunes in the city, many others stayed behind or moved back and forth between the village and jobs in the jungle and on the coast; Lagunas, Aragoto, Cuyumalca, and hundreds of other villages were as vigorous as ever at the doorstep to the new millennium. The rondas were the latest and not the final chapter in the history of transformation and renewal in the northern Andes, and yet another face of a modern world that has proved far more unruly and diverse than Alegría and others could ever have imagined.

The possibility of regional organizing was also not dead altogether. At the urging of the Catholic and Protestant Churches, a meeting was held in 1991 to form a new federation in the Bambamarca Valley. The old, exhausted federations connected to APRA and PUM would be eliminated to create the Unified Central of Rondas Campesinas of the Province of Hualgayoc. Enthusiasm about the new initiative was palpable among the 500 villagers at

Cheering the Rondas, Bambamarca, 1990

Víctor Luna, Bambamarca, 1990

the two-day gathering in the yard of the town of Bambamarca's high school. At the end of the congress, they elected a steering committee that contained villagers identified with APRA and the left, and Protestants as well as Catholics. The steering committee was sworn in with the formality of a presidential inauguration, but with a ronda twist: "Do you solemnly swear to uphold your duties with honor?" "Yes," came the response of the new leaders. "If you do, then may God and the rondas reward you. If not, may they punish you."

The ebullience lasted until the end. Men and women tumbled out of the high school toward the plaza. The sun had just set in a rapid rush over the horizon. To ward off the chill, farm couples stamped out dances to the rhythms of a band that played huaynos with a drum and three flutes made of plastic tubing, turning the street just in front of the Catholic Church and the telephone company into a dance hall. In the day's last light, the plaza hummed with "vivas" to the rondas and the strains of "Pío-Pío," a ditty from Colombia about a rooster scratching for corn that was the greatest hit that year in Peru. I had come to Bambamarca from Lima to do a story on the meeting for a Peruvian magazine. When I asked the newly elected president of the federation for his view of the future, Víctor Luna grimaced that "it's not going to be easy to keep this together." A señora in puffy skirt and straw hat interrupted us to drag the new leader out into the sea of couples twirling to the huaynos.

He joined the dance in spite of himself.

EPILOGUE

I did not know quite what to expect in 1997 when I got off American Airlines Flight 2110 from Miami at Lima's Jorge Chávez airport. The duties of teaching, writing, and family had kept me away from Peru for almost three years. As the outsized horrors of car bombs, army massacres, hyperinflation, and the cholera epidemic had receded by this time, the country seldom made the news in the United States. One of the only stories from Peru was the discovery on an Andean peak of the mummified body of Juanita, the name that archaeologists gave to this fifteenth-century sacrificial victim of the Incas. Washington pundits joked that Bill Clinton's comment after inspecting Juanita at the National Geographic Society was the best evidence yet for the boundlessness of the presidential libido.[1] "If I was a single man," gushed Clinton, "I would ask that mummy out. I'm telling you, that's the best-looking mummy I've ever seen." What many Americans knew about Peru in the mid-1990s boiled down to Juanita and *The Celestine Prophecy*. That New Age smash best-seller told the story of a beautiful young American development consultant unearthing an ancient Andean manuscript with the magical keys to spiritual enlightenment. As so often in the past, the Andes and Peru were performing their reliable role as icons of the enigmatic and the exotic, and their aura in the United States as a strange and primordial land of wisdom and mystery seemed as strong as ever.

It was the AM-PM minimarket and Dunkin' Donuts and not Incan codices that caught my attention on the way in from the airport. A sign of Peru's opening to the global economy under President Alberto Fujimori (1990–), the franchises of these and other multinationals had appeared just since my last visit in 1994; the neon glow of their signs was all the stranger to me because of my memories from the 1980s of the spooky darkness of Lima streets after the latest Shining Path bombing of the electrical system. Had the tightening of ties to the global companies and markets so transformed Peru as it appeared from the taxi window? In what other ways had Lima and the Andean interiors of Peru changed or stayed the same? And what did this mean for the rondas, which I had returned on this two-week trip to catch up on once more to finish this book? My uncertainty about these questions was heightened by that mix of nostalgia, depression, and pleasure so often a part of revisiting familiar haunts after a time away.

I was to find that the century's last decade had been a time of tectonic change for Peru. In line with the trend to free trade and markets across Latin America, Fujimori had imposed a severe austerity package to stop hyperinflation, and then moved to improve tax collection, to privatize state enterprises, and to streamline bureaucracy. By stabilizing the economy, the reforms encouraged investment from overseas, and contributed to the reactivation of mining, banking, construction, and a number of other sectors. I was happy to discover that a number of my formerly unemployed middle-class friends in Lima had found work in their chosen professions as engineers, accountants, or agronomists. A few had bought cars and joined the gleeful carnival of honking and swearing on the national capital's traffic-choked streets. The Peruvian elite had prospered under Fujimori, and a new generation, often graduates of U.S. business schools, partnered Canadian, American, Japanese, and Chinese investors in asparagus farms, shrimping, gold mines, cable TV, and other enterprises. It became de rigueur not only to have a cellular phone in the wealthy districts of San Isidro and Miraflores, but to wear it on one's belt in the airports and trendy restaurants, an unembarrassed display of status, power, and privilege in this country in which millions remained without regular telephones or for that matter even running water, sewage, and electricity.

The hope for Marxist revolution had died in Peru as elsewhere around the world. As Abimael Guzmán lived out his days alone in an island dungeon just off Lima's foggy coast, the Shining Path faded into oblivion, the defeat of the Maoist rebels sealed by the uprising of Andean villagers against them in the early 1990s. The takeover of the Japanese embassy in 1996 by the Túpac Amaru Revolutionary Movement (MRTA), the smaller of Peru's Marxist insurgencies of the 1980s, made for high drama on CNN. Yet army commandos retook the compound in a crush of bombs and bullets, a symbol of the pulverization of the myth of the guerrilla and the revolution that had inspired the best and worst in a generation of Latin Americans. After the bad experience of the violence of the Shining Path and MRTA, the growing conservatism on university campuses, and the fall of the Berlin Wall, the dream of seizing power by force of arms had vanished, a utopia unarmed, to borrow the phrasing of political scientist Jorge Castañeda.[2]

Fujimori won a landslide victory to a second term in 1995. It seemed to matter little to most Peruvians that the president's top advisor was an ex-CIA informer and drug lord lawyer, that his antiguerrilla fight jailed hundreds of innocents, or that his autocratic style verged on megalomania, with declarations about "destiny" choosing him to save the country. After the downsizing of expectations in the chaos and naked corruption of the García years (1985–90), the former university rector and talk show host looked good to many Peruvians for having kept the country from falling apart, no matter what the means. His playing up of humble roots as the child of Japanese immigrants along with handouts and public works only increased his popularity. The opposition's shortsightedness had further aided Fujimori. Instead of remolding and renewing themselves for the new times, the established parties from left to right had remained run by the same discredited caudillos—the Díez Cansecos, the Morenos, the Valle Riestras, the Belaúndes—assuring the contempt and disinterest of the vast majority of the Peruvian citizenry. In mid-1990s Peru, it seemed that the only actors to matter in national politics were Fujimori and his allies in the ever powerful military, who deployed the Military Intelligence Service to spy upon and sometimes harass or murder opponents.

Tunnel Six was my first stop in 1997. By chance, my arrival coincided with the final afternoon of the three-day celebration of the thirteenth anniversary of the village ronda committee's founding. It had degenerated by then into a drinking marathon, with a schoolteacher and several red-eyed men sitting around on kerosene drums in the House of the Rondero, guzzling the last of the beer and cane liquor. One villager informed me that the committee had sold 130 cases of beer, or 1,540 bottles. If the boozing did not exactly seem in line with the ideology of moralization and reform so much a part of the rondas, the celebration did indicate that the movement had not died. Or so the new committee president wanted to emphasize when I visited him early the next morning, the sun rising already red and hot over Ayabaca's towering Andes. A cheerful man of thirty-one, Florencio Carhuapoma lived with his wife and four children in a farmhouse just below the canal, with a grimy pile of fertilizer sacks, rice, and old tools and rags stacked in a front yard patrolled by a couple of chickens and a pig. "Many say the rondas have declined, but they still exist. The anniversary is proof. How else will people defend themselves and get along with each other? I don't think the rondas will ever disappear."

Yet Carhuapoma went on to admit a very real weakening of the rondas from the glory days when I had made my home in Tunnel Six in 1986 and 1987. The villagers no longer did a nightwatch and assemblies were infrequent, the ronda leader said. Carhuapoma believed the mission now was to organize public works. He even showed me a map of Tunnel Six made by a visiting engineer from a Swiss NGO, pointing to locations for a chapel, clinic, and asphalted streets to turn the ragtag scatter of farmhouses into a modern town. When I asked if the rondas had completed or even begun any of these projects, Carhuapoma said no, not so far, "People are not united like they used to be," he said, shrugging, and he brought me a plate of rice with a fried egg cooked by his wife over a wood fire on the dirt floor in the farmhouse kitchen, the familiar hospitality of even the very poorest in the northern countryside.

I did not find the rondas any healthier in the heartland of Chota. Although still existing in hundreds of villages there, most committees were shells of what they had been a decade before, rarely convening activities of any kind. The movement had also declined in the neighboring valleys of Cutervo and Bambamarca, and the Unified Central of Rondas Campesinas of the Province of Hualgayoc shut down in 1996 for lack of interest and participation. The rondas remained popular enough for the current Chotan mayor to have run for election under the banner of the Progressive Rondero and Popular Front of Chota. However, this linkage signaled weakness as much as strength, or at least so one man from Cuyumalca suggested to me. "The rondas belong to the poor and the countryside. Before, no town politician would have dared to run under their name, especially without consulting the committees," said Alejandro Quintana, a bricklayer and former secretary of the committee in the village where the first patrol had begun more than twenty years before.

I think the explanation for ronda weakening lay in a cluster of interrelated factors. One was division and apathy inside the committees. An avalanche of enthusiasm and participation akin to what Emile Durkheim called "collective effervescence,"[3] the rondas spread with astonishing rapidity in the late 1970s and early 1980s, at least in part due to the clarity of purpose and obvious accomplishment in their original mission of stamping out violence and theft. Their mid-1980s expansion into resolving disputes and organizing public works moved the movement onto broader, stickier terrain. It took many hours to untangle the knots of grievance and accusation in disputes over land, water, debts, and other matters, and the volume of cases seemed endless to many villagers. The best efforts could fail to satisfy one, the other, or sometimes both sides, and the most explosive conflicts could divide a village, weakening the ronda. As for the campaign of public works, real and imagined mismanagement by ronda presidents sowed division, mistrust, and infighting over control of projects with Parent-Teacher Associations, Irrigation Juntas, and other village organizations. The patrols had won a rapid victory over theft. As functions expanded beyond patrolling, the euphoria had faded, and the grind of overload, schism, and mixed outcome diminished participation and enthusiasm by the late 1990s.

The decline was not just a matter of local apathy and strife. It was also bound up with national developments, especially with the changing face of government in the age of Fujimori. Reasserting the authority of Lima and the state over society, the Fujimori government jailed dozens of ronda leaders in the early 1990s. "Now They Want to Crush the Rondas of Cajamarca," declared a 1993 headline on the latest arrests in one Lima newspaper.[4] Many village activists were rounded up on charges of beating or otherwise mistreating those accused of crimes by a ronda committee. Not all of these arrests were unjustified, for the explosiveness of drink and rivalry still sometimes spun into violence and mistreatment. Still, the motivations for most charges were clearly political. Many ronda leaders were tied to the left; jailing them on trumped-up accusations of terrorism was a way to silence criticism of authoritarianism

and of the persistence of poverty in Peru. My old Maoist friend
Oscar Sánchez was taken from his home by plainclothes policemen
in 1992, the morning after he had blasted Fujimori for suspending the Constitution and abolishing the Congress, using the radio
program *Rondas in Action* to launch the attack. Segundo Manuel
Guerrero, Jesús Ruiz Cubas, and seven leaders of the ronda federation in the San Ignacio Valley were among more than 100 other
ronderos jailed in the early 1990s. Oscar was lucky. The police released the former president of the Federation of Rondas Campesinas of the Department of Cajamarca (FRCC) after just a night in the
fetid drunk tank at the Chota station. A number of others, such as
Guerrero, spent months and even years behind bars, the majority
in the subhuman conditions of the Piccsi Prison in the desert outside Chiclayo. Concentrated in the traditional ronda strongholds
of Chota, Bambamarca, and Cutervo, the jailings had a chilling
effect, as a thinly veiled warning that the peasantry and the rondas were under the eye of a newly assertive state. "The repression
made people think twice about the rondas," Oscar admitted when
I visited him and his wife, Juana, in 1997. *Rondas in Action* was off
the air, and Oscar had himself become more guarded in his public
pronouncements.[5]

Even apparently benign government policies damaged the rondas. Political scientist Bruce Kay has underscored that the standard recipe of scaling back the state to clear the way for the
market and capitalism was not strictly applied in 1990s Peru.
Fujimori ruled through a hybrid of the populism of public works
and photo-ops and the neoliberalism of privatization and deregu-
lation.[6] The government spent more than $500 million on public
projects in poor areas in 1993 and 1994, no doubt timed to co-
incide with the reelection campaign of the president. In Tunnel
Six, I found a gaudily painted new school with a combination mini
soccer field and basketball court, and in Cuyumalca there were a
health clinic and a preschool. These projects were welcomed. Perhaps most notably in the installation of drinking water systems for
the first time in hundreds of villages, they improved the quality of
Andean life in a small way, and offered an opportunity to earn a bit
of cash. My old friends in Tunnel Six, Pastor Guaygua and Margarita Livia, the ones who had thieved to survive in the desperate
days before the rondas, even had chairs and a table in their dilapi-

dated farmhouse. Pastor had made the princely sum for Tunnel Six of fourteen dollars a day for two months, working as a mason on the new school. It was obvious, though, that the projects took time and energy away from the rondas, and in general encouraged the rural poor to look less to the movement and more to the government to solve basic needs. Because government agencies ignored the rondas in executing projects, the committees risked becoming isolated and irrelevant, even more out of the loop since many NGOs continued to bypass the rondas in their own programs to reforest, improve seed, expand irrigation, and otherwise raise living standards in what remained a deeply impoverished countryside.

Improvements in the official justice system were just as damaging to the rondas as their marginalization. Fujimori's removal in 1997 of three judges opposed to reworking the Constitution to allow him to run for a third term highlighted the subjection of the police and courts to political whim and manipulation. Corruption in connection with drug trafficking and state contracts remained a serious problem. Yet law enforcement as a whole worked much better than in the grim days of the late 1980s. Salaries had improved across the board. Although the starting wage of $200 a month still forced many policemen to moonlight, many government offices showed signs of higher morale and greater professionalism. As Florencio Carhuapoma and many other villagers themselves admitted to me in 1997, the rude and mercenary treatment once so common had diminished, as had the bald demands for bribes of the likes of the Chotan judge Manuel "Dr. How Much" Calvay.

I saw evidence of improvement in a visit to the new Chota courthouse. In contrast to the rattrap it had replaced, the building was clean and well lit, with a sunny courtyard and a glass display case with information about job openings and new laws. The pair of notoriously diffident and corrupt clerks of the old courthouse had retired, and the staff was now younger with a friendly and purposeful air of efficiency. A forty-one-year-old from the port of Pimentel near Chiclayo, Adolfo Fiestas, was one of the three judges in the courthouse, and I was impressed by his intelligence and openness. Fiestas opined that the rondas had been justified by government abuses, and he recounted an anecdote about a group of patrollers hailing and paying for a mototaxi to take him home when they found him drunk in the gutter on a Saturday night in the town of

Jaén. "We still have plenty of problems, not the least of them the lack of computers," he said, waving at the old portable Olympia typewriter on his plastic wood desk. "And yet there's no comparison between the justice system now and five years ago."

The reforms undercut the most basic raison d'être for the rondas, namely, their role in mediating conflicts. By the end of the 1980s, the justice-making of the assemblies had become the central job of the committees. A scan of ronda record books in 1997 in Tunnel Six as well as Cuyumalca showed that the case volume had fallen by more than one-half since 1992, not to mention Guir Guir, Yurayacu, Jambur, and a number of other villages that no longer held assemblies at all. When they did gather for what were still known as *arreglos,* or fix-its, the rondas were much more cautious than in the past about acting on their own. The original passion for reforming village society from within was lacking. To diminish the danger of arrest for "usurping official functions" or other charges, most committees forwarded all but the smallest conflicts to the town authorities, a more viable option given the improved odds of a modicum of efficiency and fairness from the police and courts. Flogging ceased almost completely, for fear that those disciplined would complain to the police. Although many ronda leaders accepted or were pleased about the advent of what the long-time Tunnel Six ronda secretary Natividad Domador described to me as the "time of moderation," the whip had been an instrument and symbol of ronda justice, connected to the mystique of the toughness and boldness of the peasantry in the fight for survival and redemption. The end of the tense drama of the rawhide marked the waning reality and myth of the movement's force.

Ronda decline was most evident in the realm of storytelling and legend. In Tunnel Six and elsewhere in the northern Andes in the 1980s and early 1990s, there was no end of tales about triumph over rustlers and crooked policemen, and their very abundance measured and multiplied ronda power. This had changed by 1997. Now the parable of apathy and even betrayal was the order of the day. I was told many stories, such as one from a man in the hamlet of Rojaspampa in the Chota Valley about the refusal of villagers to back their ronda president, even when the police jailed him on the false charge of beating a thief: "Once when a rondero was arrested, hundreds of us would march to the station to demand his release waving whips and machetes. Nobody bothered to do anything to help this poor guy or his wife. That's the way it is now. Envy and pettiness mean it's more likely for a villager to go to the station to pay the Sergeant to keep the guy in the slammer than to do anything to get him out." This view reminded me of José Carlos Mariátegui's 1928 claim that "myth propels men through history."[7] In contrast with the official Marxist line of Stalin and the Third International, the young intellectual and activist contended that the cold realities of exploitation and the economy can never alone explain a group of people's decision to organize for change, and the heady intoxicants of faith and belief are just as necessary to generate the energy and courage demanded by mobilization. The weakening of the ronda mythology of boldness and invincibility measured and furthered the decline of the movement, which lacked the same aura of drama and excitement as a decade before.

It struck me that disenchantment with the rondas reflected a crisis of social and political vision across the Peruvian Andes in the late 1990s. What one Peruvian commentator has called "the archaic utopia" had already vanished long before.[8] It was impossible by the end of the twentieth century to maintain faith in recovering the pre-Columbian past as the best path for the national future, as if history's clock could be turned back, or the mutual entanglement of the Western and the Andean be denied. Such a possibility was seldom thought about, much less wished for, by the overwhelming majority of villagers. The promise of redemption through socialism's triumph, whether by arms or the ballot box, had spread throughout the 1960s and 1970s, from the land invasions in Cuzco led by the Trotskyite Hugo Blanco to the Maoist activism of Daniel Idrogo and others in the Chotan rondas. It had faded even faster than it arose with the violence of the guerrillas and the corruption and infighting of leftist parties, not to mention Marxism's decline after the end of the Cold War.

Yet the half-life of the utopia of neoliberalism and the free market was proving to be just as an evanescent. It was not just leftist hand-wringing to point out that almost a decade of reform and restructuring had not eased poverty in Peru. Although the middle class and the elite might prosper as Peru wired into the global economy, the same was not true for the rest of the country. There was scant evidence for a trickle down of wealth to the brown-skinned majorities in a society in many ways still haunted and divided by the colonial legacy of painful inequality by race and class. Everywhere in the northern Andes I heard the same complaint about the impossibility of landing a decent job anywhere in the cities. "I had to come back because I was starving making only eighty dollars a month as the janitor at a Texaco station. Most poor people are as bad off as ever," explained Camilo Calle in Tunnel Six. No longer did Calle or many others in what remained the majority Peru of unwashed clothes and bodies, child labor, and adobe hovels listen to promises from Liman technocrats about development, progress, and salvation by globalization.

It had been a matter of survival that sent Cuyumalcans to the trails in 1976. The rich in Lima could afford Dobermans, electric fences, and *guachimanes,* or private security guards, to insulate themselves from increasing crime. Villagers did not have money for any of these measures; banding together in the rondas was their only way to protect life and property. As the movement's size and scope expanded in the late 1970s and early 1980s, it embodied the peasantry's highest hopes for social equality and salvation. One 1986 ballad exulted that village organizing would "end every injustice."⁹ By the late 1990s, however, one seldom heard such great expectations attached to the rondas any longer in the wake of the setbacks of justice-making together with the shrinking of faith and expectation. "Maybe the law of the poor the old-timers always used to talk about never will arrive," said former Tunnel Six ronda president Víctor Córdova when I went to visit him, Francisca, and their seven children in 1997. All of them were living in a shack of straw mat on the desert at the edge of Piura on what little Víctor made as a night watchman at the Retired State Employees' Club downtown by the banks of smelly and shrunken Chira River. I had never heard so guarded a view from this champion of the rondas and the peasant cause.

Nonetheless, I hardly want to leave the rondas as a story of failure and loss. While Peru threatened to unravel altogether in the long years from the late 1970s to the early 1990s, the northern rondas had risen in response to the incapacity of the government to protect peasants from surging violence and crime. To be sure, it was an emergency response prompted by the tremendous uncertainty and danger for thousands of villagers. But there is never a straight line from poverty and peril to mobilization, or necessarily any line at all, since the alchemy of necessity, opportunity, and initiative of organizing on a mass scale is hardly predictable. Many villagers themselves, with the characteristic bravado of the northern Andes, spoke of *decisión,* the sheer willpower of Víctor, Régulo, Eladio, Omelia, Daniel, Angélica, Oscar, Juana, Francisco, and many others whom I will always see as heroes in the rondas, no matter that they had imperfections as heroes always do. The very real accomplishments of the patrols and assemblies they built deserve to be acknowledged and remembered. "Now we can sleep peacefully, protect our health, harvest our crops only when they ripen, and raise cattle and barnyard animals, all of which was impossible before," declared a 1982 report by ronda leaders in the Bambamarca Valley that summed up the most obvious and tangible successes of the movement.[10]

The broader achievement remained a real and justified challenge to social hierarchy and power in Peru. It was no longer simply a shame and stigma to be poor, rural, and Andean. "All social movements enact a cultural politics," political theorists Sonia Alvarez, Evelina Dagnino, and Arturo Escobar remind us in a recent book about protest and mobilization in Latin America.[11] With the rise of the rondas, being a peasant was no longer felt just as lack and sadness, but also as a source of pride and celebration no less striking for being incited in part by Marxists, apristas, radical priests, and NGOs from the middle class and the cities. The mantras of multiculturalism and diversity have grown familiar and at times tiresome in the United States, at the risk of blinding us to the prerequisites of respect and understanding in a diverse society seeking to fulfill lofty promises of democracy and economic opportunity. In the solemn opinion of one Liman philosopher in 1937, "psychic degeneration" and "biological rigidity" meant that the Andean peasantry "is not, and cannot be anything but a machine." This unabashed racism and contempt persisted in the second half of the twentieth century in elitist references about the "lack of breeding" and "dirty habits" of the inhabitants of the Andean countryside.[12] The bold, sometimes brash, style of the rondas marked a refusal by northern villagers to be scapegoats for misery and backwardness. It was a movement very much connected to what philosopher Charles Taylor once called a "politics of recognition," the demand of the demonized and the marginalized to be recognized as fully human.[13]

The disappointment and cynicism of the late 1990s reflected unrealized ambitions for the rondas. The most forthright ronda supporters were nonetheless quick to point out the inroads in the struggle for the full rights of citizenship so long denied to the peasantry. "Chasing out Calvay and others showed the police and judges they could get into trouble for corruption and abuses, and that's one reason they're fairer and more polite with us now," said Alejandro Quintana on a Sunday afternoon between gulps of beer and orange soda in a cantina at the edge of Chota with me and a few others from Cuyumalca. Even those traditionally opposed to the rondas acknowledged the rondas' successes: a former military officer with gold teeth and a Rotary pin on his pinstriped suit, the Chota prosecutor Walter Silva admitted with a smile in an interview the next day that "the thought of having the rondas parade us around the plaza did make many of my colleagues think twice about bribes." It was no longer common to hear a prosecutor or any other town official address a villager by the disrespectful *tú,* much less with the condescending diminutives of "boy" or "little child." For their part, villagers were not intimidated by the authorities as in the past, when they called a policeman "boss" and "chief," or, as the ronda activist and perhaps founder Régulo Oblitas once told me, "ran away from any official like jackrabbits to hide from fear and embarrassment."

The place of the peasantry and the poor had changed in national society as well. It was obvious that Fujimori's public works and his many trips to the countryside and shantytowns were about votes and power. However, they also reflected a changing reality in which it was impossible to govern any longer in Peru as if the poor majorities did not exist. As a part of what anthropologist José Matos Mar called the "popular overflow" of migration, political violence, religious change, and social movements in the second half of the twentieth century,[14] the rondas had helped force an unprecedented measure of accountability and representation from the bureaucrats and the politicians who were supposed to serve the populace and yet had not. The gains in the struggle for recognition and citizenship were fundamental and irreversible, even if Peru's predicament remained bleak at the end of the millennium.

Any final assessment depends on the standard of evaluation. If wholesale transformation is made the measure, the rondas failed. Villagers continued to confront poverty and uncertainty no matter how far they had come. The limited achievement of even so massive a mobilization as the rondas belies the lavish claims sometimes made about the emancipatory potential of social movements. Yet dismissing the initiative for not bringing dramatic change may hold the rondas to an unreasonable standard. After all, the twentieth century will end without an instance of an approximate equality of power and opportunity having been achieved in any Latin American country (or in this one, for that matter), and even the great promise of the Cuban and Sandinista Revolutions vanished under assault from the United States and their own tyranny and incompetence. The outcome of the Mayan and other new Indian movements remains to be seen. This does not mean that one should abandon the ennobling dream of freedom and prosperity. It does force a renewed appreciation for the politics of the possible, and for those movements that made real gains for the poor and the excluded. The rondas met this standard by reducing crime and conflict, and forcing the government to pay new attention to the peasantry.

It was hard to see very far into the future. At least as far back as the rapid Inca rise through the Spanish conquest to the Shining Path's crusade for Communism, the Andes have witnessed upheavals as violent and sudden as the earthquakes for which they are famous. The end of the 1990s was not a time of protest, much less insurrection, and in this sense another reminder that there has always been much more to the region than the episodes of blood and rebellion so horrifying and fascinating to voyeuristic outsiders. At the same time, the moment pulsed with latent questions about the years ahead. Would the rondas last much longer? If so, how might the movement change in style and mission, remake itself for new times?[15] What fresh, and perhaps unexpected, forms of dissent and organizing would come into being in the Andes and Peru? Could the Andes ever be prosperous, or were the children of Tunnel Six, Cuyumalca, and hundreds of other villages destined to be the eternal losers in the national and world economy? What would be the fate of the changing but distinctive and proud traditions of the Andean countryside? "Mountains of my Peru, the Peru of the world. And Peru, at the cusp of the globe. I can only accept it," wrote the poet César Vallejo, a child of the northern Andes who fought in the Spanish Civil War and died a pauper in Paris.[16] This great early twentieth-century Peruvian intellectual understood ahead of his time that the destiny of the Andes was linked irreversibly to the nation and the rest of the planet. All the questions about the region's place in a shrinking world remain as unresolved at this century's end as they were at the beginning.

It was no easier to predict anthropology's fate. The upheavals of the late 1960s and early 1970s triggered attacks on the field for obliviousness to history, insensitivity to power, and collusion with colonialism. As part of the postmodern turn in the 1980s, the questioning extended to the politics of writing and representation, and the assumption that the anthropologist can ever completely or disinterestedly describe other cultures. The criticism sometimes edged into caricature, but it has forced us to reconsider comfortable assumptions about disciplinary righteousness. A decade in Peru sharpened my own awareness of anthropology's perils, among them of misunderstanding and willed ignorance, of the misuse of what we write, or of failing to give enough back to the people who allow us into their lives. Even what I thought would be the simple matter of writing this book became a long grind with painful moments for me and those I love best. At the same time, the rondas deserve to be recognized and remembered. I do not regret trying to chronicle the movement, or to convey a more human understanding of the Andes, peasants, and the politics of protest. As writing's shadow has lifted, moreover, it has become easier for me to see encouraging signs in anthropology, and to hope the field may contribute in a small way to comprehension, compassion, and change. These signs include the entry into the profession's ranks of more women, minorities, and people from the Third World; a concern for activism and accountability among many younger scholars; the expansion of study to encompass everything from AIDS in Africa to Caribbean sweatshops and Canadian television; the explosion of debate about race, gender, nationalism, memory, modernity, globalization, and a host of other key concepts. Do the changes of recent years in anthropology indicate renewal and reinvention, or at least life? I want to think so no matter what the potential folly of an optimistic prognosis.

Nobody broached such weighty matters on my last night in Tunnel Six. Because Víctor and Francisca had left the village five years before, I stayed this time with Francisca's mother, Margarita, who lived in her same three-room mud-walled home on the ridge together with her son Máximo, his wife, and their baby daughter. We talked by the lamplight about Víctor and Francisca, their children, the old times of a decade before when I had lived in Tunnel Six, and the latest scandals of adultery and sorcery in this village in the parched, anonymous foothills of the Andes. At about ten o'clock, Máximo appeared in the company of Natividad, the longtime ronda secretary, a pair of dark shapes in the doorway out of the unlit country night. A bit tipsy from the leftover cane liquor from the anniversary celebration, the two men were in high spirits. At Margarita's and my request, Natividad went down the hill to get his guitar to play a few songs. He came back with his battered guitar, wife, Sabina, and mother, Fedima. Natividad launched into a medley of Andean tunes, a cross-regional mix of his own making including an Ecuadoran San Juanito, Huancayan huaylash, Ayacuchan huayno, and Cajamarcan cumbia.[17] A teenager when I left Tunnel Six, Sabina was now a señora with two babies and a third on the way, but she accompanied her husband in the same high and painfully beautiful voice as ever. Máximo passed around a bottle. Everyone drank the rotgut, even the normally abstemious Margarita. I requested a ballad about the rondas. "In Tunnel Six, Jambur, Tomapampa, and Culqui, and every other place there are rondas, cleaning up the country," began this tune Natividad and Sabina had composed a decade before to a San Juanito melody. For the moment, it did not seem to matter to them or to me that the rondas no longer existed in half the places mentioned in the song.

"Long live the rondas campesinas," interjected Natividad, and then bent back over the guitar to go on with the music.

NOTES

1 It was complicated to decide whether to use names or pseudonyms in this book. I know that José Paz and many others would prefer to have their real names published, because they are proud of their protagonism in the events described. Yet I suspect those portrayed less flatteringly would prefer not to have their real names published. In most of these cases, each marked with a note when the person in question first appears in the book, I have given them pseudonyms, in a few cases also changing details about them to further protect their privacy.

2 A department is the rough equivalent of a state in the Peruvian system of administration, and each department is made up of provinces, themselves subdivided into districts.

3 This and all subsequent translations from the Spanish are mine, unless otherwise noted. The original of the agreement is in the possession of Régulo Oblitas in Cuyumalca, and it is reprinted in full in Rojas (1990:29). Chapter 1 discusses the agreement and the origins of the rondas in much more detail.

4 This figure is based on the calculations made in Starn (1992a:15).

5 The rondas against the Shining Path were initially known as Civil Defense Committees. It appears that the label of rondas was later given to these groups by the military, an effort to blunt criticism of the organizations as forced upon the peasantry by calling them by the same name as the original and more grassroots movement in northern Peru. As it turned out, the rondas in the south-central Andes took on a life of their own, and they eventually became an important force in the defeat of the Shining Path. For more on these rondas, see Starn (1993) and Degregori et al. (1996).

6 The quote from Berger comes from the frontispiece of Roy (1997).

7 The unpublished, untitled song was written by Filiberto Estela in 1983, from the village of San Antonio in the Chota Valley.

8 The untitled song was composed by the Little Workers of Santa Rosa, probably in the early 1980s.

9 Huaynos are mountain ballads especially popular with peasants.

10 A pair of bellwether books in the criticism of anthropology in the Vietnam War years were edited by Hymes (1972) and Asad (1973). Harrison (1991) is a more recent anthology in the same tradition.

11 Among the articles and books published as a result of their work are Bibler (1993), Enslin (1994), Hale (1994), Visweswaran (1994), Díaz-Barriga (1996).

12 An article by Haraway (1991) was crucial in my own thinking about the issue of knowledge and objectivity.

13 Good places to start in the large body of work on the Shining Path are Degregori (1990), Gorriti (1990), Palmer (1992), Kirk (1993), Starn (1995), and Stern (1998).

14 The song is called "Flor de retama" (The broom flower) and was composed by Ricardo Dolorier, who himself was never part of the Shining Path.

15 The many reports on Peru during the 1980s and early 1990s published by Amnesty International and Human Rights Watch–Americas (formerly Americas Watch) document the trampling of human rights by government forces. As late as 1997, a number of people falsely accused of belonging to the Shining Path, or the much smaller Túpac Amaru Revolutionary Movement (MRTA), remained in jail, and both political prisoners and common criminals continue to this day to confront lack of due process, torture, and inhumane prison conditions.

16 The authorship is uncertain, but the song, "Mamacha de las Mercedes," was most famously sung in the 1980s by folksinger Martina Portocarrero.

17 *The Other Path* is the title of a controversial book by de Soto (1989). Portes and Schauffler (1993) criticize de Soto and provide a useful summary of responses to his book. Golte and Adams (1987) are among those to have questioned de Soto for overestimating the opportunities available to the poor for advancement and prosperity through entrepreneurship in Peru. Their book is also a good introduction to the growth of Protestantism there, as well as the migration to the cities.

18 Hale (1994:6).

19 Clifford (1988:40). The descriptions of research have typically appeared either in the introduction to ethnographies by anthropologists, or in the distinctive genre of the "fieldwork account." Many of the fieldwork accounts were written by women. As Visweswaran (1994) notes, a feminist might approach these books as efforts at experimen-

tation preceding the rethinking of the politics of writing in the 1980s and ask why the mostly male group of scholars who rose to prominence in the 1980s came to be viewed as the first to think about the problem of "writing culture."

20 Ortner (1984:143).

21 I discuss the limits and possibilities of activist anthropology in Tunnel Six and elsewhere in Starn (1995). A debate between Scheper-Hughes (1995) and D'Andrade (1995) offers contrasting visions of activism and detachment in anthropology, with my sympathies far more with Scheper-Hughes.

22 This is the title of a book by Powdermaker (1966) about her fieldwork experiences in New Guinea, Mississippi, Hollywood, and Zimbabwe.

23 Marcus (1995) gives a useful look at the problems and possibilities of multisited ethnography.

24 The problems of voice and speaking for others has been the subject of much recent debate. Among the contributors have been Spivak (1988), Alcoff (1991), and a number of the contributors to Behar and Gordon (1995).

25 As part of an attempt to allow villagers to have their say about the rondas, I helped to organize a conference in 1991, in which eighteen leaders from the rondas in the northern as well as the central and southern Andes journeyed to Lima to talk about their organizing to journalists and academics at the Institute of Peruvian Studies. The proceedings were published in Starn (1993).

26 The book was Degregori, Escobal, and Marticorena (1992).

27 hooks (1990).

28 This is the title of an article by D. C. Moore (1994).

29 The quote comes from a cover story in the *New York Times Magazine* by Jonathan Goldberg, March 2, 1997, p. 32.

30 Sutton (1991) provides an interesting discussion of the issue of audience in anthropology.

31 The best statistics on the war come from Centro de Estudios y Promocion del Desarollo, Center for Development, Research and Action (DESCO) and the Instituto de Defensa Legal.

32 The world of those who have studied the rondas ranges from a German anthropologist to a Cajamarcan sociologist to a Lima lawyer. It is small enough that most of us know each other, and I am grateful in particular for the exchange of information and ideas over the years with Nora Bonifaz, Oscar Castillo, Rolando Estela, John Gitlitz, Juan Gustavo Hernández, Telmo Rojas, and Raquel Yrigoyen. The work produced by these and other analysts of the rondas includes Git-

litz and Rojas (1983), Estela (1988), Huamaní, Moscoso and Urteaga (1988), Rojas (1990), Bonifaz (1991), Zarzar (1991), Castillo (1993), Yrigoyen (1993), Castillo (1993), Hernández (1994), Huber (1995), and Pérez Mundaca (1995). Miguel Garnett (1992) has written a novel, *Rondo,* that is partly about the rondas.

33 A good place to start for debates about the relation between agency and structure are Bourdieu (1977), Giddens (1979), and Ortner (1984).

34 A reader edited by Dirks, Eley, and Ortner (1994) offers an introduction to key debates about culture, power, and history.

35 I am influenced and borrowing the phrasing of Ulf Hannerz (1989) here. Important rethinkings of the concept of culture come from Clifford (1988, 1997), Abu-Lughod (1990), and Gupta and Ferguson (1997b).

36 Among others, the work of Antonio Gramsci and Michel Foucault has been especially influential in recent thinking about power. Gramsci's most famous statement of his views on culture and the problem of hegemony was the *Prison Notebooks* (see Gramsci 1971), while Foucault's clearest statement of his understanding of power is in the second half of *The History of Sexuality,* volume 1 (1980). More recent key work that has shaped my own thinking includes Williams (1977), Haraway (1991), and Hall (1996).

37 The quote comes from the 1990 Wilderness Travel Company, catalog pp. 63–68.

38 I have discussed the problem of "Andeanism" in Starn (1991a, 1995), arguing that it reappeared in much anthropology about the Andes of the 1960s and 1970s. Mayer (1991) and the commentators on the Spanish translation of my 1991 article in the Peruvian journal *Allpanchis* (number 39, 1992) criticize the argument from a number of different angles, and my response also appears there.

39 Doughty (1968:1). In fairness, Doughty discussed issues of migration and change in later parts of the book, belying this initial assertion of the timelessness of Andean society.

40 The quote is from the opening line of Wolf's (1980:1) by now classic *Europe and the People Without History.* For a provocative if somewhat disjointed and mean-spirited attack on Wolf's book, see Taussig (1989), to which Wolf coauthored a response (Mintz and Wolf 1989).

41 Vich (1996) has studied the street clowns, Poole (1997) writes about photography, Reyes (1997) researches the drug economy, and Gill (1994) examines maids in La Paz. Reyes is strictly speaking a political scientist, but has training in anthropology, which informs the sharp-sighted analysis in his work.

42 Among many others, good examples of the new anthropology of the rural Andes are Rappaport (1990), Orlove (1991), Crain (1991), Isbell (1992), Rivera (1993), Gelles (1995), Larson and Harris (1995), Abercrombie (1997), and Albro (1997).

43 Good places to start to learn about pre-Columbian Peru are the classic works of Rowe (1946), Murra (1975, 1986), and Zuidema (1964), although see among others Gelles (1995) and Van Buren (1996) for interesting criticism of key concepts in their scholarship. Fine, more recent scholarship includes Spalding (1984), Silverblatt (1987), and MacCormack (1991).

44 Hemming (1970) offers a wonderful and vivid account of the conquest. The movie *Aguirre, Wrath of God,* directed by Werner Herzog, is a provocative cinematic view of the arrival of the Spaniards.

45 Kearney (1996) provides a provocative look at the way anthropologists have themselves further a vision of the peasantry as cut off from modernity.

46 De la Cadena (1996a:138).

47 Hannerz (1992:261). The meaning of globalization for our thinking about cultural difference and sameness turned in the 1990s into a major focus of inquiry in anthropology, and among the latest and key works are Appadurai (1996) and Gupta and Ferguson (1997a).

48 The quote comes from a 1927 article republished in Mariátegui (1972: 117). Flores Galindo (1982) has written a fine book about Mariátegui and his times.

49 Pratt (1991:33–39). As Pratt recognizes, the metaphor of the "contact zone" should not be taken to mean that the cultures that meet there are or were ever themselves static or unconnected, for they too developed and changed through intercultural conflict and encounter.

50 The song, "Mi Alfombrilla," was written in the late 1980s.

51 See Escobar and Alvarez (1992), Wignaraja (1993), Fox and Starn (1997), and Alvarez, Dagnino, and Escobar (1998) for discussions of thinking about social movements in the Third World.

52 Mushakoji (1993:xiv).

53 S. Stern (1987:34).

54 Trotskyite Blanco (1972) wrote a famous account of his involvement in peasant organizing in Cuzco. Among others, Hobsbawm (1974) and G. Smith (1989) analyze the land occupations of the 1960s and 1970s in the central Andes. García-Sayan (1982) offers a general overview of mobilizations for land, and Lynch (1992) of protests against the military government.

55 The quote comes from a book called *Underdevelopment is a State of*

Mind by Harrison (1985:73), which, disconcertingly, is still used in many college courses on public policy and Latin America.

56 Hall (1985:112).

57 I am borrowing here the title of Kearney's (1996) recent book, discussed in the text that follows.

58 An anthology edited by Shanin (1987) offers a good entrée into debates in peasant studies. The *Journal of Peasant Studies* was a major forum for debates of the 1970s and 1980s about village politics and agrarian society.

59 Wolf (1969). Besides Wolf's book, other key works in the debates about peasants and revolution were Paige (1975), Scott (1976), and Popkin (1979). Skocpol (1982) wrote a classic review essay on the topic called "What Makes Peasants Revolutionary?"

60 Kearney (1996).

61 Castells (1996).

62 Webb and Fernández (1996:208).

63 "El retorno del indio" (return of the Indian) is the title of an article by Albó (1991).

64 The story called the "The Pongo's Dream" appears in Arguedas (n.d.) and in translation in Starn, Degregori, and Kirk (1995:262).

ONE Origin Stories

1 This is a line from the poem "Noches de adrenalina" (Adrenaline nights), which appears in *The Peru Reader* (Starn, Degregori, and Kirk (1995:483).

2 Starn (1991b).

3 A common saying in northern Peru, this is also the title of a fine short book in Spanish on the rondas by Huber (1995).

4 Aguirre and Walker (1990) and Poole (1994) address the issues of rustling, banditry, and violence in the Andes. López Albujar's (1933) *Los caballeros del delito* is a fascinating early twentieth-century study of crime and punishment in the Peruvian mountains, including a particularly vivid section on the Andes of Piura.

5 Many scholars have written about Velasco and the agrarian reform. Among the important works are Lowenthal (1975), Matos Mar and Mejía (1980), and McClintock and Lowenthal (1983).

6 A model for the abolition of the haciendas as part of the project of making serfs into farmers was the Vicos Project in the central Andes of Peru. Anthropologists from Cornell University directed the

project, which involved the purchase of a hacienda, and the turning over land to the serfs. Dobyns (1971) offers an insider's assessment of this project that raises fascinating questions about the politics of anthropology, social change, development, and modernization. There is an archive of material from the Vicos Project at Cornell University.

7 I am translating *pongo* as "serf," and referring to the title of a wonderful short story by Arguedas (n.d.), translated into English in Starn, Degregori, and Kirk (1995) and discussed earlier.

8 The speech was given on June 24, which was formerly the "Day of the Indian." An excerpt of it appears in Starn, Degregori, and Kirk (1995:264–69).

9 Matos Mar and Mejía (1980:179).

10 The ballad, called "The Twenty-fourth of June," was by a rural schoolteacher from Cuzco, Gabriel Aragón, and it appears in Starn, Degregori, and Kirk (1995:270–71).

11 Thorndyke (1976) wrote a semifictional novel about the ouster of Velasco. See Lynch (1992) for a history of the last five years of the military government under General Francisco Morales Bermúdez.

12 The figures come from Gonzales and Samamé (1991:31).

13 "Peruvian pendulum" is the title of a book by Gonzales and Samamé (1991).

14 Malkki (1992:31). Deere (1990) offers a detailed history of patterns of migration in the northern mountains.

15 These are pseudonyms.

16 Basadre (1978:119, 205).

17 S. Stern (1982) provides a fine account of the policy of relocation as well as the engagement of Andeans in the colonial courts.

18 This is the title of the well-known book by Corrigan and Sayer (1985).

19 These headlines came from the front page of *El Popular*, May 15, 1983; *La República*, May 12, 1985; and *Correo*, June 9, 1983.

20 See Apel (1996) on the demography of the sierra of Piura.

21 Personal communication, March 7, 1998. De la Cadena (1996b) provides an insightful discussion of the politics of race in the Andes in a recent dissertation, soon to appear as a book from Duke University Press.

22 I discuss the issues of family and gender at length in chapter 4.

23 In a happy and unusual development, I found on returning to Cuyumalca in 1997 that most of the Oblitas children had come back to settle in the village, cobbling together a living by various contributions of farming, petty commerce, and day labor.

24 Zarzar (1991:131).

25 Gitlitz and Rojas (1983).

26 Degregori (1986).

27 Degregori (1986:52).

28 See Ansión et al. (1992) for a look at schooling in the Andes during the 1980s. Contreras (1996) also offers an insightful overview of educative and social change in the region during the twentieth century.

29 These were the words in 1986 of Agripino Domador, Víctor's father, to describe the estate of Pillo, where he was a serf before the abolition of the haciendas.

30 The figures come from Contreras (1996:40) and apply only to primary schools. They include the numbers for the cities of Piura and Cajamarca as well as the countryside, but, as Contreras notes, the fastest rate of the growth was in the rural areas, few of which had schools at all in 1920.

31 This is a line from an untitled song written in 1979 by Valentín Mejía, a ronda leader from the village of San Antonio de la Camaca in the province of Hualgayoc.

32 Alegría (1941) and Arguedas (1985).

33 "Ronderos en marcha," *Amauta*, June 5, 1986, p. 5.

34 This is from the June 24, 1969, speech by Velasco that appears in Starn, Degregori, and Kirk (1995:264).

35 The French theorist Foucault (1971) was famously concerned with the way identities may be "produced" by states. In an argument in some ways parallel to mine about "peasantness" in the mid-twentieth century, Irene Silverblatt (1995) explores how the category of "Indian" was created and imposed by the colonial state in seventeenth-century Peru, only to later become a rallying point for opposition to Iberian rule. Joseph and Nugent (1994) and Nugent (1997) also offer creative explorations of the role of states in the "production" of identity in Latin America.

36 *The Nervous System* is the title of a book by Taussig (1992).

37 This is a pseudonym.

38 Among the most provocative is Minh-ha (1989). Pratt (1992) uses "imperial eyes" as the title of her wonderful book on travel writing, and she points out in a well-known essay (1986) how many of the same tropes of discovery and mastery reappear in ethnography.

39 Quoted in Clifford (1997:281).

40 Abrams (1988:82).

41 I borrow some of this phrasing from the title of an article by Ewing (1990).

42 Silverblatt (1995:293–94).

43 These lines are part of the same song mentioned in note 14 of this chapter.

TWO Nightwatch

1 The article appears in *La República,* March 17, 1984, pp. 23–34.
2 This line comes from a song called "La ronda de La Alfombrilla" by Santos Díaz, composed in the late 1980s.
3 These numbers are approximate, and based on Starn (1992a:6–7).
4 Bonifaz (1991:165). The rise of the Shining Path and the counterinsurgency of the government had a far greater effect in terms of damage and upheaval. Yet it can be argued that the rondas were by far the larger movement in terms of participants, as the Shining Path never claimed more than 10,000 or so militants (Degregori 1990).
5 San Juanitos are a kind of country music from Ecuador, also popular in parts of northern Peru.
6 De Certeau (1984:31–32).
7 Hemming (1970) gives a vivid description of the siege of this Incan citadel.
8 Pratt (1991) provides a provocative discussion of Poma's letter. Adorno (1986) offers another assessment of it. A vitriolic essay by Urbano (1991) attacks Adorno and others for what he asserts is romanticizing and exaggerating the spirit of resistance and rebelliousness in Poma's letter and in colonial Andes in general.
9 MacCormack (1991) offers a fine treatment of religion in the Andes in the early colonial period.
10 Mario Vargas Llosa's *La ciudad y los perros* ([1967]; The City and the Dogs) is a vivid look at machismo and barracks culture inside the officers' training academy; it has been made into an excellent film by the Peruvian director Francisco Lombardi.
11 De Certeau (1984:xix, xxiii).
12 The rondas started before the military began to be sent to fight the Communist Party of Peru–Shining Path in the mountains of Ayacucho to the south. Even after the military was sent in December 1982, not many villagers from Piura and Cajamarca ended up serving in the war zone, because they were mostly stationed in northern bases that were kept up mainly in the event of conflict with Ecuador. The problem of troops' being unfamiliar with the areas where they were stationed did become an issue with the occupation of the mountains of Ayacucho by soldiers from the coast who did not speak Quechua and

often looked down upon villagers in the area as inferior and likely to be supporters of the guerrillas. See the account of navy infantrymen in Starn, Degregori, and Kirk (1995:342–47) for more on the sometimes terrible consequences of the posting of coastal troops in the Andes.

13　Paz realized this dream. In 1989, he left Tunnel Six for good to make a living selling clothes in the city.

14　"Vivo resfriadito / por cuidar mi ganadito" goes the lyric to this ballad called "Mi Alfombrilla" by José Santos Díaz Pérez, which I have translated loosely in order to preserve the rhyme.

15　The 1979 song, called "La ronda es un ejemplo" (The ronda is an example), is by Valentín Mejía from San Antonio de la Camaca in the province of Hualagayoc.

16　Contributions I have found useful in thinking about the theme of memory and history include Davis and Starn (1989), Nora (1989), Gillis (1994), and Abelmann (1996).

17　Davis and Starn (1989:2).

18　The work of White (1973) was key in rethinking the issue of objectivity in historical writing. More recent work on the question in the humanities and social sciences includes Friedlander (1992), Chandler, Davidson, and Harootunian (1994), and Megill (1994). The latter contains a debate between White and the Italian historian Carlo Ginzburg about White's claims about the "constructedness" of historical writing.

19　Benjamin (1968:257).

20　I gathered these figures through a house-to-house survey in 1987. The numbers each family reported for losses may themselves have been affected by memory's selectivity and uncertainty; but I tried to verify them through cross-checking with other villagers and ronda leaders. The results tabulated here should be viewed as a general estimate, although I believe a reasonably accurate one.

21　Nora (1989:18).

22　Taylor (1987) has written a gripping history of violence in the central provinces of Cajamarca between 1900 and 1930.

23　See Espinoza León (n.d.) for more on Froilán Alama and Rosa Palma.

24　These are pseudonyms.

25　I obtained a copy of this report from an Investigative Police officer in the Chota station. He typed it from the original for me without putting down the date of the report.

26　This song, called "Hermandad ronderil" (Ronda brotherhood), is from the late 1970s by Santos Díaz Pérez of La Alfombrilla.

27 This song, called "Los soplones" (The stool pigeons), is also by Santos Díaz.

28 See Taussig (1992) on this point.

29 The quote comes from the final page of a 1981 memorandum entitled "Apreciación de Inteligencia Nro. 02-JP-PP." It was provided to me by an officer at the station.

30 This is a pseudonym.

31 Taussig (1992:34). Scheper-Hughes (1994) describes a case of being a direct witness to violence and how she made the decision to intervene.

32 Mariátegui (1968:40).

33 The normally insightful Carlos Iván Degregori (1989) makes this incautious assertion.

34 The violations of human rights are amply documented in the many reports on Peru issued by Amnesty International and Human Rights Watch–Americas. See the sections for "Peru" in the *Amnesty International Country Report* and the *Human Rights Watch World Report* for the latest updates.

35 Stoll (1990), Burdick (1993), Stoll and Burnett (1993), and Berryman (1994) offer useful discussions of the increased influence of Protestantism in Latin America.

36 The Peruvian Dominican Gutiérrez (1988) wrote a key book on liberation theology.

37 Gitlitz (1985) offers an insightful look at church activism in the Bambamarca Valley. His account includes an examination of the church's role in the rondas.

38 This appears in *Latinamerica Press*, March 16, 1989, p. 5.

39 Olluco is a small tuber grown in much of the Andes.

40 *Cohetazos, pancazos, betazos, latigazos,* and *fuetazos* were the words in Spanish.

41 I derive this estimate from Blondet and Montero (1995:74), whose statistics are based on the period between 1981 and 1991.

42 Scheper-Hughes (1992).

43 Among the many books explaining and interpreting Foucault are Dreyfus and Rabinow (1982), Diamond and Quinby (1988), and Stoler (1995). Miller (1993) has written a controversial and interesting biography of Foucault. One of my favorite essays about the French theorist is the obituary for him by Said (1987).

44 The description appears on page 27 of Roncagliolo's article.

45 This was the title of the well-known book by Wolf (1969).

46 Lenin (1980:384–85).

47 The label of *gente humilde* for the peasantry is sometimes used by townspeople as well as villagers themselves in the Andes.

48 The interview was with General Luis Cisneros Vizquerra, a noted hard-liner with the nickname of *El Gaucho,* the Cowboy. It appeared in *El Callao* on September 26, 1986, and I quote from the reprinting of parts of it in DESCO (1989:608).

49 The telegram was dated May 18, 1979, revealing that worries about the rondas existed even before 1980. I thank the secretaries in the sub-prefecture in Chota for their help in obtaining a copy of the telegram.

THREE Nightcourt

1 For discussions on the issue of "indigenous law" in the Andes, see Tamayo Flores (1992), Wray (1993), and the essays by Iturralde, Vidal, and Stavenhagen in Stavenhagen and Iturralde (1993).

2 The proclivity to analyze "indigenous law" as primordial can be mis-leading even in cases where the practice is without doubt very old, as such categorization can ignore the way a practice can change in meaning and practice through the decades. Moore (1986) shows that "customary law" in parts of Africa was shaped and encouraged by colonial rule and in this sense far from as uncomplicated or ancestral.

3 Lynch (1990) details the history of FER and Peru's radical university politics in the 1970s.

4 Hinojosa (1992) details Maoism's major influence on the Peruvian Left.

5 These quotes come from undated flyers I obtained in 1990 and 1991, respectively.

6 Red Homeland entered the elections under the name of National Union of the Revolutionary Left (UNIR).

7 The broadsheet is undated and untitled, but appears to date to about 1980.

8 The full text of the minutes can be found in Starn (1992a:75–80).

9 The newsletter was called *El Rondero,* and these quotes come from issue no. 2, April 1980. I thank Oscar Sánchez for help obtaining it.

10 This is the title of fine essay by Dirlik (1996).

11 See Del Pino's chapter in Degregori, Coronel, et al. (1996).

12 The premise of peasant society as especially riven by conflict was most famously advanced by Foster (1960:177–78).

13 The quote appears in an excerpt from Poma's letter in Starn, Degregori, and Kirk (1995:80).

14 This quote comes from an unpublished translation of the "Proclamation of Túpac Amaru" (1781) by Jan Mannel, Department of Spanish and Portuguese, Stanford University. The proclamation and many other documents pertaining to the revolt are collected in a book published by the Comisión Nacional del Bicentenario de la Rebelión Emancipadora de Túpac Amaru (National Commission of the Bicentennial of the Emancipatory Túpac Amaru Rebellion) (1981).

15 This comes from the song "Verdades que amargan," for which the date is uncertain.

16 I thank the clerks at Chota's District Court for access to these documents.

17 Sánchez (1995) provides a history of the protest, from the perspective of a militant in Red Homeland.

18 Gitlitz (1975) and Taylor (1987) provide valuable histories of the Llaucán massacre.

19 Klaren (1973) offers a good history of the APRA and Víctor Raúl Haya de la Torre.

20 Crabtree (1992) provides a useful history of the García government and the political maneuvering of the 1980s in Peru.

21 This quote comes from a history of the rondas handwritten by Risco, which he lent to me in 1991.

22 The quote comes from the third page of an undated mimeograph called "Regulations of the Pacific Rondas of Peru" in the possession of Pedro Risco in Chota.

23 Ibid., 4.

24 Oblitas grew disenchanted with Risco and APRA in the late 1980s, as many villagers did with the economic decline under the APRA government.

25 I am grateful to Martin Lewis for explaining the reason it does not snow in the northern Andes.

26 The quote comes from the book of minutes of the Alto Cuyumalca ronda, in the possession of Régulo Oblitas in Cuyumalca.

27 This quote comes from the minutes of a September 21, 1980, meeting in the record book of the Alto Cuyumalca ronda in the possession of Régulo Oblitas.

28 The commander belonged to the Republican Guard, the branch of the police charged with borders and prisons. Chota had a prison, which is why there were Republican guards in the town.

29 The minutes appear in the same record book in the possession of Régulo Oblitas.

30 Gramsci (1971:108–10).

31 Huanambal and several other witnesses remember these as his words at the meeting.

32 The quote comes from the same record book in the possession of Régulo Oblitas.

33 The law legalizing the rondas was number 24571, issued on November 7, 1986. The decree describes the rondas as "pacific" as favored by APRA, yet in a compromise with the left APRA said the rondas were also to be "democratic and autonomous." In 1988, APRA tried to limit the operation of the rondas through Supreme Decree 012-88-IN, which required that rondas register with the police. Most ronda committees simply ignored the registration requirement. At that point, the García government was already in crisis; it did not have the power to enforce the registration requirement. In 1993, the Fujimori government issued Supreme Decree 002-93-DE. It required original rondas in northern Peru as well as the newer rondas against the Shining Path in the south-central Andes to rename themselves Self-Defense Committees, which were to be overseen by the armed forces. Few committees in the northern Andes actually followed the demand to change their name and register with the military. By that time, the rondas had weakened a great deal anyway from their heyday in the 1980s.

34 This is a pseudonym.

35 Pratt (1991) offers a brilliant and engaging discussion of the term "transculturation."

36 The marinera is music that is especially popular on Peru's northern coast.

37 The quote comes from *Americas,* a 1993 television series featuring Fuentes, and produced by WGBH in Boston.

38 Trouillot (1991).

39 *The Lettered City* (1996) was the title of Rama's well-known book.

40 Far fewer women than men came to the assemblies, and I discuss reasons for this in the next chapter.

41 The phrase "line of flight" comes from Deleuze and Guattari (1987: 89).

42 The phrase is an example of the application of agricultural terminology into ronda justice in this farm society.

43 Pratt (1992:196).

44 These passages come from an excerpt of the report reprinted in Federación de Rondas Campesinas de Cajamarca (1986:70–71).

45 *La otra cara de la luna* (*The Other Side of the Moon*) is the title of an anthology edited by Pásara and colleagues (1991) about social movements in Peru. "Ambiguities, Contradictions, and Uncertainties" is

the title of a chapter in the book by Pásara and anthropologist Alonso Zarzar, who also contributes a chapter on the rondas to the anthology. I appreciate Pásara's willingness to ask tough, deromanticizing questions. Yet I think the anthology goes too far in refusing to recognize the very real accomplishments of soup kitchens, rondas, and other movements of that decade.

46 Nedelsky (1990:163).

47 The survey was carried out in the district of Frías in 1989 by Karin Apel and Ludwig Huber with 102 respondents, reproduced here from Huber (1995:82).

Would you go to the authorities (judges, police, lieutenant governors) or the ronda campesina with the following problems?

	Rondas	Authorities
Theft, rustling	95	7
Fights, drunkenness	96	6
Family or marital problems	52	50
Slander, malicious gossip	88	14
Damages to crops or animals	85	17
Land disputes	60	42

Note: Huber and Apel do not provide data on the gender of the respondents. If the majority were men, this might account for the relatively low numbers advocating the rondas for family or marital problems. As I explain in the next chapter, men were far more reluctant than women to have the rondas turn into a tribunal for cases of domestic violence and abandonment.

48 Hernández (1994) gave more than 100 respondents a list that included the rondas, official judiciary, police and army, and district and departmental political authorities. Seventy-nine percent said they would choose the rondas first in a case of theft; 71 percent for fights; 65 percent for a family dispute; 65 percent for slander and gossip.

49 Amazonas is a department towards the jungle, a place where many Chotan villagers migrated to work and sometimes to settle for good.

50 Arguedas (1985:192). This is from "Puquio: A Culture in Process of Change," originally published in Spanish in 1964. It appears as an addendum to the English translation of Arguedas's *Yawar Fiesta*.

51 Arguedas (1985:192).

52 Mitchell (1991) provides a valuable discussion of the demise of the *varayoc* system in parts of rural Ayacucho.

53 Anderson (1983:6).

54 Arguedas (1985:192).

55 For example, Rojas (1990).

56 The name and place are pseudonyms.

57 Berg (1992) and Isbell (1992) offer interesting looks at the issue of early support for the guerrillas in the Andean countryside.

58 Among others, Isbell (1992) and Degregori, Colonel, et al. (1996) discuss the mounting rural disenchantment with the Shining Path.

59 The quote comes from Guzmán's "We Are the Initiators" speech, which appears in Starn, Degregori, and Kirk (1995:313–14).

60 I borrow this section title from the title to an interesting book by historian Mallon (1995).

61 This quote comes from an article by Ricketts called "El Perú en el diluvio," published in *Expreso,* July 29, 1990, p. 18.

62 Harvey (1989:306). Unlike Harvey, I do not think localism is necessarily or always negative or reactionary. See Massey (1994) for criticism of Harvey on this point.

63 This is a song called "En este día dichoso" (On this blessed day), by José Santos Díaz, from the late 1980s.

64 This quote comes from the speech delivered by Velasco to announce the reform, which appears in Starn, Degregori, and Kirk (1995:265).

65 The untitled song was written by Valentín Mejía of the village of San Antonio de La Camaca, and the date is uncertain.

66 See Degregori (1993).

67 The quote comes from a lecture called "Indigenous People as Emerging Actors in Mexico and Latin America," delivered on March 10, 1998, at the Council of Latin American Studies, Duke University, Durham, North Carolina. A similar view of Peru as "behind" the rest of Latin America on the ethnic question appears in Albó (1991:325).

68 Skar (1982:75).

69 I am translating *cholo* as hick in this context. Albro (1997) offers a discussion of the complex and multiple meaning of the word *cholo* in Bolivia and Peru. Both songs are untitled.

70 Vargas Llosa (1983:83) makes this claim in an article about the massacre of eight journalists in 1983 in the village of Uchuraccay.

71 An enormous literature now exists on the question of nationalism. Although nationalism was already much discussed in the late nineteenth century by scholars such as Ernest Renan, among others, it was Benedict Anderson (1983), although see also the revised edition in 1991, who coined the label of "imagined communities," underscoring the way that nations depend on the creation of feeling of shared history

and values. Other influential works include A. Smith (1979), Bhaba (1990), Hobsbawm (1990), Sommers (1991), and Chatterjee (1993).

72 Símon Bolívar and José San Martín were, respectively, Venezuelan and Argentine, but became heroes in Peru for leading the victorious War of Independence against Spain that ended in the Battle of Ayacucho in 1824. Andrés Avelino Cáceres led the resistance to the Chileans in the War of the Pacific (1879–83) and later became president, while Admiral Miguel Grau, General Francisco Bolognesi, and Colonel Alfonso Ugarte fought and died in the same war.

73 In a well-known debate about the dynamics of Peruvian nationalism, Bonilla (1987) charges Manrique (1981) and Mallon (1995) with overstating the degree and the radicalism of peasant nationalism during the War of the Pacific. Even Bonilla, however, concurs that alternative understandings of the nation arose from the conflict. Among others, Mallon (1995), Méndez (1995), Nugent (1994), and Thurner (1997) are more recent explorations of the question of nationalism in the Andes.

74 Chatterjee (1993:114).

75 "Las Rondas Campesinas," *Expreso,* June 1, 1986, p. 26.

76 Gluckman (1955:3).

77 Evans-Pritchard (1940:169).

78 Of course, many critics have argued that anthropologists of mid-century were wrong to see the Nuer and other groups as so stable. They emphasize that these groups were never as self-contained and unchanging as suggested by Evans-Pritchard and others, and they faulted these British anthropologists for downplaying the impact of colonialism in Africa. The anthology edited by Asad (1973) is a classic statement of this attack, while one edited by Comaroff and Comaroff (1993) extends the rethinking of the legacy of anthropology in Africa.

FOUR Women and the Rondas

1 Allen (1988) discusses the shifting complexities of her status during research in the village of Sonquo in her fine book *The Hold Life Has.* She relates that her adoption of a skirt was a key to her eventually being accepted as a woman.

2 Silverblatt (1987:xxviii). Spalding (1984) and Salomon (1991) offer insightful discussions of life and culture in pre-Incan society in Huarochirí.

3 Silverblatt (1987:xxviii).

4 The search for evidence of matriarchies in the ancient world was a matter of much interest in anthropology of the 1970s. For questioning of the impulses behind the search, see a by-now classic essay in feminist anthropology, Rosaldo (1980).

5 The field of feminist scholarship is large, diverse, and contentious, and feminist anthropology has become one of the most vibrant areas of anthropology over the last two decades. A few of the key works that have influenced my thinking about gender are Collier and Yanagisako (1987), Scott (1988), Ginsburg and Tsing (1990), Haraway (1991), and Massey (1994).

6 All of these figures come from Blondet and Montero (1995), a useful compendium of statistics on the status of women in Peru.

7 McPherson (1988:36).

8 The quote from Mao comes from Prazniak (1997:39). Her article is an excellent overview of Mao's thinking about the question of women in revolution.

9 Sonia Alvarez, personal communication, February 3, 1998. Alvarez (1997) develops this argument more fully in an insightful essay.

10 This group, Action for the Liberation of the Peruvian Woman (ALI-MUPER), was founded in 1973. Four other groups began at the end of the 1970s, including the Flora Tristán Center of the Peruvian Women and the Manuela Ramos Movement. These two organizations today remain among the most important of the many feminist organizations in Peru, almost all of which remain concentrated in Lima.

11 Fabj (1993) offers an interesting analysis of the Mothers of the Plaza de Mayo.

12 Collier and Yanagisako (1987:26).

13 The song was called "Cholita mía," and I could not ascertain the date or authorship. The section on "Love" in the valuable anthology of Andean songs edited by Montoya, Montoya, and Montoya (1987: 227–374) is full of lyrics on the theme of love and betrayal.

14 "Rondas en Cajamarca," *Correo*, March 25, 1980, p. 4.

15 Fox and Starn (1997:6). Although this quote comes from an introduction to this anthology that I cowrote, Fox wrote this passage, and I am therefore crediting him in the citation.

16 The names of the couple are pseudonyms.

17 The song is by Ernesto Sánchez Gallardo, "the Troubadour of Huascarán," and called "Chanca lomo."

18 Bourque and Warren (1981) was an early and important study of gender and power in the Andes. Among the many valuable studies on the subject since then are Silverblatt (1987), Seligmann (1993), De la

Cadena (1995), and Radcliffe (1996). Gill (1994) has written a fine book on the experience of rural Andean women as maids in La Paz, Bolivia.

19 P. Harvey (1994:69–70).

20 Blondet and Montero (1995:87).

21 This is a pseudonym.

22 Stavig (1995:80).

23 "Can the Subaltern Speak?" is the title of a famous essay by Spivak (1988).

24 This is a pseudonym.

25 Sapir (1949:509, 512, 576). The work of the brilliant linguist and anthropologist warns against the kind of simplistic history that imagines criticism of anthropology's traditional, homogenizing usage of the concept of culture to have developed only in the 1980s. Sapir did not deny the existence of shared meaning and tradition, yet the influence of psychology led him to insist on the inevitability as well of fragmentation, conflict, and individual diversity. Skeptical of "ruthless judgments" and "impersonal anthropological description," he advocated sensitivity to "flexible fields of cultural patterning" and the "many diverse strands" that "intercross at that point in place and time in which the individual judgment or preference is expressed" (570–73).

26 The song, "A las rondas campesinas," is by Juana Vásquez from the Chota Valley, written in the mid-1980s.

27 These are pseudonyms.

28 Stern (1995:99).

29 Gordon (1988).

30 Mohanty, Russo, and Torres (1991:5–6). Mohanty develops her argument most fully in a well-known essay republished in the same anthology, "Under Western Eyes: Feminist Scholarship and Colonial Discourses."

31 The quote comes from Mohanty's introduction to Mohanty, Russo, and Torres (1991:6).

32 The phrase was used by Gómez-Peña in a performance with Roberto Sifuentes of *The Borderama Show*, at the University of North Carolina, Chapel Hill, November 20, 1997. For more on his thinking, see Gómez-Peña (1996).

33 The first is edited by Weil (1988) and the second by Küppers (1994).

34 Blee (1991).

35 Koonz (1987).

36 Powers (1997).

37 This quote comes from page 5 of *A la Primera Asamblea de Bases de la FEDECC*, a 1982 document kindly provided to me by Lewis Taylor.

38 The quote comes from Tristán's "Women of Lima" essay in Starn, Degregori, and Kirk (1995:200), translated from the Spanish by Paul and Doris Beik. Perhaps with the romanticism of many European travelers in nineteenth-century Peru, Tristán thought that Lima women were already emancipated but that their sisters in Europe as well as the Andes were not. Pratt (1992) and Poole (1997) discuss the fascinating and sometimes contradictory writing of Tristán, and Beik and Beik have translated her Peruvian travel diaries into English (Tristán 1993).

FIVE The Rondas in the Age of the NGO

1 Campo (1996:122).

2 The NGO has only recently begun to be an object of academic study. Carroll (1992), Bebbington et al. (1993), Macdonald (1997) and Luthra (1998) offer introductions to questions raised by the work of these organizations.

3 It is possible to typologize NGOs as "intermediary" or "support" as opposed to "membership" or "grassroots." The former support work for social change among the marginalized, whereas the latter are run directly by the downtrodden. When talking about NGOs in the rest of the chapter, I refer to the "intermediary" or "support" type.

4 The concept of the "Third World" is problematic in a number of ways, not the least of them that the fact of increasing global interconnectedness belies the metaphor of separate "First" and "Third" Worlds. Escobar (1994) is one of a number of critics to question the usefulness of the term "Third World." I therefore use the term advisedly in this book, as a referent for poor countries in Asia, Africa, and Latin America.

5 The figure for Peruvian NGOs comes from a directory published by DESCO (1994). The Asociación Nacional de Centros (1991) in Lima publishes another directory of Peruvian NGOs. The figure for Latin American NGOs comes from a directory to directories of NGOs in Latin America and the Caribbean, published by the Inter-American Foundation (1995).

6 Vitillo (1997:20).

7 See my discussion of Alvarez's (1997) concept of "movement webs" later in this chapter. Keck and Sikkink (1998) also explore the possi-

bilities of these kinds of border-crossing alliances, using the case of the human rights movement.

8 I did not know it at the time, but development anthropology was then growing into a subfield of the discipline, with many anthropologists going to work for the World Bank and the U.S. Agency for International Development. For an incisive critical view on development anthropology, see Escobar (1991). Debate has continued with a response to Escobar by Little and Painter (1995).

9 The line appears in Vallejo's (1990:103) "The Black Heralds."

10 This is a pseudonym.

11 This and all the other names of the team members are pseudonyms.

12 Escobar's (1995) *Encountering Development: The Making and Unmaking of the Third World* has been a key book in the broader critical rethinking of development. Also important have been an anthology edited by Sachs (1992) and Ferguson's (1990) dissection of development in Lesotho. Pigg (1992) explores the local impact of development in Nepal in a useful essay, while Moore (n.d.) builds upon, and in some cases, seeks to rethink the new work by Escobar and other recent critics of development.

13 Escobar (1995:22).

14 Donald Moore, personal communication, September 7, 1996; see Moore (n.d.) for more on this point.

15 Llanques are sandals made of discarded tires.

16 The second-in-command was Osmán Morote, now jailed, and the house was known as the Casa Blanca, or "White House."

17 This is a quote from a speech by Shining Path chief Abimael Guzmán; it appears in Starn, Kirk, and Degregori (1995:313).

18 Among the many critics were Feder (1971), Burbach and Flynn (1980), and Bodley (1982). Sachs (1992) offers a compendium of critical views of development, many of which began to be formulated in the 1970s.

19 A collection edited by Brokensha, Warren, and Werner (1980) reflected the new thinking about development.

20 A pair of books by Smith (1991, 1996) offer a thoughtful assessment of liberation theology and its role in social movements.

21 Lernoux (1989) and Walsh (1992) offer a largely critical assessment of the rise of Opus Dei and of conservative retrenchment under John Paul II.

22 The Asháninkas are one of the largest indigenous groups in Peru's Amazon, and Brown and Fernández have written a fascinating book about them (1991).

23 Wolf (1969:xii).

24 Alvarez (1997).

25 I have changed the name and some details about the institute.

26 "El vivo vive del sonzo" was the Spanish, a line featured in the well-known ballad "Verdades que amargan" by a leading Andean balladeer, Ernesto Sánchez Gallardo.

27 I have changed the name of the center and few other details of the story.

28 The Kjarkas were a well-known Bolivian folk music group.

29 Freire (1970:9).

30 Gitlitz (n.d.).

31 I draw this quote and the discussion of PRODIA from Gitlitz (n.d.: 26–32).

32 Gilberto Rojas is a pseudonym.

33 Pratt (1991:36).

34 Alvarez (1997:107).

35 *Natacha* was a hugely popular Peruvian soap opera, broadcast in 1990.

36 A sociologist at the Institute of Peruvian Studies and the director of an NGO in Bambamarca, Castillo (1993:35) argues that instability and infighting made the rondas a poor vehicle for trying to make the basis of large-scale development projects in the countryside, but confirms that they were effective for smaller initiatives such as "village potable water systems, the construction of schools and medical posts, and trail repair."

37 An anthology edited by Gugelberger (1996) offers an assessment of testimonial literature. An example of testimonial literature from Peru is the story of Gregorio Condori Mamani and Asunta Quispé Huamán, recently translated into English (Valderrama et al. 1996) and with a fine introduction by Paul Gelles.

38 Elisabeth Burgos-Debray puts forward this view in her introduction to Merchú (1984).

39 Pratt (1991:35).

40 Visweswaran (1994:101–2).

41 In Colombia, for example, Carlos Castaño, the most powerful paramilitary leader and also a major drug trafficker, has founded an NGO called the Foundation for Peace of Córdoba.

42 Gitlitz (n.d.: 26).

43 I quote from Appadurai's lecture "The Grounds of the Nation State: Identity, Violence, and Territory," Department of Cultural Anthropology, delivered on May 4, 1998, at Duke University, Durham,

North Carolina. See Appadurai (1996) for a much fuller discussion of these issues.

SIX Leaders and Followers

1 Pratt (1992:127, 134).
2 The Republican Guard was the branch of the police charged with border and prison security.
3 Since then, it has been argued creatively by Burdick (1995) that it may be just as important for anthropologists to study in places where a social movement fails to galvanize support and to figure out the reasons why people may choose not to identify with and participate in an initiative for change.
4 Gitlitz (n.d.).
5 I do not mean to suggest that scholars have altogether ignored conflict over leadership in rural movements. A classic piece by Landsberger and Hewitt (1970) already took up the issue almost two decades ago. A more recent piece is Fox and Hernández (1989).
6 An example is an otherwise interesting article by Huamaní, Moscoso, and Urteaga (1988).
7 Quoted in Rosenbach and Taylor (1993:13). Steinbeck was referring to American presidents, but his observation applies just as well to the leaders of union organizing in California's Central Valley, whom he famously chronicled in *The Grapes of Wrath*.
8 Weber (1946).
9 Weber gives only male examples, but of course there are also plenty of cases of charismatic female leaders.
10 Varese (1968) and Zarzar (1989) have written books about Juan Santos Atahualpa. This and the larger rebellion of José Gabriel Condorcanqui, Túpac Amaru II, are discussed at length in a fine anthology edited by Stern (1987). A collection put out to mark the two hundredth anniversary of Condorcanqui's uprising provides a fascinating array of primary sources about that insurgency (Comisión Nacional del Bicentenario de la Rebelión Emancipadora de Túpac Amaru 1981).
11 The quote comes from a translation of Valcárcel's (1928) *Tempestad en los Andes* that appears in Starn, Degregori, and Kirk (1995:221).
12 Gramsci (1971:323).
13 Feierman (1990).

14 Burns (1978).

15 Stern (1982) offers a superb view of the dynamics of power in early Andean colonial society.

16 The anonymously composed song is called "Los comuneros" and appears in Montoya, Montoya, and Montoya (1987:656–57).

17 "The Tyranny of Structurelessness" is the title of the 1973 essay by Freeman, who used the pen name "Joreen."

18 Scott (1985:32). Although I admire the work of Scott, I think there is merit in the rethinking of his work by a number of critics (Kondo 1990; Mitchell 1990). As they suggest, Scott's work assumes that the poor and disenfranchised always have a neatly clear-sighted understanding of their predicament and that they would rebel against injustice if only it were not for the costs of bloody suppression. This view can romanticize the clarity of the political vision of the downtrodden and overvalue the potential of small-scale and stealthy acts of opposition for bringing change.

19 See chapter 2 for more on the "little bird."

20 Scott (1985:30–31).

21 This is a pseudonym, as is the name of the girl's father.

22 This is a pseudonym, as is the name of the store owner's wife.

23 Girard (1987).

24 Girard (1987:74).

25 Scheper-Hughes (1992). I am drawing heavily in this paragraph from her astute and moving discussion of the applicability of Girard's work to infant death in northeastern Brazil.

26 Zarzar (1991:127–28).

27 Marx (1970:737).

28 A number of urban ronda organizers inspired by the rondas campesinas to fight crime in the shantytowns and markets of Chiclayo and Piura told me the nearness of the police was a major obstacle. The proximity meant the police could break up meetings and arrest leaders much more easily than in the countryside. Although the urban rondas helped to maintain the peace in some areas in Peru, they never became as strong as their counterparts in the rural Andes.

29 The Agrarian League was the main provincial representative of the rondas in Ayabaca.

30 Huber (1995) details the history of AP and the rondas in Huancabamba.

31 The Unified Front of Rondas Campesinas of the Province of Hualgayoc was formed in 1989 as an effort to overcome partisan splits, but largely failed to do so. It was eventually dissolved. In 1991, a new effort

was undertaken to build a nonpartisan federation, and I describe at the end of the chapter the founding of what was baptized the Unified Central of Rondas Campesinas of the Province of Hualgayoc.

32 Degregori (1990:198).

33 The word for "endearments" was *cariños*.

34 The lawyer Hildebrando Castro Pozo was a leader of this party. For a fascinating look at one activist in it, Sinforoso Benites Algarobo, see Valverde (1987).

35 Deleuze and Guattari (1987).

36 A translation of Alegría's novel was published in English in 1941.

37 Vich (1997:14).

EPILOGUE

1 I am grateful to Paul Gelles for these details about Juanita.

2 This is the title of a book by Castañeda (1993) about the history of the Latin American left.

3 The great French sociologist memorably defined "collective effervescence": "At such moments this higher form of life is lived with such intensity and exclusiveness it monopolizes all minds to more or less complete extinction of egoism and the commonplace" (Durkheim 1953:92).

4 *La République,* May 26, 1993, pp. 13–15.

5 The criticism increased in 1996, when Oscar and several other former ronda leaders of Red Homeland allied with the Chota mayor, and ran, successfully, for a seat on the town council as part of the Progressive Rondero and Popular Front.

6 Kay (1996).

7 Mariátegui (1995:229). For accuracy, I have chosen not to change the original wording, although it would no doubt be more accurate to say "men and women."

8 This is the title of a book by Vargas Llosa (1996) about the work of José María Arguedas.

9 This untitled song was composed by Carmen Domador from the village of Algodonal in the Quiroz Valley.

10 The report was prepared by leaders of the Provincial Peasant Federation of Bambamarca for the first general meeting of the Departmental Peasant Federation of Cajamarca (FEDECC), a now vanished group then with ties to PUM and the Peasant Federation of Peru (CCP). I am very grateful to Lewis Taylor for giving me a copy of the report.

11 Alvarez, Dagnino, and Escobar (1998:9).

12 Deustua (1937:68).

13 The phrase "politics of recognition" comes from the title of a book by Taylor (1992).

14 *Desborde popular* (*Popular overflow*) was the title of a well-known book by Matos Mar (1983).

15 Pérez Mundaca (1995) offers a view of one interesting development in the rondas of the mid-1990s in the western part of the province of Chota. There the movement allied with the police to fight a resurgence of rustling and highway assaults, including the holdups of buses on the mountain road between Chiclayo and Chota. A change from the often hostile relation between the peasantry and police of the 1980s in the rondas, this episode marked an alliance between the committees and the official authorities, with the police even providing shotguns to the ronderos to take on the gangs.

16 This comes from a translation of Vallejo's *Human Poems* in Starn, Degregori and Kirk (1995:9).

17 Huaylash is a dance music closely associated with Peru's central Andes; cumbia is a tropical style of music that originated in Colombia.

BIBLIOGRAPHY

Abelmann, Nancy. 1996. *Echoes of the Past, Epics of Dissent: A South Korean Social Movement.* Berkeley: University of California Press.

Abercrombie, Thomas. 1997. *Pathways of Memory and Power: Ethnography and History Among an Andean People.* Madison: University of Wisconsin Press.

Abrams, Philip. 1988. "Notes on the Difficulty of Studying the State." *Journal of Historical Sociology* 1(1):58–89.

Abu-Lughod, Lila. 1990. "The Romance of Resistance: Tracing Transformations of Power through Bedouin Women." *American Ethnologist* 17(1):41–55.

Adorno, Rolena. 1986. *Guamán Poma: Writing and Resistance in Colonial Peru.* Austin: University of Texas Press.

Aguirre, Carlos, and Charles Walker, eds. 1990. *Bandoleros, abigeos y montoneros.* Lima: Instituto de Apoyo Agrario.

Alberti, Giorgio, and Enrique Mayer, eds. 1974. *Reciprocidad e intercambio en los andes peruanos.* Lima: Instituto de Estudios Peruanos.

Albó, Xavier. 1991. "El retorno del indio." *Revista Andina* 9(2):299–345.

Albro, Robert. 1997. "Virtual Patriliny: Image Mutability and Populist Politics in Quillacollo, Bolivia." *Political and Legal Anthropology Review* 20(1):73–92.

Alcoff, Linda. 1991. "The Problem of Speaking for Others." *Cultural Critique* 20:5–32.

Alegría, Ciro. 1941. *Broad and Alien Is the World.* New York: Farrar and Rineheart.

Allen, Catherine. 1988. *The Hold Life Has: Coca and Cultural Identity in an Andean Community.* Washington, D.C.: Smithsonian Institution Press.

Alvarez, Sonia. 1997. "Reweaving the Fabric of Collective Action: Challenges to 'Actually Existing Democracy' in Brazil." In *Between Resistance and Revolution: Cultural Politics and Social Protest,* Richard G. Fox and Orin Starn, eds. New Brunswick, N.J.: Rutgers University Press.

Alvarez, Sonia, Evelina Dagnino, and Arturo Escobar, eds. 1998. *Culture of Politics/Politics of Cultures: Revisioning Latin American Social Movements*. Boulder, Colo.: Westview.

Amnesty International. 1992. *Human Rights during the Government of Alberto Fujimori*. New York: Amnesty International.

Anderson, Benedict. 1983. *Imagined Communities: Reflections on the Origins and Spread of Nationalism*. London: Verso. Rev. ed. 1991.

Andreas, Carol. 1985. *When Women Rebel: The Rise of Popular Feminism in Peru*. Westport, Conn.: L. Hill.

Ansión, Juan et al., eds. 1992. *La escuela en tiempos de guerra*. Lima: CEA-PAZ.

Apel, Karin. 1996. *De la hacienda a la comunidad: la sierra de Piura, 1934–1990*. Lima: Instituto de Estudios Peruanos.

Appadurai, Arjun. 1996. *Modernity at Large: Cultural Dimensions of Globalization*. Minneapolis: University of Minnesota Press.

Arguedas, José María. 1985. *Yawar Fiesta*. Austin: University of Texas Press.

———. n.d. *El sueño del pongo*. Lima: Ediciones Salqantay.

Asad, Talal, ed. 1973. *Anthropology and the Colonial Encounter*. New York: Humanities Press.

Asociación Nacional de Centros. 1991. *Directorio de organizaciones no-gubernamentales de desarollo*. Lima: Asociación Nacional de Centros.

Barrios de Chungara, Domitila. 1978. *Let Me Speak!: Testimony of Domitila, a Woman of the Bolivian Mines*. New York: Monthly Review Press.

Basadre, Jorge. 1978. *Perú: Problema y posibilidad*. Lima: Banco Internacional del Perú.

Bastien, Joseph. 1979. *Mountain of the Condor: Metaphor and Ritual in an Andean Ayllu*. St. Paul, Minn.: West Publishing.

Baudrillard, Jean. 1983. *Simulations*. Translated by Paul Foss, Paul Patton, and Philip Beitchman. New York: Semiotext(e).

Bebbington, Anthony, et al. 1993. *Non-governmental Organizations and the State in Latin America*. London: Routledge.

Behar, Ruth. 1993. *Translated Woman: Crossing the Border with Esmeralda's Story*. Boston: Beacon.

Behar, Ruth, and Deborah Gordon, eds. 1995. *Women Writing Culture*. Berkeley: University of California Press.

Belejack, Barbara. 1996. "Latin America Online." *NACLA: Report on the Americas* 30(3):14–17.

Benjamin, Walter. 1968. *Illuminations*. New York: Harcourt, Brace, and World.

Berg, Ronald. 1992. "Peasant Responses to Shining Path in Andahuaylas." In *Shining Path of Peru*, David Scott Palmer, ed. London: Hurst.

Berreman, Gerald. 1969. " 'Bringing It All Back Home': Malaise in Anthropology." In *Reinventing Anthropology*, Dell Hymes ed. New York: Random House.

Berryman, Philip. 1994. "The Coming of Age of Evangelical Protestantism." *NACLA: Report on the Americas* 27(6):6–10.

Bhaba, Homi, ed. 1990. *Nation and Narration*. London: Routledge.

Bibler, Susan. 1993. *The Culture of Protest: Religious Activism and the U.S. Sanctuary Movement*. Boulder, Colo.: Westview.

Blanco, Hugo. 1972. *Land or Death: The Peasant Struggle in Peru*. New York: Pathfinder Press.

Blee, Kathleen, 1991. *Women of the Klan: Racism and Gender in the 1920s*. Berkeley: University of California Press.

Bloch, Marc. 1961. *Feudal Society*. Vol. 1. Translated by L. A. Mannion. Chicago: University of Chicago Press.

Blondet, Cecilia and Carmen Montero. 1995. *La situación de la mujer en el Perú, 1980–1994*. Documento de Trabajo No. 68. Lima: Instituto de Estudios Peruanos.

Bodley, John. 1982. *Victims of Progress*. Menlo Park, Calif.: Benjamin/Cummings.

Bonifaz, Nora. 1991. "Las rondas campesinas, el orden público y el orden interno: el caso de Cajamarca." In *Una ruta posible: propuestas para la I Conferencia por la Paz*. Lima: IDS.

Bonilla, Heraclio. 1987. "Comunidades indígenas y estado nación en el Perú. In *Comunidades campesinas: cambios y permanencias*, Alberto Flores Galindo, ed. Lima: Consejo Nacional de Ciencia y Tecnología.

Bourdieu, Pierre. 1977. *Outline of a Theory of Practice*. Translated by R. Nice. Cambridge: Cambridge University Press.

Bourque, Susan, and Kay Warren. 1981. *Women of the Andes: Patriarchy and Social Change in Two Peruvian Towns*. Ann Arbor: University of Michigan Press.

Brokensha, David, D. M. Warren, and Oswald Werner. 1980. *Indigenous Knowledge Systems and Development*. Washington, D.C.: University Press of America.

Brown, Michael, and Eduardo Fernández. 1991. *War of Shadows: The Struggle for Utopia in the Peruvian Amazon*. Berkeley: University of California Press.

Brush, Stephen. 1977. *Mountain, Field, and Family: The Economy and Human Ecology of an Andean Valley*. Philadelphia: University of Pennsylvania Press.

Burbach, Roger, and Patricia Flynn. 1980. *Agribusiness in the Americas*. New York: Monthly Review Press.

Burdick, John. 1993. *Looking for God in Brazil.* Berkeley: University of California Press.

———. 1995. "Uniting Theory and Practice in the Ethnography of Social Movements." *Dialectical Anthropology* 20(3–4):361–85.

Burneo, José, and Marianne Eyde. 1986. *Rondas campesinas y defensa civil.* Lima: SER.

Burns, James MacGregor. 1978. *Leadership.* New York: Harper and Row.

Calderón, Fernando, Alejandro Piscitelli, and José Luis Reyna. 1992. "Social Movements: Actors, Theories, Expectations." In *The Making of Social Movements in Latin America,* Arturo Escobar and Sonia Alvarez, eds. Boulder, Colo.: Westview.

Campo, Rafael. 1996. *What the Body Told.* Durham, N.C.: Duke University Press.

Carmack, Robert, ed. 1989. *Harvest of Violence.* Austin: University of Texas Press.

Carroll, Thomas. 1992. *Intermediary NGOs: The Supporting Link in Grassroots Development.* West Hartford, Conn.: Kumarian Press.

Castañeda, Jorge. 1993. *Utopia Unarmed: The Latin American Left after the Cold War.* New York: Knopf.

Castells, Manuel. 1996. *The Rise of the Network Society.* Cambridge: Blackwell.

Castillo, Oscar. 1993. *Bambamarca: vida cotidiana y seguridad pública.* Documento de Trabajo No. 55. Lima: Instituto de Estudios Peruanos.

Central Committee of the Communist Party of Peru. 1989. "Interview to Chairman Gonzalo." Photocopy.

Certeau, Michel de. 1984. *The Practice of Everyday Life.* Berkeley: University of California Press.

Chandler, James, Arnold Davidson, and Harry Harootunian, eds. 1994. *Questions of Evidence: Proof, Persuasion, and Reason across the Disciplines.* Chicago: University of Chicago Press.

Chatterjee, Partha. 1993. *The Nation and Its Fragments: Colonial and Postcolonial Histories.* Princeton, N.J.: Princeton University Press.

Chávez de Paz, Denis. 1989. *Juventud y terrorismo: carácteristcas sociales de los condenados por terrorismo y otros delitos.* Lima: Instituto de Estudios Peruanos.

Chernoff, John. 1979. *African Rhythm and African Sensibility: Aesthetics and Social Action in African Musical Idioms.* Chicago: University of Chicago Press.

Clifford, James. 1988. *The Predicament of Culture: Twentieth Century Ethnography, Literature, and Art.* Cambridge: Harvard University Press.

————. 1997. *Routes: Travel and Translation in the Late 20th Century.* Cambridge: Harvard University Press.

Collier, Jane, and Sylvia Yanagisako, eds. 1987. *Gender and Kinship: Towards a Unified Analysis.* Stanford, Calif.: Stanford University Press.

Collins, Jane. 1989. *Unseasonal Migrations: The Effects of Rural Labor Scarcity in Peru.* Princeton, N.J.: Princeton University Press.

Comaroff, Jean, and John Comaroff, eds. 1993. *Modernity and Its Malcontents: Ritual and Power in Postcolonial Africa.* Chicago: University of Chicago Press.

Comisión Nacional del Bicentenario de la Rebelión Emancipadora de Túpac Amaru. 1981. *La Revolución de los Túpac Amaru.* Lima: Comisión Nacional del Bicentenario de la Rebelión Emancipadora de Túpac Amaru.

Contreras, Carlos. 1996. *Maestros, mistis y campesinos en el Perú rural del siglo XX.* Documento de Trabajo No. 80. Lima: Instituto de Estudios Peruanos.

Coronel, José. 1994. "Comités de defensa: un proceso social abierto." *Ideéle* 59–60:113–15.

Coronel, José, and Carlos Loayza. 1992. "Violencia política: formas de respuesta comunera en Ayacucho." In *Perú: el problema agrario en debate / SEPIA IV,* Carlos Iván Degregori, Javier Escobal, and Benjamín Marticorena, eds. Lima: Universidad Nacional de la Amazonia Peruana and SEPIA.

Corrigan, Philip, and Derek Sayer. 1985. *The Great Arch.* Oxford: Basil Blackwell.

Crabtree, John. 1992. *Peru under García: An Opportunity Lost.* Pittsburgh: University of Pittsburgh Press.

Crain, Mary. 1991. "Poetics and Politics in the Ecuadorean Andes: Women's Narratives of Death and Devil Possession." *American Ethnologist* 18(1):67–89.

D'Andrade, Roy. 1995. "Moral Models in Anthropology." *Current Anthropology* 36(3):399–408.

Davis, Natalie Zemon, and Randolph Starn, eds. 1989. "Introduction." *Representations* 26:1–6.

Deere, Carmen Diana. 1990. *Household and Class Relations: Peasants and Landlords in Northern Peru.* Berkeley: University of California Press.

Degregori, Carlos Iván. 1986. "Del mito de Inkarrí al 'mito' del progreso: poblaciones andinas, cultura e identidad nacional. *Socialismo y Participación,* 66:49–56.

————. 1989. "Comentario a la década de la violencia." *Márgenes* 3(5–6):186–90.

————. 1990. *Ayacucho 1969–1979: el surgimiento de Sendero Luminoso.* Lima: Instituto de Estudios Peruanos.

————. 1992. "Campesinado andino y violencia: balance de una década de estudios." In *Perú: el problema agrario en debate / SEPIA VI,* Carlos Iván Degregori, Javier Escobal, and Benjamín Marticorena, eds. Lima: Universidad Nacional de la Amazonia Peruana and SEPIA.

————. 1993. "Identidad étnica, movimientos sociales y participación política en el Perú." In *Democracia, etnicidad y violencia política en los paises andinos,* Alberto Adrianzén, ed. Lima: Instituto Francés de Estudíos Andinos and Instituto de Estudios Peruanos.

Degregori, Carlos Iván, José Coronel, Ponciano del Pino, and Orin Starn. 1996. *Las rondas campesinas y la derrota de Sendero Luminoso.* Lima: Instituto de Estudios Peruanos.

Degregori, Carlos Iván, Javier Escobal, and Bejamín Marticorena, eds. 1992. *Perú: el problema agrario en debate.* Lima: Universidad Nacional de la Amazonia Peruana and SEPIA.

De la Cadena, Marisol. 1995. " 'Women Are More Indian': Ethnicity and Gender in a Community Near Cuzco." In *Ethnicity, Markets, and Migration in the Andes: At the Crossroads of History and Anthropology,* Brooke Larson and Olivia Harris, eds. Durham, N.C.: Duke University Press.

————. 1996a. "The Political Tensions of Representation and Misrepresentation." *Journal of Latin American Anthropology* 2(1):112–42.

————. 1996b. *Race, Ethnicity, and the Struggle for Self-Representation: De-Indianization in Cuzco, Peru, 1919–1991.* Ph.D. dissertation, Department of Anthropology, University of Wisconsin, Madison.

Deleuze, Gilles, and Félix Guattari. 1987. *A Thousand Plateaus: Capitalism and Schizophrenia.* Translated by Brian Massumi. Minneapolis: University of Minnesota Press.

Del Pino, Ponciano. 1991. "Los campesinos en la guerra: o de como la gente comienza a ponerse macho." In *Perú: el problema agrario en debate / SEPIA IV,* Carlos Iván Degregori, Javier Escobal, and Benjamín Marticorena, eds. Lima: Universidad Nacional de la Amazonía Peruana and SEPIA.

————. 1995. "Peasants at Arms." In *The Peru Reader,* Orin Starn, Carlos Iván Degregori, and Robin Kirk, eds. Durham, N.C.: Duke University Press.

DESCO (Centro de Estudios y Promoción del Desarollo). 1989. *Violencia política en el Perú, 1980–1988.* Vols. 1–2. Lima: DESCO.

————. 1994. *Perú: las organizaciones no-gubernamentales.* Lima: DESCO.

De Soto, Hernando. 1989. *The Other Path: The Invisible Revolution in the Third World.* New York: Harper and Row.

Deustua, Alejandro. 1937. *La cultura nacional.* Lima: Alejandro Deustua.

Diamond, Irene, and Lee Quinby, eds. 1988. *Feminism and Foucault: Reflections on Resistance.* Boston: Northeastern University Press.

Díaz-Barriga, Miguel. 1996. "Necesidad: Notes on the Discourses of Urban Politics in the Ajusco foothills of Mexico City." *American Ethnologist* 23(2):291–311.

Dirks, Nicholas, Geoff Eley, and Sherry Ortner, eds. 1994. *Culture/Power/History: A Reader in Contemporary Social Theory.* Princeton, N.J.: Princeton University Press.

Dirlik, Arif. 1996. "The Global in the Local." In *Global/Local: Cultural Production and the Transnational Imaginary.* Rob Wilson and Wimal Dissanayake, eds. Durham, N.C.: Duke University Press.

Dobyns, Henry. 1971. *Peasants, Politics, and Applied Social Change: Vicos as a Model.* Beverly Hills, Calif.: Sage.

Doughty, Paul. 1968. *Huaylas: An Andean District in Search of Progress.* Ithaca, N.Y.: Cornell University Press.

Dreyfus, Hubert, and Paul Rabinow. 1982. *Michel Foucault: Beyond Structuralism and Hermeneutics.* Chicago: University of Chicago Press.

Durkheim, Emile. 1953. *Sociology and Philosophy.* Glencoe: Free Press.

Ebert, Teresa. 1992. "Luddic Feminism, the Body, Performance, and Labor: Bringing *Materialism* Back into Feminist Cultural Studies." *Cultural Critique* (Winter):5–50.

Enslin, Elizabeth. 1994. "Beyond Writing: Feminist Practices and the Limitations of Ethnography." *Cultural Anthropology* 9(4):537–69.

Escobar, Arturo. 1991. "Anthropology and the Development Encounter: The Making and Marketing of Development Anthropology." *American Ethnologist* 18(4):16–40.

———. 1995. *Encountering Development: The Making and Unmaking of the Third World.* Princeton, N.J.: Princeton University Press.

Escobar, Arturo, and Sonia Alvarez, eds. 1992. *The Making of Social Movements in Latin America: Identity, Strategy, Democracy.* Boulder, Colo.: Westview.

Espinoza León, Carlos. n.d. *Froilán Alama: El Bandolero.* Piura: Librería Ubillús.

Estela, Rolando. 1988. *"Reconózcase a las rondas campesinas . . .": experiencias de rondas en Bambamarca.* Lima: Servicio Educativos Rurales.

Evans, Peter, Dietrich Reuschemeyer, and Theda Skocpol, eds. 1985. *Bringing the State Back In.* Cambridge: Cambridge University Press.

Evans-Pritchard, E. E. 1940. *The Nuer: A Description of the Modes of*

Livelihood and Political Institutions of a Nilotic People. Oxford, England: Clarendon.

Ewing, Katherine. 1990. "The Illusion of Wholeness: Culture, Self, and the Experience of Inconsistency." *Ethos* 18(3):251–58.

Fabj, Valeria. 1993. "Motherhood as Political Voice: The Rhetoric of the Mothers of Plaza de Mayo." *Communication Studies,* 44(1):1–18.

Feder, Ernest. 1971. *The Rape of the Peasantry: Latin America's Landholding System.* Garden City, N.Y.: Anchor Books.

Federación de Rondas Campesinas de Cajamarca. 1986. *A propósito de la autodefensa de las masas: rondas campesinas.* Chota, Peru: Federación de Rondas Campesinas de Chota.

Feierman, Steven. 1990. *Peasant Intellectuals: Anthropology and History in Tanzania.* Madison: University of Wisconsin Press.

Ferguson, James. 1990. *The Anti-politics Machine: "Development," Depoliticization, and Bureaucratic Power in Lesotho.* Cambridge: Cambridge University Press.

Flores Galindo, Alberto. 1982. *La agonía de Mariátegui: la polémica con Komintern.* Lima: DESCO.

———. 1987. *Buscando un inca: identidad y utopía en los Andes.* Lima: Horizonte.

Foster, George. 1960. "Interpersonal Relations in Peasant Society." *Human Organization* 19(4):174–84.

———. 1967. "What is a Peasant?" In *Peasant Society,* Jack Potter, May N. Diaz, and George M. Foster, eds. Boston: Little, Brown.

Foucault, Michel. 1971. *The Order of Things: An Archaeology of the Human Sciences.* New York: Pantheon.

———. 1980. *The History of Sexuality.* Vol. 1. Translated by Robert Hurley. New York: Vintage.

Fox, Jonathan, and Luis Hernández. 1989. "Offsetting the Iron Law of Oligarchy: The Ebb and Flow of Leadership Accountability in a Regional Peasant Organization." *Grassroots Development* 13(2):8–15.

Fox, Richard G., and Orin Starn, eds. 1997. *Between Resistance and Revolution: Cultural Politics and Social Protest.* New Brunswick, N.J.: Rutgers University Press.

Freeman, Joreen. 1973. "The Tyranny of Structurelessness." In *Radical Feminism,* Anne Koedt, Ellen Levone, and Anita Rapone, eds. New York: Quadrangle Books.

Freire, Paulo. 1970. *The Pedagogy of the Oppressed.* Translated by Myra Bergman Ramos. New York: Herder and Herder.

Friedlander, Saul, ed. 1992. *Probing the Limits of Representation: Nazism and the "Final Solution."* Cambridge: Harvard University Press.

García Canclini, Nestor. 1990. *Culturas híbridas: estrategias para entrar y salir de la modernidad.* Mexico City: Horizonte.

García-Sayán, Diego. 1982. *Tomas de tierra en el Perú.* Lima: DESCO.

Garnett, Miguel. 1992. *Rondo: un relato andino.* Lima: Lluvia Editores.

Gelles, Paul. 1995. "Equilibrium and Extraction: Dual Organization in the Andes." *American Ethnologist* 22(4):710–42.

Giddens, Anthony. 1979. *Central Problems in Social Theory.* Berkeley: University of California Press.

Gill, Lesley. 1994. *Precarious Dependencies: Gender, Class, and Domestic Service in Bolivia.* New York: Columbia University Press.

Gillis, John, ed. 1994. *Commemorations: The Politics of National Identity.* Princeton, N.J.: Princeton University Press.

Ginsburg, Faye. 1997. " 'From Little Things, Big Things Grow' ": Indigenous Media and Cultural Activism." In *Between Resistance and Revolution: Cultural Politics and Social Protest,* Richard Fox and Orin Starn, eds. New Brunswick, N.J.: Rutgers University Press.

Ginsburg, Faye, and Anna Tsing, eds. 1990. *Uncertain Terms: Negotiating Gender in American Culture.* Boston: Beacon.

Girard, René. 1987. "Generative Scapegoating." In *Violent Origins: Ritual Killing and Cultural Formation,* Robert Hamerton-Kelly, ed. Stanford, Calif.: Stanford University Press.

Gitlitz, John. 1975. *Hacienda, Comunidad, and Peasant Protest in Northern Peru.* Ph.D. dissertation, University of North Carolina, Chapel Hill.

———. 1985. "Twenty Years of Pastoral Experimentation: The Option for the Poor in Bambamarca, Peru." Columbia-NYU Latin American, Caribbean, and Iberian Occasional Papers, No. 4.

———. n.d. "Decline and Survival of the Rondas Campesinas of Northern Peru." Paper, Department of Sociology, State University of New York, Purchase.

Gitlitz, John, and Telmo Rojas. 1983. "Peasant Vigilante Committees in Northern Peru." *Journal of Latin American Studies* 15(1):163–97.

Gluckman, Max. 1955. *Custom and Conflict in Africa.* Oxford, England: Basil Blackwell.

Golte, Jürgen, and Norma Adams. 1987. *Los caballos de Troya de los invasores: estrategias campesinas en la conquista de Gran Lima.* Lima: Instituto de Estudios Peruanos.

Gómez-Peña, Guillermo. 1996. *The New World Border.* San Francisco: City Lights.

Gonzales, Efraín, and Lilian Samamé. 1991. *El pendúlo peruano.* Lima: Instituto de Estudios Peruanos.

Gordon, Linda. 1988. *Heroes of Their Own Lives.* New York: Viking.

Gorriti, Gustavo. 1990. *Sendero: Historia de la guerra milenaria en el Perú.* Lima: Apoyo.

Gramsci, Antonio. 1971. *Selections from the Prison Notebooks.* Translated and edited by Quintiun Hoare and Geoffrey Nowell Smith. New York: International Publishers.

Guevara, Ernesto "Che." 1967. *The Diary of Che Guevara.* New York: Bantam.

Gugelberger, Georg, ed. 1996. *The Real Thing: Testimonial Discourse and Latin America.* Durham, N.C.: Duke University Press.

Gupta, Akhil, and James Ferguson, eds. 1997a. *Anthropological Locations: Boundaries and Grounds of a Field Science.* Berkeley: University of California Press.

————. 1997b. *Culture, Power, Place: Explorations in Critical Anthropology.* Durham, N.C.: Duke University Press.

Gutiérrez, Gustavo. 1988. *A Theology of Liberation.* Maryknoll, N.Y.: Orbis Books.

Hale, Charles. 1994. *Resistance and Contradiction: Miskitu Indians and the Nicaraguan State, 1894–1987.* Stanford, Calif.: Stanford University Press.

Hall, Stuart. 1985. "Signification, Representation, Ideology: Althusser and the Post-structuralist Debates." *Critical Studies in Mass Communication* 12:91–114.

————. 1996. *Critical Dialogues in Cultural Studies.* Edited by David Morley and Kuan-Hsing Chen. London: Routledge.

Hannerz, Ulf. 1992. *Cultural Complexity: Studies in the Social Organization of Meaning.* New York: Columbia University Press.

Haraway, Donna. 1991. *Simians, Cyborgs, Women: The Reinvention of Nature.* New York: Routledge.

Harrison, Faye, ed. 1991. *Decolonizing Anthropology: Moving Further toward an Anthropology for Liberation.* Washington, D.C.: American Anthropological Association.

Harrison, Lawrence. 1985. *Underdevelopment Is a State of Mind: The Latin American Case.* Lanham, Md.: Center for International Affairs, Harvard University, and the University Press of America.

Harvey, David. 1989. *The Condition of Postmodernity.* London: Basil Blackwell.

Harvey, Penelope. 1994. "Domestic Violence in the Peruvian Andes." In *Sex and Violence: Issues in Representation and Experience.* Penelope Harvey and Peter Gow, eds. London: Routledge.

Hemming, John. 1970. *The Conquest of the Incas.* New York: Harcourt, Brace, Jovanovich.

Hernández, Juan Gustavo. 1994. *Entre democracia y violenca: aspiraciones y contradicciones de las rondas campesinas de una provincia de la sierra septentrional de los Andes Peruanos (Sihuas, Ancash).* Bachellor's thesis in the Social Sciences, Pontificia Universidad Católica, Lima, Peru.

Hinojosa, Iván. 1992. "Entre el poder y la ilusión: Pol Pot, Sendero y las utopías campesinas." *Debate Agrario* 15:15–93.

Hobsbawm, Eric. 1974. "Peasant Land Occupations." *Past and Present*, no. 62:120–52.

———. 1990. *Nations and Nationalism since 1780: Programme, Myth, Reality.* Cambridge: Cambridge University Press.

hooks, bell. 1990. *Yearnings: Race, Gender and Cultural Politics.* Boston: South End Press.

Huamaní, Giselle, Martín Moscoso, and Patricia Urteaga. 1988. "Rondas campesinas de Cajamarca: la construcción de una alternativa." *Debate Agrario* 3:63–86.

Huber, Ludwig. 1995. *Las rondas campesinas de Piura.* Lima: Instituto de Estudios Peruanos.

Husson, Patrick. 1992. *De la guerra a la rebelión: Huanta, Siglo XIX.* Lima: Centro de Estudios Regionales "Bartolomé de las Casas."

Hymes, Dell, ed. 1972. *Reinventing Anthropology.* New York: Pantheon.

Instituto de Defensa Legal. n.d. *El papel de la organización social campesina en la estrategía campesina.* Lima: Instituto de Defensa Legal.

Inter-American Foundation. 1995. *A Guide to NGO directories: How to Find over 20,000 Non-governmental Organizations in Latin America and the Caribbean.* Washington: Inter-American Foundation.

Isbell, Billie Jean. 1977. *To Defend Ourselves: Ecology and Ritual in an Andean Village.* Austin: University of Texas Press.

———. 1992. "Shining Path and Peasant Responses in Rural Ayacucho." In *Shining Path of Peru,* David Scott Palmer, ed. London: Hurst.

Joseph, Gilbert, and Daniel Nugent, eds. 1994. *Everyday Forms of State Formation: Revolution and the Negotiation of Rule in Modern Mexico.* Durham, N.C.: Duke University Press.

Kay, Bruce. 1996. "Fujipopulism and the Liberal State In Peru, 1990–1995." *Journal of Interamerican Studies and World Affairs.* 38(4):55–98.

Kearney, Michael. 1996. *Reconceptualizing the Peasantry: Anthropology in Global Perspective.* Boulder, Colo.: Westview.

Keck, Margaret, and Kathryn Sikkink. 1998. *Activists beyond Borders: Activist Networks in International Politics.* Ithaca, N.Y.: Cornell University Press.

Kirk, Robin. 1991. *The Decade of Chaqwa: Peru's Internal Refugees.* Washington: U.S. Committee for Refugees.

———. 1993. *To Build Anew: An Update on Peru's Internally Displaced People.* Washington, D.C.: U.S. Committee for Refugees.

———. 1997. *The Monkey's Paw: New Chronicles of Peru.* Amherst: University of Massachusetts Press.

Klaren, Peter. 1987. *Modernization, Dislocation, and Aprismo: Origins of the Peruvian Aprista Party, 1870–1932.* Austin: University of Texas Press.

Kondo, Dorine. 1990. *Crafting Selves: Power, Gender, and Discourses of Identity in a Japanese Workplace.* Chicago: University of Chicago Press.

Koonz, Claudia. 1987. *Mothers in the Fatherland.* New York: St. Martin's Press.

Küppers, Gaby, ed. *Compañeras: Voices from the Latin American Women's Movement.* London: Latin American Bureau.

Landsberger, Henry, and Cynthia Hewitt. 1970. "Ten Sources of Weakness and Cleavage in Latin American Peasant Movements." In *Agrarian Problems and Peasant Movements in Latin America,* Rodolfo Stavenhagen, ed. Garden City, N.Y.: Anchor Books.

Larson, Brooke, and Olivia Harris, eds. 1995. *Ethnicity, Migration, and Markets in the Andes: At the Crossroads of History and Anthropology.* Durham, N.C.: Duke University Press.

Lenin, V. I. 1980. *V.I. Lenin: Selected Works.* New York: International Publishers.

Lernoux, Penny. 1989. *People of God: The Struggle for World Catholicism.* New York: Viking.

Little, Peter, and Michael Painter. 1995. "Discourse, Politics, and the Developmental Process: Reflections on Escobar's 'Anthropology and the Development Encounter.'" *American Ethnologist* 22(3):602–10.

López Albujar, Enrique. 1933. *Los caballeros del delito.* Lima: Compañía de Impresiones y Publicidad.

Lowenthal, Abraham, ed. 1975. *The Peruvian Experiment.* Princeton, N.J.: Princeton University Press.

Luthra, Sangeeta. 1998. *The Cultural Politics of Development in the Age of NGOs.* Ph.D. dissertation, Department of Cultural Anthropology, Duke University, Durham, N.C.

Lynch, Nicolás. 1990. *Los jóvenes rojos de San Marcos: el radicalismo universitario en los años setenta.* Lima: El Zorro de Abajo Ediciones.

———. 1992. *La transición conservadora.* Lima: El Zorro de Abajo Ediciones.

MacCormack, Sabine. 1991. *Religion in the Andes: Vision and Imagination in Early Colonial Peru.* Princeton, N.J.: Princeton University Press.

Macdonald, Laura. 1997. *Supporting Civil Society: The Political Role of*

Non-governmental Organizations in Central America. New York: St. Martin's Press.

Malkki, Liisa. 1992. "National Geographic: The Rooting of Peoples and the Territorialization of National Identity among Scholars and Refugees." *Cultural Anthropology* 7(1):27–43.

Mallon, Florencia. 1983. *The Defense of Community in Peru's Central Highlands: Peasant Struggle and Capitalist Transition, 1860–1940.* Princeton, N.J.: Princeton University Press.

———. 1995. *Peasant and Nation: The Making of Postcolonial Mexico and Peru.* Berkeley: University of California Press.

Manrique, Nelson. 1981. *Las guerillas indígenas en la guerra con Chile.* Lima: CIC.

———. 1989. "La década de la violencia." *Márgenes* 3(5–6):137–82.

Marcus, George. 1995. "Ethnography In/Of the World System: The Emergence of "Multi-sited Ethnography." *Annual Review of Anthropology* 24:95–140.

Mariátegui, José Carlos. 1968. *Siete ensayos de interpretación de la realidad peruana.* Lima: Empresa Editora Amauta.

———. 1972. *Peruanicemos el Perú.* Lima: Empresa Editora Amauta.

———. 1995. "Reflections." In *The Peru Reader,* Orin Starn, Carlos Iván Degregori, and Robin Kirk, eds. Durham, N.C.: Duke University Press.

Marx, Karl. 1970. *Capital,* vol. 1. Harmondsworth, England: Penguin.

———. 1977. *Karl Marx: Selected Writings.* Edited by David McLellan. Oxford, England: Oxford University Press.

Massey, Doreen. 1994. *Space, Place, Gender.* Minneapolis: University of Minnesota Press.

Matos Mar, José. 1983. *Desborde popular y crisis del estado.* Lima: Instituto de Estudios Peruanos.

Matos Mar, José, and José Carlos Mejía. 1980. *La reforma agraria en el Perú.* Lima: Instituto de Estudios Peruanos.

Mayer, Enrique. 1991. "Peru in Deep Trouble: Mario Vargas Llosa's "Inquest in the Andes" Reexamined." *Cultural Anthropology* 6(4):466–504.

McClintock, Cynthia, and Abraham Lowenthal, eds. 1983. *The Peruvian Experiment Reconsidered.* Princeton, N.J.: Princeton University Press.

McPherson, James. 1988. *Battle Cry of Freedom: The Civil War Era.* Oxford, England: Oxford University Press.

Megill, Allan, ed. 1994. *Rethinking Objectivity.* Durham, N.C.: Duke University Press.

Méndez, Cecilia. 1995. *Incas sí, indios no: apuntes para el estudio del nacionalismo criollo en el Perú.* Documento de Trabajo No. 56. Lima: Instituto de Estudios Peruanos.

Menchú, Rigberta. 1984. *I, Rigoberta Menchú: An Indian Woman in Guatemala.* London: Verso.

Michels, Roberto. 1915. *Political Parties: A Sociological Study of the Oligarchical Tendencies of Modern Democracy.* New York: Hearst International Library.

Miller, James. 1993. *The Passion of Michel Foucault.* New York: Simon and Schuster.

Mintz, Sidney, and Eric Wolf. 1989. "Reply to Michael Taussig." *Critique of Anthropology* 9(1):25–31.

Mitchell, Timothy. 1990. "Everyday Metaphors of Power." *Theory and Society* 9:545–77.

Mitchell, William. 1991. *Peasants on the Edge: Crop, Cult, and Crisis in the Andes.* Berkeley: University of California Press.

Mohanty, Chandra Talapade, Anne Russo, and Lourdes Torres, eds. 1991. *Third World Women and the Politics of Feminism.* Bloomington: Indiana University Press.

Montoya, Rodrigo, Edwin Montoya, and Luis Montoya. 1987. *La sangre de los cerros.* Lima: CEPES.

Moore, David Chioni. 1994. "Anthropology Is Dead, Long Live Anthro(a)pology: Poststructuralism, Literary Studies, and Anthropology's 'Nervous Present.'" *Journal of Anthropological Research* 50(4):343–67.

Moore, Donald. n.d. "The Crucible of Cultural Politics: Reworking Development in Zimbabwe's Eastern Highlands." *American Ethnologist.* Forthcoming.

Moore, Sally Falk. 1986. *Social Facts and Fabrications: "Customary" Law on Kilimanjaro, 1880–1980.* Cambridge: Cambridge University Press.

Mossbrucker, Harold. 1990. *El concepto de la comunidad: un enfoque crítico.* Lima: Instituto de Estudios Peruanos.

Murra, John. 1975. *Formaciones económicas y políticas del mundo andino.* Lima: Instituto de Estudios Peruanos.

———. 1986. "The Expansion of the Inka State: Armies, War and Rebellions." In *Anthropological History of Andean Polities,* John Murra, Nathan Wachtel, and Jacques Revel, eds. Cambridge: Cambridge University Press.

Mushakoji, Kinhide. 1993. "Foreword." In *New Social Movements of the South: Empowering the People,* Ponna Wignaraja, ed. New Delhi: Vistaar.

Nader, Laura, and Harry Todd, eds. 1979. *The Disputing Process-Law in Ten Societies*. New York: Columbia University Press.

Nedelesky, Jennifer. 1990. "Law, Boundaries and the Bounded Self." *Representations* 30:162–89.

Nelson, Diane. 1996. Mayan Hackers and the Cyber-spatialized Nation-State: Modernity, Ethnonostalgia, and a Lizard Queen in Guatemala. *Cultural Anthropology* 11(3):287–309.

Nietzsche, Friedrich. 1990. *Beyond Good and Evil*. Translated by Michael Tanner. London: Penguin.

Noel Moral, Roberto. 1989. *Ayacucho: testimonio de un soldado*. Lima: Publinor.

Nora, Pierre. 1989. "Between Memory and History: *Les Lieux de Mémoire*." *Representations* 26:7–25.

Nugent, David. 1997. *Modernity at the Edge of Empire: State, Individual, and Nation in the Northern Peruvian Andes, 1885–1935*. Stanford, Calif.: Stanford University Press.

Olalquiaga, Celeste. 1992. *Megalopolis: Contemporary Cultural Sensibilities*. Minneapolis: University of Minnesota Press.

Orlove, Benjamin. 1991. Mapping Reeds and Reading Maps: The Politics of Representation in Lake Titicaca. *American Ethnologist* 18(1):3–38.

Ortner, Sherry. 1984. "Theory in Anthropology since the Sixties." *Comparative Studies in Society and History* 26:126–64.

Paige, Jeffrey. 1975. *Agrarian Revolution: Social movements and Export Agriculture in the Underdeveloped World*. New York: Free Press.

Palmer, David Scott, ed. 1992. *Shining Path of Peru*. London: Hurst.

Pásara, Luis, Nena Delpino, Rocío Valdeavellano, Alonso Zarzar, eds. 1991. *La otra cara de la luna: nuevos actores sociales en el Perú*. Lima: CEDYS.

Pásara, Luis, and Alonso Zarzar. 1991. "Ambigüedades, contradicciones, e incertidumbres." In *La otra cara de la luna: nuevos actores sociales en el Perú,* Luis Pásara, et al., eds. Lima: CEDYS.

Pérez Mundaca, José. 1995. "El nuevo eje del abigeato y bandidismo y su relación con el neoliberalismo fujimorista y el terror: la nueva etapa del movimiento rondero chotano, 1990–1993." *Extensión y Proyección Universitaria en la Universidad Nacional de Cajamarca* 1(1):82–92.

Pigg, Stacey Leigh. 1992. "Inventing Social Categories through Place: Social Representations and Development in Nepal." *Comparative Studies in Society and History* 34:491–513.

Piot, Charles. 1999. *Remotely Global: Village Modernity in West Africa*. Chicago: University of Chicago Press.

Poole, Deborah. 1997. *Vision, Race, Modernity: A Visual Economy of the Andean Image World.* Princeton, N.J.: Princeton University Press.

Poole, Deborah, ed. 1994. *Unruly Order: Violence, Power, and Cultural Identity in the High Provinces of Peru.* Boulder, Colo.: Westview.

Popkin, Samuel. 1979. *The Rational Peasant: The Political Economy of Rural Society in Viet Nam.* Berkeley: University of California Press.

Portes, Alejandro, and Richard Schauffler. 1993. "Competing Perspectives on the Latin American Informal Sector." *Population and Development Review* 19(1):33–60.

Powdermaker, Hortense. 1966. *Stranger and Friend.* New York: Norton.

Powers, Margaret. 1997. *Right-wing women in Chile, 1964–1973.* Ph.D. dissertation, Department of History, University of Illinois, Chicago.

Pratt, Mary Louise. 1986. "Fieldwork in Common Places." In *Writing Culture: The Poetics and Politics of Ethnography.* James Clifford and George Marcus, eds. Berkeley: University of California Press.

———. 1991. "Arts of the Contact Zone." *Profession* 91:33–41.

———. 1992. *Imperial Eyes: Travel Writing and Transculturation.* New York: Routledge.

Prazniak, Roxann. 1997. "Mao and the Woman Question in an Age of Green Politics: Some Critical Reflections." In *Critical Perspectives on Mao Zedong's Thought,* Arif Dirkly, Paul Healy, and Nick Knight, eds. New Jersey: Humanities Press.

Radcliffe, Sarah. 1996. "Gendered Nations: Nostalgia, Development and Territory in Ecuador." *Gender, Place, and Culture* 3(1):5–21.

Rahnema, Majid. 1990. "Participatory Action Research: The 'Last Temptation of Saint' Development." *Alternatives* 15:199–226.

Rama, Angel. 1996. *The Lettered City.* Translated by John Charles Chasteen. Durham, N.C.: Duke University Press.

Rappaport, Joanne. 1990. *The Politics of Memory: Native Historical Interpretation in the Colombian Andes.* Cambridge: Cambridge University Press.

———. 1994. *Cumbe Reborn: An Andean Ethnography of History.* Chicago: University of Chicago Press.

Reyes, Alejandro. 1997. "Compra de tierra por narcotraficantes." In *Drogas ilícitas en Colombia,* Francisco Thoumi, Sergio Uribe, Ricardo Rocha, Alejandro Reyes, Edgar A. Garzón, Andrés López, Juan Tokatlian, Manuel Hernández, eds. Bogotá: Ariel.

Rivera, Silvia. 1993. "Anthropology and Society in the Andes: Themes and Issues." *Critique of Anthropology* 13(1):77–96.

Rojas, Telmo. 1990. *Rondas, Poder Campesino y el Terror.* Cajamarca, Peru: Universidad Nacional de Cajamarca.

Rosaldo, Michelle. 1980. "The Use and Abuse of Anthropology: Reflections on Feminism and Cross-cultural Understanding." *Signs* 5(3):389–420.

Rosaldo, Renato. 1989. *Culture and Truth: The Remaking of Social Analysis.* Boston: Beacon.

Rosenbach, William, and Robert Taylor. 1993. *Contemporary Issues in Leadership.* Boulder, Colo.: Westview.

Rowe, John. 1946. "Inca Culture at the Time of the Spanish Conquest." In *Handbook of South American Indians.* Bureau of American Ethnology Bulletin 143, vol. 2. Washington: Smithsonian Institution Bureau of American Ethnology.

Roy, Arundhati. 1997. *The God of Small Things.* New York: Random House.

Sachs, Wolfgang, ed. 1992. *The Development Dictionary: A Guide to Knowledge as Power.* London: Zed Books.

Said, Edward. 1987. "Michel Foucault, 1926–1984." In *After Foucault: Humanistic Knowledge, Postmodern Challenges.* Jonathan Arac, ed. New Brunswick, N.J.: Rutgers University Press.

Salomon, Frank. 1991. "An Introductory Essay: The Huarochirí Manuscript." In *The Huarochirí Manuscript: A Testament of Ancient and Colonial Andean Religion,* Frank Salomon and George L. Urioste, trans. Austin: University of Texas Press.

Sánchez, Oscar. 1995. *El azúcar en Chota no fue dulce.* Chota, Peru: Ediciones Wayrak.

Sapir, Edward. 1949. *Selected Writings in Language, Culture, and Personality.* Edited by David Mandelbaum. Berkeley: University of California Press.

Scheper-Hughes, Nancy. 1992. *Death without Weeping: The Violence of Everyday Life in Brazil.* Berkeley: University of California Press.

———. 1994. "The Last White Christmas: The Heidleberg Pub Massacre." *American Anthropologist* 96:805–17.

———. 1995. "The Primacy of the Ethical: Propositions for a Militant Anthropology." *Current Anthropology* 36(3):409–40.

Scott, James. 1976. *The Moral Economy of the Peasant: Rebellion and Subsistence in Southeast Asia.* New Haven, Conn.: Yale University Press.

———. 1985. *Weapons of the Weak: Everyday Forms of Peasant Resistance.* New Haven, Conn.: Yale University Press.

Scott, Joan. 1988. *Gender and the Politics of History.* New York: Columbia University Press.

Seligmann, Linda. 1993. "Between Worlds of Exchange: Ethnicity among Peruvian Market Women." *Cultural Anthropology* 8(2):187–213.

Shanin, Teodor, ed. 1987. *Peasants and Peasant Societies.* Oxford: Basil Blackwell.

Shohat, Ella. 1992. "Notes on the "Post-Colonial." *Social Text* 31–32:99–113.

Silverblatt, Irene. 1987. *Moon, Sun, Witches: Gender Ideologies and Class in Inca and Colonial Peru.* Princeton, N.J.: Princeton University Press.

———. 1995. "Becoming 'Indian' in the Central Andes of 17th Century Peru." In *After Colonialism: Imperial Histories, Postcolonial Displacements,* Gyan Prakash, ed. Princeton, N.J.: Princeton University Press.

Skar, Harold. 1982. *The Warm Valley People: Duality and Land Reform among the Quechua Indians of Highland Peru.* Oslo: Universitetsforlaget.

Skocpol, Theda. 1982. "What Makes Peasants Revolutionary?" *Comparative Politics* 14(3):35–75.

Smith, Anthony. 1979. *Nationalism in the 20th Century.* New York: New York University Press.

Smith, Christian. 1991. *The Emergence of Liberation Theology: Radical Religion and Social Movement Theory.* Chicago: University of Chicago Press.

———. 1996. *Disruptive Religion: The Force of Faith in Social Movement Activism.* New York: Routledge.

Smith, Gavin. 1989. *Livelihood and Resistance: Peasants and the Politics of Land in Peru.* Berkeley: University of California Press.

Sommers, Doris. 1991. *Foundational Fictions: The National Romances of Latin America.* Berkeley: University of California Press.

Spalding, Karen. 1984. *Huarochirí: An Andean Society under Inca and Spanish Rule.* Stanford, Calif.: Stanford University Press.

Spivak, Gayatri. 1988. "Can the Subaltern Speak?" In *Marxism and the Interpretation of Culture,* Cary Nelson and Lawrence Grossberg, eds. Urbana: University of Illinois Press.

Starn, Orin. 1986. *Rondas campesinas de Paimas-Piura.* Lima: CIPCA, Comité Central de Rondas Campesinas–Tunel VI, and TAREA.

———. 1991a. "Missing the Revolution: Anthropologists and the War in Peru." *Cultural Anthropology* 6(3):63–91.

———. 1991b. "Noches de ronda." *Quehacer* 69:76–93.

———. 1992a. *"Con los llanques todo barro": rondas campesinas, protesta agraria y movimientos sociales.* Lima: Instituto de Estudios Peruanos.

———. 1992b. "New Literature on Peru's Sendero Luminoso." *Latin American Research Review* 27:212–26.

———. 1994a. "Rethinking the Politics of Anthropology: The Case of the Andes." *Current Anthropology* 35(1):13–38.

———. 1994b. "Uchuraccay y el retorno a los Andes." *Quehacer* 83:76–84.

———. 1995. "Maoism in the Andes: The Communist Party of Peru–Shining Path and the Refusal of History." *Journal of Latin American Studies* 27(2):399–421.

———. 1993. *Hablan los ronderos: la búsqueda por la paz en los Andes.* Lima: Instituto de Estudios Peruanos.

Starn, Orin, Carlos Iván Degregori, and Robin Kirk, eds. 1995. *The Peru Reader: History, Culture, Politics.* Durham, N.C.: Duke University Press.

Starr, June, and Jane Collier, eds. 1989. *History and Power in the Study of Law: New Directions in Legal Anthropology.* Ithaca, N.Y.: Cornell University Press.

Stavenhagen, Rodolfo, and Diego Iturralde, eds. 1993. *Entre la ley y la costumbre.* Mexico City: Instituto Indigenista Iberoamericano.

Stavig, Ward. 1995. *Amor y violencia sexual: valores indígenas en la sociedad colonial.* Lima: Instituto de Estudios Peruanos.

Stern, Peter. 1995. *Sendero Luminoso: An Annotated Bibliography of the Shining Path Guerrilla Movement, 1980–1993.* Albuquerque: SALALM Secetariat, General Library, and University of New Mexico.

Stern, Steve J. 1982. *Peru's Indian Peoples and the Challenge of Spanish Conquest: Huamanga to 1640.* Madison: University of Wisconsin Press.

———. 1995. *The Secret History of Gender: Women, Men, and Power in Late Colonial Mexico.* Chapel Hill: University of North Carolina Press.

———, ed. 1987. *Resistance, Rebellion, and Consciousness in the Andean Peasant World, 18th–20th Century.* Madison: University of Wisconsin Press.

———. 1998. *Shining and Other Paths.* Durham, N.C.: Duke University Press.

Stoler, Ann. 1995. *Race and the Education of Desire.* Durham, N.C.: Duke University Press.

Stoll, David. 1990. *Is Latin America Turning Protestant?* Berkeley: University of California Press.

Stoll, David, and Virginia Burnett, eds. 1993. *Pentecostal Politics in Latin America.* Philadelphia: Temple University Press.

Strong, Simon. 1992. *Shining Path: The World's Deadliest Revolutionary Force.* London: HarperCollins.

Sutton, David. 1991. "Is Anybody Out There?: Anthropology and the Question of Audience. *Critique of Anthropology* 11:91–104.

Tamayo Flores, A. 1992. *Derecho en los Andes: un estudio de antropología jurídica.* Lima: CEPAR.

Taussig, Michael. 1987. *Shamanism, Colonialism, and the Wild Man: A Study in Terror and Healing.* Chicago: University of Chicago Press.

——. 1989. "History as Commodity in Some Recent American (Anthropological) Literature." *Critique of Anthropology* 9(1):7–23.

——. 1992. *The Nervous System.* New York: Routledge.

Taylor, Charles. 1992. *Multiculturalism and "The Politics of Recognition": An Essay.* Princeton, N.J.: Princeton University Press.

Taylor, Lewis. 1987. *Bandits and Politics in Peru: Landlord and Peasant Violence in Hualgayoc, 1900–1930.* Cambridge: Center for Latin American Studies.

Thorndyke, Guillermo. 1976. *No, mi general.* Lima: Mosca Azul.

Thurner, Mark. 1997. *From Two Republics to One Divided: Contradictions of Postcolonial Nationmaking in Andean Peru.* Durham, N.C.: Duke University Press.

Trinh T. Minh-ha. 1989. *Woman, Native, Other: Writing Postcoloniality and Feminism.* Bloomington: Indiana University Press.

Tristán, Flora. 1993. *Flora Tristán, Utopian Feminist: Her Travel Diaries and Personal Crusade.* Translated and edited by Paul and Doris Beik. Bloomington: Indiana University Press.

Trouillot, Michel-Rolph. 1991. "Anthropology and the Savage Slot: The Poetics and Politics of Otherness." In *Recapturing Anthropology,* Richard Fox, ed. Santa Fe, N. Mex.: School of American Research Press.

Truman, Harry. 1964. *Public Papers of the Presidents of the United States: Harry S. Truman.* Washington, D.C.: U.S. Government Printing Office.

Urbano, Henrique. 1991. "Historia y etnohistoria andinas." *Revista Andina* 9(1):12–163.

Valcárcel, Luis. 1928. *Tempestad en los Andes.* Lima: Editorial Minerva.

——. 1950. Introduction to *Indians of Peru,* by Pierre Verger. New York: Pantheon.

Valderrama Ricardo, Carmen Escalante, Paul Gelles, and Gabriela Martínez. 1996. *Andean Lives: Gregorio Condori Mamani and Asunta Quispe Huamán.* Austin: University of Texas Press.

Vallejo, César. 1990. *The Black Heralds.* Translated by Richard Schaaf and Kathleen Ross. Pittsburgh: Latin American Literary Review Press.

Valverde, Humberto. 1987. "Sinforoso Benites Algalobos (1891–1953): líder campesino." *Apuntes de Campo* (a mimeographed publication of CEPESER, Piura) 2:11–29.

Van Buren, Mary. 1996. "Rethinking the Vertical Archipelago: Ethnicity, Exchange, and History in the South Central Andes." *American Anthropologist* 98(2):338–51.

Varese, Stefano. 1968. *La sal de los cerros.* Lima: Universidad Peruana de Ciencias y Tecnología.

Vargas Llosa, Mario. 1967. *La ciudad y los perros.* Barcelona: Editorial Seix Barral.

————. 1983. "The Story of a Massacre." *Granta* 9:62–83.

————. 1996. *La utopía arcaica: José María Arguedas y las ficciones del indigenismo.* Mexico City: Fondo de Cultura Económica.

Vich, Víctor. 1996. "Los payasos de la calle de Lima." Paper, Department of Cultural Anthropology, Duke University, Durham, N.C.

————. 1997. "Literatura latinoamericana y comunidades imaginadas: el criollismo y el indigenismo como ideologías sociales." Paper, Department of Romance Studies, Duke University, Durham, N.C.

Visweswaran, Kamala. 1994. *Fictions of Feminist Ethnography.* Minneapolis: University of Minnesota Press.

Vitillo, Robert. 1997. "NGOs: A Vital Response in an Age of Globalization." *Center Focus* (September): 19–21.

Walsh, Michael. 1992. *Opus Dei: An Investigation of the Secret Society Struggling for Power in the Roman Catholic Church.* San Francisco: Harper.

Webb, Richard, and Graciela Fernández Baca, eds. 1996. *Perú en números.* Lima: Cuánto S.A.

Weber, Max. 1946. *From Max Weber: Essays in Sociology.* Translated and edited by H. H. Gerth and C. Wright Mills. Oxford, England: Oxford University Press.

Weil, Connie, ed. 1988. *Lucha: The Struggles of Latin American Women.* Minneapolis: Prisma.

White, Hayden. 1973. *Metahistory.* Baltimore: Johns Hopkins University Press.

Wignaraja, Ponna, ed. 1993. *New Social Movements in the South: Empowering the People.* New Delhi: Vistaar.

Williams, Raymond. 1977. *Marxism and Literature.* Oxford, England: Oxford University Press.

Wills, Gary. 1994. *Certain Trumpets: The Call of Leaders.* New York: Simon and Schuster.

Wolf, Eric. 1969. *Peasant Wars of the 20th Century.* New York: Harper and Row.

————. 1980. *Europe and the People without History.* Berkeley: University of California Press.

Wray, Alberto, ed. 1993. *Derecho, pueblos indígenas y reforma del estado.* Quito: Abya-Yala.

Yrigoyen, Raquel. 1993. *Las rondas campesinas de Cajamarca-Peru: una aproximación jurídica.* Law thesis, Pontificia Universidad Católica, Lima, Peru.

Yudicé, George. 1992. "Postmodernism on the Periphery." *South Atlantic Quarterly* 92(3):543–56.

Zarzar, Alonso. 1989. *Apo Capac Huayna, Jesús Sacramentado: mito, utopía y milenarismo en el pensamiento de Juan Santos Atahualpa.* Lima: Centro Amazónico de Antropología y Aplicación Práctica.

———. 1991. "Las rondas campesinas de Piura: de la autodefensa al ¿autogobierno?" In *La otra cara de la luna: nuevos actores sociales en el Perú,* Luis Pásara, Nena Delpino, Rocío Valdeavellano, Alonso Zarzar, eds. Buenos Aires and Lima: CEDYS.

Zuidema, R. T. 1964. *The Ceque System of Cuzco: The Social Organization of the Capital of the Inca.* Leiden: E. J. Brill.

INDEX

Abrams, Philip, 65
Alama, Froilán, 82
Albó, Xavier, 32
Alegría, Ciro, 257–258
Allen, Catherine, 159
Alto Peru: and killing of rustlers, 80–85
Alvarez, Sonia, 204, 209, 271
Andeanism: and anthropology, 20; and concept of two Perus, 48–49; definition of, 19–20
anthropology: and activism, 6–7, 14, 274; and Andeanism, 19–21; criticism of, 16–17; and fieldwork, 14–19, 217; renewal of, 274–275
Appadurai, Arjun, 222
APRA, 10, 115–122, 129, 143, 147, 207, 215, 231, 234–235, 237, 248–250, 258–259; decline of, 254–255; and women, 170–171
Arguedas, José María, 34, 40, 140–143
army: influence on rondas of, 74–80; massacres by, 53, 87; and nationalism, 150
authority: types of, 227. *See also* leadership
Ayabaca, 8–10, 12, 71, 87, 89, 116, 157, 206, 224–225, 242, 246, 250, 255, 264

Bambamarca, 36, 58, 64, 69, 71, 76, 82, 90, 92, 114–116, 142, 148, 151, 169–170, 188, 207, 211, 221, 225, 241, 249, 257–260, 266, 271
Basadre, Jorge: and concept of two Perus, 48–49
Benel, Eleodoro, 82
Benjamin, Walter, 65, 81
Berger, John, 4
Berrú, Oscar, 103–104, 108
Blee, Kathleen, 185

Cabrera, Ersila, 157, 167, 187
Cajamarca, 3, 9, 14, 23–24, 31, 39, 49, 51, 53, 58, 62, 64, 79, 82, 86–87, 88–90, 96, 103–105, 109, 129, 132, 145, 150, 158, 196, 250, 265; NGOs in, 202–205, 207–209, 227, 238, 244; poverty in, 93–94; ronda federations in, 242, 247
Campo, Rafael, 193
Caro, Jorge, 61–62
Castañeda, Jorge, 263
Castells, Manuel, 31
Catholicism, 89, 153, 195, 211, 221; and gender roles, 161–162, 167, 178–179; and liberation theology, 89, 201; and native religion, 75, 89; and Opus Dei, 92; and Protestantism, 11, 140–141, 169; and the rondas, 26, 89–92, 133, 258. *See also* Christianity, Protestantism
Chota, 3, 14–15, 24, 26, 37–38, 45–

Chota (*continued*)
69 passim, 70–71, 78, 80–85, 91–93, 105–106, 113–125 passim, 127, 130, 137, 146, 159, 163, 170, 188, 205, 209–210, 214–215; decline of rondas in, 264–265, 272; and expulsion of "Dr. How Much," 97–103; land tenure system in, 141; protest in, 167–169; ronda federations in, 241, 249–251; theft in, 81
Christianity: and the rondas, 89–92, 133; and wife beating, 178–179. *See also* Catholicism, Protestantism
Chuqihuanga, Francisco, 26, 132, 224–227, 257, 271
Clifford, James, 13
Clinton, Bill, 271
Collier, Jane, 169
colonialism, 22–23, 48–49, 146–147; and anticolonialism, 96; gender, 161–162; and identity, 32, 146–147; images of, 95–96; and the "lettered city," 128; and "myth of Inkarrí"; and postcolonialism, 136; resistance to, 75; and violence, 86; and wife beating, 177
Communist Party of Peru — Red Homeland. See Red Homeland
Communist Party of Peru — Shining Path. See Shining Path
community: dream of, 140–142
Condorcanqui, José Gabriel (Túpac Amaru II), 27, 89, 114, 227–228, 230; and "myth of Inkarrí," 228; and rondas, 92
Córdova, Víctor, 10, 12, 34–35, 123, 141, 255, 270–271, 275; and problems of leadership, 228–241
Corrigan, Philip, 49
corruption: of the authorities, 50,

114–115; and "Dr. How Much," 97–100; and NGOs, 205
Cutervo, 3, 15, 36, 63, 71, 82, 142, 217–220, 257; burning of police station in, 100–103
Cuyumalca, 3, 14, 37, 109–125 passim; and founding of rondas, 52–69; and women's committee, 157, 159–169

Dagnino, Evelina, 271
Dammert, José, 90
De Certeau, Michel, 76
Degregori, Carlos Iván, 57
De la Cadena, Marisol, 51
Deleuze, Gilles, 132, 256
Del Pino, Ponciano, 113
De Soto, Hernando: and concept of "other path," 8
development: criticism of, 198, 297 n.12; rethinking of, 200–204
Durkheim, Emile, 265

Edguén, Segundo, 38, 55
education: and the "myth of progress," 57–58. *See also* writing.
El Niño, 2, 155
Escobar, Arturo, 198, 271
ethnicity: and peasant identity, 32, 147–149
ethnography: problems of, 13–16; and question of "voice," 15–16; and readability, 17
Eyde, Marianne, 214

Feierman, Steve, 230
feminism: and concept of "domestic feminism," 163; and "ethnofeminism," 183; and feminist orientalism, 183; and globalization, 165; and leadership, 233

Foucault, Michel, 96
Fox, Richard G., 171
Freeman, Joreen, 233
Freire, Paulo, 206
Fuentes, Carlos, 125
Fujimori, Alberto, 26, 31, 145, 189, 260–263, 265–267, 272

García, Alan, 116; and corruption, 50; and ronda legalization, 122
García, Margarita, 2, 170, 275
gender: in the Andes, 161–164; and power, 169–170. *See also* feminism, women
Girard, René, 240
Gitlitz, John, 207, 221, 225
globalization, 21; and the Andes, 22–23; and peasants, 30–31: and social movements, 222–223
Gluckman, Max, 154
Gómez-Peña, Guillermo, 183
Gonzales, Efraín, 41
Gordon, Linda, 182
Gramsci, Antonio, 121, 230
Guattari, Félix, 132, 256

haciendas: break-up of, 34–35, 39–41, 256; hardships on, 76; influence on rondas of, 73–78. See also *rondas de hacienda*
Hale, Charles, 5
Hall, Stuart, 28
Hannerz, Ulf, 22
Harvey, Penelope, 176
hooks, bell, 16
Huancabamba, 15, 23, 24, 152–153, 246
Hurston, Zora Neale, 21

Idrogo, Daniel, 109–125, 147, 269, 271
Idrogo, Eladio, 27–28, 31, 91, 93, 131, 159, 239, 255, 271

Irigoín, Berbelina, 52–53
Izquierda Unida. *See* United Left

Jaén, 3
Jara, Angélica, 39, 59, 77, 195
justice: and customary law, 109, 288 n.2; of the ronda assemblies, 128–136; and wife-beating, 173–183

Kay, Bruce, 266
Kirk, Robin, 5, 15, 36, 252
Koonz, Claudia, 185

leadership: burdens of, 233–235; and ritual scape-goating, 240. *See also* authority
Lenin, V. I.: and distinction between reform and revolution, 102
Lima, 36–37, 144–145, 193, 261
Llacsahuache, Martín, 114, 155, 235–237
López, Omelia, 157, 159–173, 271
Luna, Víctor, 260

Malkki, Liisa, 42
Maoism: and justice making, 108–113; and women, 165. See *also* Marxism, Red Homeland, Shining Path
Marcus, George, 15
Mariátegui, José Carlos, 86, 256, 269, and concept of "tradition," 23
Marx, Karl, 247. *See also* Marxism
Marxism, 18, 252; decline of, 254, 262–263; and Marxist anthropology, 20–21; and peasants, 120; and rondas, 24; and sexism, 250. *See also* Maoism, Red Homeland, Shining Path
memory: politics of, 81–85

Michels, Roberto, 252
Milosz, Czeslaw, 28
Mohanty, Chandra, 183
Montenegro, Rosalía: and burning of Cutervo police station, 100–101
Moore, Donald, 17, 198
myths: importance of, 269; of Inkarrí; of progress, 57

nationalism, 24, 292 n. 71; and the rondas, 149–153
Nedelsky, Jennifer, 139
neoliberalism: failure of, 269–270
nongovernmental organizations (NGOs): and corruption, 205; and "movement webs," 204–220; opinions about, 193–194; and political patronage, 205; and social movements, 202–203
Nora, Pierre, 82

Oblitas, Lino, 80–81
Oblitas, Régulo, 22, 85, 215, 271; and founding of rondas, 52–58, 64–69
Ollé, Carmen, 36
Ortiz, Máximo, 98–100

Paimas, 11, 12–13, 122
Palma, Ricardo, 57
Palma, Rosa, 82
Paz, Francisca, 29, 94–95, 139, 270, 275
Paz, José, 1–2, 31, 72
peasants: and "depeasantization," 31; and globalization, 30–31; heterogeneity of, 254; and identity politics, 32, 147; and peasant intellectuals, 230; and poverty, 33, 39–48, 93–97; reconceptualization of, 29–33
Pérez, Adolfo, 136

Piura, 3, 9–11, 13–14, 23–24, 31, 62, 79, 93, 109, 139, 145; NGOs in, 194–196, 206–207; poverty in, 94, 246; ronda federations in, 243–251; theft in, 39–48, 82
political parties: decline of, 254, 263; and rondas, 9, 248–249
Poma de Ayala, Guamán, 75, 114
Powers, Margaret, 185
Prada, Manuel González, 29
Pratt, Mary, 136, 224: and concept of "contact zones," 24, 209
Pritchard, E. E., 154
protest. See social movements
Protestantism: growth of, 11, 113, 140–141; and the rondas, 89–92, 258. See also Catholicism, Christianity

race: in Peru, 51; and racism, 271
Red Homeland, 109, 129; and justice making, 109–125; and ronda federations, 251–257; and women's organizing, 165, 170–171. See also Maoism, Marxism
religion. See Catholicism, Christianity, Protestantism
Retete, Juan, 255
Ricketts, Patricio, 145
Risco, Pedro, 116–117, 249–250
Rojas, Telmo, 53
rondas campesinas: banning of, 103; definition of, 2; distinction between northern and southern, 4, 277 n.5; and forgiveness, 88–93, 134; legality of, 290 n.33; and participation, 128–132; and reconciliation, 132–136; the Shining Path, 142–144
rondas de hacienda, 73
Rowe, John, 79–80
Ruiz, Pascual, 137–138
rustling. See theft

Samamé, Lilian, 41
Sánchez, Agustín, 129, 244, 247
Sánchez, Oscar, 252–257, 266, 271
Sapir, Edward, 178, 295 n.25
Sayer, Derek, 49
Scheper-Hughes, Nancy, 94, 240
Scott, James, 235, 300 n.18
Sendero Luminoso. See Shining
    Path
Shining Path: 4, 7, 16, 27, 88, 109;
    decline of, 262–263; and devel-
    opment, 198, 199; and rondas,
    142–144; and Senderology, 17–
    18. *See also* Maoism, Marxism
Silverblatt, Irene, 67, 160
social movements: and culture, 28;
    and globalization, 222–223; im-
    perfections of, 138; in Peru, 227;
    and "movement webs," 25–29,
    256, 204–220; as a "third way,"
    25; and women, 184–185
Spanish: and conquest of Peru,
    21–23, 273
state: as a "great arch," 49; as a
    "mask," 65; repression of rondas
    by, 266
Stavig, Ward, 177
Steinbeck, John, 226
Stern, Steve J., 180

Taussig, Michael, 62, 86
testimonios, 213
theft, 2–3, 256, 265; in Cuyumalca,
    55–58; decline of, 81–82, 95, 97;
    reasons for, 38–49; and women,
    164–165
Torres, Segundo, 217–220
transnationalism. *See* globalization
Trouillot, Michel-Rolph, 127
Tunnel Six, 1–5, 11–14, 34–35, 228–
239, 155–159; gender in, 162–163,
    189–191; justice making in,
    107–108, 134; poverty in, 94–
    96, 192–193; theft in, 39–48,
    263–264, 275
Túpac Amaru II. See Condorcan-
    qui, José Gabriel

United Left, 8–9, 250–251. *See also*
    political parties

Valcárcel, Luis, 228
Vallejo, César, 196, 274
Vásquez, Juana, 157, 252, 256–257
Velasco, Juan, 11, 59; and agrarian
    reform, 39–41, 147
Vich, Víctor, 257–258
violence: against women, 173–183;
    and the anthropologist, 85–86;
    of the government, 87–88, 278;
    and the "little-bird," 87; and
    reconciliation, 134–136; of the
    rondas, 82–93
Visweswaran, Kamala, 217

Weber, Max, 227
Wolf, Eric, 20, 102
women: before the Spanish, 160–
    161; heterogeneity of, 169; and
    wife-beating, 173–183; and
    women's committees, 159–173.
    See also feminism, gender
writing, 75; and the rondas, 125–
    128. *See also* education

Yanagisako, Sylvia, 169
Yngar, Agusto, 60, 102–103
Youngers, Coletta, 200–201, 203

Zarzar, Alonso, 53

Orin Starn is an associate professor of cultural
anthropology at Duke University. He is an editor of
The Peru Reader: History, Culture, Politics (Duke
University Press, 1995) and *Between Revolution and
Resistance* (Rutgers University Press, 1997).

Library of Congress Cataloging-in-Publication Data

Starn, Orin.
Nightwatch : the politics of protest in the Andes /
Orin Starn.
p.   cm. — (Latin America otherwise)
Includes bibliographical references and indexes.
ISBN 0-8223-2301-X (cloth : alk. paper). — ISBN
0-8223-2321-4 (pbk. : alk. paper)
1. Peasantry—Peru—Societies, etc.   2. Peasantry—
Peru—Political activity.   3. Social movements—Peru.
I. Title.   II. Series.
HD1531.P4S73   1999
322.4′4′0985—dc21   98-41295